PAYING FOR PERFORMANCE

An International Comparison

Michelle Brown
and John S. Heywood
Editors

M.E. Sharpe
Armonk, New York
London, England

Copyright © 2002 by M. E. Sharpe, Inc.

All rights reserved. No part of this book may be reproduced in any form
without written permission from the publisher, M. E. Sharpe, Inc.,
80 Business Park Drive, Armonk, New York 10504.

Library of Congress Cataloging-in-Publication Data

Paying for performance : an international comparison / edited by Michelle Brown and
John S. Heywood.
    p. cm.—(Issues in work and human resources)
    Includes bibliographical references and index.
    ISBN 0-7656-0752-2 (cloth: alk. paper) — ISBN 0-7656-0753-0 (pbk: alk. paper)
    1. Compensation management—Case studies. I. Brown, Michelle, 1960–
II. Heywood, John S. 1957– III. Series.
HF5549.5.C67 P338 2002
658.3′225—dc21   2001049221

Printed in the United States of America

The paper used in this publication meets the minimum requirements of
American National Standard for Information Sciences
Permanence of Paper for Printed Library Materials,
ANSI Z 39.48-1984.

BM (c)   10   9   8   7   6   5   4   3   2   1
BM (p)   10   9   8   7   6   5   4   3   2   1

Contents

List of Tables and Figures vii

Foreword xi

Preface xiii

1. Paying for Performance: Setting the Stage 3
   Michelle Brown and John S. Heywood

2. Performance Pay in the United States:
   Its Determinants and Effects 17
   Daniel Parent

3. Performance Pay in Canada 52
   Richard J. Long

4. France: Weitzman Under State Paternalism? 90
   Fathi Fakhfakh and Virginie Pérotin

5. Performance Pay in the United Kingdom:
   The Case of the Inland Revenue Service 115
   David Marsden and Stephen French

6. The German Experience with Performance Pay 148
   Uwe Jirjahn

7. Performance Related Pay in Australia 179
   John Shields

8. Financial Participation and Pay for Performance in Japan 214
   Takao Kato

9.	The Brazilian Case: Performance Pay as Workers' Right *Hélio Zylberstajn*	236
10.	Paying for Performance: What Has Been Learned? *Michelle Brown and John S. Heywood*	261

About the Editors and Contributors 276

Index 281

List of Tables and Figures

Tables

2.1	Mean Sample Statistics	19
2.2	Pay Method by Occupation: Quality of Employment Survey, 1977	20
2.3	Pay Method/Promotion by Occupation: National Longitudinal Survey of Youth, 1988–1990	21
2.4	Average Job Characteristics by Occupation: Quality of Employment Survey, 1973–1977	28
2.5	Average Job Characteristics by Occupation: National Longitudinal Survey of Youth, 1979 and 1982	29
2.6	Job Characteristics and Piece Rate versus Commission Contracts	31
2.7	Wage Effect of Profit Sharing Plans: NLSY	41
2.8	Cross-Tabulation of Employer and Employee Reports of Pay Methods	46
3.1	Characteristics of the Sample	62
3.2	Number of Employee Performance Pay Plans in Use, 2000	65
3.3	Incidence of Employee Performance Pay Plans by Industrial Sector, 2000	66
3.4	Employee Coverage Levels at Firms Using Each Performance Pay Plan, 2000	67
3.5	Specific Types of Employee Performance Pay Plans: Means, Standard Deviations, and Intercorrelations, 2000	74
3.6	Predictors of Total Number of Employee Performance Pay Plans	77
3.7	Predictors of Specific Performance Pay Plans	79
4.1	Incidence of Performance Related Pay Systems in France, 1992	93
4.2	Incidence of Performance Related Pay by Skill Level, 1992	94

4.3	Performance Related Pay as a Percentage of Total Pay, 1992	95
4.4	Performance Related Pay as a Percentage of Pay by Skill Level, 1992	96
4.5	Levels of Basic Pay With and Without Performance Related Pay, 1992	96
4.6	Levels of Total Pay With and Without Performance Related Pay, 1992	97
4.7	Production Function Estimation	107
4.8	Variable Definitions	110
4.9	Descriptive Statistics	111
5.1	Summary Comparison of Responses to Questions on Performance Pay (PP): Inland Revenue, 1991 and 1996	129
5.2	Estimation of the Determinants of PRP Success in the Inland Revenue	133
5.3	Changes in Indicators of the Success of PRP, 1991 and 1996	135
5.4	Changes in the Key Explanatory Variables of PRP Outcomes, 1991 and 1996	135
5.5	Stress and Receipt of Above-Average PRP, 1996	138
5.6	Estimated Determinants of Job Stress, Inland Revenue, 1996	139
5.7	Change of Mean Commitment Levels, Inland Revenue, 1991–1996	141
5.8	Link Between Commitment and Stress	141
5.9	Rotated Component Matrix	144
6.1	Proportion of Full-Time Blue-Collar Workers Receiving Performance Pay in the West German Manufacturing Sector, 1966–1995	151
6.2	Proportion of Manufacturing Establishments with Performance Pay in the Federal State Lower Saxony, 1994 and 1996	153
6.3	Movements in the Use of Performance Pay, 1994 and 1996	153
6.4	K-Means-Cluster Analysis: Means of HRM Practices Across Clusters of Firms	167
6.5	Multinomial Logit Model of HRM System Adoption	171
7.1	Manual Workers Receiving Incentive Payments, by Industry, 1949	187
7.2	Wage Incentive Payments in Australian Firms, by Industry Group and Gender, 1969	189
7.3	Types of Wage Incentive Systems in Australian Firms, by Industry, 1969	190
7.4	Workplaces Using Performance Related Pay and Employees Receiving Performance Payments, by Workplace Category, 1995	194

7.5	Workplaces Using Specific Types of Performance Related Pay, 1995	195
7.6	Performance Related Pay Provisions in Industrial Agreements, by Agreement Type, 2000	199
7.7	Proportion of Performance Pay Increase in Industrial Agreements, by Agreement Type and Sector, 2000	200
7.8	Incidence of Performance Related Pay Provisions in Industrial Agreements, by Sector and Agreement Type, 2000	202
7.9	Firms Using Specific Types of Performance Related Pay for Managerial and Nonmanagerial Employees, 1999	204
7.10	Employees Covered by Specific Types of Performance Related Pay in Firms Using Each Type, 1999	206
7.11	Performance Related Pay as a Proportion of Total Remuneration, 1999	208
8.1	Diffusion of ESOPs in All Firms Listed on the Japanese Stock Markets, 1973–1998	218
8.2	Proportion of Firms That Changed Their Pay Systems in the Previous Three Years, as of 1996 and 1999	228
8.3	Proportion of Firms That Planned to Change Their Pay Systems in the Next Three Years, as of 1996 and 1999	228
8.4	Proportion of Firms with Individual incentive Pay and Gain Sharing, 1996 and 1999	229
8.5	Perceptions of Changes in the Pay System Toward Pay for Individual Performance and Merit, 1998	230
8.6	Attitudes on Changing the Pay System Toward Pay for Individual Performance and Merit, 1998	230
8.7	Proportion of Employees Who Agreed on Pay System Changes, 1998	232
9.1	Union Density in Brazil, 1979–1999	239
9.2	Impact of Legally Provided Pay Complements and Payroll Taxes on Base Wage in Brazil, 2000	241
9.3	Structure of the Brazilian Labor Market, 1999	242
9.4	Changes in Bargaining Structure Under Provisional Measure 794, 1994–2000	246
9.5	Distribution of Firms Answering the Questionnaire, 2000 and 2001	250
9.6	Impact of Performance Pay on Productivity, Commitment, and Relations	252
9.7	Distribution of the Sample of 1,201 Performance Pay Agreements According to Industry and Region, 1995–1999	253
9.8	Transformation of Nine Qualitative Variables into Nineteen Dummy Variables	255
9.9	Estimation of the Probabilities of Bargaining Structures	256

Figures

1.1	Matrix of Performance Pay	7
2.1	Job Characteristics and Pay Methods: Quality of Employment Survey, 1973–1977	30
2.2	Fraction of Workers Paid Bonuses and Covered by a Union Contract PSID, Excluding Overtime and Commission Workers, 1976–1991	37
5.1	A Model Linking Unilateral Changes in Effort Required and Outcomes	140
8.1	Diffusion of ESOPs in Japan, 1973–1998	220
8.2	Proportion of Firms with PSPs, 1965–1992	222
8.3	Changes in Proportion of Firms with ESOPs, 1988–1997 by Industry	226
8.4	Changes in ESOP Participation Rate, 1988–1997 by Industry	227

Foreword

It may seem crass to state it so boldly, but the issue of how to get the help to do what you want them to do is *the* primary challenge in human resources—and always has been. True, personnel journals and textbooks often take up topics such as employee screening, hiring, promotion, and so forth, without direct reference to that fundamental challenge. And it is easy to become lost in the intricacies of such human-resource functions as benefit administration or grievance processing without focusing on the basic issue of getting work done.

"Pay for performance" is one answer to that primary challenge. In the absence of a pay-for-performance system, organizations might alternatively monitor employees closely or try to motivate them through a variety of noneconomic means. But pay for performance is always an option, whether used by itself or in conjunction with other motivational tools. In different periods of time and in different places, the degree to which pay for performance has been used by organizations has varied considerably. It is a mistake, therefore, to conceive of pay for performance as a new idea or to neglect the cultural and institutional setting in which it operates.

The pay-for-performance label covers a wide variety of compensation arrangements varying from simple piece rates to profit sharing and stock options. Different systems may be appropriate in different circumstances and for different occupational groups. The effects of pay-for-performance systems will vary with the specifics of the plan selected. Moreover, as is the case with other human resource policies, pay for performance can have perverse as well as salutary effects. If widespread, pay for performance may lead to economic and social externalities—impacts outside the organizations in which it is administered. Indeed, some forms of pay for performance may be encouraged or mandated by public policies, precisely because of those perceived externalities.

In this volume, Brown and Heywood have brought together a rich set of materials on pay for performance in comparative international settings. Readers will find that there is marked variation around the world in the practice of pay for performance. But there is also an increasing sense that pressures are arising in many places for added emphasis on pay for performance as an important human resource practice. Comparative research, such as that contained in the chapters that follow, create an opportunity for cross-national learning about the causes and consequences of the many forms of pay for performance. On a personal note, it is gratifying to see this volume published, since it sprang originally from one of the regular sessions of Study Group no. 9 (Pay Systems), chaired by the editor of M. E. Sharpe's Issues in Work and Human Resources book series. The Study Group, one of several sponsored by the International Industrial Relations Association in Geneva, was formed precisely to encourage the type of work embodied in these pages.

Daniel J. B. Mitchell
Series Editor

Preface

As researchers, we recognized the commonality of our interests while we were both associated with the graduate program in labor and industrial relations at the University of Wisconsin–Milwaukee (UWM). Yet, the idea for this book emerged slowly and only after Michelle Brown left UWM and returned to Melbourne in 1998. The idea became substantive following the annual meeting of the Pay Systems Study Group at the 2000 Industrial Relations Research Association meetings, in which research on performance pay from around the globe was presented. We left the Study Group that year feeling that inadequate attention was given to comparative institutions that set the agenda and limit the possibilities for performance pay, and we set out to edit a volume that recognized that comparative aspect.

We were blessed by the contacts made at the Study Group over the years. Many of the authors in this volume were introduced to us there. Moreover, the leader of the Study Group, Daniel J. B. Mitchell, was the first person we approached with our prospectus. We appreciate his support of, and his effort on, this project as well as his leadership of the Study Group.

Following the multidisciplinary tradition of the Study Group, the volume includes a diversity of academic traditions. While the largest number of contributors are economists, those in human resource management and in industrial relations have been included by design. The terminology and frameworks differ but the contributions are equally valuable when studying a subject that so clearly sits on boundaries of the traditional academic map.

Thanks go to Olaf Huebler, who put us in touch with Virginie Pérotin. We greatly appreciate a travel grant from the Faculty of Economics and Commerce at the University of Melbourne, which allowed us to work together during the fine Australian summer. Thanks to John Benson, Christina Cregan, and Roderick Iverson for making the time in Melbourne so enjoyable. Thanks also go to G. Richard Meadows and William Holahan at UWM, who have supported this project as they have so many others.

PAYING FOR PERFORMANCE

Chapter 1
Paying for Performance
Setting the Stage

Michelle Brown and John S. Heywood

Introduction

Performance pay has emerged from the curtains to take center stage in academic debates, in firm strategy, and in government policies. Previously the narrow province of specialists in compensation, it now comprises an intellectual building block for a new generation of labor economists under the heading "the economics of personnel." It concerns macroeconomists studying unemployment and the flexibility of earnings across the business cycle. Strategic specialists identify it as a critical dimension of productivity enhancing best practices, and human resource management scholars debate its fairness and influences on employee cooperation and on morale. Industrial relations experts discuss its influence on the institutions of unionization and its role in collective bargaining. Those concerned with worker participation study the complex relationship between performance pay and worker decision making. Governments promote the practice of performance pay, particularly for their own employees; and consultants sell its virtues.

The current importance attached to pay systems in each of these disciplines derives from the role they are seen to play in affecting employee and, subsequently, organizational performance. This importance in turn derives from the increasing cost and competitive pressures facing both public and private sector organizations. The amount of monies paid to employees can represent a significant proportion of the overall costs of the organization. Further, the amount of employee work effort purchased by the organization is not fixed, so organizations have an incentive to establish mechanisms that encourage employees to work in the best interests of the organization (Braverman 1974; Pencavel 1977). Most employees derive an income through the sale of their labor. This income determines the overall standard of living of the employee. Therefore, pay is central to the employment relationship, making it a potentially powerful tool in the employment relationship, particularly in the context of organizations seeking to maximize their efficiency and productivity.

Most of this study and debate remains either theoretical, divorced from actual labor market institutions, or specific to the labor market institutions of a single country. This volume presents another voice. We take for granted that the comparative labor market institutions of nations provide important constraints and incentives influencing the adoption, variety, and success of performance pay. Methods of pay successful in an otherwise equal firm in one country may fail in another country. Indeed, studying performance pay in a comparative context means that not only are the respective institutions illuminated but the accepted general wisdom of one country is revealed to be unworkable in the next.

A fundamental notion in both economics and management holds that capital and technology are highly mobile and accessible. Success is thus driven by those factors unique to an enterprise: the best location, the greatest knowledge, and the most productive workers (Wright, McMahan, and McWilliams 1994). Performance pay has elements in common both with these unique factors and with the more accessible factors. While it is an easy theoretical prospect to take a method of pay across a national border, the practical challenge can be enormous. Profit sharing is mandated in France, viewed with skepticism or as irrelevant in Germany, usually deferred in the United States, and rarely deferred in Japan. The institutions of these countries set the stage and limit the prospects for what firms can achieve from managerial strategies involving performance pay. To ignore the institutions or take a single set of institutions for granted leaves undiscovered the critical link between the variation in institutions, the resulting range of performance pay schemes and the influence on success of otherwise equal enterprises in different countries. Ultimately, ignoring that link leaves the value of respective institutions less examined, more likely to be taken for granted and thus less mutable.

The Renewed Promise of Performance Pay

Long a major weapon in the arsenal of scientific management, performance pay received far less emphasis during the third quarter of the last century.

Articles in the United States trumpeted the "domination of time rates," unions fought for solidarity wages, Japanese firms provided "seniority wages," and the centralized wage systems of continental Europe and Australia created remarkable uniformity in earnings. Yet, the institutions that limited performance pay came under increasing pressure in the last two decades of the century. International competition, privatization, a protracted recession in Japan, and an emerging single market in Europe all helped provide the pressure. Private sector unionization in the United States dropped into single digits, the Australian awards system was "deregulated"; and European governments and scholars became highly concerned with labor market flexibility, a siren sound heard even by Japanese managers. In this environment, interest in performance pay grew, as both firms and governments became more concerned with labor productivity and the ability to respond to changing external pressures. The expectation was that an appropriate compensation system that linked worker and firm objectives could be part of managing a workforce to create a competitive advantage or productive edge.

This interest infused the employment relations of governments themselves. The United Kingdom and Australia both implemented merit pay schemes for large shares of their central government activities (O'Donnell 1998; Marsden and French 1998). In the United States, much of the innovation in performance pay was done by states and localities.

The experience in local public education in the United States is illustrative. It shows not only the range of potential performance pay schemes but also the instability of such schemes, a more general theme returned to in the country chapters. The state of Tennessee developed a sophisticated statistical model identifying the effect of specific teachers on the increase in test scores of primary and secondary school students (Wright, Horn, and Sanders 1997). This effort was seen as a prerequisite for explicitly tying teacher earnings to student scores. Actual implementation of performance pay in U.S. schools typically relies on other measures of productivity. Eberts, Hollenberg, and Stone (2000) compare two similar secondary schools in the same Michigan jurisdiction, one of which explicitly rewards teachers for high student evaluations and for retention, and the other of which retains a traditional pay structure without merit pay. They found the first school successfully increased its retention rate (share of a teacher's students who stayed until the end of the course) relative to the second. They also found that the merit pay resulted in a larger rate of course failure, lower average attendance, and no increase in achievement. While the objective measure of performance increased, the ultimate success of the school did not. Indeed, Hatry, Greiner, and Ashford (1994) find that over

75 percent of all merit plans started in U.S. schools fail and are no longer in operation within a decade.

Yet schools, and government operations more generally, suffer from many of the difficulties long identified with traditional merit pay schemes. There exist multiple stakeholders, many and conflicting goals, interdependent team production, and uncertain inputs to name just a few. While these difficulties exist in the private sector as well, they may be less severe in some cases and the range of performance pay options appears higher.

Thus, the current concern about aligning the interests of workers with firms frequently focuses on a combination of financial and decision-making participation. Yet the details of how this happens depends on the labor market institutions, and it is these details that help determine success. Thus, France has mandated profit sharing largely independently of other forms of worker participation. Germany has mandated decision-making participation, but unions are skeptical of profit sharing. Japan has large degrees of both financial and decision-making participation, but both remain within the context of individual firms and company unions. U.S. firms without unions may have greater freedom to institute profit sharing than their union counterparts, but may face legal constraints on the creation of other forms of worker participation and the integration of these with profit sharing.[1] Brazil provided for profit sharing in its 1946 Constitution but took till 1995 to establish the facilitating mechanisms, including mandating it as a subject of collective bargaining, to make it legally available to organizations. Clearly, the model for transforming workplaces and the role performance pay plays must necessarily differ by country.

A Taxonomy of Performance Pay

Performance pay can be seen as a generic term that covers any system that seeks to link pay to some measure of individual, group or organizational level performance (Milkovich and Widgor 1991). The following country studies examine a range of performance pay schemes, so it is useful to review a number of taxonomies that have been developed to demonstrate the variety of ways in which pay can be linked to performance. Marriott (1957) developed a classification system that used a time frame and the relationship to output. Performance pay schemes could be:

1. Short-term output based (e.g., piece rates and bonuses)
2. Non-output based (e.g., commissions, merit pay schemes)
3. Long-term collective payment schemes (e.g., gainsharing, profit sharing).

Figure 1.1 **Matrix of Performance Pay**

		Level of Performance	
		Individual	Group
Contribution to base salary	Adds to base	Merit plans	Small-group incentives
	Does not add to base	Piece rates Commissions Bonuses	Profit sharing Gain sharing Bonuses

Source: Milkovich and Widgor (1991, 78).

More recently, Milkovich and Widgor (1991) developed a matrix of performance pay schemes (Figure 1.1) that distinguishes between the level of performance assessment (individual and group) and the relationship of performance payments to base salary (accumulating or nonaccumulating).

The level of performance assessment is important, as it influences the strength of the connection between the performance of individual employees and the rewards they receive. According to Lawler (1990), individual schemes offer the clearest "line of sight." Group schemes, on the other hand, suffer from "free-rider" problems in that all workers share in the gains, regardless of whether or not they contribute differentially to group performance. However, as will be argued in the next section, individual schemes have the potential to create "dysfunctional individualism" (Geary 1992).

Performance payments can be nonaccumulating in that the worker is required to reearn the payments each evaluation cycle (e.g., piece rates, commissions). Under an accumulating scheme, performance payments earned in one evaluation cycle roll into the base. This new (higher) base salary is used for the calculation of pay-related benefits and subsequent performance payments. Nonaccumulating schemes are seen to produce a higher average performance at a lower cost to the organization. However, they may also demonstrate a lack of commitment by the organization to its workers (Milkovich and Widgor 1992).

The choice of performance pay scheme can be made on the basis of a "best-practice" or "strategic-fit" approach (Milkovich and Newman 1998). A best-practice perspective asserts that there is a range of compensation practices that are intrinsically better than other compensation practices and that can be effectively applied in any organization, independently of the circumstances of that organization (e.g., Pfeffer 1994). In an environment of heightened domestic and international competition, performance pay is intuitively attractive to organizations and their managers and is sometimes adopted merely because a competitor uses performance pay for its workers.

A strategic-fit perspective requires the compensation system to fit with the overall business objectives of the organization. The underlying premise is that the greater the alignment between organizational conditions and the compensation system, the more effective the organization. This approach requires the organization to make an assessment of, among other things, its work force, its strategic objectives, the nature of the relations between jobs in the organization and technology in order to identify the most appropriate compensation system. There is a current body of research that examines the relationship between organizational characteristics and conditions and the form of performance pay. Some of this is reported, and added to, in the following country chapters.

Objectives of Performance Pay

At its most basic, adoption of performance pay is intended to align the interest of workers with the goals of the enterprises for which they work (Kessler and Purcell 1992). For private sector enterprises, the ultimate goal is increased profit but translation of that goal into performance pay may take many forms. For relatively simple tasks yielding easily countable output, the incentives from paying piece rates may be most successful.[2] Indeed, case studies of individual firms have demonstrated substantial gains in productivity from their adoption (Lazear 2000). Yet, the unintended consequences of piece rates may include reduced quality, increased scrap rates, or inappropriate maintenance of equipment. At least theoretically, piece rates might be modified to account for these. Thus, the "premium pay" used in Germany represents a variation on piece rates, which explicitly rewards reduced wastage or increased quality. Yet, clearly, as jobs become more complex and outputs more multidimensional, the difficulty of being formulaic increases.

Using piece rates may also introduce counterproductive strategic behavior on the part of both firms and workers. Workers may fear ratchet effects in which the firm lowers the piece rates after worker output has increased in response (Gibbons 1987). As a result of this fear, workers may exert very low effort preceding the introduction of a piece rate and agree to "simply work to rate," a specific number of units per day, after that introduction.

Many jobs simply do not result in countable pieces, and even in those that do, the pieces cannot always be readily tied to individual workers.

Again, in theory one might identify an appropriate group piece rate for the latter case, recognizing that allocation within the group is problematic. An equal allocation to all workers creates incentives to free-ride on the work of others. Moreover, in some cases the relevant "group" may not be identifiable, as the extent of interdependent production is too large.

When the ability to identify productivity is limited, an alternative could be to reward effort. Thus, the firm monitors and rewards effort. On the one hand, effort may not easily translate into productivity and so such schemes are indirect at best. On the other hand, a scheme that rewards only productivity gives little or no incentive for workers with inherently lower productivity, who might respond by exerting only the minimum effort to remain employed.[3] Many merit pay schemes depend on evaluations that include multiple subjective measures of effort. For example, the ability to complete tasks, the ability to evaluate information from a variety of sources, and the ability to apply job-related knowledge to all aspects of the job are typical measures used in merit pay schemes. Such subjective measures can be applied to a broad range of occupations and are the most common form of individual performance pay (Heneman 1992). Thus, as countries individualize the employment relationship (Kessler and Purcell 1992), the aggregate use of merit pay schemes might be expected to increase.

While these schemes may not create direct incentives for workers to increase productivity, they may create a variety of indirect incentives. First, the merit pay scheme may be valuable in setting goals and building a shared sense of purpose ultimately increasing productivity (Heneman 1992). Second, merit pay schemes, and indeed, performance pay in general, can be critical in sorting workers. Those who respond best to given set of incentives can be expected to sort into jobs and firms using those incentives. Thus, a worker who is unusually productive wants to be in a firm that explicitly rewards that productivity (Lazear 1986). Similarly, a worker who shares the goals of the firm as identified in its merit pay scheme will choose to work for that firm.

Merit pay plans rely on supervisors to provide a subjective assessment of employee performance. There is a vast literature (Milkovich and Widgor 1992; Milkovich and Newman 1998; Murphy and Cleveland 1991; Marsden and French 1998) that highlights the problems with getting supervisors to make an "accurate" assessment of employee performance and offers prescriptions to improve the operation of this aspect of a merit pay plan. More significantly, there is a concern about the appropriateness of a compensation system that focuses on the individual in the context of the increasing use of teams and team production technologies (Heneman and von Hippel 1995; Milkovich and Newman 1998). Merit pay plans focus the attentions of the employee on those aspects of the job that attract a financial reward, to the detriment of cooperative relations with coworkers and the organization (Geary 1992; Marsden and French 1998; Heneman 1992). As economists put it, there is no incentive to put forth "helping effort." Indeed, using Australian evidence, Drago and Garvey (1998) found that, as the size of the reward associated with individual performance grew, workers were less likely to cooperate by letting coworkers use their equipment, tools, or machinery. One view is that this problem can be overcome by including a performance standard that recognizes teamwork contributions (e.g., Milkovich and Newman 1998). The alternative view is that merit pay plans should be abandoned in favor of schemes that emphasize team or group performance and reward effective group performance (Drago and Turnbull 1988). A number of the following country chapters (e.g., Canada, chapter 3) demonstrate a growth in the use of group-based performance pay schemes. In Australia, a country where one might expect that group schemes would figure prominently due to the history of centralized pay determination, there are surprisingly few group schemes in operation (Morehead et al. 1997).

Another difficulty with individual merit schemes arises not from the failure to reward helping effort but from what those in human resource management call "dysfunctional individualism" (Geary 1992). While economists might identify this as incomplete contracting, the basic notion is that the inability to reward all types of productive behavior results in counterproductive behavior. Thus, an emphasis on individual performance as measured by a few indicators can actually lower enterprise performance, as employees simply meet their contractual obligations and resist extracontractual cooperation in which they might have otherwise engaged (Deakin 1991; Nolan and Walsh 1995). At its most extreme, this concern with only contractual obligations can give rise to increased performance by the measured indicators but reduced performance by more global measures.[4] In less extreme cases, workers simply lose focus on activities that might help global performance if they are not rewarded in the payment plan. Pfeffer (1998) has gone so far as to say that most U.S. individual-based merit pay plans "share two attributes: they absorb vast amounts of management time and resources, and make everybody unhappy."

The performance pay matrix contained in Figure 1.1 also includes a number of schemes that can also be regarded as organization-level schemes, for example profit sharing and employee share ownership plans (ESOP's). Interest in these types of schemes is often sparked by a concern with individual-level schemes. Organization-level schemes provide a common focal point for all employees; performance criteria are often easier to establish and have the effect of highlighting the importance of cooperation among members of the work force. These schemes also provide a mechanism for distributing the benefits of good organizational performance to employees. In France, there is a system of mandated profit sharing, though in this country the intention was to promote national savings. It is common for these schemes to exist alongside formal programs of employee participation. A financial stake in the organization is seen to reinforce the incentives to participate in organizational decision-making systems (Cressey, Eldridge, and MacInnes 1985).

A number of the chapters in this book demonstrate the use of multiple schemes, for example, Australia and Canada. These "nested" schemes (Gerhart and Milkovich 1992) are intended to provide a set of complimentary incentives to employees. In other words, an individual performance pay scheme provides an incentive to the employee to achieve individual goals, a group scheme facilitates the operation of team working arrangements, and an organization-level scheme encourages the employee to identify with and work toward the broader objectives of the organization. An alternative view (Gerhart and Milkovich 1992) is that nested schemes confuse workers by sending a set of contradictory messages. Achievement of individual objectives may well be at the expense of group or organizational level objectives.

About This Book

In the chapters that follow, an explicitly multidisciplinary approach emerges. Many of the authors draw on literature from a variety of disciplines, and there is variety among the authors' home disciplines as well. The choice to proceed in this manner is based on the view that, despite differences in terminology, the fundamental behavior and institutions being studied carry across disciplines. Thus, those from organizational behavior would identify "production interdependencies" as a reason for not using piece rates, while economists would point to "team production," meaning the same notion. At the same time, the scholar of human resource management might mistake team production for the organization of the workplace into explicit self-managed teams. While such differences in terminology raise concerns, they are outweighed by drawing from a wider range of perspectives and traditions.

The book focuses on performance pay, which, itself, can be a controversial term. By adopting the taxonomy of Milkovich and Widgor, as presented in the previous section, we hope to concentrate our efforts. While the range of potential incentive structures is very broad, we focus on those that might be identified as payment schemes. Thus, back-loaded, or deferred, compensation is thought to create incentives for workers to have longer tenure and exert effort over that tenure, yet such a scheme might reveal itself as simple time rates with tenure increments. While our authors are aware of these incentives, they typically do not examine them as performance pay. Similarly, tournaments for promotion or retention can be importantly related to compensation, yet they are considered largely outside the scope of our examination. Instead, we focus on those mechanisms that provide a more immediate link between compensation and measures of performance either of output or of input (subjective measures involved in merit pay schemes). In some cases, individual authors will focus exclusively either on performance pay linked to output (chapter 2, about the United States) or on performance pay linked to input (chapter 5, about the United Kingdom).

The specific countries we examine reflect a variety of factors. First, there is an effort to include a reasonable cross-section of industrial democracies. Second, there is a strong desire to include countries where the institutions influencing performance pay are undergoing substantial change. Thus, Australia has abandoned its centralized wage setting and Brazil has made wholesale changes in legislation toward performance pay. Third, there is an interest in reflecting a wide variety in employment relations. This contrast is illustrated by comparing the highly decentralized employment relations of the United States, the high-level bargaining and works councils of Germany, and the company unions of Japan.

Within the broad confines described in the last two paragraphs, the authors were given substantial freedom to identify the salient subjects within their own countries. The result has been a marvelous variety in focus and methodology. In chapter 2, Daniel Parent reviews the economic rationale for using performance pay linked to output and reveals the incidence of several such schemes across the U.S work force. He also highlights the critical determinants for adoption of performance pay schemes, using the detail from four individual-level data sources and isolates the influence of such schemes on the level of compensation paid to U.S. workers.

In chapter 3, Richard Long examines the overall incidence of thirteen different types of performance pay schemes among private-sector organizations in Canada: five individual, three group, and five organization-level schemes. Long then investigates the role of three sets of predictors on the incidence of each type of performance scheme. He considers the role of firm characteristics (which include competitive strategy, ownership, and organizational size) and work force characteristics (such as proportion of full-time employees, unionization, and use of outsourced labor). He particularly focuses on the impact of structural characteristics, that is, the extent to which the organization makes use of a range of "high-commitment" human resource management practices, on the form and incidence of individual, group, and organizational-level schemes.

Fathi Fakhfakh and Virginie Pérotin, in chapter 4 on France, review the incidence of a range of individual and group performance pay schemes and then concentrate on the impact of mandated and subsidized profit sharing schemes. While profit sharing was mandated in order to promote national savings, the authors demonstrate employment and productivity benefits for organizations. On the other side of the English Channel, David Marsden and Stephen French provide an analysis of performance pay in the UK public sector and then focus their attentions on the Inland Revenue Service (IRS) in chapter 5. Given the pervasive nature of performance pay in the UK public sector, they investigate the extent to which the IRS has been able to manage its operation effectively and the extent to which employees adjust their expectations of work in line with this type of compensation system.

In chapter 6 Uwe Jirjahn examines a broader set of performance pay systems for Germany but largely limits his attention to manufacturing. After revealing the incidence of such schemes, and the surprisingly widespread use of piece rates, he isolates the role performance pay plays in human resource management strategies and estimates the determinants of those strategies. In chapter 7, John Shields presents a historical portrait of performance pay in Australia that takes the reader through to current moves toward decentralization in pay determination. Highlighting the connection between the changes in institutions and the methods of pay, he presents changing patterns in the incidence of performance pay. He argues there has been no secular pattern in their use and diffusion in Australia.

In chapter 8, Takao Kato examines the continued strength of profit sharing and ESOPs in Japan. He shows that the recent economic difficulties in that country have resulted in a leveling off in the use of such plans, but not a reduction as some predicted. Interestingly, Kato presents new evidence showing a trend away from the famous "tenure wage" toward more individualized performance pay. This certainly makes Japan a country to watch.

In chapter 9, Helió Zylberstajn provides an account of the legal framework for profit and gain sharing plans in Brazil and then analyzes their incidence and impact. Although profit and gain sharing were identified as a right in the 1946 Constitution, they did not come into being until 1995. Since then, there has been a rapid increase in the use of these schemes, and Zylberstajn documents how organizations with these schemes perform with respect to a number of human resource management indicators. He examines the predictors of the form of performance pay bargaining.

Chapter 10, the final chapter, summarizes the main findings of each of the country studies. It compares and contrasts the findings under four main themes. First, the form and incidence of performance pay are examined. The country chapters provide evidence of the use of individual, group, and organization-level schemes, though often the rationale for their adoption is unexpected. Second, the chapter considers the pace of change and the extent of experimentation with performance pay schemes. Within the countries selected, we have evidence of shifts from seniority-based wages to individual performance pay in Japan and the public sectors of the UK and Australia. There has also been a growth in group and organization-based schemes in Canada and Brazil. This chapter identifies the common pressures for pay system change and contrasts the decisions made by government and organizations in response to these pressures.

Third, we examine the relationship between performance pay schemes and employee participation. In many of the countries studied, there are explicit links between these two management practices. A number of the authors demonstrate positive organizational outcomes, for example, productivity improvements, when participative programs are combined with group and organization-level performance pay schemes. Fourth, organizational characteristics are used in a number of studies to predict the incidence and form of various types of performance pay schemes. Included is consideration of the role of laws and institutions on pay system choices made by organizations in the countries studied. Chapter 10 concludes by making suggestions for future performance pay research.

Notes

1. The difficulty is embedded in the U.S. concept of unfair labor practices as defined by the National Labor Relations Act, section 8.a.2. Nonunion firms that attempt to create and direct worker organizations that have unionlike functions are prohibited, as they substitute for "more genuine," that is unionized, worker representation.

2. Piece rates are more likely to be successful in increasing profitability when inventory costs are low, demand for the good is constant, and the number of workers can easily be adjusted.

3. An audience from the United States might not see this as a problem, suggesting that the firm simply set the minimum effort to retain employment sufficiently high. Yet, in the context of alternative social norms and the resulting legislation making dismissal prohibitively expensive, that option may simply not exist in many of the other countries we study.

4. One example is the Michigan secondary school described in the earlier section, which lowered the dropout rate but failed by every other measure. Other examples include the U.S. firms Dun and Bradstreet and Sears, which faced tremendous legal

costs and customer bad will following performance pay schemes that caused employees to mislead customers. In the case of Sears, an individual performance pay plan caused mechanics to exaggerate the repairs that customers needed for their automobiles. Sales workers for Dun and Bradstreet provided fraudulent information to customers about their use of services in an effort to increase customer purchases, an action rewarded through higher commissions (see Gibbons 1998).

References

Braverman, H. 1974. *Labor and Monopoly Capital.* New York: Monthly Review Press.
Cressey, P., Eldridge, J., and MacInnes, J. 1985. *"Just Managing": Authority and Democracy in Industry.* Philadelphia: Open University Press.
Deakin, S. 1991. "Legal Change and Labour Market Restructuring in Western Europe and the U.S." *New Zealand Journal of Industrial Relations* 16: 109–122.
Drago, R., and Garvey, G. 1998. "Incentives for Helping on the Job: Theory and Evidence." *Journal of Labor Economics* 16: 1–25.
Drago, R., and Turnbull, G. 1988. "Individual and Group Piece Rates Under Team Technologies." *Journal of Japanese and International Economics* 2: 1–10.
Eberts, R., Hollenberg, K., and Stone, J. 2000. "Teacher Performance, Incentives and Student Outcomes." Staff Working Papers 00–65, W. E. Upjohn Institute for Employment Research, Kalamazoo, MI.
Geary, J. 1992. "Pay, Control and Commitment: Linking Appraisal and Reward." *Human Resource Management Journal* 2(4): 36–54.
Gerhart, B., and Milkovich, G. T. 1990. "Employee Compensation: Research and Practice." In *Handbook of Industrial and Organisational Psychology,* vol. 3, pp. 481–569, eds. H. C. Trianois and M. D. Dunnette. Palo Alto, CA: Consulting Psychologists Press.
Gibbons, R. 1998. "Incentives in Organizations." *Journal of Economic Perspectives* 12: 115–133.
———, 1987. "Piece Rate Incentive Schemes." *Journal of Labor Economics* 5: 413–429.
Hatry, H., Greiner, J. and Ashford, B. 1994. *Issues and Case Studies in Teacher Incentive Plans.* Washington, DC: Urban Institute Press.
Heneman, R. L. 1992. *Merit Pay: Linking Pay Increases to Performance Ratings.* Reading, MA: Addison Wesley.
Heneman, R. L., and von Hippel, C. 1995. "Balancing Group and Individual Rewards: Rewarding Individual Contributions to the Team." *Compensation and Benefits Review* 27: 63–72.
Kessler, I., and Purcell, J. 1992. "Performance Related Pay: Objectives and Application." *Human Resource Management Journal* 2: 16–33.
Lazear, E. 2000. "Performance Pay and Productivity." *American Economic Review* 90: 1346–1361.
———, 1990. *Strategic Pay.* San Francisco: Jossey-Bass.
———, 1986. "Salaries and Piece Rates." *Journal of Business* 59:405–431.
Marriott, R. 1957. *Incentive Payment Systems: A Review of Research and Opinion.* London: Staples Press.
Marsden, D., and French, S. 1998. *What a Performance: Performance Related Pay in the Public Services.* London: Centre for Economic Performance.
Milkovich, G. T., and Newman, J. M. 1998. *Compensation,* 6th ed. Chicago: Irwin.

Milkovich, G. T., and Widgor, A. K. 1991. *Pay for Performance: Evaluating Performance Appraisal and Merit Pay.* Washington DC: National Academy Press.

Morehead, A., Steele, M., Alexander, M., Stephen, K., and Duffin, L. 1997. *Changes At Work: The 1995 Australian Workplace Industrial Relations Survey.* Melbourne: Longman.

Murphy, K. R., and Cleveland, J. N. 1991. *Performance Appraisal: An Organizational Perspective.* Boston: Allyn and Bacon.

Nolan, P., and Walsh, J. 1995. "The Structure of the Economy and Labour Market." In *Industrial Relations: Theory and Practice in Britain,* ed. P. Edwards, 5–88. Oxford: Blackwell.

O'Donnell, M. 1998. "Creating a Performance Culture? Performance Based Pay in the Australian Public Service." *Australian Journal of Public Administration* 57: 28–40.

Pencavel, J. H. 1977. "Work-Effort, On-the-Job Screening and Alternative Methods of Remuneration." In *Research in Labor Economics* vol. 1, pp. 225–258, eds. S. W. Polachek et al. Greenwich, CT: JAI Press.

Pfeffer, J., 1998. "Six Dangerous Myths About Pay." *Harvard Business Review* (May-June): 109.

———, 1994. *Competitive Advantage Through People.* Boston: Harvard Business School Press.

Wright, M., McMahan, G. G., and McWilliams, A. 1994. "Human Resources and Competitive Advantage: A Resource Based Perspective." *International Journal of Human Resource Management* 5(2): 301–326.

Wright, S., Horn, S., and Sanders, W. 1997. "Teacher and Classroom Context Effects on Student Achievement: Implications for Teacher Evaluation." *Journal of Personnel Evaluation in Education* 11: 57–67.

Chapter 2
Performance Pay in the United States
Its Determinants and Effects

Daniel Parent

Introduction

Given the view that explicit performance pay, such as piece rates, elicits effort and reveals worker productivity through the workers choice of pay method, it would seem that such compensation would be the overwhelming choice by firms.

However, this is just not what we observe in the United States. Although not rare, compensation contracts based on explicit measures of individual performance are the exceptions more than the rule. Over the last twenty years, much of the theoretical literature devoted to the analysis of the employment relationship and to the provision of incentives has tried to rationalize this simple fact. For example, it has been argued that piece rates are not very common because of the difficulty of measuring individual output and the importance of teamwork where cohesion and cooperation are important.

This chapter surveys the empirical work on explicit performance pay in the United States focusing on two main empirical questions: What are the determinants of its use, and what are its effects, if any? To avoid simply enumerating the empirical results in the literature, I will also discuss rel-

---

Special thanks are given to the editors Michelle Brown and John Heywood for useful comments and suggestions.

evant economic models. However, readers interested in more complete theoretical surveys are referred to Gibbons and Waldman (1999) or Prendergast (1999).

The Incidence of Performance Pay

Despite a voluminous literature aimed at incorporating more "realism" into the theoretical analysis of employment relationships, relatively little empirical work has been done on the topic, especially as it pertains to the nonmanagerial workers who are the main focus of this survey. While much effort has been devoted to characterizing optimal explicit incentive contracts, it seems to this author that it took some time before people really started wondering why the use of explicit incentive schemes was not widespread. Consequently, before analyzing the determinants and the effect of pay-for-performance contracts, it would seem appropriate to show the incidence of various forms of compensation.

Table 2.1 uses four different data sets to document the extent to which workers in more or less representative samples receive some form of performance pay.[1] The least one can say about the use of explicit performance pay is not common, as fewer than 10 percent of the workers are paid either through commissions or piece rates. In fact, only in the National Longitudinal Survey of Youth (NLSY) does the percentage approach 10. In the Quality of Employment Survey (QES), the January 1977 Current Population Survey (CPS), and the Panel Study of Income Dynamics (PSID), the fraction of workers paid either a commission or a piece rate hovers around 4 percent. A likely reason for such a discrepancy is that the question on how workers are paid differs across surveys. In the NLSY workers are simply asked whether part of their earnings is based on either piece rates or commissions. In the other three data sets the question tends to be more restrictive: Workers are asked whether they are paid an hourly rate, a salary, or something else. The mutually exclusive nature of the question is such that workers paid by more than one scheme are likely to report only one which accounts for most of their earnings. Still, even with the broad NLSY definition, explicit performance pay is not ubiquitous. Yet, the fraction of workers either being paid through an explicit contract or receiving a bonus based on individual job performance (say, through a merit pay scheme) is over 20 percent in the NLSY. If we include workers on profit-sharing plans, the percentage receiving all types of performance pay is in fact close to 50 percent! Consequently one can see that most firms use performance pay other than that explicitly linked to an objective measure of individual performance.[2]

Table 2.1

Mean Sample Statistics

	CPS (January 1977)[a]	QES (1973–1977)	PSID (1984–1991)	NLSY (1988–1990)
Percentage paid				
Hourly	58.6	40.9	48.6	45.9
	(0.50)	(0.49)	(0.50)	(0.50)
Salary	37.5	51.1	38.5	54.1
	(0.48)	(0.50)	(0.49)	(0.50)
Piece rates	1.1	2.8	0.9	3.6
	(0.10)	(0.16)	(0.09)	(0.19)
Commissions	2.9	5.2	7.7	5.7
	(0.17)	(0.22)	(0.27)	(0.23)
Bonuses	8.4	—	10.6	14.1
	(0.2958)		(0.2902)	(0.35)
Profit sharing	—	0.1761	—	0.3319
Average amount of bonuses ($1,979)[a]				
For hourly paid workers	1,079.09 (1,920.24)	—	1,203.35 (2,935.30)	—
For salaried workers	2,313.05 (5237.76)	—	4,403.86 (8,921.40)	—
Sample size	4,905	724	10,803	8165

[a] Computed from workers' responses.

Tables 2.2 and 2.3 show the breakdown by occupation. Not surprisingly, most commission workers tend to be in sales-related work, while most piece rate workers tend to be operatives, although quite a few service workers report being paid according to an explicit measure of performance. In contrast, promotions, bonuses, and profit-sharing plans seem to be far more evenly distributed across occupations. From looking at Tables 2.2 and 2.3, we can immediately see that the occupations for which output appears to be easily measured are the ones where explicit incentives are most used. Consequently, we would expect measurability issues to be part of any model that tries to predict the use of such pay systems. In a related vein, another interesting feature of the tables is that it would appear that firms clearly favor providing incentives through promotions instead of using incentive schemes directly tied to a measure of performance such as piece rates or commissions. Although this is simply a restatement of Baker, Jensen, and Murphy's (1988) observation, we should nevertheless be a bit more cautious in that bonuses, which are directly based on a measure of performance, are used about as frequently as promotions.[3]

Table 2.2

Pay Method by Occupation: Quality of Employment Survey, 1977 (in percentage of occupation)

	Pay Method			
Occupation	Hourly	Salary	Piece rate	Commission
Professional and technical, except engineering technical	14.15	83.02	0.94	1.89
Engineering and science technical	28.57	71.43	0.00	0.00
Writers, artists, etc.	0.00	77.78	0.00	22.22
Managers and administrators, except farm	8.33	81.82	2.27	7.58
Sales workers	27.27	9.09	4.55	59.09
Clerical and unskilled 1[a]	27.08	64.58	0.00	8.33
Office machine operators	30.77	69.23	0.00	0.00
Secretaries	17.65	82.35	0.00	0.00
Clerical and unskilled 2[b]	46.15	53.85	0.00	0.00
Craftsmen and kindred[c]	59.02	34.43	4.92	1.64
Mechanics and repairmen	80.65	17.74	0.00	1.61
Operatives, except precision machine and textile	74.19	22.58	3.23	0.00
Precision machine operatives	68.75	12.50	18.75	0.00
Textile operators	92.31	5.13	2.56	0.00
Transport equipment operatives	63.33	16.67	10.00	10.00
Laborers, except farm	85.00	15.00	0.00	0.00
Cleaning service workers	44.44	44.44	11.11	0.00
Food service workers	80.00	20.00	0.00	0.00
Health service workers	55.56	44.44	0.00	0.00
Personal service workers	23.08	61.54	7.69	7.69

[a] From bank tellers to meter readers for utilities (Census 301 to 334).
[b] From shipping clerks to ticket agents and other miscellaneous clerks (Census 374 to 395).
[c] From auto accessories installers to machinist apprentices (Census 401 to 462).

Incentive Contracts Based on Individual Performance

In this section I will focus on explicit individual measures of performance pay, such as piece rates or commissions. As we saw in the previous section, their use is not widespread, especially in the case of piece rates. Although an explanation for this would be that individual output might simply be too costly to measure, this still leaves unanswered the question of why we observe both straight time rates or salaries and piece rates in a given well-defined industry or occupation cell. After all, if output is easy to measure for firm A, and firm A pays a piece rate, why does firm B in the same sector pay a salary instead?

After outlining the main models of choice of pay methods, I will survey evidence on the determinants of different methods. Then I will look at the

Table 2.3

Pay Method/Promotion by Occupation: National Longitudinal Survey of Youth, 1988–1990 (in percentage of occupation)

Occupation	Hourly	Salary	Piece rate	Commission	Bonus	Profit sharing	Promotions
Professional and technical except engineering technical	27.94	72.06	0.43	1.99	15.46	35.60	13.76
Engineering and science technical	42.37	57.63	0.00	5.09	9.32	41.25	18.64
Writers, artists, etc.	21.84	78.16	2.30	9.20	17.24	30.13	14.94
Managers and administrators, except farm	19.98	80.02	0.68	9.84	28.46	45.26	18.91
Sales workers	25.07	74.94	0.78	37.98	25.58	39.29	11.37
Clerical and unskilled 1[a]	43.18	56.83	1.34	3.12	13.21	44.55	16.32
Office machine operators	43.88	56.12	0.84	1.27	13.50	52.88	14.77
Secretaries	37.20	62.80	1.02	1.37	11.60	33.40	13.99
Clerical and unskilled 2[b]	48.76	51.24	1.99	1.74	10.20	42.91	14.93
Craftsmen and kindred[c]	60.32	39.68	2.67	1.60	10.68	28.12	17.97
Mechanics and repairmen	53.16	46.84	4.54	9.56	9.89	24.61	12.16
Operatives, except precision machine and textile	68.93	31.07	8.75	1.79	10.54	30.51	7.32
Precision machine operatives	60.44	39.56	36.81	1.10	9.34	37.31	10.44
Textile operators	66.67	33.33	9.76	0.71	11.43	41.57	10.00
Transport equipment operatives	50.48	49.52	3.38	8.21	13.53	32.06	10.14
Laborers, except farm	60.71	39.29	6.02	1.88	10.34	22.22	13.16
Cleaning service workers	54.46	45.55	1.49	0.50	7.43	23.35	9.90
Food service workers	52.46	47.55	0.52	1.29	7.49	13.39	11.37
Health service workers	65.99	34.01	2.03	0.51	8.63	16.05	9.65
Personal service workers	36.81	63.19	1.84	20.25	9.20	18.03	9.82

[a] From bank tellers to meter readers for utilities (Census 301 to 334).
[b] From shipping clerks to ticket agents and other miscellaneous clerks (Census 374 to 395).
[c] From auto accessories installers to machinist apprentices (Census 401 to 462).

effect explicit performance pay has on wages (and thus, indirectly, on productivity). A major issue is the identification of a true causal effect on productivity of going from an "input-based" compensation scheme, such as an hourly rate, to an "output-based" one. Finally, I also examine the incidence of bonuses based on job performance.

Determinants of Performance Pay

Theoretical Considerations

The Lazear Model

Economic theory offers a straightforward prediction when firms can observe the effort put forth by their workers: it simply does not matter whether workers are paid a piece rate or a salary.[4] Firms can enforce the first-best level of effort under either type of compensation form. To see this, consider the following simple model. A firm hires a single worker and effort e is directly related to output y by the following very simple technology:

$$y(e) = e \qquad (2.1)$$

On the other hand, the worker's utility is assumed to be separable in wages W and in the cost of effort $C(e)$:

$$U(W,e) = W - C(e) \qquad (2.2)$$

where $C(e)$ represents the worker's cost of effort. Note that effort is increasingly costly to the worker.[5] Workers can be paid either a piece rate $P(y)$ or an input-based rate $S(e)$. Assuming a competitive environment that drives profits to zero, workers will be paid their full marginal productivity. In other words, $P(y) = e$ or, under a salary, $S(e) = e$. The fact that effort is observed and thus contractible makes it possible for firms to offer either a contract in which pay is output-based, that is, it depends on y, which would be a piece rate contract, or an input-based contract in which pay is based on e, and the first-best effort level can be achieved.[6]

A more interesting and realistic case is one in which effort cannot be contracted upon but output can. Thus, individual productivity can be measured, albeit at a cost, and effort is not an issue. Then firms hire from a pool of workers who are heterogeneous in their (time-invariant) productivity y. As in Lazear (1986) or Brown (1990), different methods of pay allow workers to sort themselves among firms. The assumptions are zero expected profits, and workers know their productive ability but firms do not unless they incur a monitoring cost M. Workers can be in a firm that pays salary S which is independent of productivity y or in a piece rate firm that pays $W = y - M$.[7] Thus the worker chooses the piece rate firm if and only if:

$$y - M > S \qquad (2.3)$$

and the others choose to work in the salary firm. Provided that $M > 0$, there will be firms offering $S > 0$. These firms know they have attracted workers of lower average quality and they pay accordingly, a salary equal to the expected productivity of the self-selected workers.

Therefore, in this simplest of cases, compensation is independent of productive skills in jobs paying salaries while compensation moves one-for-one with skills in piece rates. Of course, over a longer period, promotion opportunities and the simple continuation of employment are very likely to depend on y even in salaried jobs. So the sharp distinction between "output-based" pay and "input-based" pay is likely to be blurred in reality.

Still, this simple model offers sharp predictions concerning the use of performance pay: First, more productive workers choose piece rates because only for them is it worth it to pay the measurement cost (through a reduced paycheck). Thus, proxies of worker productivity such as schooling should be positively associated with the use of piece rates. Second, the variance of output will be larger in piece rate jobs than in salaried jobs because piece rates depend on individual productivity. Third, piece rates will tend not to be offered where it is more costly to measure output. Fourth, the more heterogeneous is the work force in terms of productivity, the more there is to gain from separating the more productive from the least productive workers.[8]

The Principal-Agent Model

The principal-agent model emphasizes how risk aversion by workers combined with the inability to observe effort affects the optimal sharing of risks and the provision of incentives. The risks include machine breakdowns, weather, depressed market conditions, and so on, over which the worker has no control. These risks induce variability in output (and compensation) that the worker would like to avoid. The firm is assumed to observe output costlessly, but cannot separate the effects of the risky environment from the level of effort put forth by the worker. The best assessment it can make is that high effort is more likely when output is high than when output is low. Even that may be hard to infer if random factors become too important.

Under these conditions, the optimal contract links pay directly to output, possibly (but not necessarily) in a linear fashion in which $w = a + by$ where w is the wage and y is the output. The firm's problem is to optimally choose the incentive component b. Since there are "environmental" risks associated with the production process, we assume that output y depends linearly on both effort and a noise term ε which represents the risk element. Assuming that the firm is risk neutral while the worker is risk averse with a coefficient of risk aversion represented by r, the optimal piece rate contract sets the slope at

$$b^* = 1 / (1 + r \sigma^2 C'') \tag{2.4}$$

where σ^2 is the variance of the noise term ε representing the degree of risk involved, and C'' is the rate at which the marginal cost of effort increases.[9] Given an optimal piece rate b^*, a is then chosen to make sure that the worker earns exactly the same amount as she would earn in her next best alternative. Thus, a can be seen as the "base salary" to which is added performance pay b^*y. We can see from equation (4) that the more risk averse is the worker (i.e., the higher is r), the more muted will be the incentive component. In other words the optimal piece rate is generally lower than 1. The firm chooses b by balancing the costs and benefits of changing the strength of the incentive component. If it set $b = 1$ (all performance pay with no base), the benefit would be higher effort coming at the cost of having to compensate the worker for the added risk. In essence, the optimal contract involves *delegation* by the firm to the worker of the appropriate choice of actions to take. The firm knows that its interest conflicts with the worker's (for a given amount paid, he would like to provide as little effort as he can), so it sets up the optimal contract in such a way as to induce the worker to take the appropriate actions.[10]

Thus, unless we have "extreme" risk aversion, very high r, workers should all be paid a piece rate and pay should vary frequently. The simple facts are that (1) relatively few people are paid piece rates or commissions, and (2) people's pay does not change all the time.

Again, researchers must search for factors contributing to the low incidence of explicit performance pay. Although the firm may have a good idea of the dimension along which workers should enhance their effort, it is not clear that it can actually base compensation on that dimension. The firm will instead base the worker's pay on another measure that *appears* to be equivalent. However, as pointed out by Baker (1992), it is not clear that the worker will act in the firm's best interest by responding to the incentive that being offered. An often-cited example (e.g., in Brown 1990) is the incentive contract offered to former quarterback Ken O'Brien of the New York Jets. After a year in which he threw a lot of interceptions (and also a lot of touchdown passes—in other words, he took some risks), he was offered a contract in which final pay would be a function of many factors including how few interceptions he would throw. The end result was that O'Brien held onto the ball more than in the previous year, instead of throwing it, and, in the process, he was sacked much more often. Thus, putting such an explicit emphasis on one aspect likely turned out to be counterproductive. This is just one example among many illustrating what Kerr (1975) called "The Folly of Rewarding A, While Hoping for B."

This problem can also be formulated in a different way. Suppose a good measure of output for a particular task does exist, but workers are asked to perform many value-enhancing activities, all of which compete for the worker's limited time. If these different tasks are substitutes (e.g., if maximizing the short-term number of units produced by a machine is likely to be in conflict with its maintenance), then it may be optimal to set the piecerate slope to zero (Holmström and Milgrom 1991). The worker's pay then consists of only a base salary. Alternatively, the firm could base part of the worker's pay on the aspect of the job for which an objective performance measure exists and then base the rest on a *subjective* measure which, by its very nature, is practically impossible for a third party to verify. I will return to this aspect of performance pay when I discuss implicit incentives.

The agent principle model helps explain the use of relative performance evaluations. By the Informativeness Principle (Milgrom and Roberts 1992), the firm should use any information that reduces the noise present in the output signal (e.g., customer complaints, bad weather, other salespersons' output in the same market). One way to reduce the noise is by comparing different workers in the same job, such as salespersons operating in the same market. Given that the workers face more or less the same common risks, these can be purged through relative performance evaluation. Thus, the critical performance measure is the rank of each worker, and workers should compete for, say, performance bonuses or promotions, much as athletes do in a sports tournament (Lazear and Rosen 1981, Rosen 1986). However, tournaments may prove to be counterproductive when teamwork is important or, more generally, where the firm benefits from having people collaborate with one another. Attributing rewards based solely on the ranking of individuals may trigger "sabotage activity" (or, less spectacularly, the absence of cooperation [Lazear 1989] because one worker can benefit from decreasing another's output. Consequently, any job that involves teamwork should not be associated with explicit individual performance pay. In summary, refinements to the principal-agent model make it possible to understand some of the factors behind the low incidence of explicit performance pay.

The Role Played by Institutions

The role of unions in adopting explicit performance pay is ambiguous. On the one hand, unions tend to reduce earnings inequality, at least within unionized establishments. Indeed, the dramatic decline in the percentage of workers covered by a collective bargaining agreement (CBA) over the last thirty years has been shown to be an important factor behind the substantial increase in earnings inequality in the United States (DiNardo, Fortin, and Lemieux 1996). Thus, if unions favor wage compression, they would tend to favor time rates over performance pay. On the other hand, unions may facilitate the operation of piece rates by getting the firm to commit to a rates that need union approval to be modified. Such an outside constraint may be beneficial because firms would often be tempted to "cut the rates," or adjust the performance threshold upward, once workers reveal how difficult the job really is. Workers, knowing that firms may adjust the rates once they have all the relevant information, may reduce their effort level at the start in order to guarantee themselves higher rates in the future. This is the so-called ratchet effect (Gibbons 1987; Kanemoto and MacLeod 1992). Therefore, contractually agreed upon piece rates, because they cannot be modified at management's will, could actually provide benefits over the long run.[11]

Gender might also influence the choice of performance pay. Much of the argument rests on the lower labor force attachment by women. Because female workers are more likely to interrupt their tenure, firms should not expect deferred compensation to have a strong incentive effect on them (Lazear 1981). Consequently, as argued by Goldin (1986), female workers may be more likely than males to choose piece rates because of the lower value of the deferred portion of the compensation package. Piece rates, in effect, provide short-term incentives that may suit women better. Although the same argument might suggest that women prefer commission contracts, Geddes and Heywood (2000) argue instead that commission workers often interact on a repeated basis with customers, making the relationship long term in nature and suggesting that men should be more likely to be paid commissions.

In addition, if women prefer flexibility in their work schedule because of family responsibilities (illnesses, picking up the children at daycare, etc.), then they may choose (or firms may choose for them) jobs with minimal teamwork. If teamwork requires cohesion among the members of the team, then any disruption of the work routine due to a worker being absent might be costly to the firm. Since teamwork is likely to make the cost of measuring individual output higher, it is likely that firms may favor implicit incentives (possibly deferred compensation packages) over explicit individual incentive schemes. This, as Geddes and Heywood (2000) suggest, might be an additional factor why women are more likely than men to be paid piece rates.

The Evidence

In the previous subsection, we saw that whether firms use an explicit performance pay scheme or not will depend mainly on: (1) whether or not individual output can be measured and the cost of such measurement; (2) the monitoring technology; (3) the degree of risk aversion on the part of workers; (4) the randomness in output; (5) the level of worker skills; (6) the "complexity" of the job (e.g., the number of tasks); (7) whether part or all of the randomness associated with a particular job can be filtered out by performing relative performance evaluations; (8) union status; and (9) gender composition. Before looking at the effect of some of the factors outlined above in a multivariate context, it may be useful to show some descriptive statistics linking job characteristics to either pay schemes or occupations. Tables 2.4 and 2.5 show, using both the QES and the NLSY, the fraction of workers in each of the twenty occupations listed who reported that their job was associated with the characteristics listed. It is interesting to note that the occupations for which teamwork appears to be less important (sales, operatives) are the ones in which we find almost all the piece rate or commission workers in the samples. Figure 2.1 shows more directly that many of the factors predicted by theory go in the right direction. Teamwork clearly appears to favor salaries or hourly rates over piece rates or commissions, while multitasking is most prevalent in salaried jobs. Figure 2.1 also suggests that treating commissions as being similar to piece rates may not be appropriate: Commission work seems to be more "complex" in the sense that workers report learning more new things and having less repetitive tasks than is the case for piece work.[12]

Table 2.6 summarizes the evidence on the factors in determining explicit performance pay. It has proved challenging to provide convincing evidence, given that the variables researchers are trying to explain are categorical,

Table 2.4

Average Job Characteristics by Occupation: Quality of Employment Survey, 1973–1977 (in percentage of occupation)

Occupation	Repetitiveness	Variety of things	Worker has say	Learn new things	Teamwork	Set own pace
Professional, technical, except engineering technical	51.6	94.8	92.3	95.8	57.8	75.8
Engineering and science technical	58.4	80.7	52.9	94.6	82.5	88.4
Writers, artists, etc.	28.0	96.1	96.1	96.1	58.4	58.4
Managers and administrators, except farm	60.5	97.7	93.2	94.5	41.3	84.4
Sales workers	59.3	79.7	85.9	92.0	42.4	77.1
Clerical and unskilled 1[a]	74.9	75.5	65.0	80.8	67.1	86.9
Office machine operators	83.9	75.8	48.7	86.6	62.6	62.6
Secretaries	64.1	88.7	49.3	78.9	76.4	71.6
Clerical and unskilled 2[b]	81.1	82.0	48.8	76.5	69.3	71.7
Craftsmen and kindred 1[c]	65.5	83.4	68.8	87.7	69.2	79.7
Mechanics and repairmen	63.2	85.3	68.1	84.7	48.9	79.1
Operatives, except precision machines and textiles	77.4	52.7	45.3	56.0	66.0	54.5
Precision machines operatives	84.1	53.7	51.9	48.3	56.4	62.6
Textile operators	77.5	52.6	40.2	56.4	56.3	63.7
Transport equipment operatives	86.8	62.0	48.5	60.9	52.8	81.9
Laborers, except farm	97.6	85.4	46.1	56.9	76.4	90.7
Cleaning service workers	79.6	88.1	76.7	73.9	28.7	78.9
Food service workers	89.1	76.4	52.5	62.1	64.9	76.7
Health service workers	76.6	67.7	41.2	91.3	54.6	54.6
Personal service workers	68.8	80.1	66.5	83.4	44.3	76.7

[a] From bank tellers to meter readers for utilities (Census 301 to 334).
[b] From shipping clerks to ticket agents and other miscellaneous clerks (Census 374 to 395).
[c] From auto accessories installers to machinist apprentices (Census 401 to 462).
Cell entries represent the percentage of workers who consider their jobs to have the various features listed.

Table 2.5

Average Job Characteristics by Occupation: National Longitudinal Survey of Youth, 1979 and 1982 (in percentage of occupation)

Occupation	Autonomy	Complete task	Variety of tasks	Friendships	Deal with people
Professional, technical, except engineering technical	57.36	73.81	55.41	56.93	76.41
Engineering and science technical	61.59	78.81	56.95	58.28	65.56
Writers, artists, etc.	67.68	76.77	54.55	65.66	73.74
Managers and administrators, except farm	61.13	77.48	64.61	56.84	90.08
Sales workers	42.08	63.34	30.67	55.92	84.02
Clerical and unskilled 1[a]	32.77	65.88	30.67	49.87	72.79
Office machine operators	39.75	62.46	38.80	48.90	59.62
Secretaries	44.95	73.70	51.07	54.74	72.48
Clerical and unskilled 2[b]	39.13	67.69	37.02	49.47	63.69
Craftsmen and kindred 1[c]	47.10	71.65	47.99	56.03	46.65
Mechanics and repairmen	48.48	73.19	48.96	50.40	52.49
Operatives, except precision machines and textile	32.64	57.46	33.01	48.29	44.99
Precision machine operatives	28.92	48.59	26.51	50.20	33.33
Textile operators	31.73	59.37	33.21	47.31	33.21
Transport equipment operatives	40.25	65.50	33.25	48.50	62.25
Laborers, except farm	33.04	62.73	30.89	48.44	45.49
Cleaning service workers	34.93	64.95	27.34	40.07	33.65
Food service workers	28.26	64.37	22.19	54.45	70.57
Health service workers	37.99	68.16	39.94	62.01	82.12
Personal service workers	47.96	66.19	33.09	58.03	74.10

[a] From bank tellers to meter readers for utilities (Census 301 To 334).
[b] From shipping clerks to ticket agents and other miscellaneous clerks (Census 374 to 395).
[c] From auto accessories installers to machinist apprentices (Census 401 to 462).
Cell entries represent the percentage of workers who consider their jobs to have the various features listed.

and, as explained in Appendix 2.2, misclassification of pay methods makes it harder to measure relationships than when the variable to be explained is continuous.

Still, both Brown (1990) and MacLeod and Parent (1999a) find evidence that multitasking tends not to be associated with piece rates or commissions. In addition, MacLeod and Parent find that worker autonomy tends to go hand in hand with such explicit incentive contracts.[13] A similar result is found by Garen (1998a) in studying the determinants of salaries versus hourly rates. The result is given by Holmström and Milgrom (1994), who emphasize that delegation of authority is likely to come with output-based

Figure 2.1 **Job Characteristics and Pay Methods: Quality of Employment Survey, 1973–1977**

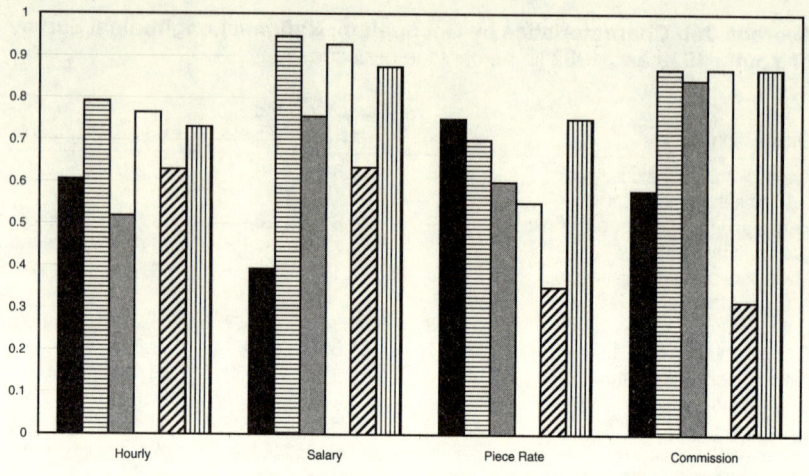

■ Repetitiveness ☰ Variety of Things ▦ Worker Has Say ☐ Learn New Things ▨ Teamwork ▥ Set Own Pace

incentives. Among other results, as reported by MacLeod and Parent and especially by Brown, teamwork appears to favor the use of hourly rates or salaries instead of explicit performance pay. This follows since teamwork means that individual output may be difficult to measure and/or cooperative behavior among workers is easier to achieve when incentives are not individual-based.

Geddes and Heywood (2000) find that, as hypothesized, women are at the same time more likely to be paid piece rates and less likely to be paid commissions than men. The argument raised by Geddes and Heywood that commission work has more of a long-term perspective than a piece rate job complements the point made in MacLeod and Parent (1999a) that output under a commission contract is very likely to be much more noisy than in piece work. Hence, it takes some time before an individual doing commission work develops the skills and contacts necessary to reduce the idiosyncratic variability in output.

The Incentive Effect of Performance Pay

In the previous section we saw that firms offering explicit individual performance pay can expect to attract and retain more productive workers. Naturally, firms expect to induce workers of a given ability level to work

Table 2.6

Job Characteristics and Piece Rate versus Commission Contracts

				Characteristics			
Papers	Gender	Presence of union	Variety of tasks	Worker autonomy	Capital intensity	Establishment size	Teamwork
Brown (1990)							
Data sets: Industry wage surveys and Dictionary of Occupational Titles (DOT)							
Pay method:							
Piece rates versus time rates	++	0	– –		0	++	
MacLeod and Parent (1999)							
Data sets: NLSY, PSID, QES, CPS							
Pay method:							
Piece rates versus hourly rates	+	0	– –	++			– –
Commissions versus salaries	– –	0	– –	++			– –
Garen (1998a)							
Data set: CPS + DOT							
Pay method:							
Hourly rates versus salaries				++			
Geddes and Heywood (2000)							
Data set: NLSY							
Pay method:							
Piece rates versus time rates/salaries	++	0					
Commissions versus time rates/salaries	– –	–					

Notes: ++ (– –) denotes strong evidence of positive (negative) association effect while + or – denotes weaker evidence.

harder by tying parts of their paychecks to an explicit measure of output. Yet, whether or not this happens depends on the existing incentives within the firm. Even when paying a straight salary, the firm can still provide some incentives to its workers by, for example, basing the continuation of the employment relationship upon past performance. Thus, a worker cannot expect to keep his job forever if he shirks continually.

That being said, it is in principle possible to assess whether commissions or piece rates have any "incentive effect" provided that we control properly for the selection process governing the choice by individuals of those types of compensation methods. In other words, the issue boils down to whether one can "purge" any estimated productivity or wage effect of its unobserved ability component. As in all evaluation problems, researchers try to answer the so-called what-if question: What would have happened to the same workers who were paid piece rates or commissions if they had been working under a time rate or a salary?

Cross-Sectional Evidence

Somewhat arbitrarily, I will focus on four specific studies carried out over the last twenty years or so. I choose as a starting point John Pencavel's (1977) work, since its publication signaled a renewed interest in the topic among economists.[14] To be sure, many studies had been carried out over the years by researchers, particularly in industrial relations. The other three studies are by Seiler (1984), Brown (1992), and Ewing (1996). Seiler and Brown use a very large sample of establishments from the Bureau of Labor Statistics (BLS) Industry Wage Surveys, each survey covering a particular industry, while Ewing uses just one wave of the NLSY.

All four studies are cross-sectional; none follow a sample of workers or firms through time. Consequently, they implicitly assume that the what-if question can be answered satisfactorily by simply comparing the average pay or productivity of incentive workers to that of the time-rated workers, conditioning out the effect of the observable characteristics present in the data. In other words, the control group made of workers not paid under an explicit pay-for-performance contract is a good approximation of the counterfactual state. This is a strong assumption considering the theoretical model outlined above, which stresses that the two types of workers are likely to be different. Of course, if the characteristics present in the data control perfectly for the difference in individual productivity, using cross-sectional data poses no particular problem. However, this is very unlikely.

All four papers find a positive relationship between the use of performance pay and the level of wages. This confirms many of the studies carried out before Pencavel.[15] Note that all four authors were aware that some selection process was involved, either on the firm side or on the worker side, the title to Pencavel's paper making explicit reference to the screening of workers by firms and Ewing being careful not to mention that the estimated relationship represents any incentive effect. Ewing, in fact, simply emphasizes that his results are consistent with the model exposited in Brown (1992), which itself is a straightforward extension of the Lazear (1986) model.

The safest conclusion from these studies is that higher productivity goes hand in hand with explicit performance pay, but that we really do not know whether the effect is because of the incentive or simply because of the selection of intrinsically more productive workers for jobs that offer explicit performance pay. Note that, from the firm's perspective, even if performance pay does not induce workers to supply a higher level of effort, the screening mechanism embodied in incentive contracts results in hiring more productive workers. Consequently, one would expect firms to use performance pay whenever a good objective measure of output exists, such as in sales. However, even when a good objective measure of productivity exists, there are situations when firms are very reluctant to put a lot of incentive pressure on just one dimension of the job. I will return to this issue later when implicit incentives are examined.

Longitudinal Evidence

Given that we can expect workers to be "positively selected" into piece rate or commission jobs, it is very important that we somehow answer the what-if question. What would have happened to workers paid piece rates had they been paid a salary or an hourly rate? Answering that question requires longitudinal data where workers are observed in both circumstances.[16] Using the so-called within-worker variation in pay methods, we can recover the incentive effect. While this is a major improvement over cross-sectional data, it is not bulletproof. First, it assumes that whatever unobserved worker characteristic (or unobserved productivity) drives the selection into incentive contracts does not change through time. Consequently, we can apply standard fixed-effect estimators in which a simple transformation of the data purges all time-invariant worker components. That assumption would be violated, for example, when both the firm and the worker are unsure about the latter's productivity, which would be inferred from observing the worker's output through time. In that case, the unobserved (to the researcher) worker productivity component would not be time invariant and could not be differenced out from the wage equation.

However, most applied researchers are willing to consider the fixed-effect assumption as a reasonable approximation to what they realize is a more complex process.

Second, not all unobserved dimensions of the wage determination process are limited to the worker. The productivity of a worker depends on how well that worker is matched with her or his current employer. Consequently, it may not be enough to have multiple observations of the same worker across jobs. One would need multiple observations within the same employment relationship. In that case, the incentive effect is identified through the changes in pay methods *with the same employer*. Now, of course, staying with the same employer does not necessarily mean that one's tasks have stayed the same: A worker's position within the firm could change, which could possibly lead to a much different job. Still, the ability to control for unobserved employer-employee matching effect likely represents a major improvement over simply controlling for unobserved worker attributes.

Three recent studies have used multiple observations of the same workers with given employers to try to identify the incentive effect of explicit performance pay. Parent (1999) exploits the three straight years in the National Longitudinal Survey of Youth, which, when combined with ability to identify each jobs separately, allows the use of fixed-effect methods to purge the estimates of some the biases caused by omitted variables, including unobserved job-match characteristics. On the other hand, Lazear (2000) uses repeated observations of workers in a single firm that changed the way it paid its workers, going from hourly rates to piece rates. The Lazear sample offers a cleaner way to identify the "true" causal effect in that the only thing that changed in that company was the pay scheme: The job (windshield installation) did not change before and after the switch. Lazear is also able to analyze the extent to which the company (Safelite Glass Inc.) retained its best employees, while the least productive ones left after change to performance pay.

Interestingly, while the data differ, the estimated average wage effects are fairly similar, a little over 6 percent for Parent and at least 9 percent for Lazear. Moreover, that portion of the cross-sectional wage differences between incentive workers and other workers that can be attributed to worker selectivity effects is also similar. In addition, Lazear shows that absenteeism decreased following the change, thus giving an added source of productivity growth. Although piece rates do seem to induce greater worker effort (despite some unresolved issues; see below), Parent finds that workers on piece rates do not appear to be earning compensating wage premiums once selection effects are taken into account.[17]

At minimum, selection effects are very important. In fact, even if there were no true incentive effects, the evidence presented in Lazear's paper shows that the overall productivity of the work force that stayed with Safelite was substantially higher than the productivity of Safelite's work force before the management switched to performance pay. Second, Parent shows that there is a great deal of heterogeneity in worker productivity in performance pay jobs. Indeed, that's partly what a piece rate contract aims to achieve, allowing the best workers to separate themselves from the least productive ones.

Finally, in perhaps the most interesting study of the three, Ichniowski, Shaw, and Prennushi (1997) use plant-level data to examine the effects of many different human resource management (HRM) practices, including performance pay, on the productivity of steel finishing lines. Their study is of particular interest because it provides evidence on the importance of complementarity of HRM practices, a point that was emphasized by Holmström and Milgrom (1994), among others. In other words, successful systems of HRM practices are likely to occur when they are well designed and implemented as a group. In particular, they find that changes in individual work practices have little effect on productivity.[18]

Bonuses and Promotions

Introduction

We can see from Table 2.1 that although workers on piece rates or commissions account for less then 10 percent of the work force, a significant fraction of workers receive either a bonus or a promotion, or both. This part of the chapter will focus only on theoretical notions that yield testable implications and the sparse evidence available. For an excellent survey of the main issues surrounding the provision of life-cycle incentives, see Carmichael (1989).

Credibility and the Use of Bonuses or Promotions:
Theory and Evidence

Despite a usable measure of worker output, the firm may choose to base pay on other dimensions of job performance that influence firm value to encourage workers to devote part of their time to aspects of the job that are not so easily measurable. Such components of pay will therefore be based on a subjective evaluation of performance leading to "merit pay," or subjectively determined bonuses, promotions, or a combination of both.[19]

It would seem that, for a variety of reasons, such arrangements would be difficult to implement. First, given the subjective nature of the performance evaluation, it is hard for a third party such as a court to enforce the terms of such a contract. The possibility for "cheating" on the terms of the implicit contract is real if the individual who performs the merit evaluation is a residual claimant to the firm's output. There is a clear incentive to underreport the worker's contribution. Anticipating this, the worker is likely not to put forth as high an effort level as if he knew the evaluation process to be "fair." Second, even when performance is not evaluated by a residual claimant, the evaluator may take actions not in the firm's interest. These include compressing the distribution of the evaluation ratings around a norm or simply overrating the poor performers because penalizing them is unpleasant. Indeed, the human resources management literature is full of cases reporting such "centrality biases" and "leniency biases."[20] In addition, because performance evaluations are subjective and thus depend on perceptions, there are incentives for workers to engage in rent-seeking activities to enhance their chances of getting good evaluations.

Before offering one argument about why bonuses and/or promotions are nevertheless quite common, note that it is not clear that the bonus measures calculated using the PSID truly reflect subjective performance rewards. However, the data show that the incidence of bonuses is much lower for workers paid on an hourly basis or paid piece rates than it is for salaried workers. In fact, in MacLeod and Parent (1999a), we argue that workers paid commissions or salaries should be treated separately from other workers for the simple reason that the output of workers on salaries and/or commissions is likely to contain a larger random element than the output of workers on an hourly rate or a piece rate. For example, a salesperson might work for long hours before closing one deal while another sale could be made very rapidly. On the other hand, working for a few more hours on an assembly line will almost certainly lead to higher output. Consequently, the bonus measure computed from the PSID, while noisy, still contains some information. In the NLSY, workers are asked directly to report whether part of their labor income was earned through performance-based bonuses. Although this does not exclude payments for team production, Brown (1990) reports that those are relatively rare. Thus, we can be relatively confident that the measures of bonuses present in the data sets reflect a subjective evaluation of performance to some extent. Assuming this is the case, the use of such evaluation is not rare. Indeed, as shown in Figure 2.2, the PSID evidence suggests that it has been increasing over time for salaried workers excluding sales workers.

By modeling a repeated game between the firm and the worker,

Figure 2.2 **Fraction of Workers Paid Bonuses and Covered by a Union Contract PSID, Excluding Overtime and Commission Workers, 1976–1991**

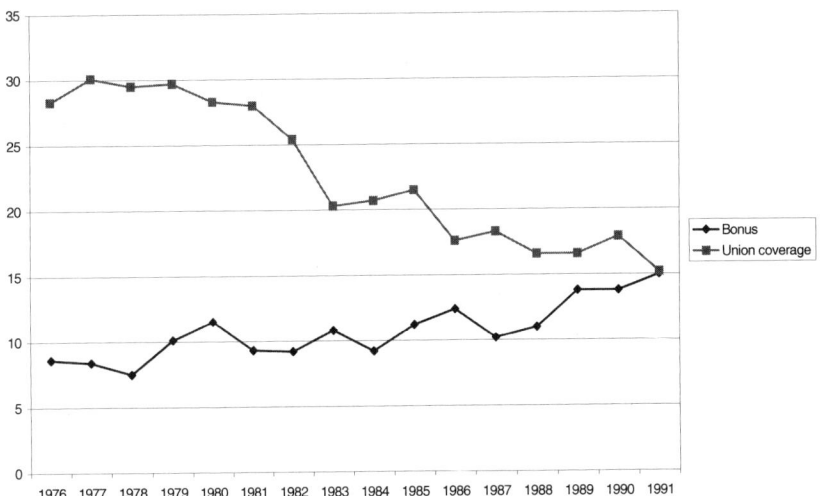

MacLeod and Malcomson (1989) show that each party will resist breaking its respective (implicit) promises only if fulfilling them creates a *surplus*. That is, one party earns at least as much as in its next best alternative and the other party earns strictly more. If that condition is met, there exists a set of nontrivial self-enforcing contracts in which both parties act honestly. This set of contracts is called self-enforcing because the promises of higher effort on the part of the worker and of rewarding such effort by the firm cannot be legally enforced.[21]

Possible sources of surplus include specific human capital and reputation effects for firm. Thus, if workers realize that the firm is cheating on its promise to reward high effort, then they may retaliate by withholding effort. Another source of surplus is involuntary unemployment. Similar to the idea of Shapiro and Stiglitz (1984), the fear of losing one's job may be sufficient to induce workers to provide effort. For that to happen, it must be the case that the workers gain strictly more than in their next best alternative; otherwise nothing would prevent them from shirking. Consequently, when workers are "abundant," for example, when we witness a relatively high unemployment rate, workers get the surplus from the relationship. The firms cannot be given the surplus because they can hire workers very easily and thus it would be very difficult for them to resist the temptation to renege on the agreement. Conversely, if workers can get jobs very easily because the labor market is tight, then it would be difficult to give them the surplus. Firms will motivate workers by paying them a bonus as part of their compensation package. Workers will trust firms to pay the bonus because the cost of replacing workers who would quit if not paid the bonus would be high for the firm. On the other hand, firms could not be trusted to pay a bonus (after observing a high effort level) when unemployment is high because the cost of replacing the workers is low. Instead, to motivate the workers, fixed wages set above the workers' next best alternative are paid and the threat of firing is used to motivate them.

Thus, there should be an inverse relationship between the use of bonuses and the unemployment rate. Strong evidence confirming this prediction is provided by MacLeod and Parent (1999a, 1999b). In the first paper, we examine the relationship between bonus incidence and the unemployment rate defined at the level of the county. In the second paper, we find even stronger evidence when we look at the relationship between the amount paid in bonuses (using the PSID) and the unemployment rate.

Although these results provide support for the incomplete contracting model of MacLeod and Malcomson, they may stem from simple rent-sharing motives. In good years (i.e., years with low unemployment), firms have higher profits and may be more willing to pay bonuses. We would feel more confident about the interpretation we give, if we could control for firm profits. While the model is certainly not a perfect substitute, it turns out that, when we include year dummies fully interacted with industry dummies to reflect the time-varying conditions in a particular industry (including demand conditions), the results actually become stronger. Still, more research in this area (with better data) seems warranted.

Unions and the Use of Bonuses

As shown in Figure 2.2, the use of bonuses appears to be on the rise since the mid-seventies. Coincidentally, the fraction of workers covered by a collective bargaining agreement has decreased over the same time period, suggesting that union coverage would tend not to be associated with the use of bonuses. Indeed, this is confirmed not only with the aggregate data but also when using a multivariate framework to control for other factors. It appears that the declining rate of unionization allows firms to provide more flexible compensation packages. Thus, given nominal wage rigidity (e.g., Bewley [1993] or McLaughlin [1999]), firms might well prefer offering workers bonuses, which are by definition temporary, instead of offering permanent wage increases, which cannot be undone so easily.

Productivity Effects of Implicit Contracts (and of Other HRM Practices)

The most compelling empirical work examining productivity effects of implicit contracts has been that of Ichniowski, Shaw, and Prennushi (1997). Although these researchers focus on one narrowly defined sector, the benefits of less unobserved heterogeneity outweigh the costs of perhaps not being able to readily generalize the results. By considering clusters of human resource management practices, they emphasize the complementarity between the different HRM practices and they can measure the individual contribution of each.

One of the HRM practices considered in their paper is the use of what they label as "line incentives," which reward not only the level of output achieved by workers on a production line but also more difficult-to-measure attributes like quality. As such, line incentive plans have common features with implicit contracts. The authors show that performance pay plans do have productivity effects, but only when used in combination with a host of other HRM practices such as flexible job assignments, training, and sharing of information. When only a subset of those other practices is used, the productivity effects of performance pay are muted.

Incentive Contracts Based on Group Performance

Instead of reviewing the large existing literature on the use of profit sharing plans, I offer new evidence suggesting (and confirming previous studies) that profit sharing does seem to "work," conditional on certain identifying assumptions. For a very comprehensive overview of the effect of profit sharing plans, readers are referred to Kruse (1993).

Why Provide Incentives Using Group Performance? Why Does it Work?

In short, researchers cannot provide compelling answers to those two questions. On the one hand, profit sharing plans suffer from the free-rider problem. Why would an individual in a group of N workers really be induced to provide effort when he will get only $1/N$ of the increased productivity or profits? Put differently, why would he not rely on the N-1 other workers' efforts to increase his wage without changing his own behavior? On the other hand, explanations based on the possible beneficial effects of profit sharing plans on team morale, worker cooperation, better internalization of the firm's objectives by the workers, and so on, suffer from the problem that they are very difficult to verify empirically.

Despite the problem of free riding, it is clear from table 2.1 that in QES and especially in the NLSY profit sharing is very common. One possibility is that firms use such plans mainly because it is tax preferred compensation, not because they think that workers' productivity will increase. Yet, basically all studies find a positive relationship between the use of profit sharing plans and either measures of productivity or workers' wages. Of course, one difficulty in assessing a causal effect is that it could well be that, while high profit firms tend to have profit sharing plans, they might earn still higher profits without them. In other word, more convincing evidence would show positive effects following a given firm's *adoption* of a profit sharing plan. Such evidence is offered in Kruse (1993). Essentially, even controlling for firms' unobserved characteristics, those that switch to profit sharing plans do seem to exhibit higher productivity. However, Kruse notes that firms adopting profit sharing plans tended to have rising productivity before the adoption of the plan. As it turns out, when Kruse (1992) controls for differential trends on productivity, results are basically left unchanged.

The Wage Effects of Profit Sharing Plans.

Given that the NLSY data do not contain firm-level data, I again use wage data to examine profit sharing plans.[22] I exploit the longitudinal dimension of the NLSY, including the fact that we know whether a worker stays in the same job or changes employers, to estimate the wage impact of such plans.[23] More precisely, I exploit the fact that I observe workers more than one time in a given employment relationship. This allows me to measure the effect of adopting a profit sharing plan in a given employment relationship.[24]

The results are shown in table 2.7. Although the coefficient changes when going from level estimation to fixed-effect estimation, there remains a statistically (and economically) significant effect of profit sharing plans in the case of men.[25] In fact, the results for men are very much in line with what researchers have previously found. Thus, the results presented here provide further evidence of the beneficial effects that profit sharing plans have on productivity. This assumes, of course, that workers are paid their marginal productivity. It could be that profit sharing plans have a wage effect but no productivity effect if firms simply use profit sharing plans as a simple way to share rents with workers. The question remains why they would do that if it has absolutely no effect on worker productivity.[26]

The absence of an association for women between profit sharing plans

Table 2.7

Wage Effect of Profit Sharing Plans: NLSY (1988–1990)

Dependent Variable: Log of Hourly Earnings

	OLS	Within worker	Within job
Part A: Men			
Profit sharing indicator	0.0811	0.0396	0.0359
	(0.0195)	(0.0134)	(0.0141)
R-squared	0.4314	0.8927	0.9434
Sample size: 4,582			
Part B: Women			
Profit sharing indicator	0.0475	0.0004	−0.0005
	(0.0125)	(0.0149)	(0.0173)
R-squared	0.4291	0.8927	0.9306
Sample size: 3,555			

Note: The R-squared statistics for the fixed-effect models are indicative only of a better fit: Without an intercept, they cannot be interpreted in the same way as in the case of models with intercepts. Other covariates include employer tenure, experience, years of completed schooling, dummies for region of residence, living in a Standard Metropolitan Statistical Area (SMSA), industry, occupation, year, health status, and union coverage.

and productivity (or at least wages) might follow from the lower labor force attachment of women, in a manner similar to that identified by Goldin (1986). If most profit sharing plans consist of contributions to pension plans (something we do not know from the NLSY data but which the work of Kruse (1992) strongly suggests), then profit sharing represents deferred compensation and, as such, provides women less incentive for effort than is the case for men.[27]

Conclusion

In this chapter I reviewed the empirical and theoretical literature on both the determinants of the methods of pay and the effects of explicit performance pay. Although the use of explicit performance pay is not very common, the data show that firms use a wide array of other tools such as profit sharing plans and bonuses, to motivate workers.

While the evidence surveyed points toward fairly large productivity effects, especially in the case of explicit incentive contracts, there remains the question of whether the identification strategies employed so far are completely satisfactory. At least, we have in the Lazear model a useful tool to help us deal with that problem, in that it makes explicit the connection between pay methods, skills, and the return to those skills. Further explorations of the implications of that model seem warranted.

Another topic that should be explored more fully is the link between profit-sharing plans and skills. Although the usual emphasis has been placed on the incentive effect of profit sharing, it might be at least as useful to consider profit sharing plans as the solution to a contracting problem. Firms would like to commit themselves to reward firm-specific skills but usually cannot, which in turn makes workers underinvest out of the concern that they will be held up. Additionally, it seems likely that if profit sharing and skill acquisition are linked, then workers will not only learn truly firm-specific skills but will also learn general skills in the process. If this is the case, then one would expect to see the wage/productivity effect of profit sharing plans carry over into subsequent employment relationships. This is, on the surface at least, a readily testable proposition which, if confirmed, would create doubt about the incentive motive for the presence of profit sharing plans.

Appendix 2.1: Data Sets

Quality of Employment Survey, 1973–1977

The Quality of Employment Survey (QES), 1973, uses a national probability sample of persons sixteen years old or older who are working for twenty or more hours a week. Three such separate surveys were conducted: in 1969–1970 (when it was named the Survey of Working Conditions), in 1973, and in 1977. The panel version used for some of the results in this paper consists of all those among the 1,455 individuals interviewed in 1972–1973 who were reinterviewed in 1977. All the usual information on wages, hours worked, industry, occupation, and so on, in addition to individual characteristics, is collected.

Of particular interest for this paper is a series of self-reported measures on many job characteristics. I make use of the following questions:

1. My job requires that I do the same things over and over. (*Variable name:* Job is repetitive).
2. I get to do a number of different things on my job. (*Variable name:* Variety of things to do).
3. I have a lot of say about what happens on my job. (*Variable name:* Worker has a lot of say about what happens on her/his job).
4. I determine the speed at which I work. (*Variable name:* Worker sets own pace).

5. My job requires that I keep learning new things. (*Variable Name:* Job makes worker learn new things).
6. My supervisor is successful in getting people to work together. (*Variable name:* Teamwork).

Answers are scaled in the following way for the first five questions:

1. Strongly disagree
2. Disagree
3. Agree
4. Strongly agree.

I recode the last two possibilities to 1 and the first two to 0. The scaling of the answers to the question about teamwork is:

1. Not at all true
2. A little true
3. Somewhat true
4. Very true.

Again, this variable is coded as 0 if the answer is 1 or 2, and as 1 if the answer is 3 or 4. The method of pay is available only for the 1977 interview. We know whether people are paid salaries, hourly rates, piece rates, or commissions, and whether or not their employer is providing them with a profit sharing plan.[28]

National Longitudinal Survey of Youth (1988–1990)

The National Longitudinal Survey of Youth (NLSY) data set surveyed 12,686 young males and females between the age of fourteen and twenty-one in 1979. In 1988, 1989, and 1990, respondents were asked whether all or part of their earnings were based on job performance. They were also asked a few questions on their work environment.

The question pertaining to pay for performance is the following:

> The earnings on some jobs are based all or in part on how a person performs the job (hand card D). On this card are some examples of earnings that are based on job performance. Please tell me if any of the earnings on your job (are/were) based on any of these types of compensation. Please do not include profit sharing or employee stock purchase plans.

1. Piece rates;
2. Commissions;
3. Bonuses (based on job performance);
4. Stock options;
5. Tips;
6. Other.

Respondents were also asked whether they had received a promotion on their current or most recent job since the last interview. Note that it is not possible to tell whether the bonuses refer to amounts paid based on the subjective discretion of the employer (say merit schemes), or whether they merely represent another form of piece rate. In the latter case, the employee gets a reward for achieving or surpassing some kind of quantitative target. A separate question was asked on whether their employer had a profit sharing plan.

Questions concerning aspects of the work environment were asked in 1979 and 1982 but not during 1988–1990. The questions asked were:

We would like to know what kind of opportunities this job offers you. (First/next) How much opportunity does this job give you (read category)—a minimum amount, not too much, a moderate amount, quite a lot, or a maximum amount? [Categories:]

1. To do a number of things (variety);
2. Deal with people;
3. For independent thought or action (autonomy);
4. Friendships;
5. To do a job from beginning to end (probe if necessary: that is, the chance to do the whole job) (complete task).

Answers are recoded to 0 if respondents answer either "a minimum amount," "not too much," or "a moderate amount," and are recoded to 1 if respondents answer either of the last two possibilities.

For each of twenty occupation cells, I compute the average of the answers in both the 1979 and the 1982 surveys. I then merge these averages to each corresponding occupation category for the 1988–1990 period. Note that the local unemployment rate contained in the NLSY (as is the case with the PSID) is measured at the level of the county.

Panel Study of Income Dynamics (1976–1991)

In the Panel Study of Income Dynamics (PSID), the sample consists of white male heads of households aged eighteen to sixty-four with positive earnings for the period 1976–1991. Individuals in the public sector who worked fewer than 500 hours are excluded. We know whether each worker is paid a piece rate, a commission, an hourly rate, or a salary (the structure of the question is very similar to the one in the QES). Interesting features of the PSID for the 1976–1991 period are that we are is able to determine whether a worker received a bonus over the last year and that workers are asked the amount of money they received from either overtime, or from commissions, or from bonuses paid by the employer. Since we cannot separately identify the amount of income derived exclusively from commissions and/or overtime work, I have had to remove these workers from the calculations.

January 1977 Current Population Survey (Validation Survey)

A subsample of workers in the January 1977 Current Population Survey (CPS) were asked questions about hours worked, union coverage, earnings, and pay methods in addition to the usual questions on labor force status, schooling, demographics, industry affiliation, and occupational status. They provided the names and addresses of their employers so that the same set of questions could be asked of them. This represents the only instance in which questions about contract form were asked in the CPS.[29] Employers (and workers) were asked whether the workers received any extra amount in addition to their regular pay.

Appendix 2.2: Measurement Problems

In the classical measurement error model in which all variables are continuous, there are two main consequences of having error-ridden measures: (1) If y, a noisy measure of the true variable y^*, is the dependent variable, the precision of the estimated parameters will be lower and the explanatory power of the model will also be lower. However, the estimated parameters will not be biased. (2) If y is the explanatory variable, its associated parameter would likely be biased toward zero, that is we would tend to falsely accept the null hypothesis of a zero effect more often than we should. Again, if y is all noise, then it follows that its associated coefficient would be zero.[30] In short, the lesson is clear: Measurement error makes it more difficult to find statistical relationships.

Now the case of measurement error of particular interest for this paper is where the variable is dichotomous (0–1). Here, the conclusion for the effect of measurement error for an explanatory variable carries through,

Table 2.8

Cross-Tabulation of Employer and Employee Reports of Pay Methods

	Employer report (same categories)				
Employee Report					
Hourly rate	0.9109	0.0753	0.0091	0.0012	0.0036
Salary	0.1297	0.8446	0.0013	0.0175	0.0069
Piece rate	0.2059	0.0000	0.7647	0.0294	0.0000
Commission	0.1238	0.1524	0.0095	0.7048	0.0095
Daily	0.2051	0.2307	0.0000	0.0000	0.5641

Source: January 1977 CPS–Percent of Number of Employee Reports.

with misclassification biasing the coefficient toward zero. However, contrary to the model with a continuous variable, if the *dependent* variable is misclassified, the parameters associated with the explanatory variables are also biased.[31]

Thus, estimation of the effect of payment method on wages faces a combination of these problems: Misclassification error of the pay methods tends to bias the estimated incentive effect toward zero, while mismeasurement of wages produces larger standard errors.

In addition, in studies of the determinants of performance pay (e.g., Brown [1990]), the estimated effects are likely to be biased toward zero because (1) the independent variables, whether they are continuous or categorical, are noisy measures, and (2) the dependent 0–1 variable is sometimes misclassified. In part because of that, it is not surprising that studies examining the determinants of pay methods often find that relatively few variables enter significantly and that the explanatory power of the model is very low.

While measurement error is a "fact of life" in empirical work, we rarely know how much of a worry it should be. We get a fairly good idea of the underlying problem from the January 1977 Current Population Survey. Using this data set, it is possible to compute a cross-tabulation of employer and employee responses to the question on method of pay. If employers and employees' responses were always identical, the diagonal elements of Table 2.8 should be equal 100 percent and the off-diagonal elements should all equal to zero. On the other hand, if employers and employees' responses were not identical, the diagonal "agreement rate" would be less then 100 percent. As Table 2.8 shows, while employers and employees seem pretty much in agreement concerning hourly rates, there exists considerable disagreement about performance pay. Again, we should not be surprised by the low explanatory power of models analyzing the determinants of performance pay.

Notes

1. See Appendix 2.1 for a detailed description of the data sets used.
2. This, of course, assumes that firms use profit sharing or bonuses as incentive devices.
3. Two caveats here: Although the question on bonuses in the NLSY makes explicit reference to job performance, respondents are not asked to make any difference between their individual performance and team performance. Second, promoted workers may also report that they were paid bonuses. On that last point, about a third of the workers reporting being paid a bonus also reported having received a promotion since the previous interview.
4. I use the term "piece rate" here to encompass both true piece rate contracts and commission contracts. As emphasized by Lazear (1986), any form of pay method that links pay to an objective measure of output is, in fact, a piece rate contract.
5. That is, $C'(e) > 0$ and $C''(e) > 0$.
6. The socially efficient level of output is such that the total so-called social surplus is maximized. This is given by the choice of e, which maximizes the difference between total output and total cost, $y(e) - c(e)$. Using the fact that $y(e) = e$, we get that the socially efficient effort level is such that the marginal cost of output, $C'(e)$, is equal to the marginal productivity of effort, 1 (output increases by 1 per unit of effort).
7. This is the wage paid to the worker because it represents her true productivity when monitoring costs are netted out.
8. See Lazear (1986) for a proof.
9. See Prendergast (1999) for a more general formulation in which both objective and subjective performance measures are used to determine the optimal incentive contract.
10. In a related vein, see Garen (1998b) on the issue of how control of the work routine will be assigned when the cost of measuring output varies and how this affects the provision of incentives.
11. See also Lazear (1986) for a "solution" to the problem of underprovision of effort by the worker when the firm cannot commit not to renegotiate the rates.
12. In fact, MacLeod and Parent (1999a) put piece rate and hourly rated workers in one group and commission and salaried workers in another.
13. Even though Figure 2.1 would suggest that, contrary to the theory, multitasking is prevalent in commission work relative to piece rate or hourly rated jobs, such is not the case when we compare commissions with salaries, which is the comparison made in MacLeod and Parent (1999a).
14. Indeed, Pencavel (1977) starts his paper by citing Alfred Marshall's Principles to illustrate that economists used to be interested in the notions of "intensity and diligence of worker effort manifested by workers" before essentially leaving this field to industrial relations researchers.
15. See either Pencavel (1977) or Seiler (1984) for the specific references.
16. Strictly speaking, this is not necessary. One could still identify the true causal effect of piece rate contracts with cross-sectional data provided there existed an exogenous determinant of that form of payment that played no direct role in the log wage equation. It is very difficult, a priori, to think of such a credible exclusion restriction.
17. In addition, Parent (1999) estimates a simple model of the covariance structure

of wages to identify the main sources of the larger observed variance of wages for incentive workers. Seiler (1984) had previously observed the same phenomenon and conjectured that it reflected the greater risk (of output variability) faced by incentive workers. Assuming risk aversion, those workers paid piece rates require a compensating differential. This would partly explain the wage premium enjoyed by incentive workers, the rest of it being due to effort inducing effects. By decomposing the wage into a worker-specific component reflecting the underlying heterogeneity of worker productivity and a "true" residual term, Parent (1999) showed that the variance in wages for incentive workers was accounted for by the worker component to a much greater extent than was the case for other workers. This result is not consistent with incentive workers being compensated for higher risks. In fact, it turns out that the variance net of the worker component, which would better reflect income risk, is actually larger for hourly and salaried workers than it is for piece rate workers.

18. See also Athey and Stern (1998) on the topic of complementarity and on how to devise the appropriate empirical framework in the presence of such complementarities.

19. As opposed to bonuses paid to workers who surpassed a certain quantitative target, such as is often the case in sales work.

20. See Prendergast (1999) for a list of references.

21. Another line of argumentation has raised the point that firms may penalize themselves by not rewarding superior performance when it occurs. Take the example of a firm deciding whether or not to promote a worker to a different job in the organization. The implicit agreement here is that the worker expects to get a promotion under the condition that she performs well. Assuming that the efficient assignment of that worker (efficient in the sense that the worker's productivity is higher in the new job) implies that the worker should be promoted, the firm would actually penalize itself by not allowing the worker to realize her potential for greater productivity. See Prendergast (1993) for a complete treatment.

22. It is not possible to know the exact nature of the plan (cash based or deferred based plan, such as a pension fund in which firms put a percentage of their profits).

23. In levels, the model I estimate is:

$$W_{ijt} = X_{it}\Gamma + Z_{ijt}\beta + PS_{ijt}\delta + \alpha_i + \theta_{ij} + \varepsilon_{ijt}$$

where W_{ijt} is the log hourly wage of individual i in job j at time t, X_{it} is a vector of individual characteristics which may be time-varying, Z_{ijt} is the vector of time-varying job-match attributes (e.g., tenure with the current employer), and PS_{ijt} is a dummy (0–1) indicator for a profit sharing plan. The other terms represent unobserved components of variance which may be correlated with the observable characteristics. As is well known, estimating equation (5) in levels may produce a biased estimate of δ if profit sharing plans tend to be offered to intrinsically more productive individuals (high α's) or to workers in particularly good matches (high θ's). Consequently, one can alleviate the unobserved worker quality problem by estimating equation (5) in differences or by transforming the variables so that they are expressed in deviations from individual means form. Although unobserved fixed worker attributes are purged doing this, we may still have a bias stemming from unobserved job-match characteristics. Consequently, it would be even better to use differences within jobs so as to eliminate all time invariant unobserved components.

24. This is, of course a so-called fixed-effect regression—"fixed" because it purges all time-invariant components of productivity.

25. Moreover, the decrease in the magnitude of the coefficient likely results in part from misclassification of the profit sharing dummy. See Appendix 2.2 for more details.

26. Note also that, given the short time dimension of the NLSY panel, I did not include lagged dummy indicators for the presence of profit sharing plans in previous years, which would have reduced the sample size considerably. The idea of including lagged dummy indicators is that the positive productivity effect of profit sharing plans may take some time to develop, as the evidence in Kruse (1993) suggests. Thus, the measured effects shown in Table 2.5 may actually represent a lower bound of the true effects.

27. One way to assess this conjecture would be to re-estimate the same models, but with women who are past their childbearing years, either because they have already had the number of children they planned to have or because of their age.

28. See MacLeod and Parent (1999a) for details on dealing with the likely endogeneity of the job characteristics questions when estimating methods of pay.

29. Mellow and Sider (1983) provide a thorough analysis of the data set.

30. I say likely because, although true when y is the only explanatory variable, it cannot be generalized when y is one of many explanatory variables. In practice, however, one encounters an attenuation bias even in the multivariate models.

31. See Hausman, Abrevaya, and Scott-Morton (1998) for a proof.

References

Athey, S., and Stern, S. 1998. "An Empirical Framework for Testing Theories About Complentarity in Organizational Design." Mimeograph, Department of Economics, Massachusetts Institute of Technology, Cambridge.

Baker, G. P. 1992. "Incentive Contracts and Performance Measurement." *Journal of Political Economy* 100: 598–614.

Baker, G. P., Jensen, M. C., and Murphy, K. J. 1988. "Compensation and Incentives: Practice vs. Theory." *Journal of Finance* 43: 593–616.

Bewley, T. F. 1993. "A Depressed Labor Market, as Explained by Participants." Mimeograph, Yale University, New Haven, CT.

Brown, C. 1990. "Firm's Choice of Method of Pay." *Industrial and Labor Relations Review* 43: 165–182.

———. 1992. "Wage Levels and Method of Pay." *Rand Journal of Economics* 23: 366–375.

Carmichael, H. L. 1989. "Self-Enforcing Contracts, Shirking and Life Cycle Incentives." *Journal of Economic Perspectives* 3: 65–83.

DiNardo, J., Fortin, N., and Lemieux, T. 1996. "Labor Market Institutions and the Distribution of Wages, 1973–1992: A Semiparametric Approach." *Econometrica* 64: 1001–1044.

Ewing, B. 1996. "Wages and Performance-Based Pay: Evidence from the NLSY." *Economics Letters* 51: 241–246.

Garen, J. 1998a. "Self-Employment, Pay Systems, and the Theory of the Firm: An Empirical Analysis." *Journal of Economic Behavior and Organization* 36: 257–274.

———. 1998b. "Some Law and Economics of Employment: Incentives, Investment, and Control of the Work Routine." Mimeograph, Gratton College of Business and Economics, University of Kentucky—Lexington.

Geddes, L. A., and Heywood, J. S. 2000. "Gender and Incentive Pay: Individual Data." Mimeograph, Department of Economics, University of Wisconsin—Milwaukee.

Gibbons, R. 1987. "Piece Rate Incentive Schemes." *Journal of Labor Economics* 5: 413–429.

Gibbons, R., and Waldman, M. 1999. "Careers in Organizations." In *Handbook of Labor Economics,* vol. 3, eds. O. Ashenfelter and D. Card. Amsterdam: North Holland.

Goldin, C. 1986. "Monitoring Costs and Occupational Segregation by Sex: A Historical Analysis." *Journal of Labor Economics* 4: 1–27.

Hausman, J., Abrevaya, J. and Scott-Morton, F. 1998. "Misclassification of the Dependant Variable in Discrete-Response Setting." *Journal of Econometrics* 87: 239–269.

Holmström, B., and Milgrom, P. 1991. "Multi-Task Principal-Agent Analysis: Incentive Contracts, Asset Ownership, and Job Design." *Journal of Law, Economics, and Organization* 7: 24–52.

———. 1994. "The Firm as an Incentive System." *American Economics Review* 84: 972–992.

Ichniowsky, C., Shaw, K., and Prennushi, G. 1997. "The Effects of Human Resources Management Practices on Productivity: A Study of Steel Finishing Lines." *American Economic Review* 87: 291–313.

Kanemoto, Y., and MacLeod, W. 1992. "The Ratchet Effect and the Market for Second-Hand Workers." *Journal of Labor Economics* 10: 85–92.

Kerr, S. 1975. "On the Folly of Rewarding A, While Hoping for B." *Academy of Management Journal* 18: 769–783.

Kruse, D. 1992. "Profit Sharing and Productivity: Microeconomic Evidence from the United States." *Economic Journal* 102: 24–36.

———. 1993. *Profit Sharing: Does It Make a Difference?* Kalamazoo, MI: W. E. Upjohn Institute.

Lazear, E. P. 1981. "Agency, Earnings Profiles, Productivity, and Hours Restrictions." *American Economic Review* 71: 606–620.

———. 1986. "Salaries and Piece Rates." *Journal of Business* 59: 405–431.

———. 1989. "Pay Equality and Industrial Politics." *Journal of Political Economy* 97: 561–580.

———. 2000. "Performance Pay and Productivity." *American Economic Review* 90: 1346–1361.

Lazear, E. P., and Rosen, S. 1981. "Rank-Order Tournaments as Optimal Labor Contracts." *Journal of Political Economy* 89: 841–864.

MacLeod, W. B., and Parent, D. 1999a. "Job Characteristics and the Form of Compensation." In *Research in Labor Economics,* vol. 18, pp. 177–242, ed. S. Polachek. Stamford, CT: JAI Press.

———.1999b. "Job Characteristics, Wages, and the Employment Contract." *Federal Reserve Bank of St. Louis Review* 81: 13–29

MacLeod, W. B., and Malcomson, J. M. 1989. "Implicit Contracts, Incentive Compatibility, and Involuntary Unemployment." *Econometrica* 57: 447–480.

McLaughlin, K. J. 1999. "Are Nominal Wage Changes Skewed Away from Wage Cuts?" *Federal Reserve Bank of St. Louis Review* 81: 117–132.

Mellow, W., and Sider, H. 1983. "Accuracy of Response in Labor Market Surveys: Evidence and Implications." *Journal of Labor Economics* 1: 331–144.

Milgrom, P., and Roberts, J. 1992. *Economics, Organizations, and Management.* Englewood Cliffs, NJ: Prentice Hall.

Murphy, K. J. 1999. "Executive Compensation." In *Handbook of Labor Economics,* vol. 3, eds. O. Ashenfelter and D. Card. Amsterdam: North Holland.

Parent, D. 1999. "Methods of Pay and Earnings: A Longitudinal Analysis." *Industrial and Labor Relations Review* 53: 71–86.

Pencavel, J. H. 1977. "Work Effort, On-the-Job Screening, and Alternative Methods of Remuneration." In *Research in Labor Economics,* vol.1, pp. 225–258, ed. R. Ehrenberg. Greenwich, CT: JAI Press.

Prendergast, C. 1993. "The Role of Promotion in Inducing Specific Human Capital Acquisitions." *Quarterly Journal of Economics* 108: 523–534.

———. 1999. "The Provision of Incentives in Firms." *Journal of Economic Literature* 1: 7–63.

Rosen, S. 1986. "Prizes and Incentives in Elimination Tournaments." *American Economic Review* 76: 921–939.

Seiler, E. 1984. "Piece Rate vs. Time Rate: The Effect of Incentives on Earnings." *Review of Economic and Statistics* 60: 363–376.

Shapiro, C., and Stiglitz, J. E. 1984. "Equilibrium Unemployment as a Worker Discipline Device." *American Economic Review* 74: 433–444.

Chapter 3
Performance Pay in Canada

Richard J. Long

Introduction

In recent years, many commentators have argued that changes to traditional compensation systems have become crucial for effective business performance, and that the use of performance pay for work groups and the organization as a whole should be a fundamental part of this change (Schuster and Zingheim 1992; Wilson 1995). The underlying basis for this argument is that, as the organizational environment has become more dynamic, technological processes more complex, employees more skilled and highly educated, and competitive strategies more dependent on innovation and flexibility, traditional organization structures and management practices are no longer adequate.

The traditional organization is characterized by narrowly defined jobs, centralized decision making, heavy reliance on rules and procedures, and a hierarchical structure of management to enforce these rules and procedures. Commentators now argue for structures characterized by empowered employees equipped with the information and knowledge to exercise wide latitude in performing a wide array of job duties, often as part of a self-managing work team. In order to foster the teamwork, cooperation, and commitment to the organization necessary to make this approach successful, employee pay that focuses on performance at the team and organizational levels is essential (Lawler 1992; MacDuffie 1995; Levine 1997).

Firms that have all these elements have had a variety of labels applied to them, including "Theory Y" (McGregor 1960), "organic" (Burns and Stalker 1961), "human resources" (Miles 1975), "high involvement" (Lawler 1992), "high performance" (Betcherman, et al. 1994), "the mutual gains enterprise" (Kochan and Osterman 1994), and "high commitment" (Wood 1996), but their commonalties are so great that they are virtually interchangeable. "High involvement" is the label used for this form of organizational structure in this chapter.

While all these authors are clear in urging the use of pay based on team or organizational performance, the role of individual performance pay is somewhat more ambiguous. In general, most advocates of high involvement management oppose the use of piece rates, as they focus employee behavior on a very narrow set of performance criteria at the individual level, and do nothing to foster cooperative behavior or commitment to the overall objectives of the firm. Other types of individual performance pay, such as merit raises, may be inappropriate where individual performance is difficult to separate from the performance of other employees. Indeed, a wide array of research suggests that although many employers support the concept of merit raises, they are often very dissatisfied with the underlying appraisal processes used to assess individual performance levels, and some firms have even abandoned them (Long 2002).

However, Canadian performance pay deserves more study. Although there is considerable evidence about the use of certain performance pay plans, such as profit sharing and employee stock plans, there has been no systematic study of the full spectrum of performance pay plans in Canada. This chapter presents the results of a recent survey of 240 Canadian companies, including the incidence of thirteen specific types of performance pay plans, their extent of employee coverage, and the factors associated with their adoption. Five of the pay plans were geared to individual performance (piece rates, sales commissions, merit raises, merit bonuses, and special incentives), three to group/team performance (gain sharing, goal sharing, and other team-based pay), and five to organizational performance (profit sharing, stock bonuses, stock purchase, stock options, and other organizational performance pay plans).

This chapter addresses two main questions: (1) What is the incidence and employee coverage of various types of performance pay in Canada? 2) What factors are associated with the adoption of performance pay by Canadian firms? Where baseline data exist, trends in the use of performance pay will also be discussed.

Possible Explanatory Factors

Three sets of company characteristics were examined as possible explanatory factors—structural characteristics, work force characteristics, and general characteristics of the firm. The first set focused on the degree to which the firm had structural characteristics consistent with a "high-involvement" approach to management. The expectation was that high-involvement organizations would be more likely to have pay plans based on group/team and organizational performance than traditional organizations, but not necessarily more individual performance pay.

High-Involvement Management and Performance Pay

To date, there has been relatively little empirical research focusing on the relationship between managerial strategy and performance pay. Wood (1996) examined whether or not there was any relationship between high-commitment management and use of various types of pay systems in a sample of 135 British manufacturing firms. He hypothesized that pay based heavily on individual output or performance (such as piece work or merit bonuses) would be negatively related to high-commitment management, while group and organizational-based pay would be positively related. In his view, by focusing workers' attention only on the immediate job cycle, output-based pay inhibits the broader employee perspective that is necessary for enhanced employee participation in the workplace, while individual merit bonuses detract from the teamwork needed for high-commitment management. In contrast, group and organizational-based pay systems focus on the broader picture and encourage teamwork.

Overall, Wood's data provided only limited support for his hypotheses. Individual bonus systems were negatively related to high-commitment management, but no other significant relationships were found. However, one possible explanation for the lack of the other expected relationships was that changes to pay systems may lag introduction of high-commitment management, which was at an early stage of development in many firms during the study period (1986–1990). It may also be that the implementation of tax incentives for profit sharing (which was the major organizational pay plan found in Wood's sample) by the British government during the early 1980s may have caused increased adoption of profit sharing in all types of firms, not just high-commitment firms.

Although Wood found no association between profit sharing and high-involvement management in his British sample, four Canadian studies and five studies conducted in the United States, Australia, and Germany do suggest such an association. An analysis by Long (1989) of data collected from 946 establishments by the Economic Council of Canada in 1985 found profit sharing positively associated with numerous characteristics of high-involvement management, including job enrichment, work teams, quality circles, and problem-solving groups. In a second study, Long (1997) found that the managerial philosophy of top management was a key predictor of the incidence of profit sharing. In the third Canadian study, profit sharing was found to be positively associated with the presence of work teams and negatively with hierarchical control (Wagar and Long 1995). In the fourth study, Long (2001) found a positive relationship between gain/profit sharing and a flexible, high-involvement organizational structure in a sample of forty-four large Canadian manufacturing firms.

In the United States, Osterman (1994) found that profit sharing was significantly more common in firms using "innovative work practices," such as work teams. Similarly Gittleman, Horrigan, and Joyce (1998) found profit sharing positively related to an index of "alternative work practices," such as work teams and quality circles. More recently, Freeman, Kleiner, and Ostroff (2000) found that firms with "employee involvement" were significantly more likely to have profit sharing and other forms of shared compensation. Studies in Australia (Drago and Heywood 1995) and Germany (Heywood, Hubler, and Jirjahn 1998) have also found evidence that profit sharing is related to mechanisms for employee involvement.

Other Factors Affecting Performance Pay

A number of studies have identified factors that may be linked to a firm's choice of particular performance pay plans. For example, C. Brown (1990) examined the process by which firms choose whether to adopt individual performance pay, and if so, what type. He suggested that three alternatives available to employers are piece rates, merit raises based on appraised performance, and "standard pay" that does not incorporate any performance dimension. He argued that the use of each plan can be predicted by the cost of using it.

According to Brown, a key issue is the cost of monitoring employee performance, which is assumed to be higher in large organizations. It follows, he argued, that piece rates (which are assumed to reduce the need for monitoring of employees and thus to decrease supervisory costs) will be more attractive to large firms. In addition, the fixed costs of adopting and maintaining a piece rate system can be spread across more employees in a larger firm, and larger firms are more likely to have the long production runs of standardized output that are most amenable to use of piece rates.

Other factors Brown hypothesized to affect use of piece rates included the organization of jobs, and the level of performance variability within jobs. Jobs that are designed to include only a narrow range of duties, performed repetitively, are more amenable to piece rates, and jobs for which performance is heavily dependent on a high level of effort and/or skill would also benefit, he argued, from a system that provides differential rewards depending on output levels. On the other hand, output measurement difficulties make some jobs less amenable to piece rates. Examples include jobs of a complex nature, jobs where performance quality is a key factor but is difficult to measure, and jobs for which a high level of interdependence (or team work) is required for task completion.

Brown also discussed whether unionization plays a role in the choice of individual payment plans. He argued that merit pay based on supervisory appraisals will be opposed by unions because of potential for arbitrary use and divisiveness among members but the case for piece rates is not so clear. Piece rates do create the potential for divisiveness through inequality of pay, but may be considered preferable to merit raises, since piece rates are assumed to be more objective. Of course, even with piece rates, there is potential for arbitrary supervisory behavior, as supervisors may favor some employees by assigning them to jobs with "loose" rates, while assigning out-of-favor employees to jobs with "tight" rates. In addition, management may arbitrarily cut piece rates once workers increase their productivity. For these reasons, Heywood, Hubler, and Jirjahn (1998) suggest that a key intervening variable is the level of trust and cooperation between labor and management—trust being essential to employee acceptance of piece rates. However, this is not likely to prevail in classical organizations with traditional adversarial labor-management relationships.

C. Brown (1990) tested some of these relationships in a large sample of U.S. firms that employed at least 200 persons. He found unionized firms more likely to have standard rates (and less likely to have merit pay) than nonunion firms, but no less likely to have piece rates. Larger firms were more likely to use piece rates and standard pay, but less likely to use merit raises. As expected, piece rates were less likely to be used for jobs with a variety of duties, and for which measuring work quality was difficult.

Drago and Heywood extended Brown's discussion of possible determinants of performance pay plans by adding theory based on "strategic choice" literature, "where managers select wage incentives as part of a larger system for managing and motivating the work force" (1995, 508), and by discussing group and organizational incentives in addition to individual performance pay. Under strategic choice, the key to the use of performance pay is a desire on the part of management to transform a traditional (adversarial) system of employee-management relations into a more cooperative system, with a greater mutuality of goals between employees, management, and owners. This perspective focuses particularly on group- and organization-based performance pay to further this transformation.

Strategic choice theory predicts that larger firms will be more likely to institute performance pay, because they are more likely to have the compensation specialists in house to initiate, design, and manage performance pay. In addition, job security may be higher in larger organizations. This is relevant because workers may be reluctant to embrace pay schemes that increase productivity if this increased productivity may result in "working themselves out of a job." This understandable concern would be less severe in firms that offer more job security, either because these firms are able to increase sales as productivity increases, because they are in sectors that are growing in demand, or because they employ a "buffer" of contingent employees who can be laid off without affecting the core work force. Larger firms would also be more able to respond to productivity increases by attrition, or redeployment of "surplus" personnel to other areas of the firm.

Turning to unions, traditional labor theory posits that unions will oppose incentive systems in favor of standard rates to promote solidarity and reduce arbitrary wage differences (Freeman 1982). However, strategic choice theory suggests that unions may not oppose performance pay—particularly group and organization based pay—if there is a cooperative union-management relationship characterized by mutual trust. From an employer point of view, this cooperative relationship, along with favorable group norms, is also essential in order to avoid free-rider problems that might otherwise arise with group- and organization-based pay systems.

As mentioned earlier, the argument about mutual trust also applies to piece rate systems. Without mutual trust, it will be very unlikely that workers will raise output in response to piece rates, since they will be concerned that management would then simply reduce the rates. Moreover, changes will need to be made to the system as production requirements or technology changes, but will be very difficult to make in a context of mutual distrust (Heywood, Hubler, and Jirjahn 1998).

What is the empirical evidence? In a series of closely related studies, the determinants of piece rates have been estimated in Australia (Drago and Heywood 1995), the United Kingdom (Heywood, Siebert, and Wei 1997), Hong Kong (Heywood and Wei 1997), and Germany (Heywood, Hubler, and Jirjahn 1998). Overall, unionization did not affect the incidence of piece rates, except in the United Kingdom where a significant negative relationship was found, a result that Ng and Maki (1994) also found in

Canada. Establishment size was significantly positively related, except in Hong Kong where there was no relationship. In all cases except Australia, employment stability was negatively related to piece rates. Interestingly, the strongest finding of these researchers, which prevailed in all four samples, was that firms with a high proportion of female workers are significantly more likely to have piece rates. They go on to aver that this result, although consistent with previous research (C. Brown 1990; Belman and Heywood 1992), has yet to be definitively explained.

Heywood and his colleagues also examined profit sharing in their Australian and German samples. In neither country was there any relationship between company size and profit sharing, consistent with studies in Canada (Long 1989; Wagar and Long 1995) and the United States (Cheadle 1989; Kruse 1996). However, other studies in a variety of countries have shown a positive relationship between size and profit sharing, including studies in Canada (Jones and Pliskin 1997; Long 1997), Britain (Gregg and Machin 1988; Poole 1989), Italy (Biagioli 1993), and Germany (Carstensen, Gerlach, and Hubler 1992; Fitzroy and Kraft 1995). Only one study, conducted in Britain (Estrin and Wilson 1989), has found a significant negative relationship.

Heywood, Hubler, and Jirjahn (1998) found that unionization was significantly negatively associated with profit sharing in Germany, a result also found by researchers in Canada (Long 1989; McMullen, Leckie, and Caron 1993; Betcherman et al. 1994; Ng and Maki 1994; Wagar and Long 1995; Jones and Pliskin 1997), in the United States (Cheadle 1989; Kim 1998; Cooke 1994), and in Britain (Poole 1989). However, other studies in Canada (Long, 1997), Britain (Estrin and Wilson 1989), the United States (Kruse 1993), Germany (Carstensen, Gerlach, and Hubler 1992), and Australia (Drago and Heywood 1995) have shown no association, while one British study has shown a positive association (Gregg and Machin 1988).

Perhaps the most interesting study on this issue is that by Kruse (1996), who, in his cross-sectional analysis of U.S. data, found that unionization was significantly negatively related to the incidence of profit sharing. However, when he used a longitudinal design to examine factors affecting adoption of profit sharing by U.S. firms over the period 1975–1991, he found that union firms were not less likely to adopt profit sharing than nonunion firms. This may suggest that attitudes of U.S. unions and unionized employers toward profit sharing have changed in recent years.

In relation to employee share ownership, Kruse (1996) found that larger firms had both a significantly higher incidence of employee stock plans and a higher adoption rate during the period 1975–1991. He also found that unionized firms had a significantly lower incidence of employee stock plans, but that there was no significant difference in adoption rates during the period 1975–1991. Long (1992) found that employee stock plans were much more common in large, publicly traded Canadian firms. In their analysis of Canadian data collected in 1986–1987, Jones and Pliskin (1997) also found stock plans significantly more common in large firms, but less common in unionized firms. Overall, however, Kruse and Blasi (1997) note that research has not yet uncovered factors that explain a major part of the variation in the use of stock plans.

The current study will examine the role of a variety of factors suggested by this earlier work, along with several other relevant factors. Five work force characteristics will be examined—the proportions of employees who are: full-time, highly educated, and managerial, and who are union members, along with the proportion of the firm's labor requirements that are contracted out. In discussing their possible relevance, however, it should be noted that each factor may affect performance pay differently, depending on whether the pay plan is geared to performance at the individual level or to performance at the group or organizational level.

This discussion is further complicated by the likelihood that the same variable may relate differently to different types of individual performance pay. For example, a greater proportion of managerial employees may imply less use of piece rates, but a greater use of merit pay. The rationale is that an output-based control system (piece rates or sales commissions) should require less managerial monitoring than a behavior-based control system (merit raises, merit bonuses). In this vein, Eisenhardt (1989) found that U.S. retail stores making more use of sales commissions had a significantly lower supervisory ratio than other stores, while Banker et al. (1996) found that introduction of an individual sales bonus system led to a significant reduction in supervisory ratio. In their British sample, Heywood, Siebert, and Wei (1997) also found a strong negative relationship between output-based pay and the supervisory ratio.

Firms with more part-time employees may feel a need to motivate and control these employees through output-based pay, since these employees may have a lower commitment to the organization than full-time employees. A more highly educated work force should encourage the use of more merit pay (although not necessarily piece rates or commissions), because firms will be anxious to maximize the performance value of these employees. A more unionized work force will reduce the use of all types of individual performance pay. Firms that contract out a major portion of their labor requirements may not find individual performance pay as worthwhile for the remaining employees, as this relatively small group will constitute a small portion of total labor costs, relative to firms that do not contract out.

Relating these factors to group/organization based performance pay, it is less likely that firms with many part-time employees will feel it worthwhile to utilize pay plans that are relatively long term in nature. Drago and Heywood (1995) found that firms with a greater proportion of casual workers were less likely to have profit sharing. A more highly educated work force should encourage the use of group or organizational performance pay, since more complex behavior will likely be expected from these employees. A more unionized work force will likely have less group or organizational performance pay, due to traditional union preferences for fixed wages and member solidarity, which could be threatened by increased commitment to the employer. Firms that contract out more of their labor requirements will have less group or organizational performance pay, since these plans will be spread over fewer employees. Firms with more managers could either have more group or organizational performance pay, if the need for more managers signifies more complex behavior in the organization, or less group or organizational performance pay, if the need for more managers signifies an organization that emphasizes managerial control of employees, rather than reward-based control. In fact, Long (1994) found that Canadian manufacturing firms with gain sharing and/or profit sharing had 31 percent fewer managers than firms without these plans.

In addition to these work force characteristics, several other characteristics of the firm will be examined—industrial sector, nature of ownership, size, growth rate, geographical dispersion, and the firm's competitive strategy. The following relationships are tentatively proposed. Firms in the manufacturing sector will be more likely to have piece rates, and those in the retailing sector will be more likely to have sales commissions. Publicly traded firms will be more likely to have employee stock plans, since the infrastructure is in place for these plans. Large firms are more likely to have all types of performance pay. Rapidly growing firms are more likely to have stock plans, since stock plans will be more attractive to employees in these firms, and they help to conserve capital for growth purposes. Firms that are more geographically dispersed will use more organizational performance pay, in order to ensure that employees are committed to organizational objectives. Firms that utilize innovator competitive strategies will be more likely to have group and organizational performance pay, to encourage the goal based innovative employee behavior that is desired in these organizations.

Sample and Variable Measures

Data Collection and Sample

Surveys were mailed to 1,744 companies or business units that had a head office in Canada, based on a list generated by Dun and Bradstreet. This list was designed to include only commercial enterprises, and excluded organizations such as hospitals, universities, and government departments. Small enterprises (those with fewer than 200 employees) were also excluded, since they are less likely to have the range of compensation systems and practices that are of interest in this study (Drago and Heywood 1995). A random sampling of industrial sectors was incorporated into the selection procedure.

The survey procedure involved several steps. First, all companies were telephoned, to verify their mailing addresses and to obtain the name of the individual in charge of human resources for the organization. Surveys were then mailed to those individuals, during the summer of 2000. If a response was not received within three to four weeks, a follow-up telephone call was made to encourage participation in the survey, and additional surveys were sent out, if the original had been lost. Overall, surveys were received from 246 companies, for a response rate of about 14.1 percent. Six companies were eliminated because they did not fall within the parameters of the study or had too much missing data.

Table 3.1 shows the main characteristics of the sample. As can be seen, 5 percent of the respondents were primarily focused on the resource sector, 36 percent on the manufacturing sector, and the remainder on various service sectors. Nearly half the firms were publicly traded on a stock exchange. About 44 percent were independent business units, while most of the remainder were subsidiary units of larger Canadian or foreign enterprises. Most companies had substantial geographical dispersion, with only 9 percent having just one work site, while nearly two-thirds reported having at least five geographically separated work sites. The number of persons employed at the firms ranged from 240 to 30,000, with a mean size of 1,914 and a median of 911. In all, the firms in this sample employed 459,423 people. Just over half these firms had at least some unionized employees.

Variable Measures

The incidence of performance pay plans and the extent of employee coverage at each firm were measured by asking respondents to indicate the

Table 3.1

Characteristics of the Sample

Characteristic	Number of firms	Percentage of sample
Industrial sector		
• Resources	11	5
• Manufacturing	86	36
• Electricity/gas	6	3
• Wholesale/retail	28	12
• Accommodation/food	7	3
• Transportation	21	9
• Communication	15	6
• Finance/insurance	30	13
• Other services	36	15
Ownership		
• Publicly traded	113	47
• Independent Canadian firm	105	44
• Subsidiary of Canadian firm	37	16
• Subsidiary of foreign firm	63	26
Geographical dispersion		
• One work site	21	9
• Two to five work sites	67	28
• Six to ten work sites	47	20
• Eleven to forty-nine work sites	63	26
• Fifty or more work sites	42	19
Number of employees		
• Fewer than 500	28	12
• 500 to 999	99	41
• 1,000 to 1,999	59	26
• 2,000 to 4,999	34	15
• 5,000 or more	20	8
Union status		
• Unionized	130	54

percentage of the nonmanagerial work force covered by thirteen different performance pay plans, clustered into three categories based on whether the performance pay was related to the performance of individual employees ("individual performance pay"), performance of specific subunits, work groups, or teams ("group performance pay"), or performance of the organization as a whole ("organizational performance pay"). Within each category, several specific types of performance pay were listed, along with a brief definition of each type. Details can be found in Appendix 3.1.

Characteristics of the Firm

A number of general characteristics of the firm were measured. These included industrial sector, ownership of the firm, total number of employees, growth in employment during the previous five years, the geographical dispersion of the firm (in terms of the number of physically separate workplaces in Canada), and competitive strategy.

Based on the Miles and Snow (1978) strategic typology, the following item was used to assess competitive strategy: "The success of this organization depends more on the continual introduction of new products and services than on efficient production of existing products and services." The Likert-type response scale ranged from 1 ("disagree strongly") to 7 ("agree strongly"). A higher score indicates a more innovative "prospector" strategy, while a lower score suggests a more conservative "defender" strategy. This item was adapted from Ng and Maki (1994) and Lee (1998).

Structural Characteristics

Four variables were used to assess structural characteristics of the firm: high involvement, job scope, proportion in the HR department, and proportion in teams. High involvement was measured by fifteen items (which are provided in Appendix 3.1) The scale was created by summing these items and dividing by fifteen. This scale had a Cronbach's alpha reliability of .85, a very satisfactory level (Nunnally 1967). In data analysis, the four items measuring "job scope" were also included as a separate subscale, and its alpha reliability was .77, again a very satisfactory level.

Two other structural indicators were used. One variable asked respondents to indicate the percentage of the work force that worked in "self-managing work teams or project teams." The other variable took the percentage of the total work force that was employed in the central HR department of the organization. In using this measure, it was reasoned that firms with a strong HR department were likely to have the expertise and capability to support the more complex compensation structures occasioned by the extensive use of performance pay. This may also indicate a higher importance placed on human resources within the organization.

Work Force Characteristics

Five variables were used as indicators of the nature of the work force and work force policies in place at a given organization. They were the percentages of the total work force that were full time, had university degrees, were managerial employees, and were unionized, and the proportion of the organization's total HR or labor requirements that were outsourced or contracted out.

Incidence of Performance Pay in Canada

This section of the paper reports the current incidence of the various performance pay plans in Canada. In addition, where possible, attempts will be made to identify trends in usage. While baseline data, utilizing comparable samples and survey procedures, are not available for all performance pay plans, useful data are available for some of them, particularly gain sharing, profit sharing, and employee stock plans.

The great majority of firms (94 percent) reported that they used at least one of the thirteen performance pay plans for at least some of their employees. As Table 3.2 shows, most firms (70 percent) had from two to five plans, with 21 percent reporting one or none, and 10.4 percent reporting six or more plans. One firm reported nine plans. The mean number of plans in use was 2.9, and the median was three plans. The most commonly used category of plan was individual performance pay (utilized by 88 percent of the sample companies), followed by organizational performance pay (utilized by 52 percent of firms), while only a minority of firms (36 percent) utilized group performance pay. Relatively few firms (about 21 percent) used all three categories of performance pay.

Individual Performance Pay

At one extreme, only 12 percent of firms reported having no pay plans based on individual performance. At the other extreme, just one firm reported having all five plans, while another twelve reported four plans. Overall, the mean number of plans was 1.8, and the median was 2.0. As can be seen in Table 3.3, the most commonly used plan was merit raises, used by 72 percent of the firms, followed by merit bonuses (37 percent of firms), special incentives (29 percent), sales commissions (27 percent), and piece rates (11 percent). Table 3.3 also provides a breakdown by industrial sector. Where a chi-square test indicates a significant difference between sectors for a given pay plan, the "total incidence" percentage for that plan has been bolded.

Overall, piece rates were used quite rarely. They were concentrated most heavily in the manufacturing and resource sectors, where two-thirds of the piece rate plans were found, and were not found at all in the wholesale/

Table 3.2

Number of Employee Performance Pay Plans in Use, 2000

Number of performance pay plans	Number of firms	Percentage of sample
• None	14	6
• One	37	16
• Two	63	26
• Three	42	18
• Four	37	16
• Five	23	10
• Six	14	6
• Seven	6	3
• Eight	2	1
• Nine	1	0.4

retail, electricity/gas, and accommodation/food sectors. As Table 3.4 shows, very few plans covered all nonmanagerial employees, and the mean employee coverage among firms using piece rates was 43 percent.

Few quantitative data are available to assess trends in use of piece rates in Canada. However, an analysis of collective bargaining agreements (in bargaining units of at least 500 employees) showed a gradual decline during the period 1987 to 1993, from 13.5 percent of contracts to 10.3 percent (Chaykowski and Lewis 1995). In the current study, the incidence of piece rates in unionized firms was 12.3 percent, and 10.1 percent in nonunion firms, which may suggest that no further decline in their use has taken place.

Sales commissions were used by just over a quarter of the firms in the sample. Their use varied significantly across industrial sectors, being found most commonly in the communications sector (where they were used by 60 percent of the firms) and the wholesale/retail and finance/insurance sectors. However, among firms using commissions, employee coverage was quite low, with 83 percent of users covering fewer than half of their employees. The mean coverage level was 20 percent.

Pay raises based on employee merit were the most commonly used form of performance pay, used by 72 percent of the firms in the sample. There was no significant variation across industrial sectors in usage. Among firms using merit raises, employee coverage was high, averaging 73 percent, and just over half of the users covered all of their nonmanagerial employees. Only 28 percent of users included less than half of their employees in merit raises.

Table 3.3

Incidence of Employee Performance Pay Plans by Industrial Sector, 2000 (in percentages)

Type of Performance Pay Plan	Resources (11 firms)	Manufacturing (86 firms)	Electricity/ Gas (6 firms)	Wholesale/ Retail (28 firms)	Accom./ Food (6 firms)	Transportation (21 firms)	Communication (15 firms)	Finance/ Insurance (30 firms)	Other services (36 firms)	Total incidence[a] (239 firms)
Plans based on individual performance										
• Piece rates	18	19	—	—	—	14	13	7	6	**11**
• Sales commissions	—	25	17	43	17	19	60	40	11	**27**
• Merit raises	73	68	67	79	50	62	67	80	81	72
• Merit bonuses	27	28	50	43	33	19	47	57	44	**37**
• Special incentives	18	26	—	18	67	33	27	43	36	**29**
Plans based on group or team performance										
• Gain sharing	46	14	17	18	—	5	—	20	11	**14**
• Goal sharing	27	14	17	29	—	24	33	14	14	18
• Other group plans	9	12	—	32	17	5	20	23	14	16
Plans based on organizational performance										
• Profit sharing	46	38	—	25	—	38	27	27	31	32
• Stock bonus plans	9	5	17	—	—	10	—	7	—	4
• Stock purchase plans	27	15	33	18	33	19	47	27	17	21
• Stock option plans	9	8	17	4	—	—	33	13	11	10
• Other organizational performance plans	9	5	—	—	—	—	7	10	6	5

[a] Boldface total incidence percentages indicate significant differences between industrial sectors, chi square tests, $p < .05$, two-tailed.

Table 3.4

Employee Coverage Levels at Firms Using Each Performance Pay Plan, 2000 (in percentages)

Type of Performance Pay Plan	Fewer than Half of Nonmanagers Covered	50–99% of Nonmanagers Covered	All Nonmanagers Covered	Mean Nonmanagerial Coverage
Plans based on individual performance				
• Piece rates	46	46	8	43
• Sales commissions	83	17	—	20
• Merit raises	28	19	53	73
• Merit bonuses	50	15	35	51
• Special incentives	44	9	47	57
Plans based on group or team performance				
• Gain sharing	41	27	32	56
• Goal sharing	35	28	37	61
• Other group plans	49	21	30	50
Plans based on organizational performance				
• Profit sharing	21	12	67	78
• Stock bonus plans	20	10	70	80
• Stock purchase plans	6	10	84	92
• Stock option plans	35	8	57	68
• Other organizational performance plans	18	9	73	88

Bonuses based on merit were provided by 37 percent of the firms. This varied significantly across industrial sectors, ranging from 57 percent of firms in the finance/insurance sector to 19 percent of firms in the transportation sector. Employee coverage also varied substantially, with 35 percent of users covering all nonmanagerial employees, and 50 percent covering less than half of their employees.

Special incentives were utilized by 29 percent of firms. They were used by two-thirds of the firms in the accommodations/food sector, and by 43 percent of firms in the finance/insurance sector, but were seldom used in the wholesale/retail, resources, and electrical/gas sectors. Among firms using special incentives, employee coverage varied dramatically, with nearly half of users covering all employees, while 44 percent covered less than half of their employees. The mean coverage level was 57 percent.

Group or Team Performance Pay

While most firms (64 percent) reported having no group or team-based performance pay at all, there were six firms that reported having all three types. About 27 percent of firms reported having one type, and 7 percent reported two types. As shown in Table 3.3, the three types of group performance pay were approximately equal in popularity, with gain sharing used by 14 percent of firms, goal sharing by 18 percent, and other group plans by 16 percent.

Use of gain sharing varied significantly across industrial sectors. Nearly half of firms in the resource sector utilized gain sharing, while it was not used at all in the communication and accommodations/food sectors. Among firms using gain sharing, employee coverage varied greatly, with 32 percent of users extending it to all nonmanagerial employees, and 41 percent of users to less than half of their employees. The mean coverage level was 56 percent.

Several other studies have examined the use of gain sharing in Canada over the past 15 years or so. The Economic Council of Canada conducted two large-scale surveys, one in 1985 (Long 1989) and a follow-up in 1991 (Betcherman, Leckie, and Verma 1994). These studies included smaller firms than the present survey (establishments with 50 employees or more, mean size 278 employees, median of 104), but did include a broad cross-section of industrial sectors. They found that 8 percent of Canadian firms had gain sharing in 1985, and that this proportion had not changed by 1991. Based on dates of adoption, the 1985 study indicated that popularity of gain sharing had been increasing since 1973, with a large spike during 1979–1985, when 70 percent of the plans had been implemented. One possible explanation for this spike is posited by Long and Warner (1987), who have argued that the severe recession of the early 1980s served as a catalyst for many firms to reexamine their traditional approaches to management, and to experiment with a variety of innovative work practices, including gain sharing.

In a survey of very large Canadian firms (mean size 7,000 employees, median 3,030) conducted during 1990–1991, Long (1993) found a much higher adoption level, 20 percent. However, it is possible that this apparent discrepancy may be due to the size difference of the two samples, since the Long (1993) sample found the incidence of gain sharing much higher in large firms. The size range of the current survey (mean 1,914 employees; median 911) falls between these two surveys.

In a survey of medium to large companies conducted in 1995, The Conference Board of Canada (Isaac 1995) found that about 11 percent of their sample had gain sharing, but another 5 percent were planning to implement it "soon." Data on attrition rates of Canadian gain sharing plans (Long 1989) indicated that 17 percent of the firms with gain sharing plans in 1980–1985 discontinued them during that period. If that is the case, an incidence of perhaps 13 to 14 percent by 2000 could be projected on the basis of the Isaac study, which is consistent with the results actually found in the current survey. The results on goal sharing indicated that 18 percent of firms had such a plan, with no significant variation across industrial sectors. Employee coverage ranged widely, with 37 percent of users covering all employees, and 35 percent covering less than half. The mean employee coverage was 61 percent. Beyond goal or gain sharing, 16 percent of firms reported use of some other type of group plan, and usage did not vary significantly across industrial sectors. Some 30 percent of users covered all employees, while 49 percent covered less than half. Mean coverage level was 50 percent.

Organizational Performance Pay

While just over half of all firms had some form of organizational performance pay, none reported more than three of the five types. However, this is not surprising since three of the plans were variations of stock plans, and most firms would not have more than one of these.

Overall, as can be seen in Table 3.3, the most popular form of organizational performance pay was profit sharing, utilized by 32 percent of firms. Stock purchase plans were utilized by 21 percent of firms, stock options by 10 percent, and stock bonuses by 4 percent. Overall, about 27 percent of firms used some type of stock plan. The largest group of users (19 percent) had just one stock plan, while 7 percent had two stock plans and one firm had all three. A small number of firms (5 percent) had some type of organizational performance plan other than stock plans or profit sharing.

Employee profit sharing showed no statistically significant variation across industrial sectors, but tended to be most heavily concentrated in the resources, manufacturing, and transportation sectors, and was not used at all in the electricity/gas and accommodation/food sectors. Among firms using profit sharing, employee coverage was high, with two-thirds of users covering all their employees. Overall, the mean coverage level was 78 percent.

What is the trend in profit sharing? Comparable surveys conducted in 1985 (Betcherman and McMullen 1986) and in 1993 (Wagar and Long 1995) indicated a doubling of the use of profit sharing during that eight-year period. Long (1992) found that 17.3 percent of Canadian firms had profit sharing in 1989–1990, while a comparable study by the Economic Council of Canada conducted in 1991 showed 18 percent. A 1993 survey

(Betcherman, Leckie, and Verma 1994) showed 21.6 percent adopted profit sharing. The 32 percent adoption level in the current study seems to point to a rather dramatic continued increase in the popularity of employee profit sharing in Canada, despite the lack of public policy measures to encourage adoption. In Canada, unlike many other countries, profit sharing carries no particular tax advantages (Tyson 1996).

About a fifth of the firms in the sample had stock purchase plans. Although there was no significant difference in utilization across sectors, they were most common in the communication sector (where they were used by nearly half of all firms), and least common in the manufacturing sector. Among users, employee coverage was very high, with 84 percent of users including all employees, and a mean coverage level of 92 percent. In contrast, stock bonus plans were rarely used, with just 4 percent of firms having such a plan, and no significant variation across sectors. Among users, coverage was high, with 70 percent of users including all employees, and the mean employee coverage level was 80 percent.

There is a considerable body of evidence regarding the use of employee stock plans in Canada. For example, a 1986 study of its members by the Toronto Stock Exchange (1987) revealed that 23 percent had some type of broad based employee stock plan. By 1989–1990, Long (1992) found that 37 percent of the publicly traded firms in his sample had broad-based stock bonus or purchase programs. The Conference Board of Canada (Isaac 1995) found that about 43 percent of publicly traded firms had broad based employee stock purchase plans by 1995. The current study found that the exact same proportion—43 percent—of publicly traded corporations currently have stock bonus and/or stock purchase plans, suggesting that the growth in these plans may have tailed off in recent years, after a rapid expansion during 1987 to 1995. Although the reasons for this rapid expansion are not entirely clear, it was quite likely influenced by the dramatic upsurge in popularity of employee ownership in the United States experienced during the late 1970s and 1980s (Kruse and Blasi 1997).

Interestingly, once stock option plans are included with stock bonus and stock purchase plans, results reveal that the percentage of publicly traded firms with stock plans has continued to increase in Canada, reaching 48.7 percent by 2000. However, not surprisingly, employee stock plans are much less common in companies that are not publicly traded corporations. For example, in his 1989–1990 study of mostly small to medium-sized companies, Long (1992) found that only about 4 percent of privately held corporations had employee stock bonus or purchase plans. The current study showed little change in this, with just 4.8 percent of unlisted companies having employee stock bonus and/or purchase plans, although when stock option plans are included, this proportion increases to 7.1 percent.

These results suggest that there has been major growth in the use of stock option plans. Until the 1990s, stock options were a common component of executive compensation, but were almost never granted to nonmanagerial employees. However, since 1989, when PepsiCo Inc granted all employees stock options worth 10 percent of their salary, "an estimated 2,000 [US] companies have instituted their own broad based option plans" (Capell 1996, 80). In Canada, Isaac (1995) found that about 4.4 percent of her sample of medium to large Canadian companies had provided stock options or stock grants (bonuses) to at least some of their nonmanagerial employees.

In the current sample, about 10 percent of firms report providing stock options to their nonmanagerial employees. Usage is much higher among publicly listed companies—17 percent—and much lower among unlisted companies (3 percent), where these plans are still rare. There was a high concentration in the communications sector, where they are used by about a third of firms, and they were not used at all in the transportation or accommodation/food sectors. Among users, employee coverage was generally high, with 57 percent of users extending stock options to all employees, and a mean employee coverage of 68 percent.

The incidence of stock options in the current study accords well with a recent study conducted by the Conference Board of Canada, which found that just under 10 percent of firms provided broad-based stock option plans in 2000 (D. Brown 2001). Overall, the results of both studies indicate a rather dramatic increase in the use of employee stock option plans in Canada during the past few years, possibly following from their popularity in the United States. One reason for their popularity relative to stock purchase or bonus plans is that stock options can be issued to employees at no direct cost to the firm (although there may ultimately be some cost to existing shareholders in terms of share dilution), and at no cost to employees. Unlike stock purchase plans, employees do not need to lay out any investment, nor do they suffer losses if share prices decline.

The popularity of stock options is likely to be accelerated by changes in Canadian income tax laws announced in 2000, which remove the previously unfavorable income tax treatment of stock options. Instead of becoming liable for income taxes at the time of exercise, Canadians are now liable only at the time of the actual sale of the exercised shares. This brings Canadian tax treatment of stock options in line with treatment in the United States.

Turning to organizational plans other than stock or profit sharing, results (in Table 3.3) revealed use by only a few firms (5 percent), with no significant variation across sectors. Among users, employee coverage levels were high, with 73 percent of users including all employees, and a mean employee coverage of 88 percent.

Patterns of Adoption

An important issue briefly touched on earlier in the chapter is whether performance pay plans serve as substitutes or complements to one another. For example, firms that wish to stimulate employee performance through the use of individual performance pay could do so either through output-related pay (such as piece rates or sales commissions), or through merit pay based on appraised performance. Use of both types, even where appropriate, could simply represent a costly duplication. Similarly, if employees already receive group performance pay, use of individual performance pay may not only be a costly redundancy, but may also negate the philosophy of team work and cooperation that the group system is intended to foster. These examples reflect the substitution argument.

The essence of the complementarity argument is that combining several types of performance pay can result in a compensation system that captures the advantages of each type of performance pay, while minimizing the deficiencies of each plan. For example, the linkage between individual employee performance and reward is very evident in individual performance pay plans, but less so in group plans, and even less so in organizational plans, where the potential for free riding is very high (Jones, Kato, and Pliskin 1997). On the other hand, focusing on rewarding only individual performance could lead to a variety of negative outcomes, including narrowly self-interested employee behavior, lack of cooperation among employees, and little concern for the overall success of the organization. Group or team-based pay plans might engender close cooperation among employees within individual work units, but could lead to lack of cooperation or even conflict with other organizational units. However, these problems might be averted by also incorporating organizational performance pay into the compensation system. Thus, under the complementarity argument, one would expect positive relationships between the three categories of performance pay plans, while the substitutability argument would suggest negative relationships.

There is, however, a third possibility, which will be labeled the *independent benefits argument*. Under this argument, each category of performance pay delivers a set of specific independent benefits, which may or may not be useful to a given organization. Here, the decision to utilize individual, group, or organizational performance pay is based on the firm's analysis of the balance between the benefits accruing to the organization from adopting a given category of performance pay and the costs of implementing and operating that system. Under this argument, one would expect to find no relationship between the use of one category of performance pay and the use of another.

So what do the data indicate? In fact, analysis revealed significant positive relationships between all three categories of performance pay. Firms that had a greater number of individual performance pay plans also had a greater number of group pay plans ($r = .22$, $p < .001$) and organizational plans ($r = .19$, $p < .001$). Similarly, firms with more group plans also had more organizational plans ($r = .16$, $p < .01$), as well as more individual plans. These results provide support for the view that many firms see the three categories of performance pay plans as complements to one another.

However, might this be different *within* performance pay categories? As discussed earlier, one would expect firms with output related pay (such as piece rates or sales commissions) to have a lower need for performance pay related to appraised performance (such as merit raises or merit bonuses). As another example, if one group plan, such as gain sharing, is in place, wouldn't another be seen as superfluous? Also, why have a stock plan if you already have profit sharing? Within performance pay categories, one might expect much stronger support for the substitutability argument, since pay plans in each of the three categories are, by definition, aimed at the same type of employee performance behavior—focusing on individual performance objectives, group performance objectives, or organizational performance objectives.

The independent benefits argument, however, could also come into play. Firms may use two or more performance pay plan within the same category if they perceive that each performance pay plans delivers different benefits to the organization, focuses on different aspects of the relationship between performance and pay, or has different shortcomings. For example, stock plans may have the potential to create high employee identification with the organization, but the connection between performance and reward is less predictable for stock plans than for profit sharing. Moreover, profit sharing can be designed to include all employees, while a stock purchase plan will include only those employees who choose to purchase stock. Thus, an organization may choose to utilize both of these plans, one or the other, or neither, based on a cost benefit analysis of each.

In order to examine this issue, Table 3.5 provides the correlations

Table 3.5

Specific Types of Employee Performance Pay Plans: Means, Standard Deviations, and Intercorrelations, 2000

Type of Performance Pay Plan	Mean	SD	Piece rates	Sales commissions	Merit raises	Merit bonus	Special incentives	Gain sharing	Goal sharing	Other group Plans	Profit sharing	Stock bonus	Stock purchase	Stock option
Plans based on individual performance														
• Piece rates	4.64	17.35	—											
• Sales commissions	5.46	15.75	−.03	—										
• Merit raises	52.42	44.97	−.2[a]	.03	—									
• Merit bonuses	18.97	35.59	−.11[b]	.01	.23[a]	—								
• Special incentives	16.83	35.33	−.06	−.08	.11[b]	.08	—							
Plans based on group or team performance														
• Gain sharing	7.94	24.32	−.06	.01	−.09	−.03	−.06	—						
• Goal sharing	11.11	28.89	−.02	−.03	.09	.20[a]	.02	.12[b]	—					
• Other group plans	7.84	23.89	.00	.11	.15[b]	.11[b]	.03	.13[b]	.33[a]	—				
Plans based on organizational performance														
• Profit sharing	24.55	41.32	.04	.13[b]	.13[b]	.02	.02	.09	.13[b]	.03	—			
• Stock bonus plans	3.38	17.86	−.05	.04	.04	.12[b]	−.08	−.06	.16[a]	−.06	.05	—		
• Stock purchase plans	19.39	38.99	−.02	.08	.08	.11[b]	−.02	−.02	.07	.00	−.07	.16[a]	—	
• Stock option plans	6.6	24.26	−.07	.15[b]	.15[a]	.13[b]	−.11	−.09	−.02	−.08	.13[b]	.05	.10	—
• Other organizational performance plans	4.05	19.14	−.06	.14[b]	.14[a]	.17[a]	.05	.04	.07	.03	−.02	.06	.03	.04

[a] Indicates statistical significance at the 1 percent level.
[b] Indicates statistical significance at the 5 percent level.

between all thirteen performance pay plans (as measured by the percentage of employees covered by each plan). As can be seen, of the twenty-three within-category correlations, just two are significantly negative, while seven are significantly positive. This result thus provides very little support for the substitutability argument, with just two exceptions. As expected, firms using piece rates are in fact significantly less likely to use merit systems (merit raises or merit bonuses) based on appraised performance.

Beyond these two relationships, the bulk of evidence appears to favor the independent benefits argument, although there appears to be some evidence of complementarity even within performance pay categories. For example, firms with merit raises were more likely also to have merit bonuses. Firms using one group pay plan were also significantly more likely to have one of the others. Firms with stock purchase plans were also more likely to have stock bonus plans, and firms with profit sharing plans were more likely also to have stock option plans.

Most of these relationships make sense in terms of various aspects of complementarity, such as complementarity of administration. For example, both merit raises and merit bonuses depend on a performance appraisal system. Stock purchase plans and stock bonus plans depend on an infrastructure geared for valuation and sale of company stock. Many of the administrative issues for operating group pay plans are common across different types of group pay. A different type of complementarity is also evident for merit raises and merit bonuses, whereby merit bonuses are often used to continue to motivate employees who are no longer eligible for merit raises because they are at the top of their pay ranges.

Across the performance pay categories, numerous patterns of complementarity emerge. For example, merit raises and merit bonuses were both significantly related to numerous forms of group and organizational performance pay, suggesting that firms may be attempting to temper the individualistic focus that might otherwise be engendered by individual performance pay. Sales commissions were related to organizational performance pay, although not to group pay. Goal sharing and "other" group plans were both significantly related to forms of individual and organizational pay. Profit sharing and stock bonus plans were both significantly related to forms of individual and group performance pay, while stock purchase, stock options, and "other" organizational performance plans were related to forms of individual performance pay.

No patterns of substitutability across categories were found, but two pay forms appeared to be used independently of forms in other categories. Neither piece rates nor gain sharing showed any significant relationships to pay forms outside their categories.

Predictors of Total Number of Plans

What factors predict the extent to which firms have adopted performance pay plans? Three sets of variables were used as potential predictors—characteristics of the firm, structural characteristics, and work force characteristics. Multiple regression analysis (ordinary least squares) was used to ascertain the effects of each of these variables on the total number of performance pay plans used by each firm, and the resulting coefficients are shown in Table 3.6.

As can be seen, five significant factors were identified. Consistently with expectations, high-involvement firms had a higher total number of performance pay plans than other firms, as did larger firms and publicly traded firms, while firms with higher unionization had fewer performance pay plans. Outsourcing of labor requirements was positively related to number of performance pay plans. Together, these variables explained 23.5 percent of the variation in the total number of performance pay plans utilized by a given firm.

However, the picture changes somewhat when examining predictors of individual, group, and organizational performance pay plans. As Table 3.6 shows, three factors—unionization, size, and labor outsourcing—predicted the number of individual performance pay plans that firms adopted, explaining 19.3 percent of the variation. Firms with high levels of unionization adopted far fewer individual performance plans than did other firms, while larger firms and firms with more outsourcing of labor requirements were more likely to have individual performance plans than other firms.

Four factors—high involvement management, industrial sector, competitive strategy, and labor outsourcing—significantly predicted the total number of group performance plans adopted by firms, explaining 7.5 percent of the variation. Firms that practiced high-involvement management, firms in the retail/wholesale sector, and firms with more labor outsourcing were more likely to have group plans, while firms with a prospector competitive strategy were less likely to have them.

Five factors—high involvement, public listing, growth, employee education, and work teams—significantly predicted the total number of organizational performance plans in use, explaining 29.9 percent of the variation in adoption. High-involvement firms, publicly traded firms, rapidly growing firms, and firms with greater proportions of highly educated employees and employees in work teams were more likely to have organizational performance pay plans than other firms.

Many of these findings are consistent with expectations. For example, high-involvement firms had more group and organizational performance

Table 3.6

Predictors of Total Number of Employee Performance Pay Plans

Company characteristics	Total number of performance pay plans	Total number of individual performance pay plans	Total number of group performance pay plans	Total number of organizational perf pay plans
Characteristics of firm				
• Competitive strategy				
—Prospector	−.03	−.02	−.14[a]	.06
• Industrial sector				
—Manufacturing	.03	.06	−.02	.01
—Retail/wholesale	−.02	−.06	.16[a]	−.06
• Ownership				
—Publicly traded	.13[a]	.03	−.01	.31[b]
—Foreign subsidiary	−.06	−.02	−.04	−.08
• Size and growth				
—Employment total	.15[a]	.19[b]	−.02	.10
—Employment growth	.10	.00	.10	.15[b]
—Geographical dispersion	—	.09	.09	—
Structural characteristics				
• High involvement	.24[b]	.08	.14[a]	.21[b]
• Job scope	−.02	.06	−.12	.10
• Proportion in HR department	.04	.01	.08	.02
• Proportion in teams	.04	−.03	.03	.13[a]
Work force characteristics				
• Proportion full-time	−.01	.00	−.01	.05
• Proportion with degrees	.08	.08	.00	.15[a]
• Proportion managerial	−.10	−.08	−.09	−.01
• Proportion outsourced	.15[a]	.14[a]	.13[a]	.04
• Proportion unionized	−.30[b]	−.41[b]	−.04	−.01
r-squared	.235	.193	.075	.299

[a] Indicates significance at the 5 percent level.
[b] Indicates significance at the 1 percent level.

pay than other firms. Unionized companies had less individual performance pay, as expected, but not less group or organizational performance pay, where expectations had been less clear. Publicly listed firms and firms experiencing rapid employment growth were more likely to have organizational performance pay, consistent with expectations.

Some findings were partially consistent with expectations. For example, firms with more highly educated employees were more likely to have organizational performance pay, as expected, but not group or individual performance pay, as had also been expected. Large firms had more individual performance pay, as had been expected, but not more group and organizational performance pay. Firms with more outsourcing of their labor requirements were less likely to have individual performance pay, as expected, but not less likely to have group or organizational performance pay. Firms with more teams were more likely to have organizational performance pay, but surprisingly, no more likely to have group performance pay, and no less likely to have individual performance pay.

Some findings were inconsistent with expectations. For example, it had been expected that a broad job scope might make individual performance pay less viable, thus increasing the attractiveness of group or organizational performance, but no such effects were found. It was posited that geographically dispersed organizations might desire more performance pay, in order to lend cohesion to far-flung operations, but again, there was no such relationship. It had been thought that firms with a greater proportion of full-time employees might find it worthwhile to have more performance pay, especially group and organizational pay, but no such results were found. It had been suggested that firms with more innovative competitive strategies might see performance pay as a mechanism to encourage employee innovation and creativity, but this was not evident, and in fact, firms with a prospector strategy were actually less likely to have team-based pay.

Predictors of Specific Performance Pay Plans

What factors predict the use of each specific type of performance pay? Multiple regression analysis (ordinary least squares) was again used to identify significant predictors, and resulting coefficients are shown in Table 3.7. The measure of performance pay used was the percentage of employees at each firm covered by a given form of performance pay.[1]

As can be seen, there was at least one significant predictor for every type of performance pay, with the exception of individual special incentives. However, the amount of variation explained was relatively low for two pay plans—gain sharing and stock bonuses—amounting to about 2.3 percent in each case. For the other ten performance pay plans, the independent variables explained from 5.8 percent of the variation (for profit sharing) to 34.8 percent (for merit raises).

Predictors of Individual Performance Pay Plans

The most commonly used performance pay plan—merit raises—had six significant predictors. By far the most important predictor was unionization level. Consistently with expectations, unionized firms were much less likely

Table 3.7

Predictors of Specific Performance Pay Plans

	Individual performance pay plans					Group performance pay plans			Organizational performance pay plans				
Company characteristics	Piece rates (27 plans)	Commissions (64 plans)	Merit raises (171 plans)	Merit bonus (88 plans)	Special incentives (70 plans)	Gain sharing (34 plans)	Goal sharing (43 plans)	Other group plans (37 plans)	Profit sharing (75 plans)	Stock bonus (10 plans)	Stock purchase (50 plans)	Stock option (23 plans)	Other plans (11 plans)
Characteristics of firm													
• Competitive strategy													
—Prospector	−.02	.13a	−.22b	.04	.07	−.02	−.04	−.03	−.01	.05	.00	.09	.03
• Industrial sector													
—Manufacturing	.25b	−.02	.15a	−.06	−.01	.02	−.02	.01	.20b	−.01	−.01	.04	.09
—Retail/wholesale	−.03	.34b	.01	−.02	−.09	−.02	.04	.31b	−.03	−.05	.00	.00	−.07
• Ownership													
—Publicly traded	.00	.12a	.13a	−.02	.03	−.11	−.03	.03	.01	.15a	.35b	.09	−.02
—Foreign subsidiary	−.17b	.02	.03	−.04	.03	−.05	−.09	.04	−.08	.02	−.11a	−.03	.15a
• Size and growth													
—Employment total	−.04	−.01	−.09	.07	.02	−.02	.05	−.06	.04	.06	.20b	−.02	−.03
—Employment growth	−.10	−.05	−.02	.11	−.05	−.03	.17b	.19b	.02	−.02	.12a	.12a	.16a
—Geographical dispersion	−.10	.14a	.16b	.07	.08	−.03	.08	.08	−.06	.04	.02	−.12a	.11a
Structural characteristics													
• High involvement	−.04	−.01	−.09	.13a	.05	.02	.33b	.11	.16a	.08	.06	.09	.01
• Job scope	−.15a	−.01	.13a	.01	−.02	.01	−.21b	.03	−.04	.06	.11a	.21b	.02
• Proportion in HR department	−.03	−.03	−.05	.20b	.00	.11	.13a	.02	−.04	.03	.04	.04	.21b
• Proportion in teams	.00	−.02	−.07	−.11	.06	.06	−.03	.00	.08	.08	.08	−.03	.00

(continued)

Table 3.7 *(continued)*

	Individual performance pay plans					Group performance pay plans			Organizational performance pay plans				
Company characteristics	Piece rates (27 plans)	Commissions (64 plans)	Merit raises (171 plans)	Merit bonus (88 plans)	Special incentives (70 plans)	Gain sharing (34 plans)	Goal sharing (43 plans)	Other group plans (37 plans)	Profit sharing (75 plans)	Stock bonus (10 plans)	Stock purchase (50 plans)	Stock option (23 plans)	Other plans (11 plans)
Work Force characteristics													
• Proportion full-time	.07	.00	−.09	−.01	−.04	.11	−.19[b]	−.03	.01	.03	.03	.02	.06
• Proportion with degrees	.01	.04	.22[b]	.03	.05	.11	−.03	−.01	.00	.04	−.05	.20[b]	.17[b]
• Proportion managerial	.01	−.14[a]	−.03	.02	−.03	−.01	−.05	−.03	−.05	−.04	.12[a]	−.10	.04
• Proportion outsourced	.07	.12	.03	.06	−.04	.02	.14[a]	.05	.04	−.06	.02	−.13[a]	−.01
• Proportion unionized	.03	−.11[a]	−.40[b]	−.23[b]	−.09	.15[a]	−.01	−.05	−.10	−.08	.02	.03	−.02
r-squared	.105	.221	.348	.139	—	.023	.162	.133	.058	.023	.271	.183	.152

[a] Indicates statistical significance at the 5 percent level.
[b] Indicates statistical significance at the 1 percent level.

to use merit raises than nonunion firms. Firms employing a prospector strategy were also less likely to use merit raises, while firms that were publicly traded, were geographically dispersed, had broad job scope, and had higher proportions of full-time and highly educated employees were more likely to use merit raises.

Six factors also predicted the use of sales commissions. Firms that were in the retail/wholesale sector, were publicly listed, were geographically dispersed, and used a prospector competitive strategy were more likely to use sales commissions, while those with more managers and unionized employees were less likely to utilize them. Together, these factors explained 22.1 percent of the variation in use of sales commissions.

Two types of individual performance pay plans each had three significant predictors. Merit bonuses were most likely to be found in firms with low unionization, a high-involvement managerial strategy, and a strong human resources department, and these factors explained about 14 percent of the variation in their usage. Piece rates were found most commonly in the manufacturing sector, and in firms that had narrow job scope, while foreign subsidiaries were less likely to have piece rates, and these three variables explained just over 10 percent of variation in their usage.

Predictors of Group Performance Pay Plans

Goal sharing plans were used more extensively in high-involvement firms; rapidly growing firms; firms with larger HR departments and more labor outsourcing; and, perhaps surprisingly, firms with a higher proportion of part-time employees. They were used less extensively in firms with a broad job scope. Gain sharing had just one significant predictor and was used more extensively in unionized than in nonunion firms. "Other" group plans had two significant predictors and were used more extensively in retail/wholesale firms and rapidly growing firms.

Predictors of Organizational Performance Plans

Stock purchase plans had six significant predictors. The most important predictor was whether the firm was publicly traded. Larger firms, rapidly growing firms, those with more managers, and those with broad job scope were also more likely to have stock purchase plans, while foreign subsidiaries were less likely to have them. The predictors together explained about 27 percent of the variation in their use. Stock option plans were used more extensively in firms that were growing rapidly, had jobs with broad scope, and had highly educated employees, and less often in geographically dispersed firms and those with more labor outsourcing. The variables explained about 18 percent of the variation.

Stock bonus plans had just one significant predictor and were used more extensively in publicly traded firms. Profit sharing plans were used more extensively in high-involvement firms and manufacturing firms. "Other" organizational performance plans had five significant predictors. The variables explained 15.2 percent of their variation, and they were used more extensively in firms with strong HR departments, highly educated employees, geographical dispersion, and rapid growth, and in foreign subsidiaries.

Overall Patterns

Looking at the predictors, it can be seen that all three sets of characteristics are important. General characteristics of the firm were related to ten pay plans, structural characteristics to eight pay plans, and work force characteristics to eight pay plans. Among the characteristics of the firm, ownership was related to six types of pay plans, as publicly traded firms were more likely to have stock bonus or purchase plans, and were also more likely to utilize merit raises and sales commissions. Foreign subsidiaries were less likely to use piece rates and stock purchase plans, but more likely to use "other" organizational pay plans.

Industrial sector was related to five pay plans, as manufacturing firms were more likely to have piece rates, merit raises, and profit sharing, while retail/wholesale firms were more likely to have sales commissions and "other" group pay plans, possibly in the form of group commissions or sales bonuses geared to branch or regional sales. Competitive strategy was related to two pay plans, as firms with a prospector strategy were more likely to use sales commissions but less likely to use merit raises. Rapidly growing firms were more likely to have goal sharing, "other" group pay plans, stock purchase, stock options, and "other" organizational pay plans. Rather surprisingly, company size had very little impact, being related only to stock purchase plans. Geographical dispersion had somewhat more impact, being positively related to commissions, merit raises, and "other" organizational pay plans, and negatively to stock options.

Structural characteristics were related to eight pay plans. Firms with a high-involvement managerial strategy were more likely to have merit bonuses, goal sharing, and profit sharing plans. Firms having jobs with broad scope were more likely to have merit raises, stock purchase, and stock options, but less likely to have piece rates. Firms with larger human resource departments were more likely to have merit bonuses, goal sharing, and organizational performance plans other than profit sharing or stock plans.

Work force characteristics were significantly related to eight pay plans, and by far the most important of these was the unionization level. Highly unionized firms were less likely to have sales commissions, merit raises, and merit bonuses, but more likely to have gain sharing. Firms with highly educated employees were more likely to have merit raises, stock options, and "other" organizational pay plans. Firms with more full-time employees were less likely to have goal sharing plans, while firms with more managers were more likely to have employee stock purchase plans and less likely to utilize sales commissions.

Conclusions

While nearly all Canadian firms use some form of performance pay, individual performance plans continue to be the most popular form, particularly merit raises, which was the only specific type utilized by a majority of firms. However, organizational performance plans appear to have experienced a dramatic growth during the last quarter of the twentieth century, to the point where over half of the firms in this sample had some form of broad-based organizational performance pay, and more than a third had some form of group- or team-based pay. The specific forms of performance pay that seem to have grown most rapidly are profit sharing plans, stock plans (especially stock options), and goal sharing plans.

What accounts for this rapid growth? Since Canada has no particular tax or public policy measures in place that would induce firms to adopt these pay practices, Canadian firms must be adopting these plans based on their perceived benefits to the organization. Indeed, an increasing body of evidence suggests that various group and organizational pay plans have the potential to significantly enhance organizational effectiveness (Kruse and Blasi 1997; Jones, Kato, and Pliskin 1997), particularly if applied in combination with a high-involvement organizational model (Lawler 1992; MacDuffie 1995; Levine 1997; Appelbaum et al. 2000).

As firms attempt to find ways to become more responsive, flexible, innovative, and productive within an increasingly complex and dynamic organizational environment, many are moving toward the high-involvement model (Betcherman, et al. 1994; Osterman 1994; Gittleman, Horrigan, and Joyce 1998; Freeman, Kleiner, and Ostoff 2000). As they do so, it becomes evident to them that a crucial component of this process is the adoption of "new" pay practices that focus on group and organizational performance

(Long 2002). This explanation is certainly consistent with the findings in this study, where high-involvement organizations had adopted significantly more group and organizational performance plans than had other firms.

It is interesting to note, however, that firms are not abandoning individual performance plans entirely as they add group and organizational performance plans. Indeed, firms with more group plans and organizational plans were also likely to have more individual pay plans, suggesting that many firms see these pay practices as complements, not substitutes, for one another. The only exception to this is in regard to piece rates and merit pay, which are apparently seen as substitutes.

Overall, some results of this study were consistent with expectations, while others were somewhat surprising. As expected, characteristics of the firm, structural characteristics, and work force characteristics all played a role in predicting the incidence of performance pay. Large firms were likely to have more individual performance pay plans, as expected, but not more group or organizational plans, and company size played a surprisingly small role in predicting the incidence of specific types of performance pay. As expected, high-involvement organizations had more group and organizational performance pay than traditional organizations, but not more individual performance pay. Unionization was strongly negatively related to individual performance pay, as expected, but did not affect the total number of group or organizational performance pay plans.

One interesting finding is in regard to the (lack of) relationship between the use of work teams and group or team-based performance pay. Although firms using more work teams did have a higher number of organizational pay plans, they did not have a higher number of group or team-based performance pay plans. It is possible that these firms do not view team-based pay as an important element in the success of work teams, and that organizational performance pay is sufficient to foster the teamwork and cooperation required, or it may simply be that the implementation of team-based pay is lagging the introduction of work teams. With the baseline data provided in this study, future research can provide a clearer view of these issues.

Appendix 3.1: Variable Definitions

A. The incidence of performance pay schemes was based on the following question: Please estimate the percentage of employees ... who are covered by each of the performance pay systems listed below:

Pay Systems Geared to the Performance of Individual Employees

1. Piece rates (pay based on the number of units produced or processed)
2. Sales commissions (pay based on the number of units sold)
3. Merit pay raises (pay increases based on appraised employee performance)
4. Merit pay bonuses (bonuses based on appraised employee performance that do not raise annual pay)
5. Special-purpose cash incentives (e.g., attendance bonuses; suggestion bonuses, etc)

Pay Systems Geared to the Performance of Specific Subunits, Work Groups, or Teams (but not the organization as a whole)

6. Gain sharing plans (bonuses based on group/subunit/team productivity gains or cost improvements)
7. Goal sharing plans (bonuses based on the group/subunit/team achievement of specified performance goals/objectives)
8. Other group or team bonuses (e.g., group/subunit/team piece rates; group sales commissions; other group pay plans)

Pay Systems Geared to the Performance of the Organization as a Whole

9. Profit sharing (a formal system to share organizational profits)
10. Share bonus plans (provision of company shares at no cost to the employee)
11. Share purchase plans (a formal program to provide company shares to employees at a discounted rate)
12. Share options (provision of stock options to employees)
13. Other organizational performance plans (e.g., other long-term financial incentives linked to corporate performance)

B. "High involvement" was measured using a set of fifteen items that tapped various aspects of the organization structure, including job scope, coordination process, control mechanism, communication, and leadership/decision making. The response scale utilized a seven-point Likert-type scale.

1. Most jobs in this organization require a high level of skill, knowledge and ability to accomplish them. (job scope)
2. Most jobs in this organization are narrow in scope with a very limited range of responsibilities and duties. (job scope—reverse-scored)
3. For most jobs in this organization, individuals have considerable latitude in planning and organizing their work activities. (job scope)
4. Most jobs in this firm are highly repetitive. (job scope—reverse-scored)
5. Coordination of work activities is carried out mainly by managers/supervisors. (coordination—reverse-scored)
6. In this organization, there is a strict hierarchy of authority that is almost always followed. (coordination—reverse-scored)
7. There are a great many rules in this organization. (control—reverse-scored)
8. In this organization, rules are considered largely unnecessary, since employees will act responsibly even without them. (control)
9. Management believes that because most employees are committed to and enjoy their jobs, they will work effectively even without supervision. (control)
10. In this organization, communication flows freely up, down, and across the organization. (communication)
11. In general, management believes that it is not necessary for employees to have any more information beyond that required to perform their jobs. (communication—reverse-scored)
12. The *main* role of a supervisor at this firm is to ensure that employees are doing their jobs. (leadership style—reverse-scored)
13. The main role of a supervisor at this firm is to facilitate and support employees in carrying out their assigned duties. (leadership style)
14. In this organization, even small matters have to be referred to someone higher up for final decision. (decision making—reverse-scored)
15. When decisions are made in this organization, there is usually a significant amount of participation by employees. (decision making)

Note

1. Note that the full sample of firms was used in the estimation. Thus, those firms that reported they did not make use of a particular pay scheme were identified as having 0 percent of employees covered. Obviously, the estimates then combine the influence of the factors on adopting a particular pay scheme and the influence of the factors on expanding the coverage of a particular pay scheme. It would seem there is no particular

difference in the theoretical influence that the factors should have on these two decisions of adopting or expanding a particular scheme.

References

Appelbaum, E., Bailey, T., Berg, P., and Kalleberg, A. L. 2000. *Manufacturing Advantage: Why High Performance Work Systems Pay Off.* Ithaca, NY: ILR Press.
Banker, R. D., Lee, S., Potter, G., and Srinivasan, D. 1996. "Contextual Analysis of Performance Impacts of Outcome-Based Incentive Compensation." *Academy of Management Journal* 39: 920–948.
Belman, D., and Heywood, J. S. 1992. "Wages, Incentive Schemes, and the Role of Gender." *Review of Social Economy* 50: 149–162.
Betcherman, G., Leckie, N., and Verma, A. 1994. "HRM Innovations in Canada: Evidence from Establishment Surveys." Working Paper Series No.QPIR 1994–3. Kingston, ON: Industrial Relations Centre, Queen's University.
Betcherman, G., and McMullen, K. 1986. *Working with Technology: A Survey of Automation in Canada.* Ottawa: Canadian Government Publishing Centre.
Betcherman, G., McMullen, K., Leckie, N., and Caron, C. 1994. *The Canadian Workplace in Transition.* Kingston, ON: IRC Press.
Biagioli, M. 1993. "An Econometric Investigation of Employee Financial Participation in Enterprise Results in a Sample of Large Italian Firms." Unpublished paper, Faculta di Economia e Commercio, University of Modena, Italy.
Brown, C. 1990. "Firms' Choice of Method of Pay." *Industrial and Labor Relations Review* 43: 165–182.
Brown, D. 2001. "Stock Options Grow." *Canadian HR Reporter* 14: 1–10.
Burns, T., and Stalker, G. 1961. *The Management of Innovation.* London: Tavistock.
Capell, K. 1996. "Options for Everyone." *Business Week,* July 22: 80–84.
Carstensen, V., Gerlach, K., and Hubler, O. 1992. "Profit Sharing in German Firms: Institutional Framework, Participation, and Microeconomic Effects." Paper presented at the WZB Workshop, Institutional Frameworks and Labor Market Performance. Berlin: Hanover University.
Chaykowski, R., and Lewis, B. 1995. *Compensation Practices and Outcomes in Canada and the United States.* Kingston; ON: IRC Press.
Cheadle, A. 1989. "Explaining Patterns of Profit Sharing Activity." *Industrial Relations* 28: 387–400.
Cooke, W. N. 1994. "Employee Participation Programs, Group-Based Incentives, and Company Performance: A Union-Nonunion Comparison." *Industrial and Labor Relations Review* 47: 594–609.
Drago, R., and Heywood, J. S. 1995. "The Choice of Payment Schemes: Australian Establishment Data." *Industrial Relations* 34: 507–531.
Eisenhardt, K. M. 1989. "Agency-and Institutional Theory Explanations: The Case of Retail Sales Compensation." *Academy of Management Journal* 31: 488–511.
Estrin, S., and Wilson, N. 1989. "Profit Sharing, the Marginal Cost of Labour, and Employment Variability." London: London School of Economics, Department of Economics.
Fitzroy, F., and Kraft, K. 1995. "On the Choice of Incentives in Firms." *Journal of Economic Behavior and Organization* 26: 145–160.
Freeman, R. B. 1982. "Union Wage Policies and Wage Dispersion Within Establishments." *Industrial and Labor Relations Review* 36: 3–21.
Freeman, R. B., Kleiner, M., and Ostroff, C. 2000. *The Anatomy of Employee Involve-*

ment and Its Effects on Firms and Workers. Cambridge, MA: National Bureau of Economic Research.

Gittleman, M., Horrigan, M., and Joyce, M. 1998. "Flexible Workplace Practices: Evidence from a Nationally Representative Survey." *Industrial and Labor Relations Review* 52: 99–115.

Gregg, P. A., and Machin, S. J. 1988. "Unions and the Incidence of Performance Linked Pay Schemes in Britain." *International Journal of Industrial Organization* 6: 91–107.

Heywood, J. S., Hubler, O., and Jirjahn, U. 1998. "Variable Payment Schemes and Industrial Relations: Evidence from Germany." *KYKLOS* 51: 237–257.

Heywood, J. S., Siebert, W. S., and Wei, X. 1997. "Payment by Results Systems: British Evidence." *British Journal of Industrial Relations* 35: 1–22.

Heywood, J. S., and Wei, X. 1997. "Piece Rate Systems and the Employment of Women: The Case of Hong Kong." *Journal of Comparative Economics* 25: 237–255.

Isaac, K. 1995. *Compensation Planning Outlook 1996.* Ottawa: Conference Board of Canada.

Jones, D. C., Kato, T., and Pliskin, J. 1997. "Profit Sharing and Gain Sharing: A Review of Theory, Incidence, and Effects." In *The Human Resource Management Handbook, Part I,* eds. Lewin, D., Mitchell, D., and Zaidi, M. A. Greenwich, CT: JAI Press, pp. 153–174.

Jones, D. C., and Pliskin, J. 1997. "Determinants of the Incidence of Group Incentives: Evidence from Canada." *Canadian Journal of Economics* 30: 1027–1045.

Kim, S. 1998. "Does Profit Sharing Increase Funds' Profits?" *Journal of Labor Research* 19:351–370.

Kochan, T., and Osterman, P. 1994. *The Mutual Gains Enterprise: Forging a Winning Partnership Among Labor, Management, and Government.* Boston: Harvard Business School Press.

Kruse, D. L. 1996. "Why Do Firms Adopt Profit Sharing and Employee Ownership Plans? *British Journal of Industrial Relations* 34: 515–538.

Kruse, D. L. 1993. *Profit Sharing: Does It Make a Difference?* Kalamazoo, MI: W. E. Upjohn Institute.

Kruse, D. L., and Blasi, J. R. 1997. "Employee Ownership, Employee Attitudes, and Firm Performance: A Review of the Evidence." In *The Human Resource Management Handbook, Part I,* eds. Lewin, D., Mitchell, D. J. B., and Zaidi, M. A. Greenwich, CT: JAI Press, pp. 113–152.

Lawler, E. E. 1992. *The Ultimate Advantage: Creating the High Involvement Organization.* San Francisco: Jossey Bass.

Lee, S. 1998. "Organizational Flexibility in Korean Companies: Rules and Procedures on Managerial Discretion and Employee Behaviour." *International Journal of Human Resource Management* 9: 478–493.

Levine, D. I. 1997. "Team Production." In *The Human Resource Management Handbook, Part I,* eds. Lewin, D., Mitchell, D. J. B., and Zaidi, M. A. Greenwich, CT: JAI Press, pp. 35–62.

Long, R. J. 1989. "Patterns of Workplace Innovation in Canada." *Relations industrielles* (Industrial Relations) 44: 805–826.

———. 1992. "The Incidence and Nature of Employee Profit Sharing and Share Ownership in Canada." *Relations industrielles* (Industrial Relations) 47: 463–486.

———. 1993. "New Information Technology and Employee Involvement." *Proceedings of the Administrative Sciences Association of Canada (Organizational Behaviour Division)* 14: 161–170.

———. 1994. "Gain Sharing, Hierarchy, and Managers: Are They Substitutes?" *Proceeding of the Administrative Sciences Association of Canada (Organization Theory Division),* 15: 51–60.

———. 1997. "Motives for Profit Sharing: A study of Canadian Chief Executive Officers." *Relations industrielles* (Industrial Relations) 52: 712–723.

———. 2001. "Pay Systems and Organizational Flexibility." *Canadian Journal of Administrative Sciences,* 18:25–32.

———. 2002. *Strategic Compensation in Canada.* Toronto: Nelson Thompson Larning.

Long, R. J., and Warner, M. 1987. "Organizations, Participation, and Recession: An Analysis of Recent Evidence." *Relations industrielles* (Industrial Relations) 42: 65–90.

MacDuffie, J. P. 1995. "Human Resource Bundles and Manufacturing Performance: Organizational Logic and Flexible Production Systems in the World Auto Industry." *Industrial and Labor Relations Review* 48: 197–221.

McGregor, D. 1960. *The Human Side of Enterprise.* New York: McGraw-Hill.

Miles, R. E. 1975. *Theories of Management: Implications for Organizational Behavior and Development.* New York: McGraw-Hill.

Miles, R. E., and Snow, C. 1978. *Organizational Strategy, Structure, and Process.* New York: McGraw-Hill.

McMullen, K., Lelkie, N., and Caron, C. 1993. *Innovation at Work: The Working with Technology Survey, 1980–91.* Kingston, ON: IRC Press.

Ng, I., and Maki, D. 1994. "Trade Union Influence on Human Resource Management Practices." *Industrial Relations* 33: 121–135.

Nunnally, J. C. 1967. *Psychometric Theory.* New York: McGraw-Hill.

Osterman, P. 1994. "How Common Is Workplace Transformation and Who Adopts It?" *Industrial and Labor Relations Review* 47: 173–188.

Poole, M. 1989. *The Origins of Economic Democracy: Profit-Sharing and Employee-Shareholding Schemes.* London: Routledge.

Schuster, J. R., and Zingheim, P. 1992. *The New Pay: Linking Employee and Organizational Performance.* New York: Lexington Books.

Toronto Stock Exchange. 1987. *Employee Share Ownership at Canada's Public Corporations.* Toronto: Toronto Stock Exchange.

Tyson, D. E. 1996. *Profit Sharing in Canada: The Complete Guide to Designing and Implementing Plans That Really Work.* Toronto: John Wiley and Sons.

Wagar, T. H., and Long, R. J. 1995. "Profit Sharing in Canada: Incidence and Predictors." *Proceedings of the Administrative Sciences Association of Canada (Human Resources Division)* 16: 97–105.

Wilson, T. B. 1995. *Innovative Reward Systems for the Changing Workplace.* New York: McGraw-Hill.

Wood, S. 1996. "High Commitment Management and Payment Systems." *Journal of Management Studies* 33: 53–77.

Chapter 4

France
Weitzman Under State Paternalism?

Fathi Fakhfakh and Virginie Pérotin

Introduction

In the late 1990s, about one-third of nongovernment employees in France (27 percent of all employees) were covered by a profit sharing plan, while only about 15 percent of employees were paid according to individual performance and less than 10 percent according to small-group performance. Profit sharing has been the dominant form of performance-related pay in France for at least fifteen years, and will be the focus of this chapter.

France has one of the oldest and most extensive sets of legal provisions encouraging profit sharing, and is one of the OECD countries where this pay system is most widespread (see Estrin et al. 1997). However, most French commentators do not think of profit sharing primarily as performance related pay in the sense of an incentive. One reason for this is that profit sharing is more than a pay system. Profit sharing gives employees residual rights to the firm's surplus, which makes it a form of financial

---

The authors thank the French Ministry of Labor and INSEE for access to data from the following surveys: *Enquête sur le coût de la main d'oeuvre et la structure des salaires en 1992*, (1992 Survey of labor costs and pay composition), *Enquête sur les relations professionnelles et négociations d'entreprises* (Workplace industrial relations and bargaining survey), and *Enquête annuelle d'entreprise* (Annual enterprise survey). The views expressed in the chapter are the authors' own and do not necessarily reflect the positions of the ILO (the Industrial Labour Office), INSEE, or the French Ministry of Labor. We are grateful to Muneto Ozaki for helpful comments.

participation, like employee stock ownership. Another reason is that the incentive features of profit sharing were largely unrecognized in France until recently. In public policy debates, profit sharing has appeared primarily as a way to redistribute productivity gains and to encourage workers to save.

Profit sharing has been practiced at least since the late nineteenth century in France but became a subject of public policy in the wake of post–World War II reconstruction. The original objective of the policy, as promoted by French president Charles de Gaulle, was to share the wealth resulting from postwar growth as widely as possible. Such sharing was designed to help workers save in order to build their own homes, and in the process promote a "third way" of cooperative relations between workers and management. This approach was part of a broader context in which unemployment, old age, and sickness were to be taken care of within compulsory, state-subsidized insurance systems. The first law encouraging cash profit sharing was passed in 1959, and deferred profit sharing plans were introduced in 1967 and made mandatory in medium-sized and large firms. The basic features of this legislation are still in place today, although the procedures for setting up a profit sharing plan and having it approved for tax relief have been much simplified. Interestingly, the management-worker cooperation and participatory objectives evoked by De Gaulle never became a major aspect of the system (see, e.g., Vaughan-Whitehead 1992; Balligand and De Foucauld 2000). The 1967 legislation was clearly designed for redistribution and links tax concessions to deferment of payments for several years in order to encourage saving. Incentives to save were attached even to cash profit sharing plans when the 1959 legislation was revised in the 1980s and 1990s.

Despite a growing interest in employee participation, the savings aspect continues to dominate debates on financial participation in France today (see Balligand and De Foucauld 2000). Thus, profit sharing and employee stock ownership are considered possible sources of working capital for firms and possible bases for supplementary pension plans. Other views of profit sharing, such as Weitzman's (1984) hypothesis that it could increase employment by depressing the marginal cost of labor, have had very little impact on the French debate. Even though French profit sharing plans fit those of Weitzman's model much more closely than do U.S. plans, his hypothesis is usually dismissed without much debate by French scholars and policymakers. Yet recent evidence suggests that in practice the system has most of the effects hypothesized in the economic literature, including Weitzman-style effects on labor demand.

Using national survey data on the composition of pay, we examine the incidence of different types of performance related pay in France by gender and skill in the next section. The remainder of the chapter concentrates on profit sharing, its features in the French context, and empirical evidence regarding its effects on productivity and employment. The institutional and legal context will be outlined in the third section, together with a short description of the profit sharing plans currently in existence. We summarize theoretical hypotheses about the effects of profit sharing and review the empirical evidence in the fourth section. The fifth section presents new estimations of the effects of profit sharing on establishment productivity using the French industrial relations survey. Conclusions are drawn in the final section.

Incidence of Performance Related Pay in France

The most recent information on the incidence of performance pay in France is the 1992 Survey of Labor Costs and Pay Composition (*Enquête sur le coût de la main d'oeuvre et la structure des salaires en 1992*, or Composition of Pay Survey). This survey covers a nationally representative sample of approximately 150,000 employees in the public and private sectors (see Appendix 4.1). The survey gives information on the share of employees' pay that took the form of variable or fixed bonuses in 1992 (e.g., performance-related pay, bonuses for particularly demanding or hazardous working conditions, and Christmas bonuses). Three forms of performance pay are identified in the survey, including pay linked to individual performance, such as piece rates, sales commissions, or merit pay; pay linked to group performance; and pay linked to establishment or firm performance (enterprise performance), such as profit sharing and discretionary bonuses granted by firms when business is good.

France has a national minimum wage, and national industry-level wage bargaining that sets wage scales and certain bonuses for the employees covered. Individual firms have to comply with industry-level agreements and the national minimum wage, but also have an obligation to bargain annually on wages (though there is no obligation to settle).[1] Bonus systems related to individual or group performance, as well as bonuses relating to enterprise performance but not related to subsidized profit sharing plans, may have been adopted as a result of those annual negotiations or been set up by the employer without negotiation. Voluntary subsidized profit sharing plans are normally negotiated (see below), and the contracts cover several years.

Table 4.1 shows the incidence of the three types of payments—related to individual, group, and enterprise performance. In 1992, one employee

Table 4.1

Incidence of Performance Related Pay Systems in France, 1992
(percentage of employees)

	Men and women	Women	Men
Based on individual performance	15.33	13.37	16.54
Based on group performance	5.00	4.02	5.61
Based on establishment or firm performance	20.62	16.57	23.14
N	131,578	50,476	81,102

Source: Computed from the 1992 Survey of Labor Costs and Pay Composition (*Enquête sur le coût de la main d'oeuvre et la structure des salaires en 1992*).
Note: The same employee may earn components related to all three levels of performance.

in five received enterprise performance pay, 15 percent received pay linked to individual performance, and only 5 percent received group performance pay. As a point of comparison, 26 percent of employees received bonuses for demanding or hazardous working conditions. Information from the exhaustive surveys of compulsory profit sharing plans carried out by the French Ministry of Labor indicates that the Composition of Pay survey underestimates the incidence of enterprise performance pay (probably because respondents do not always include bonuses received under the compulsory profit sharing scheme as enterprise performance pay). Thus, according to the French Ministry of Labor, compulsory profit sharing schemes alone covered 22 percent of all employees in 1992 (26 percent outside government; see Fagnot 1999). At the time of the survey, individual performance pay was dominated by two systems—piece rates in manufacturing and various forms of merit pay, which had been on the increase in the 1980s but seems to have leveled off more recently. Unfortunately, the survey does not allow us to distinguish between these two very different pay systems.

The survey also allows us to examine the incidence of performance pay by gender (see Table 4.1).[2] A substantially lower proportion of women receive all three types of performance related pay. This pattern can be observed for other types of bonuses as well (e.g., for demanding or hazardous working conditions). For individual and group performance pay, this difference could be related to technological factors. Occupational segregation could mean that women are more often found in occupations where asymmetries of information and output measurement problems are too severe to make performance related pay an effective incentive. However, this argument does not apply to enterprise performance pay systems, suggesting

Table 4.2

Incidence of Performance Related Pay by Skill Level, 1992 (percentage of employees)

	Blue-Collar	Clerical	Supervisory	Technical	Professional/Management
Based on individual performance	18.45	12.65	14.79	15.35	13.66
Based on group performance	5.77	4.00	6.07	5.85	4.13
Based on establishment or firm performance	21.22	16.84	26.53	23.91	21.98
N	49,449	38,429	11,454	11,643	19,053

Source: Computed from the 1992 Survey of Labor Costs and Pay Composition (*Enquête sur le coût de la main d'oeuvre et la structure des salaires en 1992*).
Note: The same employee may earn components related to all three levels of performance.

that other factors may be involved. These include segregation of women into enterprises that are less likely to practice performance pay or into industries that are less unionized, or exclusion of women from performance pay schemes due to indirect discrimination. For example, in a given enterprise a scheme may exclude certain departments or posts that happen to be primarily staffed by women, or may not cover part-time or temporary employees.[3]

Consistently with the incidence of performance pay by gender, Table 4.2 shows that clerical workers, the skills group where the proportion of women is highest, are the least likely to receive performance pay. The two groups most often covered are supervisory staff for group and enterprise performance bonuses, and technical staff (all three forms of performance related pay). Blue-collar workers are the most likely to receive individual performance pay, but come third or fourth among the five groups for the incidence of other types of performance pay.

As a percentage of pay, the three types of bonuses reach rather similar levels (5–7 percent of pay) for employees covered by a performance pay system (see Table 4.3). Women receive a slightly lower proportion of their pay in the form of individual or group performance pay than men (and women's pay is on average about 80 percent of men's pay in France; see Meurs and Ponthieux 2001). Men and women receive about the same share of their pay in the form of enterprise performance pay (the share may even be slightly higher for women). This pattern may be due to subsidized profit sharing schemes, under which the criteria for determining each employee's share of

Table 4.3

Performance Related Pay as a Percentage of Total Pay, 1992

	Men and women	Women	Men
Based on individual performance	6.69	5.52	7.27
Based on group performance	5.77	5.31	5.97
Based on establishment or firm performance	4.74	4.97	4.63
N	131,554	50,470	81,084

Source: Computed from the 1992 Survey of Labor Costs and Pay Composition (*Enquête sur le coût de la main d'oeuvre et la structure des salaires en 1992*).
Note: Average percentage of pay computed only over employees covered by a given pay system. The same employee may earn components related to all three levels of performance.

the overall part of profit allocated to employees must be identical for all the employees covered. The only individual parameters, other than the level of pay, that may be considered in determining individual allocations are absenteeism and seniority. The effect may be more egalitarian than individual performance pay, which may reflect subjective performance measures that are more easily influenced by prejudice. Under voluntary subsidized profit sharing, union confederations tend to negotiate provisions for equal payments across the board, regardless of pay levels, absenteeism, or seniority.

As Table 4.4 shows, managers and professional employees covered by performance pay receive markedly higher percentages of pay in that form than other skill groups. This could reflect the use of different forms of payment for managers. It may also be the case that employees with the highest levels of pay are less averse to risk and more willing to have variable pay. While clerical employees are the least likely to receive performance pay, the corresponding share of their remuneration is commensurate with the shares of other nonmanagement groups. However, note that manual workers, the most likely to receive individual performance pay, get a share of their remuneration similar in that way to what other skills groups get, but a lower share of their pay in other forms of performance pay.

Finally, the 1992 survey allows comparisons of total pay and basic (fixed) pay. Table 4.5 presents a univariate comparison of average basic pay. Pay related to individual and group performance appears to substitute for fixed pay the employees covered would otherwise receive. The employees not receiving those forms of performance pay have significantly higher (fixed) wages. The same pattern is observed with bonuses for hazardous work. For enterprise performance pay, it is the other way around. Employees not covered by a plan have lower basic wages. This is consistent with the

Table 4.4

Performance Related Pay as a Percentage of Pay by Skill Level, 1992

	Blue-Collar	Clerical	Supervisory	Technical	Professional/ Managerial
Based on individual performance	6.43	6.17	6.20	6.75	8.82
Based on group performance	4.62	6.32	6.85	5.69	7.90
Based on establishment or firm performance	3.94	4.84	4.13	3.72	7.65
N	49,449	38,429	11,454	11,643	19,053

Source: Computed from the 1992 Survey of Labor Costs and Pay Composition (*Enquête sur le coût de la main d'oeuvre et la structure des salaires en 1992*).
Note: Average percentage of pay computed only over employees covered by a given pay system. The same employee may earn components related to all three levels of performance.

Table 4.5

Levels of Basic Pay With and Without Performance Related Pay, 1992

	Without		With	t
Based on individual performance	105,749	>	102,165	7.04[a]
Based on group performance	105,420	>	101,843	3.93[a]
Based on establishment or firm performance	102,584	<	115,196	31.03[a]

Source: Basic pay is pay net of performance related bonuses. Computed from the 1992 Survey of Labor Costs and Pay Composition (*Enquête sur le coût de la main d'oeuvre et la structure des salaires en 1992*).
[a] Statistically significant at the 1 percent level.

legislation concerning subsidized profit sharing, which prohibits substituting profit sharing for fixed wages. However, multivariate estimations of wage equations with panel data suggest such a substitution does take place over time, as lower wage increases are negotiated in firms that have profit sharing plans (Mabile 1998). In any case, lower fixed wages need not imply lower total pay. As Table 4.6 shows, all forms of performance-related pay are associated with higher levels of total pay, on average, on the basis of the same type of univariate tests performed on basic wages.

Profit Sharing: Legislation and Plan Characteristics

The bulk of profit sharing in France comes under two subsidized schemes, though individual firms also have pay linked to enterprise performance

Table 4.6

Levels of Total Pay With and Without Performance Related Pay, 1992

	Without		With	t
Based on individual performance	125,441	<	130,966	9,85[a]
Based on group performance	125,780	<	135,949	11,90[a]
Based on establishment or firm performance	120,858	<	147,190	50,70[a]

[a] Statistically significant at the 1 percent level. Computed from the 1992 Survey of Labor Costs and Pay Composition (*Enquête sur le coût de la main d'oeuvre et la structure des salaires en 1992*).

which they choose not to register as subsidized plans, perhaps because they find the rules applying to subsidized schemes too constraining. The older subsidized scheme introduced in 1959—*intéressement* (profit sharing)—is voluntary, while the plan introduced in 1967 and confusingly named *participation* (participation in profits) is compulsory in medium-sized and large firms and voluntary in small ones. The legislation was unified and simplified in 1986 and revised in 1990 and 1994, though the main aspects of the schemes have remained the same throughout.

Under both subsidized schemes, the share of profit to be allocated to employees is defined by a set formula which appears in the contract instituting the scheme. All profit sharing payments are exempt from social security and social welfare contributions as well as corporate tax.[4] In principle, both types of plan are matters of contract between the firm and its employees. However, in the case of *participation* there is often no negotiated contract, since the scheme is compulsory for many firms and the law leaves little room for negotiation over the terms of the plan. Most profit sharing contracts cover one firm or establishment, but an increasing number cover several firms together, for example if they form part of the same conglomerate.

Voluntary Subsidized Profit Sharing (**Intéressement**)

This scheme was introduced in 1959 but really took off after the legislation was revised and simplified in 1986.[5] It is a cash-based form of profit sharing, under which employees receive at least one annual payment based on last year's firm or establishment performance. The contracts are signed for a period of three years and are normally negotiated, though in small firms where neither union delegates nor a works council is present the proposed contract can be ratified by a two-thirds majority of the work force.[6] The contract defines the formula for calculating employees' share of profits, the rules for employee eligibility, the rules for distributing the employees' share among individual workers, and the arrangements for keeping employees informed of firm performance.

Under *intéressement,* the share of profit to be allocated to employees can be based on any one indicator of establishment or firm performance or on a combination of indicators, such as profit and measures of product or service quality. However, a vast majority of contracts (80 percent in 1997) define accounting profit as the sole indicator of performance.[7] Most employees have to be eligible—the only restriction allowed concerns seniority and is minimal (six months). The way individual payments are calculated has to be the same for all individuals covered by one contract, though some flexibility is allowed (e.g., several contracts can be negotiated for different parts of the same firm).[8] Individual payments may, but need not, vary according to wages, absenteeism, and/or seniority. Identical individual payments have been favored by the main union confederations (see Vaughan-Whitehead 1995) and have been adopted by larger firms. In any case, individual payments may not exceed 20 percent of basic (fixed) wages, a limit rarely reached. In addition to exemptions from corporate tax, social security, and welfare contributions, employees can get personal income tax relief on *intéressement* payments if the money is deposited in a regulated company savings plan account for a minimum of five years.[9]

When it was first instituted, *intéressement* was a rather cumbersome scheme to set up. As a result, the plan did not spread very fast. By the end of the 1960s there were about 200 plans, and the number grew less than 10 percent annually in the 1970s. In the early 1980s the number of schemes increased more quickly, by almost 20 percent a year, but the main period of expansion was the late 1980s, especially after registration procedures for tax purposes were greatly simplified in 1986. In that period, the number of *intéressement* plans grew by 40 percent a year and reached almost 10,000, covering more than 2 million employees (about 10 percent of all employees) by 1990 (see Pérotin 1994). In 1990 the obligation to have a *participation* profit sharing plan in firms with 100 or more workers was extended to all firms with 50 or more workers, so that the number of *intéressement* schemes leveled out for a few years before growing slowly again. In 1997, more than 3 million employees were covered by *intéressement* plans in some 15,000 firms.

On average, *intéressement* bonuses vary little over time as a proportion of wages and have remained about 2–4 percent, regardless of variations in the legally permitted maximum. The figure was 3.3 percent in 1997—roughly one month of minimum wage per employee on average in companies that made profit sharing payments. However, payments have always been substantially higher in smaller firms—especially those firms that were too small to have a compulsory *participation* plan (see Fakhfakh and Mabile 1999). For example, in 1997 *intéressement* payments represented on average 6 percent of the wage bill in those firms with fewer than 10 employees that had profits to share, as against 2.9 percent in firms with 2,000 employees or more. Because payments are often distributed according to wage levels, there are differences in the levels of bonuses paid to employees in different skills groups. In 1997 the average bonus received by professional and management employees was about twice as high as that for manual workers.[10] Inequality is especially great in small firms, where the plans are not negotiated with unions or with a works council.

Compulsory Profit Sharing Plans (Participation)

Participation is a deferred profit sharing scheme that is mandatory in all firms with fifty employees or more, and may be adopted voluntarily in smaller firms. The features of the plans are precisely defined in the law, which leaves little flexibility to negotiating parties in individual firms or groups of firms. Every year, the plan allocates to employees a share of the profits in excess of 5 percent of assets that is proportional to half the share of the wage bill in value added, according to the following formula

$$PS = (1/2) \text{ (Profit } - 5\% \text{ } K) \text{ } (WL/VA) \tag{4.1}$$

where *PS* is the total amount of (net taxable) profit allocated to employees, *K* is total assets, *WL* is the gross wage bill, and *VA* is value added.[11] Firms wishing to distribute a larger share of profit can do so provided their *participation* contract is approved by the Ministry of Labor; a substantial proportion of these firms are workers' cooperatives.

All employees with at least six months' seniority are eligible. Individual bonuses are proportional to wages, up to a maximum specified in the law.[12] These bonuses may be invested in shares of the company; in other stock; or in fixed-interest accounts in individual employees' names for a period of three to five years, or eight years if no *participation* contract has been negotiated. If there is a contract, it must specify how bonuses are to be invested during the deferment period. In addition to the exemption from corporate tax, social welfare contributions, and social security that would otherwise apply to *participation* bonuses, extra tax relief is granted to firms that plow back profits as well as to those that choose to pay out to employees a higher share of profit than specified in the statutory provision.

Only 50 percent of the tax concessions applicable to *participation* bonuses apply to sums that are paid out to employees before the five-year deferment period.

The number of *participation* contracts was stable at around 10,000 from the 1970s to 1990; after the obligation to have a scheme was extended to smaller firms, it grew to about 16,000 in 1995. In 1997, 5 million employees were covered by *participation* plans in 19,000 firms. Despite the legal obligation, not all firms with fifty employees or more had plans. It has been suggested that many of the firms that did not have plans made no profit (see Balligand and De Foucauld 2000).

The level of *participation* payments is similar to that of *intéressement*. In 1997, *participation* payments represented 4.2 percent of the wage bill in firms that had sufficient profit to make payments. This level matches other Organization for Economic Cooperation and Development (OECD) countries outside Japan and the United Kingdom (see Estrin et al. 1997). Note, however, that, in the 6,000 French firms that have both types of profit sharing schemes, employees receive a larger portion of pay in profit sharing. Profit sharing payments also represent a sizable share of profit for the firms concerned. *Participation* payments alone amounted to 10 percent of net taxable profit on average in 1997, with a median level of 14 percent of profit. As with *intéressement,* payments from *participation* represent a higher proportion of wages in firms with fewer than fifty employees (e.g., 6.2 percent of wages in firms with fewer than 10 employees in 1997, as against 3.3 percent in firms with 2,000 employees or more). Part of this difference may come from the fact that a number of small firms with *participation* schemes are workers' cooperatives, which pay out higher than statutory bonuses.

Empirical Evidence on the Effects of Profit Sharing in France

Profit sharing has been thought to have two main effects—on productivity (and therefore on firm performance) and on employment.[13] Profit sharing should affect productivity because of its incentive features and by inducing attitudinal changes in employees. This hypothesis has been tested for *intéressement* on several French data sets, with remarkably consistent results across specifications and estimation methods. The hypothesis put forward by Weitzman (e.g., 1984) and before him by Vanek (1965), that profit sharing increases labor demand without creating inflation has never been popular with French policymakers or researchers. As a result, it has not been as frequently tested in France as elsewhere, even though the form of profit sharing considered by Vanek and by Weitzman almost exactly matches *intéressement* plans. We now review the French empirical evidence on each of these two hypotheses.

Productivity Effects

Profit sharing is thought to improve productivity by creating a direct coincidence of interest between firm owners and employees. Employees have incentives to work more and better and to cooperate with colleagues and management. As a result, information flows may increase both horizontally and upwards and organizational effectiveness may improve. In addition, long-term profit sharing may give employees greater incentives to acquire human capital and may decrease employee turnover. Against these expectations, profit sharing could induce employees to free-ride on the efforts of others because of the collective nature of the scheme. This problem may be overcome if employees realize the benefits of cooperation over time or engage in mutual monitoring. It may not even arise if there are strong bonds among employees, for example due to employee participation in decisions. Information and participation in decision making are generally thought to improve the effects of profit sharing on productivity, because of the complementary nature of the two forms of participation.[14]

These effects can be tested by estimating a production function which includes either a dummy variable indicating the presence of profit sharing or a variable giving the level of profit sharing payments or the percentage of pay they represent. Three French studies have taken the latter option. Defourny, Estrin, and Jones (1985) estimate both constant elasticity of Substitution (CES) and Cobb-Douglas production functions on data from about 500 workers' cooperatives observed in 1978–1979. In addition to profit sharing, employee capital ownership and the share of cooperative members in the work force are controlled for. The estimation uses instrumental variable methods to account for the endogeneity of the level of payments, and profit sharing is found to have a positive and mildly significant effect on productivity. Estrin, Jones, and Svejnar (1987) estimate translog functions by ordinary least squares (OLS) and instrumental variables on the same data set and reach similar conclusions. All the other French studies use Cobb-Douglas specifications, which seem to fit French data well. Cahuc and Dormont (1992) estimate a Cobb-Douglas function by generalized least squares (GLS) on a balanced panel of 565 manufacturing firms observed over four years (1986–1989) instrumenting the level of profit sharing payments with fitted values from a Tobit estimation of an equation explaining the level of those payments. Profit sharing is found to have a positive, significant effect in all their estimations, with and without instrumentation.

Among studies using dummy variables, three use different parts of the same data set from INSEE and the French Ministry of Labor (INSEE/MoL) or the same part of the data set but with different estimation methods and sets of controls. The major advantage of the INSEE/MoL data is that it covers a large, annually representative sample of firms in all industries, the whole data set being an unbalanced panel with firms entering and exiting the sample every year. Pérotin and Robinson (1998) use three years (1988–1990) of the unbalanced panel of about 5,000 manufacturing and construction firms in the data set. The specification allows profit sharing to affect factor elasticities as well as the overall level of total factor productivity and controls for skills, market share, and the presence of a *participation* plan. It is estimated by instrumental variables methods, and the presence of *intéressement* is found to increase productivity by 8.7 percent. This result is confirmed by another set of estimations using the same data set with a larger set of controls and accounting for possible reverse causality. Estrin et al. (1999) estimate a productivity effect of 8.4 percent and find the adoption of *intéressement* to be unrelated to average labor productivity in the two years preceding the introduction of the scheme. The positive and significant effect on productivity remains when the presence of profit sharing is endogenized in the production function estimation using fitted values from a probit estimation. Finally, Fakhfakh and Pérotin (2000) select a longer, five-year portion of the same data (1986–1990). The production function (with factor elasticities effects and controls for market share, skills, and wage levels) is estimated by GLS with a correction for selection bias, in order to deal with possible reverse causality issues and take into account the unbalanced nature of the panel. Profit sharing is found to have a 7 percent effect on average on productivity. However, the estimated effect is substantially higher in firms also required to have *participation* plans, suggesting the two types of plans are complements.

Two studies using much smaller data sets yield similar results. Using a sample of 116 manufacturing firms in 1983–1985, Vaughan-Whitehead (1992) estimates a Cobb-Douglas production function by weighted least squares to correct for heteroskedasticity and finds *intéressement* increases productivity by 8.6 percent. Fakhfakh (1998) uses GLS on a three-year (1987–1989) balanced panel of ninety-four large firms as well as production possibilities frontier estimations and finds *intéressement* has a productivity effect of about 9 percent over the long run. Both studies include extensive sets of controls. In particular, both studies control for the presence of employee share ownership, a variable unavailable in the IN-SEE/MoL data.

An effect of the same magnitude is again estimated using the most recent French data set, the Workplace Industrial Relations and Bargaining Survey. This data set comprises information for 1992 on a representative cross-section of 3,000 establishments in the trading sector (see Appendix 4.1). Wherever possible, information was obtained not only from management but also from employee representatives (union delegates if there were some in the establishment). Fakhfakh (1997) uses the subsample of firms for which answers concerning the presence of profit sharing plan are available from both sides. In a third of cases, employees and management gave different answers, and the probability of this happening is significantly related to the absence of management-employee communication. In weighted least squares estimations (to correct for heteroskedasticity) the presence of profit sharing is associated with a productivity increase of 7–8 percent when worker representatives indicated there was a plan—even if management disagreed—but with no effect if only management indicated there was a plan and worker representatives were unaware of it. This suggests that adequate information and workplace communication are essential to the incentive effects of profit sharing. Poor communication and information could also reveal deeper management-employee conflicts. Vaughan-Whitehead (1992) finds that the climate of management-employee relations affects worker satisfaction more strongly than the quality of information or the level of profit sharing payments, and it is likely that worker satisfaction influences productivity.

Rather than looking at productivity itself, two other studies examine the effect of *intéressement* on factors which should affect productivity. Using GLS with corrections for sample selection, Brown, Fakhfakh, and Session (1999) estimate the effect of the presence of profit sharing and employee ownership on absenteeism on an eleven-year, unbalanced panel of about 130 large manufacturing firms. Both forms of financial participation are associated separately and jointly with significant reductions in the number of days lost. Profit sharing and employee share ownership are also found to be associated with lower employee turnover by Vaughan-Whitehead (1992) with two years of data on 116 manufacturing firms.

Employment Effects

The micro aspect of the hypothesis put forward by Vanek (1965) and Weitzman (1984)—the only one that can be tested in the absence of an economy in which all firms practice profit sharing—can be summarized as follows. Profit sharing firms regard only the fixed part of pay as the marginal cost of labor, because the share of profit allocated to employees is not affected by the firm's level of employment. Firms only have to provide for the fixed part of pay when hiring extra employees. For a given level of total pay, the marginal cost of labor will therefore be lower in profit sharing firms and labor demand will be higher.

Cahuc and Dormont (1992) estimate a recursive model in which management and union bargain over a payment related to firm performance and the share of the payment in total pay may then affect employment, and find profit sharing to have no significant effect. The other two studies testing for employment effects on French data examine the effect of the presence of profit sharing as well as its level. If the Vanek-Weitzman hypothesis is correct, we should observe a generally higher demand for labor in firms that have profit sharing. In addition, profit sharing payments should not have the same negative effect on employment as does the fixed part of pay. Vaughan-Whitehead (1992) estimates labor demand equations for skilled workers and for unskilled workers over two years of data for sharing and nonsharing firms, allowing employment to depend on both the presence or absence of an *intéressement* plan and on the share of profit sharing payments in pay. The presence of profit sharing is positively and significantly associated with higher employment levels for skilled workers but not for unskilled workers. In both equations the ratio of profit sharing payments to total earnings has a negative and significant coefficient, but the absolute value is considerably smaller than the negative and significant coefficient for the fixed wage. Vaughan-Whitehead interprets the finding as suggesting a positive employment effect though not of the Weitzman type.

Estrin et al. (1999) estimate two different labor demand equations by instrumental variables. One equation includes a dummy variable indicating the presence of profit sharing and shows profit sharing influencing employment positively and significantly. This result could be caused both by the productivity increases associated with profit sharing and by Weitzman-style effects. Another equation limits the sample to only profit sharing firms and includes the fixed wage and the share of profit sharing payments in pay as separate variables in order to test whether bonuses enter the marginal cost of labor in those firms. Unlike the fixed wage, which has a negative, significant coefficient with the expected magnitude, the share of profit sharing payments has no effect on employment, suggesting that sharing firms only regard the fixed wage as the marginal cost of labor, as Weitzman expected. Related estimations confirm this result (Biagioli et al. 1999). In conjunction with this finding, wage equations estimated by Mabile (1998) suggest that profit sharing could positively affect employment in the Vanek-Weitzman way. A few years after profit sharing has been introduced, the presence of a plan has a negative effect on the level of fixed wage increases, so that the fixed wage eventually becomes lower in profit sharing firms, even though total pay is higher than in nonsharing firms.

Overall, findings on the relationship between profit sharing and employment are mixed for France, as they have been for other countries (see, e.g., OECD 1995), though very few tests have been done on French data. Yet, the finding that profit sharing is associated with productivity increases is so robust that a positive overall association between profit sharing and labor demand seems plausible. The most recent findings suggest that there is an employment effect, part of which could be due to a mechanism of the type hypothesized by Vanek and Weitzman. This would be logical given that the design of *intéressement* plans conforms to the schemes considered in the hypothesis.

New Estimations of the Effect of Profit Sharing on Productivity

Some of the findings we reviewed in the previous section suggest that in France profit sharing may be implemented together with other forms of financial participation and participation in decisions as well as employee information schemes, and that these forms of participation may affect the relationship between profit sharing and productivity. The only existing estimates including controls for employee share ownership were based on small samples, and no test of the interactions between financial and nonfinancial participation in their effects on productivity has ever been performed on French data. In this section, we report estimations using the Workplace Industrial Relations and Bargaining Survey, which includes information about several forms of employee participation and information schemes on a large representative sample of firms in all industries of the trading sector (see Appendix 4.1 for a description of the data set).

We estimate a Cobb-Douglas production function that takes the following general form:

$$\text{Log } Q = A + \alpha_1 \, PS + \alpha_2 \log K + \alpha_3 \log L \quad (4.2)$$
$$+ (\alpha_4 + \delta PS) X + Z\beta + U$$

where Q is value added, A is a constant, and K and L are assets and employment respectively, Z is a vector of controls and U is an error term.

In the absence of the term $(\alpha_4 + \delta PS) X$, the coefficient α_1 will give an estimate of the elasticity of total factor productivity with respect to the presence of profit sharing, which is hypothesized to shift the whole production function upward. The specification also allows profit sharing to interact with certain control variables in order to test for the possibility that the effects of profit sharing are strengthened by the presence of firm policies. Here δ is the coefficient of the joint effect of profit sharing with firm policy X on productivity, in addition to the effects profit sharing and policy X may have separately (estimated with α_1 and α_4, respectively).

As in Fakhfakh (1997), we select firms where answers regarding the presence of *intéressement* are available from both the management and the employee side. We use two profit sharing variables. The variable PS indicates the presence of a plan that worker representatives know about, whether or not management also report the plan to exist. The variable "*PS* according to management only" indicates that managers report the existence of a plan that workers' representatives did not know existed. In addition to profit sharing, we look at the effect of employee share ownership and at institutions for employee information, participation, and voice—quality circles, suggestions groups, shop meetings, and autonomous teams. We also allow for some of these channels of employee information and influence to interact with the presence of profit sharing to test for complementarity between financial and nonfinancial participation. The equation is estimated by ordinary least squares.[15]

The results are reported in Table 4.7 for three different specifications. Model 1 includes only profit sharing in addition to capital, labor, and controls for skills; model 2 also includes controls for employee share ownership and other forms of employee information and participation; and model 3 allows those other forms of participation to interact with profit sharing. The estimated factor elasticities have the expected magnitudes, and profit sharing plans that worker representatives know about are associated with an estimated 7–8 percent increase in productivity, which is consistent with the other results reported above for France (as expected, plans that only managers are aware of have no significant effect). However, the estimated effect of profit sharing decreases by one percentage point as controls for other forms of participation are introduced (model 2), which suggests that their omission had caused a slight bias. The only other plan that is found to have a significant (and positive) effect on productivity is employee share ownership (8 percent). Other forms of employee involvement (information and participation) have no significant effect either separately or taken together: an F-test shows their coefficients to be jointly insignificant. Introducing interactions between profit sharing and other forms of participation

Table 4.7

Production Function Estimation
Dependent Variable: Value Added Ordinary Least Squares 1992—$N = 978$

Variable	Model 1	Model 2	Model 3
Intercept	4.48[a]	4.50[a]	4.50[a]
	(56.97)	(55.63)	(53.23)
Log capital	0.17[a]	0.17[a]	0.17[a]
	(15.99)	(16.04)	(15.93)
Log labor	0.84[a]	0.83[a]	0.83[a]
	(58.94)	(57.06)	(56.82)
PS	0.08[b]	0.07[b]	0.08
	(2.74)	(2.18)	(1.32)
PS according to management only	0.017	0.005	−0.001
	(0.36)	(0.11)	(0.01)
Employee share ownership		0.08[b]	0.08[b]
		(2.49)	(2.50)
Quality circles		0.04	0.09[b]
		(1.31)	(2.17)
Suggestions groups		0.01	0.02
		(0.18)	(0.49)
Autonomous teams		0.03	−0.01
		(0.70)	(0.25)
Regular meetings		−0.02	−0.04
		(0.57)	(0.95)
Percentage professionals and management	0.87[a]	0.84[a]	0.85[a]
	(8.50)	(8.19)	(8.30)
Percentage blue collar	−0.15[a]	−0.16[a]	−0.15[a]
	(2.69)	(2.87)	(2.70)
PS × quality circles			−0.10[c]
			(1.76)
PS × suggestions groups			−0.03
			(0.53)
PS × autonomous teams			0.07
			(0.91)
PS × regular meetings			0.04
			(0.59)
Industry dummies	Yes	Yes	Yes
R^2	0.9640	0.9644	0.9645

Note: Absolute *t*-values in parentheses.
[a] Statistically significant at the 1 percent level.
[b] Statistically significant at the 5 percent level.
[c] Statistically significant at the 10 percent level.

(model 3) only yields one mildly significant effect—having profit sharing together with quality circles negatively affects productivity. Taken together, the interactions variables have no significant effect (an F-test supports the hypothesis that their coefficients are jointly insignificant) and the coefficient of the profit sharing variable even becomes insignificant.

These findings suggest that profit sharing is associated with increased productivity when communication in the firm is good enough for employee representatives to know about the plan, and that employee share ownership also increases productivity and should be taken into account when investigating the effect of profit sharing. Effective communication may matter more than the precise channels it takes, since F-tests do not support the inclusion of variables indicating the presence of nonfinancial forms of participation and employee information as such in the specification. Those forms of employee involvement are correlated with the presence of a profit sharing plan that employees know about. This may explain why the effect of profit sharing becomes insignificant when interaction terms are introduced, but F-tests do not support the inclusion of these terms either. It is possible that these forms of employee voice play little role in firms where there is active establishment-level employee representation, as is probably the case in our sample. The sample is made up of those firms in which an employee representative could be found and felt sufficiently well informed to answer the question regarding profit sharing. In these firms, indirect employee representation may be regarded as more effective than other forms of voice, as suggested by Ben-Ner and Jones (1995).

Conclusion

The dominant form of performance related pay in France is profit sharing. With the support of old and extensive legislation and substantial tax incentives, profit sharing now covers about one-third of employees in the trading sector. Compared with other forms of pay related to performance, profit sharing is also more egalitarian, which may be due to the restrictions imposed by the legislation on differences of treatment among employees under profit sharing plans as well as to the fact that individual plans are normally negotiated.

Profit sharing has always been regarded in France as a means of redistribution and as encouragement for employees to save. This view is so central that, in the last decade or two, profit sharing, company savings plans and employee share ownership schemes have all been subsumed in the public debate under the term *épargne salariale* (employee savings plans). Originally, the legislation did aim to promote employee-management cooperation and employee participation. This aspect never fully materialized in the successive laws, but national union confederations were sufficiently concerned about the possible introduction of employee participation (which they opposed) to remain skeptical toward profit sharing for years. As public policy regarding profit sharing and financial participation is being reexamined, the neglected dimension of employee participation in decisions and governance is receiving some renewed attention (see, e.g., Balligand and De Foucauld 2000). Participation in decisions and governance may resolve the moral hazard problem faced by employees under profit sharing as they take on income risk that depends on decisions they have no part in, such as investment decisions. As such it may be a way for unions to ensure that their members' interests are taken into account. Some of the empirical results of French studies also suggest that at least limited forms of participation condition the effect of profit sharing on productivity. The findings we have presented here confirm the importance of employee information and communication and suggest in particular that profit sharing has a substantial effect on productivity in firms with active statutory employee representation and union voice.

The productivity effects of profit sharing are little discussed, if at all, in the French policy debate. Yet the empirical findings are remarkably consistent and robust across data sets, specifications and methods of estimation. Although profit sharing was not introduced for its incentive features, it has been associated with productivity increases of 6–9 percent in France. Findings about employment effects are much more tentative, but the estimated productivity effects lead us to expect that profit sharing plans should be associated with higher labor demand. Some of the most recent work suggests that effects of the Weitzman type could be observed, in which profit sharing increases labor demand by introducing a wedge between pay and the marginal cost of labor. This suggestion has been rejected in French debates in the past, but is perfectly reasonable given that French profit sharing plans of the *intéressement* type are nearly identical to those considered by Weitzman.

Appendix 4.1

Data Sources

The *Enquête sur le coût de la main d'oeuvre et la structure des salaires en 1992* (Survey on Labor Costs and Pay Composition 1992) was carried out by the national statistics institute (INSEE) in 1993. The survey covered a representative sample of about 16,000 establishments of the public and

Table 4.8

Variable Definitions

Value added	Value added (standard accounting definition) in French francs 000s.
Capital	Fixed assets at book value in French francs 000s.
Labor	Number of employees.
PS	Dummy variable equal to 1 if the establishment has an *intéressement* scheme the employee representative knows about in 1992 (0 otherwise).
PS according to management only	Dummy variable equal to 1 if the establishment has an *intéressement* scheme according to the manager, but not according to the employee representative in 1992, and 0 otherwise.
Employee share ownership	Dummy variable equal to 1 if employees own part of the capital of the company in 1992, and 0 otherwise.
Quality circles	Dummy variable equal to 1 if there were quality circles or problem-solving groups in the establishment in 1990 and/or 1991 and/or 1992 (0 otherwise).
Suggestions groups	Dummy variable equal to 1 if there were suggestions groups negotiated under the *Auroux* laws in the establishment in 1990 and/or 1991 and/or 1992 (0 otherwise).
Autonomous teams	Dummy variable equal to 1 if there were autonomous teams in the establishment in 1990 and/or 1991 and/or 1992 (0 otherwise).
Regular meetings	Dummy variable equal to 1 if there were regular shop, team, or unit meetings in the establishment in 1990 and/or 1991 and/or 1992 (0 otherwise).
Percentage professionals and management	Proportion of professional and management-level employees (*cadres*) in the work force.
Percentage blue collar	Proportion of blue-collar workers in the work force.
Industry dummies	Dummy variables for industries (two-digit level French classification).

private sectors and about 150,000 employees in those establishments. The data set includes information on enterprise policies, overall labor costs, and the skills distribution of the work force, as well as individual data on seniority, occupation, working time, and the level and composition of pay for the employees covered.

Among pay items that do not form part of the basic, fixed wage, the survey distinguishes eight types of bonuses. In addition to performance-related pay and pay for hazardous work, the survey identifies extra pay items proportional to wages or set at a fixed level, such as seniority bonuses; exceptional bonuses granted because of enterprise events; payments related to the employee's private life (e.g., getting married or supporting dependent children); and compensation for layoff or early retirement.

The French *Enquête sur les relations professionnelles et négociations*

Table 4.9

Descriptive Statistics (subsample used in the estimations)

Variable Name	Mean	Standard Deviation
Value added	3,506,412.34	15,991,533.28
Capital	16,842,446.84	99,494,043.48
Labor	5,769.01	18,918.60
PS	0.54	0.50
PS according to management only	0.11	0.32
Employee share ownership	0.25	Dummy variable
Quality circles	0.44	Dummy variable
Suggestions groups	0.30	Dummy variable
Autonomous teams	0.15	Dummy variable
Regular meetings	0.77	Dummy variable
Percentage professional and management	0.13	0.16
Percentage blue collar	0.41	0.34
PS × quality circles	0.26	Dummy variable
PS × suggestions groups	0.19	Dummy variable
PS × autonomous teams	0.09	Dummy variable
PS × regular meetings	0.43	Dummy variable

d'entreprise (Workplace Industrial Relations and Bargaining Survey) was run in 1993 by the private polling company BVA for the French Ministry of Labor. It covered a representative sample of 3,000 establishments with fifty employees or more in all industries and sectors except for agriculture and government (but including state-owned enterprises). Interviews were held with the managing director or human resource manager and, in 1800 establishments, employee representatives. The data set comprises firm-specific information and data on industrial relations (including information on informal management-employee discussions in establishments where there was no union delegate), employee involvement plans, work organization, and pay policies.

Much of the industrial relations survey can be merged and matched with the composition of pay survey and with the *Enquête annuelle d'entreprise* (Annual Enterprise Survey) run by INSEE, which provides the economic information we used to carry out our estimations. Table 4.8 shows the variable definitions, and Table 4.9 shows the descriptive statistics for the data used in those estimations.

Notes

1. For an overview of French industrial relations, see, e.g., Hyman and Ferner (1998).

2. Information by ethnic group is not available in France; collection of data on ethnic origin is prohibited.

3. This type of problem has been observed with employee involvement plans (see Dickens 1999). For the UK, Pérotin and Robinson (2000) find that employee participation has a greater effect on productivity when it is associated with equal opportunities policies.

4. As a result, the firm will pay FF1 for each FF1 received by the employee in the form of profit sharing payments, as against approximately FF1.75 for each FF1 of net pay outside profit sharing (taking into account welfare and social security contributions paid by employers and by employees, but not personal income tax).

5. The main subsequent revisions in 1990 and 1994 concerned comparatively minor aspects, such as the maximum percentage of pay that could be paid in the form of bonuses under the scheme, eligibility rules, and the relationship with wage bargaining.

6. Firms with fifty employees or more must have a works council in France.

7. The latest Ministry of Labor figures available concern 1997 and are quoted from Fagnot 1999, unless otherwise specified.

8. However, having different contracts for different skills groups, which was allowed for a few years, no longer is possible due to the inequality it created.

9. About one-third of the total value of *intéressement* bonuses was deposited in company savings plans in 1997. That year, nearly half of the companies that had *intéressement* plans also had regulated savings plans.

10. However, wage differences between these groups are greater. The use of other criteria such as absenteeism and seniority for calculating profit sharing bonuses and the practice of equal bonuses in certain large firms mitigate wage inequality.

11. This formula may have been chosen to approximate distributing half of profit according to the "contributions" of capital and labor to production, since in conditions of perfect competition and with a Cobb-Douglas technology and constant returns to scale, factor shares in value added would be proportional to their marginal revenue products and sum up to 1.

12. The part of wages that is taken into account to determine an individual employee's profit sharing payment should not exceed a level (defined with reference to other variables of French social policy) that is equivalent to about eight times the minimum wage in 2001 and the profit sharing payment itself should not exceed a limit equivalent to approximately twelve months of minimum wage.

13. See Kruse (1993) and OECD (1995) for surveys of the empirical literature.

14. Reviews of these arguments can be found (e.g., in Ben-Ner and Jones (1995) and Pérotin and Robinson [1998]).

15. A Breusch-Pagan test led us to reject the hypothesis that the residuals might be heteroskedastic (Chi square$_{(14)}$ = 15.55).

References

Balligand, Jean-Pierre, and de Foucauld, J. B. 2000. *L'épargne salariale au coeur du contrat social. Rapport au Premier Ministre* (Placing employee savings plans at the heart of the social contract—A report to the Prime Minister). La Documentation française (Government of France Publication), January, http://www.ladocfrancaise.gouv.fr/ftml/0040010.46/html/0000.htm.

Ben-Ner, Avner, and Jones, Derek C. 1995. "Employee Participation, Ownership and Productivity." *Industrial Relations* 34: 532–554.

Biagioli, Mario, Curatolo, Salvatore, Gerlach, Knut, and Hübler, Olaf. 1999. "The Effects of Profit sharing on Labour Demand." In *The Impact of Profit sharing in Europe,* eds Virginie Pérotin and Andrew Pendleton. Cheltenham, U.K., and Northampton, MA: Edward Elgar, forthcoming.

Brown, Sarah, Fakhfakh, Fathi, and Sessions, John. 1999. "Absenteeism and Employee Sharing: An Empirical Analysis Based on French Panel Data, 1981–1991." *Industrial and Labor Relations Review* 52: 234–251.

Cahuc, Pierre, and Dormont, Brigitte. 1992. *Les effets de l'intéressement en France: La productivité plutôt que l'emploi* (The effects of profit sharing in France: Productivity rather than employment) *Economie et Statistique* 257: 45–56.

Defourny, Jacques, Estrin, Saul, and Jones, Derek C. 1985. "The Effects of Workers' Participation on Enterprise Performance: Empirical Evidence from French Cooperatives." *International Journal of Industrial Organization* 3: 197–217.

Dickens, Linda. 1999. "Beyond the Business Case: A Three-Pronged Approach to Equality Action." *Human Resource Management Journal* 9: 9–19.

Estrin, Saul, Jones, Derek C., and Svejnar, Jan. 1987. "The Productivity Effects of Worker Participation: Producer Cooperatives in Western Economies." *Journal of Comparative Economics* 11: 40–61.

Estrin, Saul, Pérotin, Virginie, Robinson, Andrew, and Wilson, Nick. 1997. "Profit sharing in OECD Countries: A Review and Some Evidence." *Business Strategy Review* 8: 27–32.

———. 1999. "Profit Sharing Revisited: British and French Experience Compared," mimeograph, London Business School.

Fagnot R. 1999. *De bons résultats pour la participation et l'intéressement versés en 1998* (High profit sharing payments made under *intéressement* and *participation* plans in 1998). *Premières Synthèses,* No. 34.2, August.

Fakhfakh, Fathi. 1998. "Sharing Schemes and Productivity." *Advances in the Economic Analysis of Participatory and Labor-Managed Firms* 6: 115–134.

———. 1997. *Quand l'intéressement passe inaperçu....* "(When Profit Sharing Goes Unnoticed....." *Travail et Emploi* (Work and employment) 71: 53–63.

Fakhfakh, Fathi, and Mabile, J. 1999. "France." In *The Impact of Profit Sharing in Europe,* eds. Virginie Pérotin and Andrew Pendleton. Cheltanham, UK and Northampton, MA: Edward Elgar, forthcoming 2002.

Fakhfakh, Fathi, and Pérotin, Virginie. 2000. "The Effects of Profit Sharing Schemes on Enterprise Performance in France." *Economic Analysis* 3: 93–112.

Hyman, Richard, and Ferner, Anthony. 1998. *Changing Industrial Relations in Europe.* Oxford, UK, and Malden, MA: Blackwell.

Kruse, Douglas L. 1993. *Profit Sharing: Does It Make a Difference?* Kalamazoo, MI: W. E. Upjohn Institute for Employment Research.

Mabile, J. 1998. *Intéressement et salaires: Complémentarité ou substitution?*(Are profit sharing payments and wages complements or substitutes?) *Economie et Statistique* 316–317: 45–61.

Meurs, Dominique, and Ponthieux, Sophie. 2001. *Une mesure de la discrimination dans l'écart de salaires entre hommes et femmes.* (A measurement of discrimination in the gender wage gap.) *Economie et Statistique* 337–338: 135–158.

Organization for Economic Cooperation and Dvlopment (OECD). 1995. "Profit Sharing in OECD Countries." In *Employment Outlook,* 139–169.

Pérotin, Virginie. 1994. *Quelles sont les entreprises qui adoptent l'intéressement?* (Which firms adopt profit sharing?) *Problèmes économiques* (Economic Issues). No. 2372, April, pp. 24–28.

Pérotin, Virginie, and Robinson, Andrew. 2000. "Employee Participation and Equal

Opportunities Practices: Productivity Effect and Potential Complementarities." *British Journal of Industrial Relations* 38: 557–583.

———. 1998. "Profit Sharing and Productivity: Evidence from Britain, France, Germany and Italy." *Advances in the Economic Analysis of Participatory and Labor-Managed Firms* 6: 135–162.

Vanek, Jaroslav. 1965. "Workers' Profit Participation, Unemployment and the Keynesian Equilibrium." *Weltwirtschaftliches Archiv* (World Economic Archive) 94: 206–214, reprinted in *Advances in the Economic Analysis of Participatory and Labor-Managed Firms,* vol. 2, 1987, eds. D. C. Jones and J. Svejnar, pp. 5–11. JAI Press, Greenwich, CT.

Vaughan-Whitehead, Daniel. 1995. *Workers' Financial Participation. East West Experiences.* Geneva: International Labor Office.

———. 1992. *Intéressement, participation, actionnariat.* (Profit sharing and employee share ownership). Paris: Economica.

Weitzman, Martin. 1984. *The Share Economy.* Cambridge, MA: Harvard University Press.

Chapter 5

Performance Pay in the United Kingdom

The Case of the Inland Revenue Service

David Marsden and Stephen French

Performance Related Pay in British Public Services

Perhaps the most important change in pay systems in Britain during the last fifteen years has been the spread of performance related pay (PRP) from the private to the public sector. This has occurred against a background of privatization of former public sector activities and fundamental changes in public management. In the early 1980s, the Megaw (1982) inquiry into Civil Service pay acknowledged that the longstanding provisions for withholding annual salary increments in the case of poor performance were rarely if ever used. By the late 1990s, virtually all Civil Service employees were covered by PRP schemes of various kinds, as were significant numbers of employees in local government, education, and health services. According to a survey conducted for the Institute of Personnel and Development in 1997, public sector organizations were just about as likely to use individual performance pay for their managers as were private

---

This research was conducted at the Centre for Economic Performance, London School of Economics, with a grant from the Anglo-German Foundation and additional financial support from the CEP. If you wish to correspond with the authors, please write to David Marsden at d.marsden@lse.ac.uk.

firms (Richardson/IPD 1999). Approximately 37 percent of public managers, compared to 43 percent of private managers, received individual performance pay, a difference that was statistically insignificant. Among nonmanagerial employees the gap had greatly narrowed: about one-fifth of public sector organizations used it, compared to about one-third of private sector organizations.

The change has provoked considerable public debate about whether private sector pay systems are appropriate for public employees, and it is one that is still not resolved as opposition by public employees and their unions remains strong. Broadly speaking, there have been three families of arguments suggesting performance pay in the public sector may be inappropriate. According to the first, the goals of public sector work are too diffuse and often contradictory, especially when they are set by conflicting levels of government and management. According to the second, public employees do jobs that are not amenable to objective measurement, and public service managers lack the skills to conduct proper subjective evaluations. According to the third, performance pay, and particularly individual performance pay, is inconsistent with the idea of public service.

Evaluating the effects of performance pay in the British public services involves assessing a moving target. Since the first schemes were introduced in the late 1980s, there has been a very considerable learning curve, and one can see policy measures that respond to each of the three types of argument just mentioned. In this chapter, we look at the introduction of performance pay in the British public services in light of these three types of arguments. It is a history of experimentation and learning from past mistakes, pursued with a degree of consistency unusual for postwar British public policy.

The first argument has been developed most forcefully by Jean Tirole (1994) and Susan Rose-Ackerman (1996). They stress that one peculiarity of the public sector is that there are "multiple principals." In principal-agent incentive theory, the "principal" purchases labor services from the "agent." A common explanation for performance pay is that the principal needs to design incentives that will motivate the agent to deliver the desired standard or type of performance when close supervision is not feasible. In the public sector, the principal might be the central government, a particular ministry, or any of a number of different levels of government. These may set incompatible, and sometimes contradictory, goals, and this creates a lack of clarity as to performance objectives. It also creates the possibility for the agent to play one principal against another. As will be seen in the short history that follows, there has been considerable effort to clarify the goals of many departments by establishing them as semi-independent agencies with much clearer lines of accountability.

The second argument relates to individual employees' objectives. A great deal of public service work is not readily amenable to objective measures of individual output or performance. Applying inappropriate objective measures is likely to lead to the familiar problems of biasing performance towards those tasks that can most easily be measured, as stressed by Holmstrom and Milgrom (1991). Many of the public service unions have argued that this will lead to an emphasis on the quantitative rather than qualitative aspects of public employees' performance. Chatting to a patient may contribute a lot to their well-being and may even speed recovery, but it is likely to conflict with quantitative performance targets. In the course of our research, we learned that job placement advisors in the Employment Service considered it their job to help job seekers find suitable work. This was often not possible in the allotted time for interviews. The need to balance quantitative and qualitative aspects of performance puts a lot of stress on subjective performance evaluations by line managers, which has been the dominant pattern of performance pay: appraisal-based pay. However, line managers have often lacked the necessary skills to appraise in a way that is considered fair, and may also lack the necessary information. Ambiguity in their own objectives also makes it more difficult for them to appraise their staff.

The public service argument is one that has surfaced in many forms. In part, it reflects the quality versus quantity choice. It also reflects the idea that the work undertaken in public services differs from that in private services. Although it has to be paid for, it is delivered on the basis of individual need or entitlement rather than individual ability to pay. This breaks the immediate link between the service and its price, and so it seems inconsistent to base rewards on marginal increments in public servants' efforts. Such views may be even more strongly held among the many professionals working in the public services. Their training will often have instilled ideas of appropriate levels of professional performance that should be provided independently of direct management supervision. Finally, many public services involve a high degree of employee commitment.

All three factors have influenced policy. In our short narrative of developments in the British public services we shall bring out the progressive attempts to clarify organizational objectives and to reduce the impact of conflicting and changing principals. This will also bring out some elements of the second argument. However, in examining the second two, we propose to draw on our study of performance pay at the Inland Revenue (the tax service in the U.K.) in 1991 and 1996–1977 (Marsden and French 1998, chapter 2) to explore whether employees have adapted to the new types of pay systems (Marsden and French 1998). Writing about the impact of norms of fairness on pay, John Hicks once remarked that no system of wages, when called into question, will ever be found to be fair, but that when pay systems become established, they gain the sanction of custom. Then a pay system "becomes what is expected; and (admittedly on a low level of fairness) what is expected is fair" (Hicks 1974, 65).

Thus, one might ask whether public employees are becoming more accustomed to performance management and performance pay. As they do so, its negative consequences should diminish over time.

Recent History of Pay System Reforms in the British Public Service

In Britain, from the mid-1980s there has been a clear central strategy for public management reform. At the same time, personnel costs have been tightly controlled. Elliott and Dufus (1996) show that, during the 1980s and 1990s, earnings growth for white collar public service occupations was generally below that in the private sector, particularly after 1981. Nevertheless, apart from a few exceptions, cost cutting has not been allowed to subvert the wider search for higher levels and different types of performance.

Turning to the strategies for personnel management reform in the public services, one can see that the period after the Megaw report on civil service pay (1982) was one of a series of major cumulative changes in the organization of pay and performance systems across the public services. These benefited from a degree of consistency in reform policies over two decades that has been quite unusual. It has also survived the change from a Conservative to a Labor government in 1997, as Tony Blair's government has made its intention clear to press ahead with performance management and performance pay for school teachers, coupled with further pay reforms in the National Health Service (NHS). Such consistency of approach has provided the opportunity for policymakers and public service management to learn from early mistakes and to adapt performance management systems in the light of experience.

Several elements have been important in the development of performance management and performance pay systems since the Megaw report (1982). They are summarized as follows:

1. Devolution of management decisions to business units for which performance indicators can be established;
2. Devolution of pay and personnel management to the same units;
3. Improvements in the design of organizational performance indicators for public services;
4. More systematic and more open performance appraisal of individual employees;
5. Increased recognition of performance appraisal as part of the prospective setting of employees' goals rather than as retrospective evaluation;
6. Increased sophistication in the design of performance management systems and recognition of potential dysfunction.

The first element responds to the need to simplify the role of the principal in the relationship between the government and public service delivery. The second relates to devolving employee performance management to the individual units responsible for providing public services on a day-to-day basis. The subsequent points relate to improving the validity and reliability of performance indicators. In this area there has been a considerable amount of organizational learning, as can be seen in the progression from the first crude performance indicators toward a better link between goal setting and performance evaluation. All this has taken place against a background of rigorous cost controls.

Agencies and the Devolution of Responsibilities for Personnel Management

Behind the spread of performance management in Britain has been the restructuring of public service organizations and the devolution of greater management responsibility to units with clearer outputs. "Privatization" affected most of the commercial activities for which a readily identifiable market existed, such as rail and air transport, coal mining, and the utilities. More important among the public services has been the identification of particular activities and their assignment to business units or "agencies" responsible for their delivery, and "contracting out" certain noncore services that could be provided by independent firms, such as refuse collection, and some ancillary services for schools and hospitals. The basic philosophy for this was outlined in the then government's "Next Steps" report (Efficiency Unit 1988).

The report identified three main priorities for the reform of civil service management:

1. The work of each department should be organized so as to focus on the job to be done, with systems and structures to enhance the effective delivery of policies and services;
2. The management of each department should ensure the staff has the relevant experience and skills for the tasks essential to effective government;
3. There should be a real and sustained pressure on and within departments for continuous improvement in value for money.

In most cases, agencies were the chosen vehicle for the reorganization. They were to become the focus for carrying out the executive functions of government, within a policy and resources framework set by a government department.

Devolution of Pay and Performance Management

Given the high share of staff costs in total costs, an essential accompaniment to devolution of general management has been the delegation of responsibility for pay and personnel management. The framework for this was set up by the Civil Service (Management Functions) Act of 1992, which defined the broad scope for pay delegation to include: (1) Pay and grading structures, (2) "customized" performance pay arrangements for particular groups of staff, (3) probation arrangements, (4) starting pay for particular groups of new staff, (5) redundancy schemes, and (6) disciplinary procedures. However, the Treasury retained significant powers of budgetary control over the agencies, and influence over the design of performance schemes. By April 1994, 24 out of 91 agencies identified in the "Next Steps" report had pay delegation, representing about 58 percent of civil service employment (IRS 1993). With delegation, there has emerged increasing diversity of pay and conditions among civil servants who, in the early 1980s, had been covered by a system of national agreements.

Within the National Health Service, analogous changes have taken place, with the establishment of NHS hospitals as locally managed NHS trusts competing to provide services within the NHS "internal market."[1] Just as the agencies are managed by a chief executive, so the NHS trust hospitals have altered their management structures in the same direction. These reforms too represented a radical break with the past. When the NHS Management Inquiry reported in 1983, it noted that there had been no major review of internal hospital management for thirty years since the 1954 Bradbeer Report (Griffiths 1983).

By April 1, 1994, about 96 percent of hospital and community health services were being provided by 482 self-governing trusts, with a fifth wave of NHS trusts completing the process by April 1995. Trusts are allowed to determine their pay and conditions locally, although existing employees are allowed to remain on the preexisting "Whitley" national pay and conditions (IDS 1995). According to a September 1997 survey, about 38 percent of NHS trust employees were on local trust contracts, although mostly they had retained national pay and conditions, with fewer than 20 out of over 500 trusts moving to locally determined pay (IDS 1998).

In schools, the equivalent change came with Local Management of Schools, introduced gradually from 1988 with the passing of the 1988 Education Reform Act. Local Management required schools to take over responsibilities from local authorities, transferring many powers to the schools' governing bodies. These have played an important part in the administration of performance pay for head teachers since the 1991 salary structure was introduced. Thus, for the civil service, hospitals, and schools, the major structural reforms in management were in place by the mid-1990s after five years of radical restructuring.

Learning Effects with Performance Targets and Indicators

An essential element in delegation of management responsibilities within the public services to agencies lies in developing suitable performance targets, measuring their achievement, and making the results public. These are seen to play an essential role both for managing the relationship between government and its departments and agencies, and as an instrument of internal performance management. There has been a rapid growth in the use of public service performance indicators since the early 1980s (Smith 1990). Examples include the 1981 code of practice for the publication of local authority annual reports (Department of the Environment 1981) and the Department of Health and Social Security (DHSS) 1983 "Grey Book" of indicators for the National Health Service (Griffith 1983). More recently, many such indicators have become more widely accessible, and it is now possible for visitors to NHS trust hospitals to pick up a copy during their visit and see how their hospital compares on a very wide range of quality indicators with other hospitals. The National Audit Office (NAO) has also played an important role in monitoring the performance of parts of the public service, and has encouraged the development of sophisticated information systems to assist management. For example, both of the two civil service organizations that we have studied, the Inland Revenue and the Employment Service, were commended by the NAO for their use of performance benchmarking between local offices (NAO 1989). To assist Local Management, starting in 1991, the government developed a national framework for schools, including a national curriculum, a system for assessing school performance, publication of comparative performance tables, and external evaluation by inspectors from the Office for Standards in Education (Ofsted).

There is a large literature on the potential dysfunctions of performance indicators. These include that managers will use their superior local knowledge to engage in "creative accounting" to deceive ministers (Smith 1990). Performance may be biased toward those items that are most easily measured, usually quantity over quality. When there is a multiplicity of indicators, it may not be easy to determine which ones should be given priority, and there is a temptation in the public services to give greatest attention to those likely to attract media coverage, such as clearing hospital waiting lists. If one additionally ties management and staff rewards to such performance indicators, there is even greater temptation to manipulate them, but also there is the temptation to operate them so as to avoid sanction rather than to achieve reward, a practice that may discourage higher performance.

These dysfunctions are inherent dangers in any management information system, and several of them can be seen in our case study of performance pay. What is also striking is the scope for learning from past mistakes. For example, the Inland Revenue had by 1996 changed a number of features that appeared to demotivate staff in the scheme that was in operation in 1991. Most notably, any reference to a "quota" on performance payments (and by implication on good appraisals) had vanished, and instead of appraisal on a standard set of criteria, individual staff established their own performance targets in agreement with their line managers. Thus, in theory at least, if an employee's job demands did not fit well into a standard description, or if employees' ability levels varied, allowance could be made in determining their performance targets. Further reforms of civil service performance pay are currently in negotiation.

Another important feature of public service performance management to emerge from our study has been the key role played by judgmental targets. Although often expensive to compile, they have the advantage of greater sensitivity to aspects of performance that are not easily measured, and where performance is multifaceted, they avoid compressing it into a single scale of measurement. This can be seen at two levels. At the organizational level, there has been quite widespread use of judgmental performance indicators in the form of Ofsted reports on schools' performance. Our study of performance pay for head teachers shows that many school governing bodies and head teachers used implementation of their proposals, and the achievement of school development plans as a criterion of head teachers' performance (Marsden and French 1998). Most did this in preference to objective statistical indicators such as exam pass rates.

The same principle has been applied in the performance appraisals of individual public servants, stressing line manager judgments over possible objective performance measures. In the early days of performance pay, as in the civil service and Inland Revenue schemes of the late 1980s and early 1990s, managerial judgments acted as a kind of proxy for objective indicators. Staff were evaluated according to a predetermined set of performance criteria, almost as if their performance on each criterion could be scaled. In more recent schemes, the emphasis has shifted to line managers' agreeing to work goals with individual staff and then assessing how well they have met them some time later. In principle, it is possible to adapt judgments of performance to the demands of each worker's job and to the abilities of each worker. Thus judgment intervenes both in the choice of work targets and in the assessment of performance. In practice, it is unlikely that work targets in any large organization could ever be wholly individualized, and most of the respondents to our study were skeptical of this possibility. Nevertheless, judgment does allow a margin of adaptation to the circumstances of individual jobs and staff, and allows more recognition of qualitative dimensions of work as agreed between line managers and their staff.

Allowing greater scope for management judgment exposes individual staff to possible discrimination and favoritism, hence the importance, and acceptance, of measures to ensure a high degree of procedural justice in the operation of performance management. Here too one can see a degree of learning in the operation of schemes. In the early 1980s, appraisals were confidential, and an important step with the introduction of performance pay was to move to open reporting. In addition, increased attention has gone into monitoring the distribution of appraisal scores and sharing such information with trade unions and professional associations. As will be seen later, it is not clear how far greater measures to ensure procedural justice have been successful.

Another area of learning supported by our research has been some modification of the early emphasis on performance pay as a financial incentive as distinct from an essential part of effective employee-management goal-setting within public service organizations. Much of the debate about performance pay has been dominated by the intuitively appealing, but questionable idea that people will work better if better work leads to better pay. This idea also has strong theoretical support from the disciplines of economics, in the theory of incentives, and from organizational psychology, notably from expectancy theory (Vroom 1964). There is, however, a problem in many public service activities. Even if it is possible to identify "high fliers," good organizational performance depends on the work of the many, and identifying fine gradations of high performance among the many who are working hard and effectively is very difficult. Thus, for many, the attribution of performance rewards can appear arbitrary and unfair and so damage rather than encourage performance. It may therefore be that if performance pay actually does raise performance, as our study suggests it may do, then it does so by channels other than financial incentives. The most obvious alternative is that it works through the appraisal system by forcing line managers to clarify the work goals of their staff, and that the "many" work better when they know what management wants them to do. Thus, increasing emphasis has been devoted to the improvement of performance appraisal, a good example of this being in the Inland Revenue.

Such learning has been possible because of the long period over which public service management reforms have been sought and the consistency with which successive governments have pursued them.

Cost Control Maintained

While the pursuit of performance management has been a long-term strategy in the British public service, it would be wrong to overlook the role of cost pressures on management to raise efficiency by other means. In a recent study, Winchester (1996) summarized the effects of government "cash limits" on public services as forcing managers to find savings. He cites a number of responses, including: (1) use of early retirement to cut staff and recourse to agency staff to deal with peak loads; (2) a more restrictive approach to the use of premium rates for overtime and unsociable hours; (3) hiring less qualified staff to take such tasks away from qualified staff (e.g., use of health care assistants to relieve qualified nurses); and (4) leaving more vacancies unfilled, which saves on pay costs and increases work loads of remaining staff.

Although performance management has had pride of place, the need to work within cash limits has slowed progress in some areas. For example, the introduction of performance pay for classroom teachers in 1993 through the awarding of "excellence points" probably failed as much because none of the extra money the pay review body had urged for its success was available as because of opposition from the teachers' professional associations. Likewise, local pay determination for NHS hospital trusts was partly delayed because the amount of money available was too small (Bach and

Winchester 1994). However, lack of money is not the whole story. In the NHS trust hospitals in our 1998 study (Marsden and French 1998, chapter 5), performance pay was made self-financing. In December 1998, the government announced plans to introduce performance management for classroom teachers, combined with an offer of a major revaluation of teachers' salaries, but opposition to it remains strong (DfEE 1998).

In summary, the reform of performance management in the public services has progressed furthest in the civil service, whereas reforms in the NHS and in schools are still very much in progress. Although there have been periodic tensions between reforming performance management and cost control, successive governments have managed to keep their sights on performance objectives.

Have Public Employees Adapted to the New Pay Systems? A Case Study of the Inland Revenue

Despite initial opposition, one might think that employees would gradually come to terms with new pay and performance management systems. First, staff turnover brings a gradual renewal of the work force, and new employees are unlikely to be wedded to previously long-established pay principles. There might also be an element of self-selection. Those who preferred the old system of management may have chosen to work in the public service. There is some evidence from Germany that risk-averse employees are more likely choose public service jobs, as Luhmann and Mayntz's survey of school leavers found those opting for public service jobs to be *leistungsfähig aber risikoscheu* (competent but risk averse) (Mayntz 1985). Likewise, those who do not like public service conditions are more likely to quit for private sector jobs. Second, as people become socialized into their work environment, they are likely to grow to accept its prevailing norms. We know, for example, that affective organizational commitment often increases with length of service (Meyer and Allen 1997). Third, as employees get to know a new pay system and understand how it works, they learn to predict what patterns of behavior will lead to rewards, and they may learn how to work the system to their own benefit. Fourth, as line managers learn how to operate new systems, particularly appraisal-based ones, it is likely that they will make them operate more equitably and more predictably for all concerned.

For all these reasons then, one might expect initial opposition to new pay systems to decline as time passes. Our study (Marsden and French 1998, chapter 2) of performance pay at the Inland Revenue (which oversees tax collection) offers a unique opportunity to trace the impact of performance pay over time in the British public services. Because this was part of a wider study covering the Employment Service, primary and secondary schools, and National Health Service trust hospitals, we are also able to make a judgment about how typical is the response of tax service employees of those of other public servants. Our analysis draws on data collected in a study of the Inland Revenue scheme in 1992 by Marsden and Richardson (1991, 1994), and in a wider study of the public services in 1996–1997 by Marsden and French (1998).

Background on the Schemes at the Inland Revenue

The Inland Revenue set up its first PRP scheme in 1988. Although the scheme came in as part of the pay agreement with the then Inland Revenue Staff Association (IRSF), the union had been told that without it there would no pay agreement.

The key principle of the scheme was that performance pay should be awarded on the basis of appraisals of individual staff by their line managers. The performance assessment used the standard civil service performance criteria (then thirteen in all), which were applied alike to employees in all jobs. These were rather rigid and not suited to many jobs, and took no account of the differing abilities of different employees some of whom might work hard but not perform outstandingly well. On the basis of this, employees were awarded a "box marking," ranging from Box 5 for unsatisfactory performance to Box 1 for outstanding performance. In 1988, about 7 percent overall got Box 1, about 40 percent Box 2 and about half got Box 3 ("fully meets the normal requirements of the grade"). Only 2 percent got Box 4 and none got Box 5.

Performance awards took the form of movements along the existing pay scale, resulting in accelerated increments for those who received performance awards. Those with Box 1 got an accelerated increment, and those with Box 2 in two successive years got half an increment. Awards were incorporated into basic salary and were pensionable. The amount of money for performance pay was set in the 1988 agreement at roughly the equivalent of 25 percent of the staff receiving performance awards.

A number of defects emerged in the 1988 scheme; some of these were confirmed by our research, which was carried out with close collaboration from unions and management. First of all, many employees thought the scheme unfair because it took too little account of the aptitudes of individual employees and the fixed criteria were poorly adapted to many jobs. This was tackled in the 1993 scheme by agreeing to a "contract" with each individual employee. This consisted of a set of performance objectives for the year, agreed with the person's line manager, and because it was personalized, in theory at least, it should be better adapted both to individual capabilities and differences between jobs. The contract system was intended to be more flexible and to take account of the idea that even less able employees need to be motivated to perform well. Employees were then assessed at the end of the year against the objectives agreed upon at the beginning.

A second important change was to eliminate what had become known as the quota. It might be good union practice to get management to be specific about the size of the pot available for performance pay and thus to restrict the scope for management to cut the pay bill by being tighter on performance appraisals. Nevertheless, as confirmed by Marsden and Richardson (1994), this was perceived as an arbitrary ceiling on the box markings available for good performance. In the 1993 scheme, management made it clear that good performance would be rewarded no matter how many performed well, and line managers were instructed not to apply quotas on good assessments.

The new scheme operated against a background of increasing work loads, and it was partly designed to support these. The most significant among these was "Self Assessment" for taxpayers. Under these provisions, the self-employed assumed greater responsibility for working out their own tax (correctly). There were also some staff reductions, and the privatization of the data processing operations and the valuation arm became the Valuation Agency. Staff were given an incentive to accept an increased workload if they could get their jobs classified as "extra-loaded," which applied to about a fifth of them. This entitled them to more highly geared performance rewards: A "succeed" in an "extra-loaded" post was worth an "exceed" in a normally-loaded post, and an "exceed" in an "extra-loaded" post brought about 1 ½ percentage points extra pay compared with the same in a normally loaded post. The top managers we spoke to in 1996 and 1997 were of the view that work loads had increased, and this was also the view of a substantial minority of the line managers included in our sample. At the time of writing, 2000–2001, the 1993 scheme was being renegotiated.

Our present study is based primarily upon questionnaires sent to employees including line managers in the Inland Revenue in 1991 and 1996. In both cases the questionnaires were sent after the scheme had been in operation for about three years (1988 and 1993, respectively). For the first survey we had the active support of both management and union, but for the second, management declined to be involved, and we relied upon the cooperation of the union for member addresses. Since union membership is high, we believe the possible biases to be small. For the first survey, staff were allowed to complete the questionnaires during work hours, but not the second, so the response rate was about 60 percent the first time and about half that the second time, giving about 2,400 and 1,200 usable replies, respectively. On both occasions, questionnaires were completed anonymously and returned to the researchers in sealed envelopes. It was not possible therefore to undertake a panel survey. The full texts of the questionnaires and methodological notes can be found in Marsden and Richardson (1992) and Marsden and French (1998).

An Overview of Employee Reactions to Performance Pay, 1991 and 1996

Despite initial hopes of some of the union officials who followed our study that it would provide a "silver bullet" to kill performance pay, in fact, it revealed both positive and negative features. As shown in Table 5.1, among the most striking on the positive side were that nearly 60 percent of respondents thought that the principle of linking pay to performance was a good one, and a similar percentage disagreed when the same question was posed negatively, that it was fundamentally unfair. Also on the positive side, four-fifths of employees said they understood why they were awarded their most recent appraisal, and around two-thirds thought it a fair reflection of their performance. Also high in both years were the percentages of employees expressing high levels of affective commitment to their office and expressing the view that they contributed to an important public service (Table 5.1)

In 1991, the scheme was also generating many problems; most notably, employees believed it was unfair in its operation. Many employees believed there was a quota on good assessments and that no matter how well they performed, they would not get a high appraisal score. There was also a widespread belief that line managers were guilty of favoritism in their assessments (over a third in 1991). These views are interesting because they reveal a degree of distrust of both higher management, who were believed to apply a quota in order to save money, and line managers, who were believed to have their favorites and so not to be trustworthy to operate the scheme fairly.

The early scheme was also seen to be divisive. Over 60 percent said it caused jealousies among the staff, over half thought it undermined morale, and nearly 30 percent thought it undermined cooperation among staff. Finally, many staff members thought it unfair because they did not have enough scope in their jobs to improve their performance.

A first reaction to these results might be that they are "teething prob-

Table 5.1

Summary Comparison of Responses to Questions on Performance Pay (PP): Inland Revenue, 1991 and 1996 (N 1991 = 2422; N 1996 = 1192)

Question: Percent Replying "Agree"	1991	1996
Pay and work orientations		
PP is a good principle.	57	58
I contribute to an important public service.	62	56
Personal satisfaction of my work is enough incentive.	63	32
Improved goal-setting and higher productivity		
PP makes managers set work targets more clearly.	27	32
I understand why I was awarded my most recent performance assessment.	79	79
It was a fair reflection of my performance.	66	64
Of which: Line manager views		
PP has increased quantity of work done.	22	42
Caused many to work beyond job requirements.	15	37
PP has increased quality of work done.	19	17
Relations with management		
Management use PP to reward their favorites.	35	57
There is a quota on good assessments.	74	78
PP has made me less willing to cooperate with management.	10	30
Of which: Line manager views		
PP has reduced staff willingness to cooperate with management.	20	45
Motivation and relations with colleagues		
PP an incentive to work beyond job requirements.	21	18
PP causes jealousies.	62	86
PP has undermined morale.	55	81
Discourages helping colleagues with work difficulties.	28	63
Of which: Line manager views		
PP is bad because staff have insufficient control in their jobs.	46	57
Commitment and work atmosphere		
Feel "part of the family" in my current office.	62	56
Feel "part of the family" in the Inland Revenue.	35	16
Feel a strong sense of commitment to my current office.	58	53
Feel a strong sense of commitment to the IR.	41	35

lems." After all, the 1991 replies in Table 5.1 also show that not many thought PRP had led managers to set work goals more clearly, which is surely essential for an effective PRP scheme. The perceived divisiveness might also be the result of worries by inexpert line managers that, if they were seen to be overly generous by their own managers, they would be penalized. Possibly the perceived favoritism arose because line managers rewarded those on whose cooperation they most depended, again for fear of being penalized by their own superiors should their office not perform well. Thus, as management become more expert in operating the system, one might expect some of the perceived unfairness to subside. Likewise, one might expect those who approve of the principle to increase over time as they come to recognize the unfairness of the previous system which had many stuck at the top of their pay scales, and rewarded performance only through the limited number of promotion opportunities. Thus, one might expect Inland Revenue staff to follow the path of the health service managers studied by Dowling and Richardson (1997) as these appeared to come to terms with, and accept, their new performance management system.

Turning to the replies for 1996, we observe a dramatic worsening in the perceptions of unfair operation and of their negative effects on aspects of work behaviour. Again from Table 5.1, the percentage believing PRP causes jealousies rose from 62 percent to 86 percent, and the percentage thinking it undermined morale increased from 55 percent to 81 percent. The percentage who thought it discouraged colleagues from assisting each other more than doubled. The line managers who thought it made staff less willing to cooperate with management more than doubled, rising from 20 percent to 45 percent of line managers.

There was also a marked decline in the measures of intrinsic satisfaction, as the percentage who thought the intrinsic satisfaction of their work enough incentive to work hard halved, dropping from 63 percent to 32 percent. Some of the commitment measures, especially those expressing commitment to the Inland Revenue rather than their current office, also showed a steep decline. These variables differ somewhat from those relating to jealousies, morale, and cooperation. We observed a decline, but it may not necessarily be attributed to the operation of PRP. On the other hand, the jealousies, morale, and cooperation questions relate to the causal attributions by the employees themselves.

On the more positive side for management, the top management views that productivity levels had been sustained and possibly improved were borne out by the reports of a substantial minority of line managers. Of line managers, 42 percent thought PRP had led staff to work harder, and nearly as many thought it had caused staff to work beyond their job requirements. Although subjective, these views should not be set aside lightly, because these are the people who carry out the objective setting and performance appraisals of individual employees. They are a minority, but the question was phrased in such a way that the alternative lumped together "no view," "no change," and "working less hard." Also on the positive side for management was that there was a small increase in those believing PRP had improved goal setting, and the great majority still understood the reasons for their latest rating, and around two thirds still thought it fair.

There was therefore little sign that Inland Revenue staff had grown more accustomed to PRP, as one might have expected. Despite management's attempts to improve the working of PRP, by getting rid of the quota, and the efforts to improve individual assessments, employee reactions deteriorated sharply over the five years. The deterioration was such that the government's own committee on the future of performance pay in the civil service concluded, citing this and other evidence, that the IR scheme was "ineffective and discredited" in the eyes of the staff (Makinson 2000, 2).

Given that both the 1988 and the 1993 schemes appeared to conform to current personnel management ideas of "best practice," the question of why this should be so arises.

Causes of Change

In analyzing the underlying causes of these changes, we propose to use a model developed by Marsden, French, and Kubo (2000), which was based on the full sample of public service organizations covered in 1996–1997. This model applies the broad principal-agent framework, and treats the effects of PRP as arising from the positive incentive effects of financial reward and clearer target setting, and the negative demotivating effects arising from poorly conducted goal setting and appraisals. It also suggested that organizational commitment could reduce the likelihood of moral hazard by employees. Logistic regressions estimated the determinants of PRP success, including as controls organizational dummies for each of the different public service organizations (Inland Revenue, Employment Service, NHS trust hospitals, and schools), ISCO ("International Standard Classification of Occupations," devised by the International Labor Office, Geneva) one-digit occupations, and gender and length of service in the organization. Mostly, the latter were not significant. The authors found that the effects of PRP on motivation and work performance across the public services could be explained by a model that stressed five key sets of variables. These consisted of: (1) an *incentive* effect of performance rewards (monetary and recognition); (2) a positive effect from line managers setting work *goals* more effectively; (3) a negative effect from *badly conducted appraisals* which left employees feeling they could not get PRP even if they perform well; (4) a positive support from *organizational commitment* (which seemed to counteract short-term demotivating effects); (5) a negative effect deriving from the hostility to PRP of those in *professional occupations* who resented line-manager interference.

Table 5.2 shows the results of estimating the determinants of nine key measures of motivation and the success of the Inland Revenue Service performance pay scheme. In addition to the controls highlighted above, the determinants include eight variables from Table 5.1, measuring the quality of communication, the fairness of the system and worker commitment.[2]

The variables were derived from questionnaire responses, and so there are inevitably questions about how far we can separate cause and effect, and how far we can separate the influence of different variables attributed to different questions. We chose output variables that reflected *employee attributions* of the effects of PRP, thus all the questions chosen here asked employees for their views about specific likely effects of PRP on their willingness to perform in certain ways and on that of their colleagues and management. The input, or causal, variables asked for their appraisal marks that determine PRP, for their experiences of the appraisal process, and some questions about the relationship between their intrinsic motivation and belief in professional standards and PRP, and about commitment.

As Table 5.2 shows, those who do better than average and feel their last appraisal was fair report greater success and those who anticipate a poor appraisal report worse success. Those with greater intrinsic motivation and greater commitment to the organization tend to report greater success, as do those who felt targets were set clearly.

We tested whether the parameters of the above model were the same in 1991 as in 1996 by using a shift dummy for the year, and interacting year dummies with the coefficients for each explanatory variable.[3] The original coefficients on the variables had nearly always the same sign, and very few of the interactions were statistically significant, suggesting stability across the years.

Changes in Values of Independent Variables

Having established the basic model and ascertained that it is largely unchanged between 1991 and 1996, we now ask whether the changes between the two years can be explained by changes in the key explanatory variables. Tables 5.3 and 5.4 summarize the key changes respectively in the outcome and explanatory variables.

It is likely that the changed distribution of performance rewards has affected the number of employees responding positively. We chose to measure the incentive effect of PRP by considering those who get above average awards largely because under the 1993 system everyone got performance pay because it had replaced length of service increments which continued to function under the previous scheme. In effect we are comparing the 45 percent who got Box 2 or Box 1 in 1991, with the 31 percent who got "Exceed" or better in 1996. On the other hand, the rewards in 1996 were more highly geared especially for those in "extra-loaded"

Table 5.2

Estimation of the Determinants of PRP Success in the Inland Revenue

	Rewards good work	Good principle	Work beyond job requirements	Show more initiative in my work	Raised my awareness of organization's objectives	Causes jealousies among the staff	Undermines team working	Management operates a quota	Reduced my wish to cooperate with management
Dummy 1=96	−.90[a] (0.108)	.45[a] (0.091)	.22 (0.117)	−.01 (0.112)	−.74[a] (0.091)	1.08[a] (0.109)	1.30[a] (0.089)	−.20 (0.105)	1.13[a] (0.122)
Gets above average PRP#	.47[a] (0.102)	.42[a] (0.096)	.77[a] (0.119)	.60[a] (0.114)	.21[b] (0.095)	.36[a] (0.103)	−.03 (0.099)	.09 (0.107)	−.30[b] (0.153)
Managers set targets more clearly ##	.43[a] (0.046)	.27[a] (0.041)	.50[a] (0.053)	.43[a] (0.050)	.57[a] (0.042)	−.07 (0.044)	−.07 (0.042)	−.20[a] (0.047)	−.24[a] (0.058)
Doubt I'll get a good appraisal ##	−.37[a] (0.042)	−.23[a] (0.038)	−.14[b] (0.049)	−.17[a] (0.047)	−.07 (0.038)	.19[a] (0.041)	.23[a] (0.040)	.52[a] (0.046)	.39[a] (0.060)
My last appraisal was fair	.18[a] (0.049)	.008 (0.040)	−.04 (0.055)	−.05 (0.052)	.06 (0.041)	−.12[a] (0.045)	−.08 (0.041)	−.14[a] (0.052)	−.41[a] (0.053)
There is a standard for the job	−.28[a] (0.053)	−.26[a] (0.050)	−.70[a] (0.058)	−.71[a] (0.056)	−.10[b] (0.048)	.09 (0.051)	.13[a] (0.050)	.20[a] (0.053)	.14 (0.072)
Intrinsic motivation sufficient ##	.14[a] (0.041)	.12[a] (0.035)	.16[a] (0.048)	.07 (0.046)	.05 (0.035)	−.06 (0.039)	−.09[a] (0.036)	−.04 (0.043)	−.20[a] (0.048)
Affective commitment Factor 1	.25[a] (0.050)	.15[a] (0.043)	.34[a] (0.057)	.38[a] (0.055)	.20[a] (0.043)	−.14[a] (0.047)	−.12[a] (0.044)	−.16[a] (0.051)	−.45[a] (0.061)
Goal commitment: Factor 2	−.01[a] (0.044)	−.09[b] (0.040)	−.097 (0.050)	−.20[a] (0.047)	.03 (0.040)	.10[a] (0.042)	.004 (0.041)	.03 (0.047)	.03 (0.057)

(continued)

Table 5.2 (continued)

	Rewards good work	Good principle	Work beyond job requirements	Show more initiative in my work	Raised my awareness of organization's objectives	Causes jealousies among the staff	Undermines team working	Management operates a quota	Reduced my wish to cooperate with management
N	3123	3118	3125	3120	3118	3126	3126	3124	3123
Chi 2	746.98	356.86	534.56	580.53	452.76	327.46	506.82	383.59	699.96
Sig level	a	a	a	a	a	a	a	a	a
Percentage correct	75.01%	64.54%	81.16%	78.93%	66.14%	71.10%	69.73%	76.85%	85.22%

Note: Dependent or outcome variables in the top row ("agree" = 1), and independent or input variable in left hand column. The figures show the logit coefficients. Standard errors are shown in parentheses. Regression is weighted by sample fractions. # denotes binary variable. ## denotes binary variable scaled from 1 = disagree strongly to 5 = agree strongly. Includes control dummies for occupation, length of service, and gender, not shown in the table.
[a] Indicates those significant at the 2 percent level.
[b] Indicates those significant at the 5 percent level.

Table 5.3

Changes in Indicators of the Success of PRP, 1991 and 1996

	1991 Mean % agree	1996 Mean % agree	Changes, 1991–1996
Rewards good work	41	19	−
Good principle	57	58	=
Made me willing to work beyond job requirements	22	17	−
Made me willing to show more initiative in my work	27	20	−
Raised my awareness of organization's objectives	57	38	−
Causes jealousies among the staff	62	85	+
Undermines team working	28	63	+
Management operates a quota	74	77	+
Reduced my wish to cooperate with management	10	30	+

Table 5.4

Changes in the Key Explanatory Variables of PRP Outcomes, 1991 and 1996

	IR, 1991 Mean	1996 Mean	1991 % Agree	1996 % Agree	Change 1991–1996
Gets above average PRP (dummy)	0.45	0.31			−
Managers set targets more clearly	2.81	2.69	27	32	−/+
Doubt I'll get a good appraisal	3.18	3.60	45	63	+
My last appraisal was fair	3.42	3.38	66	64	=
There is a standard for the job	4.01	4.03	82	84	=
Intrinsic motivation	3.47	2.64	63	32	−
IR 1991 and 1996, Affective commitment	.029	−.060			−
IR 1991 and 1996 Goal/financial commitment factor 2	−.010	.021			+

posts. The relatively large drop in those getting above-average pay combined with the large coefficients on that variable confirm its importance.

The big investments by higher management in revamping performance appraisal appear to have had only a small effect. Despite the shift from standard criteria to individually negotiated performance agreements, there was only a small change in the percentage reporting that performance management led to managers setting work targets more clearly (Table 5.4). In the same vein, there was little change in the percentage reporting that they thought their last appraisal was a fair reflection of their performance.

Against this, there was a steep increase in the numbers doubting they would get a good appraisal even if they performed well, and also decreases in intrinsic motivation and commitment. It might seem there is a contradiction, in that most workers felt their appraisals were fair and yet they doubted they would get good appraisals even if they performed well. The likely cause is that most people continued performing as before, got average appraisals, and accepted them as fair assessments. They had not aspired to get "Exceed," and did not feel unfairly deprived.

Two points need to be explored further. First, the shift dummy for 1996 is really no more than a statement of ignorance capturing the general direction of movement. Second, despite the evidence of employee demotivation, there was a doubling of the percentage of line managers reporting that PRP had led staff to work harder: from 22 percent to 42 percent. This suggests we need to look more closely at the position of line managers and of the appraisal system.

Performance Outcomes: Line Manager Views

Line managers have a critical position in appraisal-based performance pay both because they help set the employee work objectives at the most concrete level and because they appraise how well they have been achieved at the end. Replies to our survey indicated two routes through which appraisals could raise performance. The first follows much of the psychological literature, which attests to the positive effect of good goal setting on performance (Locke and Latham 1990). This stresses the positive motivational effect; but there is also the possibility that appraisals are used to pressure employees into working harder, and this brings out a negative threat effect. There was evidence of both routes in the replies we received.

Line managers were asked a number of questions about the effects of PRP on the work of other employees in the Inland Revenue. These included whether performance pay has caused staff to work harder (beyond job requirements) and whether it has made staff less cooperative with management. As shown in Table 5.1, line mangers are more likely in 1996 than in 1991 to report that performance pay has increased the work done and that it has reduced willingness of staff to cooperate with management. To see whether such line manager judgments were influenced by their own personal experience of being appraised for PRP, we ran similar logistic regressions to those on table 5.1 with the line manager judgments of other staff as the dependent variable. Mostly the coefficients on receipt of PRP and on the conduct of appraisal were nonsignificant, which given sample numbers of around 850, means we can discount such influence. On balance therefore, one can conclude that line managers' views on other employees' performance were not unduly colored by the operation of PRP for their own pay and performance.

Increased Stress and PRP

The line manager judgments that many staff are working harder as a result of PRP could reflect two processes. Employees may be working harder because they feel positively motivated by the rewards for individual performance and clearer work goals. Alternatively, they may be doing so because they feel pressured by the goal-setting process and the linking of their rewards to line management appraisal. There may also be a mixture of the two, as different employees have different experiences of performance management. Clearly, the evidence of demotivation in the replies suggests that substantial numbers may feel pressured.

The questions asked in 1996 enable us to explore this issue. One indicator would be whether employees found that PRP had caused them more stress in their work, and whether they believed staff were pressured into accepting performance objectives without the opportunity to agree to them with their line managers. Another might be found in signs of risk-averse behavior, for example, in seeking to negotiate work targets that were unlikely to result in penalties, and a belief that one needs to be clever to negotiate easy objectives.

To test the first effect, we included responses to the question about PRP causing more stress in the basic model. This variable was available only in 1996 and was entered in a version of the estimations in Table 5.2 that included interactions of each independent variable. Inclusion of a stress variable has little overall effect on the role of other variables in model, but its own coefficients are mostly strong and significant. Feeling that PRP has caused more stress makes employees significantly less likely to believe PRP rewards good work or to approve of the principle of PRP, and more likely to judge its consequences adversely. Those feeling more stress were significantly more likely to report jealousies, undermined team working, reduced cooperation with management, and increased work hours. While these results are based only on the 1996 sample, they deserve further exploration.[4]

Who Feels More Stress?

The feeling of greater stress is quite widely spread among employees at the Inland Revenue (Table 5.5). Even among those who got above average

Table 5.5

Stress and Receipt of Above-Average PRP, 1996

	Ordinary PRP	Gets above-average PRP
	%	%
PM caused more stress in my job:		
Strongly disagree	3.8	4.8
Disagree	20.4	28.7
Neutral	9.6	12.1
Agree	40.0	33.1
Strongly agree	26.2	21.3
Total	100.0	100.0

PRP awards, more than half (54.4 percent) thought it had increased stress. Among those who got only average PRP awards, the belief that it caused stress was even stronger, with 66.2 percent agreeing it had.

To explore the correlates of employees feeling that PRP had caused them greater stress in their jobs, we estimated a logistic regression with the reporting of greater stress being the dummy dependent variable (see Table 5.6). The same occupational and demographic controls were used as in previous table 5.2, but none proved statistically significant at the 5% level. Also nonsignificant were the measures of getting above average performance pay, and of managers setting targets more clearly and being sufficiently informed about their subordinates' work. In contrast, a number of other variables came to the fore that revealed employees' feeling that they had been pressured into accepting objectives, and that their jobs lacked scope for them to perform well. They also thought that those who got good appraisals did so because they were clever at negotiating their performance agreements, and that for their part, they were more concerned to avoid a "not met" appraisal than to achieve an "exceed." In other words, for these employees, PRP appeared to be more about management imposing tougher performance standards that they felt they could not meet than a positive incentive, and the financial element was there to sanction them should they fail.

Overall, those who feel stress has gone up as a result of performance pay feel that management has been pressing staff against their will to raise effort. They experience this as a punishment-centered approach which induces risk-averse behavior. This could be heightened by the feeling that staff are less willing to help each other, so that one is more on one's own when faced with difficult situations at work. The feeling that many are in

Table 5.6

Estimated Determinants of Job Stress, Inland Revenue, 1996

Dependent variable: PRP has caused me greater stress in my job (dummy).	B	Standard error
My last appraisal was a fair reflection of my performance.	−.183**	(.078)
Staff feel pressured into accepting performance objectives set by management without discussion.	.310**	(.073)
In agreeing objectives, I am more concerned to avoid a "Not Met" than to aim for an "Exceed."	.138*	(.067)
The staff who gain "Exceeds" are those who are cleverest at negotiating their Performance Agreements.	.145**	(.064)
The nature of my present job makes it very hard for me to get an "Exceed."	.149*	(.076)
PRP has made staff less willing to assist colleagues experiencing work difficulties.	.248**	(.066)
Staff suffering illness or personal distress lose out under Performance Management.	.307**	(.078)
Were you able to agree your last Performance Agreement with your manager? (yes/no)	−.265	(.313)

The figure show logit coefficients. Significance: **2%, *5%. Standard errors are shown in parentheses. Regressions are weighted by sample fractions. Questions coded on a five-point Likert scale. Regression includes control dummies for occupation, length of service and gender not shown in the table.

$N = 1025$, % correct 70.7, chi squared $= 202.2$, Cox and Snell $r^2 = 0.179$, Nagelkerke $r^2 = 0.244$

Figure 5.1 **A Model Linking Unilateral Changes in Effort Required and Outcomes**

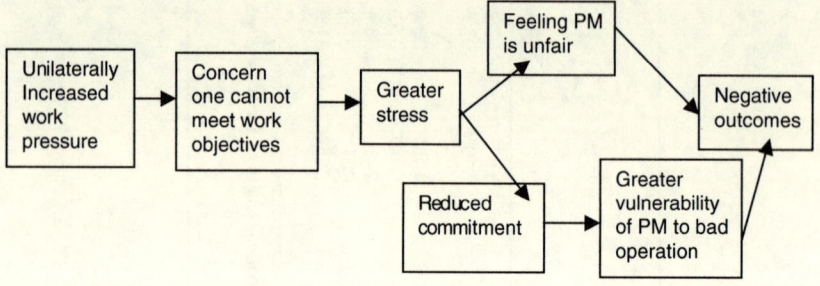

jobs that do not enable them to raise their performance probably contributes to the cynical belief that getting easy targets rather than improving performance is the best way to get rewarded. In sum, these results would be consistent with the causal connection suggested in Figure 5.1 that concern over meeting stated objectives increases stress.

Commitment

Do demotivation and a feeling of greater stress matter to the organization if performance levels are rising? Although research to date has not established any firm empirical link between organizational commitment and employee performance, it is certainly plausible that high levels of commitment will induce employees to use their discretion in work to benefit their organization, and to refrain from opportunistic behavior. Guest has found in his own survey work that organizational commitment has declined with the introduction of performance related pay.[5] The same appears to have occurred at the Inland Revenue.

Affective commitment levels to both the Inland Revenue as a whole and to the employee's workplace fell between 1991 and 1996, whereas the more financially oriented types of commitment increased in value (Table 5.7)

Although we can measure it only for 1996, there appears to be a strong link between the feeling that PRP has caused stress and differences in levels of organizational commitment as suggested in Figure 5.1. The data in Table 5.8 show that those who feel increased stress report lower levels of affective commitment.

Can we assess the cross-sectional link between stress and commitment with the over time change in commitment levels between 1991 and 1996? One link comes with responses to the item "Even if my performance is

Table 5.7

Change of Mean Commitment Levels, Inland Revenue, 1991–1996

		Mean[a]	Variance
Three-factor model			
Commitment to Inland Revenue	1991	.04579	1.04553
	1996	−.09485	.89317
Commitment to one's office	1991	.05792	.96100
	1996	−.11998	1.06036
Financial commitment	1991	−.02162	1.08593
	1996	.04479	.81981
Two-factor model			
Affective commitment	1991	.04548	1.03741
	1996	−.07195	.91763
Goal/financial commitment	1991	.02883	1.04241
	1996	.05139	.79868

Note: N 1991 = 2,422; N 1996 = 1,192.
[a] Mean across whole sample is zero.

Table 5.8

Link Between Commitment and Stress

	Causes stress	Mean	Variance
Commitment to Inland Revenue	Yes	−.10231	.90425
	No	−.08376	.87790
Commitment to office	Yes	−.28250	1.15061
	No	.14896	.80860
Financial commitment	Yes	.03818	.91467
	No	.05964	.65770

Note: Commitment scale based on whole sample, 1991–1996. N (yes) = 740; N (no) = 437.

good enough, I doubt I'll get an Exceed/Box 1 or 2". This item played an important part in the model set out earlier, and in 1996 it correlated with perceived stress until the other stress-related variables were included. Between 1991 and 1996, the share of employees doubting they would get an award increased by nearly half, from 45 percent to 63 percent. This reinforces the interpretation that it is the involuntary nature of the increased performance that lies behind the feelings of demotivation and divisiveness, and that increased output owes more to the goal-setting process than the incentive of greater individual rewards.

Given the limited evidence linking organizational commitment and performance, one could well ask whether management should care about the decline in commitment. One reason emerges from the model discussed earlier. There it appeared that organizational commitment, and affective commitment in particular, attenuated some of the negative consequences of poorly conducted appraisals and goal setting. Commitment acts like a great stabilizer, making motivation less vulnerable than it might be to feelings that management has acted unfairly. Thus, a reduction in commitment levels could be expected to make employee motivation less resilient in the face of strained relations with management.[6]

Conclusion

Apart from the negative evidence that employees did not grow accustomed to the new pay system despite considerable management efforts to improve its operation, the study raises an interesting question about whether or not performance pay itself was responsible for the decline in employee motivation and the feelings of divisiveness. Alternatively, performance pay might have acted like a lightning conductor, and became the focus of employee resentment at unilaterally demanded increases in performance levels. Any other payment system might have attracted similar ire. Two points deserve mention.

First, although it is difficult on the basis of a single organization to distinguish between the two interpretations, there was considerable variation among three public sectors covered in the earlier work with respect to line manager estimates of whether PRP had caused the quantity of work to increase (Marsden and French 1998). If PRP were acting as a lightning conductor for an unpopular imposed increase in effort levels, then this would be most likely in the other organizations in which line managers associated PRP with their staff working harder. In the hospital with individual performance pay an even higher percentage of line managers responded saying it had caused employees to work harder. Yet, compared with the Inland Revenue, the positive motivational judgments were stronger, and the negative judgments of demotivation and divisiveness were weaker. This suggests that PRP has been more than just a lightning conductor for general discontent.

Second, the scheme in force in 1996 was designed to accommodate increased workloads and reward these by means of "extra-loaded" posts that covered about one-fifth of our sample. This provision increased the gearing of the incentive offered under the scheme. While this may have increased the incentive effect, it may also have increased the salience of inadequate appraisals and goal setting, as these will have caused employees to doubt their chances of earning performance increments. The big increase in those believing that even if their performance warranted additional reward they would not get it was a clear sign of this.

The most plausible interpretation of events at the Inland Revenue then is that PRP has been used as the vehicle through which management has sought to increase performance, and in particular, to increase productivity. That has been experienced by many employees as pressure rather than incentive because of the key role played by the appraisal and goal-setting process, which is an essential part of the type of performance pay scheme. In that respect, one could say that the then government and its senior management achieved their objectives by means of PRP. However, there remains a key concern over the sustainability of this increase, a concern expressed to us by some senior managers themselves. Such concerns seem justified in the light of the erosion of organizational commitment at the Inland Revenue, and the inflation of performance indicators that occurred at the Employment Service (see note 6). In the year 2000, Inland Revenue management and unions began talks on further major changes to performance management including the possibility of team incentives as proposed by the government's Makinson Report (2000). These discussions proved protracted and were still in progress at the time of writing. The concern about sustainability is also reflected in the fact that management and unions are currently in the process of a major overhaul of the system.

Appendix 5.1: Derivation of the Commitment and Intrinsic Motivation Variables.

The measures of commitment used in Table 5.2, and subsequently, were modeled on questions close to those of Meyer and Allen (1997) and Pec-

Table 5.9

Rotated Component Matrix

	Component	
	Affective	Financially oriented
Being in the IR means a lot to me.	0.823	0.000
I would be happy to spend the rest of my life working at the IR.	0.780	−0.016
I am emotionally attached to the organization.	0.722	−0.101
Working in the IR, I am contributing to an important public service.	0.570	0.120
I feel like part of the family in my current office.	0.510	0.022
It is unfair to use PRP to retain staff.	−0.019	0.982
I could just as easily become attached to another organization.	−0.592	0.134

Note: Extraction method: Principal Component Analysis. Rotation method: Varimax with Kaiser Normalization.

cei and Guest (1993). We asked whether being in the Inland Revenue meant a lot to the employees; whether they would be willing to spend the rest of their lives working there; whether they could become equally attached to another organization; whether they felt they were contributing to an important public service; whether they did or did not feel emotionally attached to the organization; and whether it would be fair to use PRP simply to stop staff from leaving. Two factors emerged from our factor analysis, broadly "affective" commitment and financially oriented commitment. Believing that PRP should not be used to retain staff part of the standard commitment question about whether one would seriously consider leaving for a bit more money elsewhere. Those who would consider leaving for a bit more money could be expected to tolerate managers awarding PRP in order to retain staff. The rotated factor loadings are shown in Table 5.9. The commitment scales in Tables 5.7 and 5.8 brought in the additional distinction between commitment to one's immediate office or workplace and commitment to the Inland Revenue, the organization as a whole.

For intrinsic motivation, we asked whether people considered that the satisfaction from doing their jobs well was sufficient incentive to perform well.

Notes

Many of the data used in this paper were collected for joint research by David Marsden and Ray Richardson (Marsden and Richardson 1994) and by David Marsden and Stephen French (Marsden and French 1998). Full details of the questionnaire and the sample can be found in Marsden and Richardson (1992), and Marsden and French (1998).

1. At the time of writing, the NHS system was in the process of reform.
2. The authors have compared the estimations for the Inland Revenue with those for the full public sector sample and find very few coefficients that differ between the two samples and conclude that the two estimations regimes are broadly similar. This comparison is available from the authors.
3. In order to determine whether the estimation applied to the Inland Revenue was the same for both years, we interacted each variable with a year dummy. Nearly all the interactions were statistically insignificant. This suggests that the same underlying causal model linking incentive and appraisal effects to PRP outcomes applies in both years.
4. The estimations that add the extra variable on stress to the 1996 data are available from the authors. The significance tests are all at the 5 percent level.
5. We are grateful to David Guest, Kings College London, for pointing this out to me.
6. A second reason why the organization might be concerned about demotivation and stress even when performance levels are rising is the employees may become cynical about their incentives and begin to engage in gaming behavior. According to a series of reports in the *Guardian* newspaper, there occurred a serious inflation in a key indicator of performance, the number of job placements, by the Employment Service (*Guardian,* March 29. 1997; April 1, 1997; and April 16, 1997). What had begun as a minor abuse arising from the gray area surrounding what counts as a job placement switched into a widespread practice involving both employees and management which inflated job placements by up to 30 percent nationally. Taking these reports with our own survey evidence suggests that the employees divorced their normal work of advising job seekers from the numbers game required for performance pay. Once the numbers game took off, those who would normally have been strict about what they counted as placements would have been penalized for falling behind the placement rates of their colleagues.

References

Bach S., and Winchester, D. 1994. "Opting Out of Pay Devolution? The Prospect for Local Pay Bargaining in UK Public Services." *British Journal of Industrial Relations* 32: 263–282.

Department for Education and Employment (DfEE). 1998. *Teachers: Meeting the Challenge of Change.* Cm 4164. London, HMSO (Her Majesty's Stationery Office), December.

Department of the Environment (1981). *Local Authority National Reports.* London: Department of the Environment.

Dowling, B., and Richardson, R. 1997. "Evaluating Performance-Related Pay for Managers in the National Health Service." *International Journal of Human Resource Management* 8: 348–366.

Efficiency Unit. 1988. *Improving Management in Government: The Next Steps.* Report to the Prime Minister. London, HMSO.
Elliott, R. F, and Dufus, K. 1996. "What Has Been Happening to Pay in the Public Service Sector of the British Economy? Developments over the Period 1970–1992." *British Journal of Industrial Relations* 34: 51–85.
Griffiths, R. 1983. *NHS Management Inquiry.* London: Department of Health and Social Security.
Hicks, J. R. 1974. *The Crisis in Keynesian Economics.* Oxford: Blackwell.
Holmstrom, B., and Milgrom, P. 1991. "Multitask Principal-Agent Analysis: Incentive Contracts, Asset Ownership, and Job Design." *Journal of Law, Economics and Organization* 7: Special Issue 24–52.
IDS. 1995. *Pay In the Public Services. Review of 1994: Prospects for 1995.* London: Incomes Data Services.
IRS (Industrial Relations Services). 1993. *Agenda for Delegation in the Civil Service.* IRS Employment Trends, 549. London: Industrial Relations Services, December.
Locke, E. A., and Latham, G. P. 1990. *A Theory of Goal Setting and Task Performance.* Englewood Cliffs, NJ: Prentice Hall.
Makinson, J., Chair. 2000. *Incentives for Change: Rewarding Performance in National Government Networks.* London: Public Services Productivity Panel, HM Treasury.
Marsden, D. W., and French, S. 1998. *What a Performance: Performance Related Pay in the Public Services.* London: Centre for Economic Performance.
Marsden, D. W., French, S., and Kubo, K. 2000. "Why Does Performance Pay Demotivate? Financial Incentives versus Performance Appraisal." *Centre for Economic Performance Discussion Paper No. 476,* November 2000. London: London School of Economics.
Marsden, D. W., and Richardson, R. 1994. "Performing for Pay? The Effects of 'Merit Pay' on Motivation in a Public Service." *British Journal of Industrial Relations* 32: 243–262.
———. 1992. "Motivation and Performance Related Pay in the Public Sector: A Case Study of the Inland Revenue." *Centre for Economic Performance, Discussion Paper No. 75,* London: School of Economics.
Mayntz, R. 1985. *Soziologie der öffentlichen Verwaltung* (Sociology of the public service). Heidelberg: Müller Juristischer Verlag (dritte überarbeitete Auflage)
Megaw, J., Chair. 1982. *Inquiry into Civil Service Pay: Report.* Cmnd 8590, London: HMSO.
Meyer, John P, and Allen, Natalie J. 1997. *Commitment in the Workplace: Theory, Research and Application.* Thousand Oaks, CA: Sage.
National Audit Office (NAO). 1989. *Manpower Planning in the Civil Service.* Cm 398, HMSO, London.
Peccei, R., and Guest, D. 1993. "The Dimensionality and Stability of Organisational Commitment," Centre for Economic Performance Discussion Paper No. 149, London: London School of Economics, May.
Richardson, R./IPD. 1999. *Performance Pay Trends in the UK Institute of Personnel and Development Survey Report No. 9,* London: Institute of Personnel and Development. September.
Rose-Ackerman, S. 1996. "Altruism, Nonprofits, and Economic Theory." *Journal of Economic Literature* 34: 701–728.
Smith, P. 1990. "The Use of Performance Indicators in the Public Sector." *Journal of the Royal Statistical Society,* Series A 153: 53–72.
Tirole, J. 1994. "The Internal Organisation of Government." *Oxford Economic Papers* 46: 1–29.
Vroom, V. 1964. *Work and Motivation.* New York: John Wiley and Sons.

Winchester, D. 1996. "Recent Changes in Pay Determination in the British Public Sector." Paper presented to the Anglo-German Foundation conference on Pay Reform and Job Modernisation in the Public Sector, London: London School of Economics, December 12–13.

Chapter 6
The German Experience with Performance Pay

Uwe Jirjahn

Introduction

This chapter investigates performance pay in German manufacturing establishments. In the first section, it focuses, in particular, on pay-for-performance schemes for blue collar workers. In the second section, typical forms of performance pay such as piece rates and premium pay are described. Moreover, three types of reward systems are distinguished, namely incentive systems based on individual performance, incentive systems based on group performance, and incentive systems based on whole-firm performance. Descriptive statistics about the use of the various methods of pay are provided.

The third section discusses the theoretical determinants of performance pay and reviews German empirical studies estimating those determinants. Examining the determinants of payment schemes is important for several reasons. First, these studies provide information about the conditions under which payment schemes succeed and about the mechanism through which payment schemes influence firm performance. Second, the studies recognize that the pattern of observed payment schemes need not be efficient.

This chapter builds upon joint research done with John S. Heywood, Olaf Hübler, and Gesine Stephan. I am also grateful to Michelle Brown, Peter Kaukewitsch, Wolfgang Meyer, and Friedhelm Pfeiffer for helpful comments. All remaining errors are my own.

Market failures, distributional conflicts, and slack within firms can be critical determinants of incentive schemes. On the one hand, the German evidence confirms findings from other countries, with firm size, the organization of work, and gender playing predictable roles. On the other hand, the German industrial relations system plays an important and unique role in determining the use of performance pay. Industrial relations in Germany are characterized by a dual structure of employee representation. Works councils provide a highly developed mechanism for establishment-level participation while collective bargaining agreements are negotiated between unions and employers' associations on an industrial level. The empirical studies (Heywood, Hübler, and Jirjahn 1998; Heywood and Jirjahn 2000) show that there exists an important interaction between these components of the industrial relations system. Even though particular work practices must be negotiated between works councils and managers on the establishment level, these practices are more easily negotiated when substantial distributional conflicts are moderated outside the firm. This interaction effect, as it applies to performance pay, has not been well recognized in debates about the relative efficiency of centralized collective bargaining.

Previous examinations of performance pay in Germany estimated the determinants of single payment schemes. An alternative approach is developed in the fourth section, which recognizes that the various methods of linking pay and performance are part of a broader human resource management (HRM) strategy that consists of interrelated work practices. Through cluster analysis, it is shown that individual-based piece rates are an element of an HRM strategy characterized as traditional mass production. In contrast, group-based incentives and profit sharing are elements of HRM strategies relying on a participative organization of work and on regular training for blue-collar workers. Having identified alternative HRM strategies, the determinants of the choice among the various strategies are estimated. Industrial relations, product markets, incentives for managers, and complementarities between skilled blue-collar work and skilled white-collar work emerge from the analysis as important determinants.

Forms of Performance Pay

A first look at the use of performance pay can be obtained from *Statistisches Bundesamt* (official German statistics). The data of the *Gehalts-und Lohnstrukturerhebung* (wage structure samples) are drawn as a two-stage random sample from all establishments in the complete manufacturing sector and parts of the service sector. In Table 6.1 we report the percentage of full-time blue-collar workers in the West German manufacturing sector receiving performance pay for the years 1966, 1972, 1978, 1990, and 1995. The survey identifies two typical forms of performance pay: piece rates and premium pay. Piece rates reward workers for units of output. Premium pay also may reward the quantity of output or the speed of completion but is more often linked to the quality of workmanship or the sparing use of raw materials. The survey distinguishes between workers with regular performance pay and workers only occasionally remunerated by performance pay. As Table 6.1 shows, the percentage of blue-collar workers receiving performance pay has not changed dramatically over the last thirty years. Nonetheless, a large share of workers receive performance pay, more than a quarter of men and more than a third of women. In total, 21 percent of male blue-collar workers received pay for performance on a regular basis in 1966, and 22 percent in 1995. In comparison, 29 percent of female blue-collar workers received pay for performance on a regular basis in 1966 and 30 percent in 1995. Adding those occasionally receiving such pay raises these measures several percentage points for each gender. More detailed information on piece rates and premium pay is available only for 1990 and 1995. As seen in Table 6.1, the gender differences in those years are due to the higher proportion of women remunerated by piece rates. Finally, both men and women are more frequently remunerated by piece rates than by premium pay.

Note that the absence of both piece rates and premium pay need not imply the complete absence of performance pay. There are other forms of performance pay such as profit sharing. These alternative pay-for-performance schemes are not identified by the survey. Moreover, there are different forms of piece rates and premium pay. They can be based either on individual performance or on group performance, a distinction not made in the official statistics.

More detailed information on the use of pay for performance in firms can be obtained from the "Hannover Panel" (Brand et al. 1996), a four-wave establishment panel with data from manufacturing establishments in the German federal state of Lower Saxony. The survey population consists of all manufacturing establishments with at least five employees. The sample is stratified according to firm size and industry. The data was collected by a German survey and research institute, using a questionnaire to guide personal interviews. Those interviewed were the owner, top manager, or head of the personnel department. The number of firms taking part in the panel study has declined over the four waves: from 1025 in 1994, to 849 in 1995, to 721 in 1996, and finally to 709 in 1997.

Information on pay-for-performance schemes is available in the first (1994) and the third wave (1996). The survey questions identify (1)

Table 6.1

Proportion of Full-Time Blue-Collar Workers Receiving Performance Pay in the West German Manufacturing Sector, 1966–1995 (Percentage of workers)

Method of Pay	1966 Men	1966 Women	1972 Men	1972 Women	1978 Men	1978 Women	1990 Men	1990 Women	1995 Men	1995 Women
1. Performance pay (piece rates and/or premium pay)	20.7	29.0	19.3	29.6	19.5	31.6	23.0	33.5	22.2	30.0
a. Only piece rates	n.a.*	n.a.	n.a.	n.a.	n.a.	n.a.	13.0	23.8	13.2	19.2
b. Only premium pay	n.a.	n.a.	n.a.	n.a.	n.a.	n.a.	9.4	8.8	8.5	9.5
c. Piece rates and premimum pay	n.a.	n.a.	n.a.	n.a.	n.a.	n.a.	0.6	0.9	0.5	1.3
2. Remuneration occasionally based on performance pay	7.6	8.9	4.9	8.3	2.5	5.1	5.3	6.8	4.4	5.7
Number of cases	3,445,010	1,105,220	3,796,850	1,236,870	3,340,528	1,006,715	3,570,395	887,200	2,904,599	633,600

Note: Author's calculations based on official German statistics (Statistisches Bundesamt).
* Not available.

whether or not the establishment uses piece rates based on individual performance and/or based on group performance; and (2) if the establishment does use a piece rate, whether or not that rate is a group piece rate. Correspondingly, the questions identify (1) whether or not the establishment uses individual-based and/or group-based premium pay and (2) if the establishment does use a premium pay, whether or not it is group-based. Moreover, it is identified whether or not target based schemes are used. Workers remunerated by a target-based scheme receive a fixed wage rate. They are expected to reach a certain performance goal. If they consistently overperform or underperform, the wage rate will be adjusted, but such adjustments happen only periodically. Pay, therefore, is discontinuously linked to performance. Finally, it is asked whether or not there is profit sharing for employees.

Table 6.2 contains information on the proportion of establishments using the various pay for performance schemes for the years 1994 and 1996.[1] The proportion of establishments with piece rates is similar for both years: 19 percent in 1994 and 18 percent in 1996. Group-based piece rates are less frequently used. The proportion of establishments with group piece rates is about 5 percent in both years. Therefore, at least 14 percent of the firms in 1994 and 13 percent in 1996 use individual-based piece rates. Also, the proportion of establishments using premium pay is similar for both years: 17 percent in 1994 and 16 percent in 1996. Group premium pay is used less frequently, with about 5 percent of the firms using it in 1994 and about 4 percent in 1996. The share of establishments using target-based schemes is 13 percent in 1994 and 8 percent in 1996. Finally, 17 percent and 14 percent of the establishments, respectively, have profit sharing plans for employees in 1994 and 1996. In sum, 46 percent of the establishments use at least one of the various payment schemes in 1994 and 42 percent in 1996.

Table 6.3 shows changes in the use of performance pay between 1994 and 1996. While 14.6 percent of the establishments in the first and the third waves use piece rates in both years, 8.4 percent change their use of piece rates between 1994 and 1996. Of that 8.4 percent, 4.8 percent use piece rates in 1994 but drop them by 1996, and 3.6 percent newly adopt them in 1996. A similar pattern can be observed for the other pay-for-performance schemes. About 11 percent of all establishments use premium pay in both years, 7 percent only in 1994 and 5 percent only in 1996. About 8 percent of all establishments use profit sharing in both years, 9 percent only in 1994 and 7 percent only in 1996. Clearly, there exists substantial instability in the firms using particular payment schemes. For five of the six categories of performance pay, the proportion of firms using

Table 6.2

Proportion of Manufacturing Establishments with Performance Pay in the Federal State Lower Saxony, 1994 and 1996 (percentage of establishments)

Method of pay	1994	1996
Piece rates for blue-collar workers (individual and/or group based)	19.4	18.2
Piece rates for blue-collar workers (group based)	5.2	5.3
Premium pay for blue-collar workers (individual and/or group based)	17.0	16.1
Premium pay for blue-collar workers (group based)	4.7	4.4
Target based schemes for blue-collar workers (e.g., quota wage)	13.1	8.3
Profit sharing for employees	17.4	14.7
Number of observations	1,016	720

Note: Author's calculations based on the first and the third wave of the Hannover Panel. Multiple answers are possible.

Table 6.3

Movements in the Use of Performance Pay, 1994 and 1996 (percentage of establishments)

Method of pay	No use in 1994 and 1996	Use only in 1994	Use only in 1996	Use in 1994 and 1996
Piece rates for blue-collar workers (individual and/or group based)	77.0	4.8	3.6	14.6
Piece rates for blue-collar workers (group based)	91.7	2.9	2.8	2.5
Premium pay for blue-collar workers (individual and/or group based)	77.0	6.7	5.0	11.2
Premium pay for blue-collar workers (group based)	92.4	3.1	2.5	2.0
Target based schemes for blue-collar workers (e.g., quota wage)	81.4	10.4	5.2	3.1
Profit sharing for employees	76.3	8.9	6.7	8.1

Note: Author's calculations based on the first and the third wave of the Hannover Panel. Number of observations = 714.

the scheme in both years is less than the proportion using it in one year alone.

In sum, substantial use is made of a variety of methods for linking payment to performance. Pay-for-performance schemes can be linked to particular performance dimensions, such as the quantity of output, or to broader performance measures. They can be based on individual performance, group performance, or firm performance. Moreover, payment can be continuously or discontinuously linked to performance. This variety of pay-for-performance schemes sets the stage for exploring the determinants of performance pay in Germany.

Determinants of Performance Pay

This section discusses the determinants of performance pay in Germany. The focus is both on the theoretical determinants and on four recent German empirical studies. The studies by Heywood, Hübler, and Jirjahn (1998) and Hübler and Jirjahn (1998) are each based on establishment data from the first wave of the Hannover Panel. Heywood and Jirjahn (2001) investigate the determinants of pay for performance with the first and the third wave. Jirjahn and Stephan (2000) use matched employer-employee data from manufacturing firms in Lower Saxony. The discussion is organized around five large sets of determinants: the organization of work and production technology, job security and tenure, gender, industrial relatioand product markets and management incentives.

Organization of Work and Technology of Production

Individual-based performance pay presupposes that individual output can be identified. When the organization of work is characterized by team production, identifying a worker's individual contribution is difficult. Moreover, when workers perform multidimensional tasks, individual performance measures are often unavailable for all dimensions. These dimensions may include building long-term relationships with customers, helping other workers on the job, improving product quality, and asset maintenance. When the productivities of employees are mutually dependent, sharing schemes provide incentives for cooperation (Drago and Turnbull 1988) and reduce rent-seeking influence activities that are harmful to firm performance (Itoh 1992). However, even if the workers' outputs are mutually independent, tasks may be multidimensional. For example, individual performance may depend on both the quantity and the quality of produced output. Holmström and Milgrom (1991) argue that many firms offer low-powered incentives to workers because performance pay distorts the allocation of effort across tasks. Piece rates induce workers to exert effort increasing quantity but to neglect quality. However, profit sharing stands as an alternative to both low-powered incentives and piece rates. Even in the presence of a free-rider problem and income risk, it may have advantages as it does not distort the allocation of effort across tasks (Jirjahn 2000). Profit sharing provides incentives to exert effort in all activities that are relevant to the firm's profit. In contrast to low-powered incentives, it may elicit greater total effort. In sum, it can be expected that sharing schemes induce positive incentive effects especially in situations where workers cooperation is important or where tasks are complex and multidimensional.[2] Teamwork and multitasking should be associated with the use of sharing schemes. Individual-based incentives, and especially piece rates, may have advantages when workers perform less complex tasks with lower skill requirements. Compared to pure time rates, it can be expected that piece rates elicit greater effort and induce self-selection by attracting more productive workers (Lazear 2000).[3]

Heywood and Jirjahn (2001) present evidence that when jobs require skilled blue-collar workers (as opposed to unskilled), the use of individual-based piece rates is less likely and the use of profit sharing is more likely. Moreover, establishments with direct employee involvement in the firm's investment decisions are less likely to use piece rates and are more likely to use profit sharing. This fits theoretical considerations as workers paid by the piece are less likely to make appropriate establishment wide decisions and, instead, consider what helps them increase their individual output. In contrast, profit sharing induces cooperation by aligning the interests of employer and workers. This interpretation also fits the finding that profit sharing is positively associated with product and process innovations (Askildsen, Jirjahn, and Smith 2000).[4] Finally, the organization of work has a direct impact on the choice of payment schemes. Establishments with work teams in production are more likely to use group piece rates, group premium pay, and profit sharing (Heywood and Jirjahn 2001).

Large-scale production makes performance pay more likely. First, in large firms it is more difficult to monitor workers' efforts. Therefore, pay is often linked to output-related performance measures. Second, establishing and administering pay-for-performance schemes involves fixed costs, and the fixed costs per worker decrease with the number of employees receiving performance pay. Empirical evidence in Germany shows that the likelihood of individual-based and group-based piece rates and premium pay increases with establishment size (Heywood and Jirjahn 2001). There is also weak evidence that the likelihood of profit sharing increases with establishment size (Hübler and Jirjahn 1998). However, the significance of the coefficient depends on the specification of firm size. As Kruse (1996) notes, there are two opposite effects of firm size on the use of profit sharing. On the one hand, firm size may exert a positive impact because profit sharing also involves fixed costs that can be spread over a larger number of workers. On the other hand the free-rider problem becomes more severe in larger firms.

Job Security and Tenure

The relationship between job security and performance pay depends critically on the type of payment scheme. Evidence from Australia (Drago and Heywood 1995) and from the United Kingdom (Heywood, Siebert, and Wei 1997) shows that pay-for-performance schemes such as piece rates are more likely in establishments using layoffs. This evidence carries over to Germany where Heywood and Jirjahn (2001) find that long-term stable employment has a negative impact on the use of individual-based piece rates and premium pay. These findings suggest that pay-for-performance schemes such as piece rates and premium pay are associated with short-term employment relationships. Indeed, Goldin (1986) argues that contemporaneous incentive schemes are alternatives to deferred compensation. Deferred compensation rearranges the earnings profile by paying workers less than their marginal product early in their tenure and more than their marginal product late in their tenure (Lazear 1981). Thus, long-expected tenure is a prerequisite for the use of deferred compensation. Consequently, establishments with frequent layoffs are more likely to use contemporaneous incentive schemes because workers fearing layoffs will not be motivated by deferred compensation.

Employment stability plays a different role when the incentive effects of a payment scheme require trust and cooperation. Obviously, employment stability is of particular importance for profit sharing. Possible solutions to the free-rider problem rely on repeated games between the employees (MacLeod 1988) or on mutual monitoring and peer pressure (Kandel and Lazear 1992). Moreover, the employer has to build a reputation for reporting profits honestly. The reputation mechanism is based on a repeated game between employer and employees. Hence, profit sharing should be associated with long-term employment relationships. This prediction has been confirmed for Germany. Employment stability exerts a positive impact on the use of profit sharing (Heywood, Hübler, and Jirjahn 1998; Heywood and Jirjahn 2001). Additionally, establishments relying on promotions as incentive schemes are more likely to use profit sharing. Promotions are associated with long-term employment relationships because they motivate only workers with a long tenure.[5]

Trust may play a role not only for profit sharing but also for piece rates. Workers will withhold effort when they fear an increase in performance standards after a period of good performance. However, the link between this ratchet effect and job security or tenure is ambiguous. On the one hand, long-term employment relationships foster trust. On the other hand, workers with short-term employment relationships are less likely to fear the ratchet effect because they are not affected by a future increase in performance standards (Milgrom and Roberts 1992, 232–236). The negative link between employment stability and the use of individual-based payment schemes found by Heywood and Jirjahn (2001) fits the second view. In contrast, Jirjahn and Stephan (2000), find that blue-collar workers with a longer tenure are more likely to receive piece rates.

Gender

The weight of international studies show that firms with high percentages of women are more likely to use piece rates (Drago and Heywood 1995; Heywood, Hübler, and Jirjahn 1998).[6] Goldin (1986) argues that women are sorted out of deferred compensation schemes and into jobs with contemporaneous incentive schemes because of their shorter expected tenure. Heywood and Wei (1997) emphasize an alternative explanation. Even when both spouses work, women are disproportionately responsible for household production. This disproportionate responsibility requires more flexibility between work and family. For example, women are more likely to take time off for illness of a child or other family members. Jobs without production interdependencies between workers allow such flexibility. Because these jobs are characterized by low costs of measuring individual performance, they are suitable for performance pay based on individual performance. While both hypotheses stress the women's disproportionate responsibility for household production, they differ in the time horizon referred to. The focus of the first hypothesis is on long-term breaks of individual work careers whereas the second hypothesis is related to ongoing short-term breaks of work (flexibility).

Heywood and Jirjahn (2001) find a significant positive impact of the share of women on the use of individual-based piece rates and premium pay but not on the use of group-based piece rates and premium pay. These results appear at odds with Goldin's hypothesis. If shorter expected tenure requires contemporaneous incentives, women should be disproportionately paid by both individual-based and group-based payment schemes. The results, instead, fits the hypothesis that women need more flexibility between work and home. If women are sorted based on teamwork (dependencies between workers), high shares of women should be associated with individual-based pay. Women should not be associated with group-based schemes because these schemes reflect technologies requiring teamwork. Thus, German data confirms that from Australia showing that establishments with high shares of women are more likely to use individual piece rates but less likely to use group pay (Drago and Heywood 1995). Both the Australian and the German studies find that establishments with a high share of women are more likely to use profit sharing. To the extent that profit sharing is associated with long-term employment relationships and with teamwork, this finding may argue not only against Goldin's hypothesis but also against the claim that women are less valuable in teamwork.

Jirjahn and Stephan (2000) confirm that female blue-collar workers are more likely to receive piece rates than male blue-collar workers. While workers with longer tenure are more likely to receive piece rates, the hypothesis that women sort into jobs with piece rates due to their responsibility for household production is partly supported. Female employees with children are more likely to be remunerated by piece rates, whereas there is no impact of children on the use of piece rates for male employees. Interestingly, women are more likely to receive pay-for-performance schemes, even controlling for tenure and for the presence of children. Jirjahn and Stephan test a third hypothesis: Women who are subject to discrimination will sort into payment schemes associated with less arbitrariness in performance appraisals. Subjective performance evaluations by superiors provide discretion in performance appraisals. This discretion may result in performance appraisals based on the superiors' subjective opinions and preferences. In contrast, piece rates are based on "objective" performance measures (Milkovich and Newman 1996) and therefore provide better protection against discrimination. This hypothesis is supported by the finding that piece rates increase the hourly wages of German women more than for German men and thereby close the gender earnings gap. These results support related work from the United States, finding that piece rates have a stronger impact in increasing the wages of blacks than the wages of whites (Belman and Heywood 1988).[7]

Industrial Relations

Pay-for-performance schemes based on "objective" performance measures may also suffer from employer opportunism. As noted above, a well-known example is the ratchet effect. Workers will withhold effort when they fear that the employer will increase the performance standards of a piece rate scheme after a period of good performance. Similarly, the incentive effects of profit sharing are weak when employees fear that managers will be slack in improving firm efficiency or that the employer will not honestly report the firm's profit. Cooperation and trust, therefore, appear crucial for payment schemes to provide the desired incentive effects (Heywood, Hübler, and Jirjahn 1998). On this score, the German industrial relations system plays a unique role.

Industrial relations in Germany are characterized by a dual structure of employee representation through works councils and unions (Müller-Jentsch 1995). Works councils provide a highly developed mechanism for establishment-level participation. This establishment-level participation is formally independent of the process of centralized collective bargaining between unions and employers' associations on an industrial level. Moreover, codetermination by works councils and collective bargaining by unions address different domains.

The rights of the councils are laid down in the Works Constitution Act (WCA). The WCA was introduced in 1952 and reformed in 1972 and 1989. Note that employee involvement through works councils is entirely separate from the system of board-level codetermination—workers on the board of directors (FitzRoy and Kraft 2000). Councils are elected by the entirework force of establishments with five or more permanent employees. However, their creation depends on the initiative of the firm's work force. Hence, councils are not present in all eligible German firms. Councils have full codetermination rights on a broad set of issues which include the introduction of new payment methods, the fixing of job and bonus rates, and the introduction and use of technical devices designed to monitor employee performance. The councils have less strong consultation rights in matters such as changes in equipment and working methods that affect job requirements. Their participation rights include the provision of financial and economic information. The WCA ties works councils to the general obligation to cooperate with management "in a spirit of mutual trust . . . for the good of the employees and of the establishment."

There are two major explanations as to why codetermination may improve economic efficiency. First, councils exert a collective voice in the sense of Freeman and Medoff (1984). Many working conditions are workplace public goods, and councils communicate worker preferences to management helping to optimize their provision. Second, works councils with codetermination rights prevent employers from engaging in opportunistic behavior (Smith 1991; Freeman and Lazear 1995). Of course, there may be other solutions to the danger of employer opportunism. Under some circumstances repeated games and reputation concerns may induce an employer to act honestly (Bull 1987). However, the reputation mechanism fails if an employer overly discounts the future loss of trust and cooperation. In this situation a council with veto rights can prevent an employer from opportunism. Moreover, the reputation mechanism fails if employees do not have enough information to verify whether or not an employer behaves honestly (Kreps 1990). This suggests that the comprehensive information rights of the works council and the reputation mechanism may be complementary in some situations. Hence, codetermination fosters workers' cooperation and provides a mechanism to increase the economic surplus of the firm. Such surplus enhancing work practices include pay for performance schemes. Evidence from Heywood, Hübler and Jirjahn (1998) supports this notion. They find that the presence of a works council exerts a positive impact on the use of piece rates. Moreover, Heywood and Jirjahn (2001) show that establishments with works councils are more likely to use individual-based and group-based piece rates and premium pay. Thus, those German establishments with works councils have in place a mechanism to build trust and share information, making the adoption of performance pay more likely.

Collective bargaining agreements play a different role both in determining pay and in the presence of performance pay. Agreements are usually negotiated between unions and employer associations on a broad industrial level. They regulate wage rates and general aspects of the employment contract such as working hours. While firms that are members of an employers' association and that have union members are covered by the collective bargaining agreement, employers may have an incentive to pay the negotiated wage rate also to employees who are not union members. This incentive results because otherwise those employees would join the union (Fitzenberger and Franz 1999). Note that collective agreements define minimum standards. Of course, covered firms are free to pay wages or to improve working conditions above the level specified by the agreements.

Often collective agreements contain more or less detailed regulations concerning the design of piece rate schemes and premium pay whereas profit sharing usually is not regulated (Bispinck 2000). Note that piece rates and premium pay are the more traditional pay-for-performance schemes, as shown in Table 6.1. Although profit sharing has a long academic tradition in Germany, it has never been broadly adopted (Carstensen, Gerlach, and Hübler 1997). In sum, unions are sceptical concerning profit sharing. The dominant Metal Workers Union (IG Metall) has always strongly resisted profit sharing. An exception has been the Construction Workers Union (IG Bau), which has more willingly accepted profit sharing.

Substantial debate continues over the economic effects of Germany's centralized collective bargaining. Opponents claim centralized bargaining is insufficiently responsive to the local conditions of the firm. According to this point of view, the reorganization of work from specialized tasks to multitasking and flexible production further contributes to the inefficiency of centralized collective bargaining (Lindbeck and Snower 1997). However, it remains a question exactly which aspects of firm policy face inflexible restrictions imposed by centralized agreements. Of particular interest here is the role centralized bargaining plays in the adoption of performance pay. Our preceding discussion suggests that individual schemes, and particularly individual-based piece rates, are not suitable for multitasking, as they distort the allocation of effort across the several tasks. In contrast, group incentives or sharing schemes provide incentives to exert effort in all activities that are relevant to the performance of the group or to the performance of the firm (Jirjahn 2000). Even if individual performance measures are available, payment schemes based on broader performance measures such as firm performance may be advantageous as flexible production implies that the nature of tasks change frequently. Frequent changes in the nature of tasks require frequent revisions of reward systems based on narrowly defined performance measures. However, the fixed costs of establishing and administering such reward systems work against frequent revisions of those reward systems and make them less suitable for flexible production. In sum, it appears that the reorganization of work toward multitasking makes the use of group-based incentives and sharing schemes more likely.[8]

Does centralized collective bargaining hinder or foster the use of particular types of performance pay? Hübler and Jirjahn (1998) show that establishments covered by collective bargaining agreements are more likely to use individual-based and group-based premium pay. Heywood and Jirjahn (2001) find that covered establishments are more likely to use group-based piece rates and less likely to use profit sharing.

The interpretation of the negative link between collective bargaining and profit sharing is not clear-cut. One explanation might be that profit sharing is difficult to negotiate on a central level because firms are heterogeneous and an appropriate design of a sharing scheme depends on firm-specific factors. This interpretation fits with work by Franz et al. (2000). The firms in their study claimed that collective bargaining agreements could be an important obstacle to the introduction of more flexible payment schemes. However, they provide no information about the mechanism through which the centralized bargaining system might hinder the use of particular payment schemes.

The negative link between the coverage by a collective agreement and profit sharing may simply reflect the unions' attitudes. Empirical studies for the United States and the United Kingdom suggest that unions often oppose profit sharing (Lindop 1989; Eaton and Voos 1992). Unions might fear the dispersion of earnings across firms. However, evidence from the United States shows that unions' attitudes toward profit sharing can change over time. Profit sharing may become a union objective in an era of concession bargaining when this profit sharing is important for the competitiveness of firms. In the United States, unions cooperated in the 1980s with the introduction of sharing schemes to reduce labor cost growth and to increase employment growth (Bell and Neumark 1993). Correspondingly, Kruse (1996) shows for the United States that the negative correlation between profit sharing and unionization disappears in longitudinal data. The future will show whether we will observe similar findings for Germany, but, as already mentioned, most German union remain skeptical of profit sharing.

Collective bargaining in Germany not only has a direct impact on the use of performance pay but also a less recognized indirect effect, which turns out to be quite important. Although codetermination and collective bargaining are formally independent there are important linkages. The interaction between collective bargaining and codetermination brings us back to the works councils. The WCA aims to restrict distributional conflicts at the establishment level, with works councils subject to a general peace obligation and not given the right to strike or negotiate over wages. If council and management fail to reach agreement, they appeal to an internal arbitration board *(Einigungsstelle)* or to the labor court. Despite this, formal and informal establishment-level negotiations play an important role. Councils can use their codetermination rights on social or personnel matters to obtain employer concessions on issues where they have no legal powers (Müller-Jentsch 1995, 60). If an employer and a works council fail to reach an agreement, the council can threaten to be uncooperative in areas where its consent is necessary. Codetermination strengthens the workers' bargaining power by weakening the employer's position in case of a disagreement. Hübler and Jirjahn (2000) present a bargaining model showing that this rent-seeking behavior of works councils results not only in higher wage rates but also in less productive work practices. Works councils are more likely to improve efficiency when the opportunities for rent-seeking behavior are restricted. There are several reasons why rent-seeking activities of the works councils are more restricted in establishments covered by collective bargaining agreements. First, establishment-level bargaining undermines the unions' power and contributes to dispersed earnings across firms. Second, because of the centralized bargaining system, unions are more interested in the industrywide employment levels than are the parties within an individual firm (Svejnar 1982). Therefore, a union will provide a council with expertise to strengthen the council's position against an opportunistic employer but it will try to restrict rent-seeking activities of the council.

Efficiency-enhancing work practices are more likely to be negotiated by management and works council when substantial distributional conflicts are moderated by unions and employers' associations outside the firm

(Freeman and Lazear 1995). The presence of a works council exerts a positive impact on the use of piece rates and profit sharing within the industrial relations regime covered by collective bargaining agreements but not within the uncovered industrial relations regime (Heywood, Hübler, and Jirjahn 1998). Heywood and Jirjahn (2001) find a positive link between works councils and the use of individual-based piece rates, individual-based premium pay and profit sharing for covered establishments but not for uncovered establishments. Correspondingly, Hübler and Jirjahn (2000) present evidence of a positive impact of councils on productivity within the covered regime but not in the uncovered regime. Conversely, the impact of works councils on wages is less strong in covered establishments than in uncovered establishments (Jirjahn and Klodt 1999; Hübler and Jirjahn 2000). In sum, the evidence supports the view that councils are less engaged in rent-seeking and more engaged in improving efficiency when a firm is covered by a collective agreement.

Several policy implications emerge from these findings. First, German works councils have attracted considerable international attention as an alternative form of worker participation to promote industrial democracy and economic performance. Indeed, the evidence from Germany shows that there is a positive link between works councils and the use of performance pay. However, the economic effect of works councils depends on the industrial relations system. A positive impact of works councils on performance pay and productivity can be found only in establishments covered by centralized collective bargaining agreements. Policies to encourage councils (including those by the European Commission) should take into account the absence of an influence within uncovered establishments. Moreover, it is certainly questionable whether or not councils would have a positive influence in decentralized systems of collective bargaining.

Second, relating pay to performance has been hailed as a major step toward alleviating unemployment in Germany and increasing the competitiveness of German firms. Opponents of centralized collective bargaining claim it imposes inflexible restrictions on firms. However, a negative link between the coverage by collective bargaining agreements and the use of performance pay can only be found in the case of profit sharing. The interpretation of this negative link is not clear. In contrast, coverage by a collective agreement has a positive impact on the use of the other individual-based and group-based payment schemes examined. In sum, there is little evidence that centralized collective bargaining hinders the use of performance pay.[9]

Moreover, centralized collective bargaining has an important indirect effect on firm performance in general and on performance pay in particular.

It reduces distributional conflicts on the firm level. Even if changes in the organization of work or in the method of pay must be negotiated on the establishment level, these changes are more easily negotiated when distributional conflicts are largely settled outside the firm. The decentralization of collective bargaining would imply that works councils become less effective in promoting trust and cooperation, and in turn, the use of performance pay.

Product Markets and Management Incentives

In addition to distributional conflicts and distrust between management and workers, slack and agency problems may hinder the introduction of performance pay. Incentives to overcome slack within a firm can be provided through aligning the compensation of managers to the firm's profit or through product market competition. Establishments with a profit-sharing plan for executive managers are more likely to use piece rates, premium pay, and profit sharing (Heywood and Jirjahn 2001). Industrial concentration has a negative impact on the use of piece rates and premium pay in Germany. Evidence from Australia confirms that product market competition exerts a positive impact on the use of performance pay (Drago and Heywood 1995). These results confirm the hypothesis that product market competition forces management to reduce slack and improve efficiency (Nickell 1999).

The nature of product markets also influences the entire human resource management (HRM) system of firms. A common typology distinguishes between mass production and lean manufacturing (e.g., Milgrom and Roberts 1995). Mass production is characterized by exploiting economies of scale with standardized products. In contrast, lean manufacturing is characterized by exploiting economies of scope with a broader range of more specialized products. Production adjusts quickly to changing markets and consumer demands. Arthur (1992) and MacDuffie (1995) show that mass production and lean manufacturing are based on distinct HRM systems. Mass production relies on narrowly defined tasks with low skill requirements. Lean manufacturing relies on workers performing a variety of tasks with high skill requirements. Firms with lean manufacturing are more likely to use participative work practices. Moreover, our preceding discussion suggests that the distinct HRM systems belonging to the respective business strategies should rely on distinct incentive schemes. Individual-based piece rates are more suitable for mass production, whereas group-based payment schemes and profit sharing are more suitable for lean manufacturing. Which business strategy is better depends, in part, on the respective product market structure. Therefore, different HRM systems and different types of payment schemes should be associated with different market structures. Heterogeneous consumer demands in an international market require a high degree of flexibility. Osterman (1994) finds evidence that firms are more likely to have a flexible work organization when they are selling their products in international markets.

Bertrand (1999) stresses another effect of product market competition that is relevant for the use of incentive schemes in firms. Firms in highly competitive product markets are more likely to renege on implicit contracts with their employees. Employers only care about their future reputation and behave honestly when they place a high value on future cooperation and trust. Other things being equal, HRM practices that require high-trust relationships are less feasible in highly competitive product markets. This effect of competition works against the slack reducing effect. For the United States, Kelly (1996) shows that the choice of a participative HRM system positively correlates with the firm's market power while Ichiniowski and Shaw (1995) obtain mixed results. It remains unclear what impact product market competition has on participative work practices in Germany. When the reputation mechanism does not work, the dual industrial relations system may protect workers from employer opportunism. Confirming this logic, Heywood and Jirjahn (2001) find a positive impact of industrial concentration on the use of profit sharing in the uncovered industrial relations regime but not in the covered regime.

Performance Pay and Human Resource Management Systems

Earlier studies examining performance pay in Germany focus on the determinants of single payment schemes. For example, they examine the determinants of whether or not firms adopt profit sharing. However, firms do not choose a single work practice. They choose a system consisting of more or less interrelated and internally consistent practices. In this section, we investigate pay-for-performance schemes as elements of broader HRM systems which interact with other HRM practices such as work teams and training. First, typical bundles of HRM practices are identified. Second, the determinants of the different HRM systems are estimated. The empirical analysis uses the third wave (1996) of the Hannover Panel because this wave contains the most detailed information on the personnel policy of the establishments.

Types of HRM Systems in German Manufacturing Firms

The analysis focuses on the HRM practices for blue-collar workers. Dummy variables for the organization of work, communication, training and payment schemes provide the basis for a cluster analysis. Organization, the complexity of tasks and production interdependencies between workers, is proxied by the presence of work teams with expanded involvement in decision making and increased responsibility. Communication and the information flow between management and workers is measured by the presence of regular meetings that inform workers about the economic situation of the establishment. Regular continuous training for blue-collar workers captures investments in the workers' human capital. Finally, all variables for the pay-for-performance schemes described in the second section are included: piece rates, group piece rates, premium pay, group premium pay, target-based schemes, and profit sharing for employees. Several interaction effects between these variables can be expected to be revealed by the cluster analysis.

Work teams and meetings. Workers organized in production teams have to perform a variety of tasks. These workers need information about changing markets and consumer demands to adjust their allocation of effort across tasks. Conversely, employees working in teams possess useful knowledge for the managers' business decisions.

Participative organization of work and training. Worker participation is associated with increased skill requirements (Adams 2000). Workers perform a broad set of tasks, and delegating decisions to them presupposes that they comprehend important elements of the production process. Social interaction is greater, and workers need to be trained in social competences. A participative organization of work also supports training because it provides opportunities for learning by doing.

Participative organization of work and method of pay. Group-based payment schemes and profit sharing induce cooperation of the work force by aligning the employer's and the workers' interests. This is particularly important when tasks are multidimensional, teams are self-managed, and workers are involved in the firm's decision making. Conversely, a participative organization of work may help overcome free-rider problems associated with collective incentive schemes. Teams and meetings provide opportunities for mutual monitoring and peer pressure. Moreover, the information flow between management and workers fosters trustful and cooperative relationships that make the use of performance pay feasible.

Training and method of pay. Since workers financially participate in productivity improvements, performance pay provides incentives for work-

Table 6.4

K-Means-Cluster Analysis: Means of HRM Practices Across Clusters of Firms

Cluster Variable	HRM			
	System 1	System 2	System 3	System 4
Profit sharing for employees	7.96**	10.26	29.35**	20.75
Piece rates (individual and/or group based)	0.00**	100.00**	0.00**	100.00**
Group-based piece rates	0.00**	11.54*	0.00**	50.94**
Premium pay (individual and/or group based)	8.71**	16.67	23.37**	47.17**
Group-based premium pay	1.00**	3.85	5.43	28.30**
Target-based schemes	6.22**	3.85**	10.33	24.53**
Work teams	17.16**	10.26**	84.78**	81.13**
Meetings	25.87**	25.64**	73.91**	62.26**
Regular training	6.72**	11.54**	55.43**	41.51**
Number of cases in the cluster	402	78	184	53

Note: * $p < 0.1$, t-test, ** $p < 0.05$, t-test comparing the mean for the cluster to the mean for the rest of the sample. An approximation t-test for unequal variances was used when indicated by a statistically significant F-test for equality of sample variances. Author's calculations based on the third wave of the Hannover Panel.

ers to participate in training activities. However, workers will acquire a broader set of skills only if they perform a broader set of tasks and if their remuneration is based on broader performance measures. Hence, we expect that group-based incentives and profit sharing induce workers' cooperation with training activities. Moreover, profit sharing makes the employees' remuneration flexible by aligning it with firm profit. Profit sharing contributes employment stability and fosters the workers' willingness to share the cost of firm-specific training. Conversely, training may improve the incentive effects of profit sharing when workers comprehend the firm's business strategy and the managers' decision making.

We now examine these interrelationships. Table 6.4 describes the four HRM systems identified by the cluster analysis. Tests determine whether the mean for a variable in a cluster is statistically above or below the mean for the rest of the establishments. This technique helps us determine the unique characteristics of a cluster (see Arthur 1992, 496). HRM system 1 is characterized by means of all HRM practices that are significantly below those for the rest of the establishments. Note that 56 percent of all establishments in the sample belong to this cluster. This cluster stands as a base of comparison. HRM system 2 can be labeled the traditional system of mass production. The means of the variables for work teams, meetings, and training are significantly below the means for the rest of the sample while the mean for the piece rate variable is significantly above that for the rest of the establishments. All the firms in this cluster use piece rates. At least 88 percent of these piece rate schemes are individually based. HRM system 3 and HRM system 4 represent alternative versions of lean manufacturing. Both clusters are characterized by means for work teams, meetings, and training above those for the rest of the establishments. However, they differ in the use of performance payment schemes. Establishments in HRM system 3 use profit sharing more frequently than the rest of the sample, and we label this HRM system lean manufacturing with profit sharing. Establishments in HRM system 4 use group-based payment schemes more frequently than the rest of the sample, and we label this HRM system lean manufacturing with group incentives. Note that establishments in this cluster also use target-based schemes more frequently. This result fits the theoretical argument that target-based schemes help overcome the free-rider problem (Petersen 1992).

Determinants of HRM Systems

According to our preceding discussion, the determinants of HRM systems can be broken into the following categories: industrial relations, product markets and managerial incentives, the nature of production technology, employment stability, and gender. We now use the available proxies to test the role of these determinants.

Previous studies based on the Hannover Panel showed a positive impact of works councils on the use of performance pay. Moreover, industrial relations based on trust and cooperation may foster employer provided training (Gerlach and Jirjahn 1999). The link between works councils and a participative organization of work is less clear-cut.[10] On the one hand, works councilors may fear the loss of power if employees directly communicate with managers. On the other hand, workers fearing job loss due to technological change do not reveal information about potential productivity enhancing innovations. In this case a works council may engender the trust that makes a participative organization feasible. Therefore, we expect that the presence of a works council will have a positive impact on the choice of HRM system 2, while the impact on the use of systems 3 and 4 is ambiguous. We also test for the effects of collective bargaining coverage. First, we will determine whether there is evidence that centralized collective bargaining imposes restrictions on the reorganization of work. Second, our preceding discussion suggests an important indirect effect of centralized bargaining. Even if the introduction of HRM practices must be negotiated on the establishment with works councils, these changes are more easily negotiated when substantial distributional conflicts are moderated on a central level by unions and employers' associations. Dummy variables for the various combinations of council presence and coverage by a collective agreement are constructed to distinguish the direct and indirect effects: works council by coverage by a collective agreement, works council by no coverage by a collective agreement, and no works council by coverage by a collective agreement.

Product markets and management incentives are captured in several variables. The presence of profit sharing for executive managers reduces agency problems by aligning the interests of managers and owners. If HRM practices increase profits, they are more likely to be implemented when managerial profit sharing is in place. Similarly, product market competition may induce managers to reduce slack. However, the impact of competition on the choice of HRM systems that require trust and cooperation is ambiguous. Trustful relationship between management and workers may be more feasible when there is less external pressure. Two variables capture competition: First, each establishment reports whether or not increasing market share is at the heart of the corporate strategy. Second, industrial concentration figures (sales of six largest firms as share of total) as measured by official German statistics are matched to thirty-two industrial sectors identified by the survey. Further, changing markets and consumer demands are proxied by a dummy variable equal to 1 if the international market is the most important market for the establishment. Since international markets require a high degree of flexibility, a positive impact on the use lean manufacturing can be expected.

A number of variables capture the nature of production. First, three dummy variables for broad industrial groups are included. Second, a dummy variable equal to 1 if the production machinery is of the newest level is included. Third, we control for firm size as measured by the number of employees as the fixed costs of establishing and administering a HRM system can be spread over more workers. Since the focus is on blue-collar workers, the proportion of blue-collar workers within an establishment is included in the analysis. Additionally, we include a dummy equal to 1 if the establishment is a single firm, not part of a multiestablishment firm. Establishments that are part of a larger firm have better access to information on innovative HRM practices. Fourth, we include the percentage of university and college graduates to capture complementarities between skilled blue-collar labor and skilled white-collar labor.

Employment stability is proxied by a dummy variable equal to 1 if the employment level at the end of 1995 is not below the employment level at the end of the two previous years. Finally, we control for the proportion of female employees.

A multinomial logit model (see Greene 1997, 914–917) is estimated to investigate the determinants of the HRM systems. A similar approach has been used by Ichniowski and Shaw (1995). Let x_i denote the vector of characteristics of establishment i and let β_j denote the vector of coefficients. There are four HRM systems ($j = 1, 2, 3, 4$). Using the normalization $\beta_1 = 0$, the probability that firm i chooses HRM system j is

$$\text{Prob}(HRM_i = 1) = \frac{1}{1 + \sum_{k=2}^{4} exp(\beta_k' x_i)} \quad (6.1)$$

$$\text{Prob}(HRM_i = j) = \frac{exp(\beta_j' x_i)}{1 + \sum_{k=2}^{4} exp(\beta_k' x_i)}, j = 2, 3, 4 \quad (6.2)$$

We can compute the log-odds ratios

$$\ln[\text{Prob}(HRM_i = j)/\text{Prob}(HRM_i = 1)] = \beta_j' x_i \quad (6.3)$$

The results are shown in Table 6.5. Works councils exert a positive impact on the use of HRM system 2 in both covered establishments and uncovered establishments. A combination of works council presence and coverage by a collective bargaining agreement exerts a positive impact on the choice of lean manufacturing with group-based incentive schemes (HRM system 4). No effect of the industrial relations variables can be found on the use of HRM system 3. Furthermore, there is no isolated effect of coverage by collective bargaining agreements on the choice of HRM systems. In sum, there is a positive link between works council presence and the traditional system of mass production. However, there is also evidence that the dual structure of industrial relations plays a positive role for the reorganization of work toward flexible production. Works councils, do indeed, foster the use of innovative HRM practices when substantial distributional conflicts are moderated outside the firm.

Incentives for managers are an important predictor for the choice of HRM system. Profit sharing for executive managers exerts a positive impact on the use of HRM systems 3 and 4. Industrial concentration exerts

Table 6.5

Multinomial Logit Model of HRM System Adoption

Variable	HRM System 2	HRM System 3	HRM System 4
Constant	−5.340	−1.243	−10.226
	(4.961)**	(2.109)**	(5.751)**
Proportion of women	1.198	0.341	0.794
	(1.807)*	(0.695)	(0.912)
Proportion of blue-collar workers	1.700	−0.068	5.081
	(1.863)*	(0.124)	(3.482)**
Proportion of university and college graduates	−4.939	2.484	8.330
	(1.267)	(1.332)	(2.646)**
Production technology at the newest level	−0.030	0.377	0.311
	(0.100)	(1.815)*	(0.844)
Firm size (number of employees)	0.003	$0.003 \cdot 10^{-1}$	0.004
	(1.815)*	(0.751)	(3.483)**
Firm size squared	$-0.001 \cdot 10^{-3}$	$-0.002 \cdot 10^{-5}$	$-0.001 \cdot 10^{-3}$
	(1.148)	(0.515)	(2.607)**
Firm is no subsidiary and has no subsidiaries	0.082	−0.398	−0.148
	(0.273)	(1.902)*	(0.394)
Works council * collective agreement	0.901	−0.132	1.106
	(1.971)**	(0.492)	(1.648)*
Works council * no collective agreement	0.942	−0.041	0.300
	(1.782)*	(0.117)	(0.347)
No works council * collective agreement	0.355	0.122	0.216
	(0.653)	(0.408)	(0.228)
Employment level in 1995 not below the level in each of the two previous years	−0.765	0.020	−0.203
	(2.558)**	(0.100)	(0.560)
Profit sharing for executive managers	0.397	0.541	1.189
	(1.416)	(2.703)**	(3.116)**
Management plans to increase the market share of the firm	0.559	0.091	0.178
	(1.985)**	(0.454)	(0.506)
Industrial concentration	−0.029	0.008	−0.014
	(2.167)**	(1.156)	(1.050)
International market is the most important market	0.037	0.524	−0.184
	(0.102)	(2.073)**	(0.423)
Industry dummies	Yes		
Log likelihood	−641.235		
Number of cases	658		

Note: T-statistics are in parentheses, * $p < 0.1$, ** $p < 0.05$. Author's calculations based on the third wave of the Hannover Panel.

a negative impact on the use of HRM system 2, while there is a positive effect of a strategy to increase the market share. These findings support the notion that competition forces management to reduce slack. However, concentration and increasing the market share have no impact on the use of lean manufacturing systems. In contrast, selling products in international markets has a positive impact on the use of HRM system 3. This confirms the hypothesis that production for international markets requires a high degree of flexibility.

There is a positive effect of new technology on the use of HRM system 3 and a positive effect of the proportion of employees with university or college degree on the use of HRM system 4. These findings support the contention that skilled blue-collar labor complements modern machinery and skilled white-collar labor. Firm size and the proportion of blue-collar workers have a positive impact on the use of the HRM systems 2 and 4. No impact of these variables can be found on the use of lean manufacturing with profit sharing. In the case of profit sharing there may be two opposing effects of firm size. On the one hand, the fixed costs of this payment scheme can be spread over more workers. On the other hand, the free rider problem is more severe in larger firms. Firms that are not part of multifirm establishments are less likely to choose HRM system 3.

The proportion of female employees has a positive impact on the use of HRM system 2 but not on the choice of the HRM systems 3 and 4. This result complements the finding by Heywood and Jirjahn (2001) that German establishments with a high proportion of women are likely to use individual-based payment schemes but not group-based incentive schemes.[11] Finally, our proxy for employment stability is negatively associated with the use of HRM system 2. This fits the view that shorter-term employment relations lend themselves to immediate rewards systems and less investment in training.

Concluding Observations

Several findings of the present study of Germany complement studies from other countries. Firm size exerts a positive impact on the use of performance pay. Establishments with a high proportion of women are more likely to use individual-based piece rates. Group-based incentives and profit sharing are components of innovative HRM systems that rely on teamwork, information sharing, and regular training for workers. In contrast, individual-based piece rates are part of the traditional system of mass production. National product market competition exerts a positive impact on the use of this traditional system, whereas firms selling their products in international markets are more likely to use an innovative HRM system.

Germany has an industrial relations systems that is distinct from most other countries and this has implications for the use of various forms of performance related pay. The interaction effect between works councils and collective bargaining plays an important role. Works councils may foster trust and cooperation within firms. However, this requires that councils be engaged more in efficiency enhancing activities than in rent-seeking activities. Therefore, works councils exert a positive impact on the use of performance pay only when substantial distributional conflicts are moderated outside the firm between unions and employers' associations. This fits as part of a larger ongoing discussion on the efficiency or inefficiency of centralized collective bargaining. A direct positive impact of collective bargaining can be found on the use of individual-based and/or group-based piece rates and premium pay, whereas there is a negative impact on the use of profit sharing. However, in case of profit sharing the interaction effect with codetermination works against this negative direct effect. Councils exert a positive impact on the use of profit sharing in covered firms but not in uncovered firms.

Examining the choice of HRM systems we found that the presence of works councils is associated with a more traditional HRM system. However, there is also evidence that councils in covered establishments exert a positive impact on the use of a innovative HRM system relying on group incentives and/or target-based schemes. No effect of industrial relations can be found on the choice of the HRM system relying on profit sharing. These explorative results clearly call for further research. In particular, the traditional skepticism of unions and the ability of councils to create trust deserve a careful case-by-case examination.

Notes

1. It should be stressed that when using sample weights (which only correct for the stratification by establishment size) the proportion of establishments with performance pay is smaller than that in the unweighted statistics. However, the pattern for the various payment schemes is similar whether or not using sample weights. Based on sample weights, for 1996 we obtain: 8 percent of the establishments with piece rates, 2 percent with group piece rates, 7 percent with premium pay, 1 percent with group premium pay, 9 percent with target-based schemes, and 11 percent with profit sharing. In sum, 28 percent of the establishments used at least one of those payment schemes in 1996.

2. Most German studies find that profit sharing is associated with increased firm performance (see Carstensen, Gerlach, and Hübler 1997). Using data from firms in the metalworking industry, FitzRoy and Kraft (1987) obtain a positive impact of profit

sharing on total factor productivity. However, reestimating the effect of profit sharing on value added, they demonstrate significant selection effects (FitzRoy and Kraft 1995). Firms are more likely to use profit sharing when there are large productivity effects of this incentive scheme. Using data from the Hannover Panel, Jirjahn (1998) finds a positive link between profit sharing and subjective measures of profitability.

3. Jirjahn and Stephan (2000) use a matched employer-employee data set containing detailed information about the individual worker's qualification. Blue-collar workers remunerated by piece rates receive significantly higher hourly wage rates. This result confirms other international studies (see Prendergast 1999, 16–18). In contrast, studies with establishment data obtain mixed results for Germany. Kraft (1991) finds no significant impact of piece rates on total factor productivity, whereas FitzRoy and Kraft (1995) find a positive impact of piece rates on value added in firms not using profit sharing. Hübler and Klodt (1995) show that there are positive effects of piece rates and premium pay on sales, while Jirjahn (1998) obtains a negative impact of piece rates on value added. On the one hand, these results fit partly to theoretical consideration. On the other hand the results should be interpreted with some caution. Piece rates are used typically for blue-collar workers who perform simple jobs. If a study does not effectively control for the complexity of tasks and for the workers' human capital, the piece rate variable will reflect these factors. This can result in an insignificant or even negative coefficient of the piece rate variable. This possibility clearly calls for further research taking into account unobserved factors that have a positive impact on the use of piece rates but a negative impact on the establishment's performance.

4. There is some evidence that profit sharing is more likely in establishments with a production technology that is not of the most recent vintage (Heywood and Jirjahn 2001). This result, together with the finding by Askildsen, Jirjahn, and Smith (2000), suggests that firms modernizing their technology use profit sharing as an incentive scheme to ensure the cooperation of the work force.

5. However, there is an alternative interpretation. Promotions acting as tournaments give incentives for mutual sabotage activities that result in reduced efficiency (Lazear 1989). Workers remunerated by profit sharing also share this efficiency loss (Itoh 1992). Therefore, profit sharing reduces sabotage activities resulting from tournaments within establishments.

6. Using individual data, Booth and Frank (1999) find that women are less likely to receive performance pay. However, Geddes and Heywood (2000) show that these contrasting findings can be reconciled. Typically the studies failing to find the traditional positive relationship between women and performance pay use broad measures of performance pay which include bonus schemes and profit sharing.

7. Contrast these results with those discussed by Parent (chapter 2 in this volume), suggesting that women gain less from piece rates in the United States.

8. Lindbeck and Snower (1997) provide a somewhat contrasting argument. They argue that centralized collective bargaining follows the rule "equal pay for equal work." Different workers performing the same tasks receive the same wage. This rule presupposes that tasks are clearly defined and that workers within a task have similar abilities and qualifications, but multitasking implies that there are diverse combinations of tasks and that particular tasks are performed by heterogeneous workers. Therefore, the incentives for multitasking should depend on the respective worker's combination of tasks and on the respective worker's abilities. Obviously, this argumentation presupposes that incentives for multitasking can be based on the worker's individual performance. However, our theoretical argumentation and previous empirical studies suggest that multitasking is associated with the use group incentives or sharing schemes.

9. Franz and Pfeiffer (2001) emphasize evidence that collective agreements impose restrictions on the adjustment of the wage level.
10. Addison, Schnabel, and Wagner (1997) find a negative correlation between work teams and works councils with the first wave of the Hannover Panel. However, Müller-Jentsch (1995, 70) notes that weak work councils are more likely to resist the introduction of management-led participation. Strong councils are self-confident enough to moderate a participative organization of work.
11. The author experimented with various cluster solutions as dependent variables. There was sometimes a significantly positive relationship between the proportion of women and the lean manufacturing system using profit sharing. This finding accords with that of Heywood and Jirjahn (2001).

References

Adams, C. P. 2000. "Shopfloor Decision Making in U.S. Manufacturing," Working paper, University of Wisconsin–Madison.
Addison, J. T., Schnabel, C., and Wagner, J. 1997. "On the Determinants of Mandatory Works Councils in Germany." *Industrial Relations* 36: 419–445.
Arthur, J. B. 1992. "The Link Between Business Strategy and Industrial Relations in American Steel Minimills." *Industrial and Labor Relations Review* 45: 488–506.
Askildsen, J. E., Jirjahn, U., and Smith, S. C. 2000. "Works Councils and Environmental Investment: Theory and Evidence from German Panel Data." Working Paper, University of Hannover, Germany.
Bell, L., and Neumark, D. 1993. "Lump Sum Payments and Profit Sharing Plans in the Union Sector of the United States Economy." *Economic Journal* 103: 602–619.
Belman, D., and Heywood, J. S. 1988. "Incentive Schemes and Racial Wage Discrimination." *Review of Black Political Economy* 17: 47–56.
Bertrand, M. 1999. "From the Invisible Handshake to the Invisible Hand? How Import Competition Changes the Employment Relationship." NBER Working Paper No. 6900.
Bispinck, R. 2000. *Tarifentgelt nach Leistung und Erfolg: Regelungen in ausgewählten Tarifbereichen.* (Performance related pay: Evidence from collective agreements). *WSI Informationen zur Tarifpolitik* (Economic and Social Institute's *Information on Collective Bargaining*), No. 43.
Booth, A., and Frank, J. 1999. "Earnings, Productivity, and Performance-Related Pay." *Journal of Labor Economics* 17: 447–463.
Brand, R., Carstensen, V., Gerlach, K., and Klodt, T. 1996. "The Hannover Panel." Discussion Paper No. 2, University of Hannover, Germany.
Bull, C. 1987. "The Existence of Self-Enforcing Implicit Contracts." *Quarterly Journal of Economics* 52: 147–159.
Carstensen, V., Gerlach, K., and Hübler, O. 1997. "Profit Sharing in Germany." Working Paper, University of Hannover, Germany.
Drago, R., and Heywood, J. S. 1995. "The Choice of Payment Schemes: Australian Evidence," *Industrial Relations* 34: 507–531.
Drago, R., and Turnbull, G. K. 1988. "Individual and Group Piece Rates Under Team Technologies." *Journal of the Japanese and International Economies* 2: 1–10.
Eaton, A., and Voos, P. B. 1992. "Unions and Contemporary Innovations in Work Organization, Compensation, and Employee Participation." In *Unions and Economic Competitiveness,* eds. L. Mishel and P. B. Voos. Armonk, NY: M. E. Sharpe, 173–215.

Fitzenberger, B., and Franz, W. 1999. "Industry-Level Wage Bargaining: A Partial Rehabilitation—The German Experience." *Scottish Journal of Political Economy* 46: 437–457.
FitzRoy, F. R., and Kraft, K. 2000. "Co-Determination, Efficiency, and Productivity." Working Paper, University of Essen, Germany.
———. 1995. "On the Choice of Incentives in Firms." *Journal of Economic Behavior and Organization* 26: 145–160.
———. 1987. "Cooperation, Productivity, and Profit Sharing." *Quarterly Journal of Economics* 102: 493–504.
Franz, W., Gutzeit, M., Lessner, J. Oechsler, W. A., Pfeiffer, F., Reichmann, L, Rieble, V., and Roll, J. 2000. *Flexibilisierung der Arbeitsentgelte und Beschäftigungseffekte* (Flexibility of Payments and Employment Effects) Documentation No. 00–09, Centre for European Economic Research, Mannheim, Germany.
Franz, W., and Pfeiffer, F. 2001. *Tarifbindung und die ökonomische Rationalität von Lohnrigiditäten* (Collective Bargaining and the Economic Rationale for Wage Rigidities) Discussion Paper No. 01–01, Centre for European Economic Research, Mannheim, Germany.
Freeman, R. B., and Lazear, E. P. 1995. "An Economic Analysis of Works Councils." In *Works Councils—Consultation, Representation and Cooperation in Industrial Relations,* eds. J. Rogers and W. Streeck. Chicago: University of Chicago Press, 27–52.
Freeman, R. B., and Medoff, J. L. 1984. *What Do Unions Do?* New York: Basic Books.
Geddes, L. A., and Heywood, J. S. 2000. "Gender and Incentive Pay: Individual Data." Working Paper, University of Wisconsin–Milwaukee.
Gerlach, K., and Jirjahn, U. 1999. "Employer Provided Further Training: Evidence from German Establishment Data." Working Paper, University of Hannover, Germany.
Goldin, C. 1986. "Monitoring Costs and Occupational Segregation by Sex: A Historical Analysis." *Journal of Labor Economics* 4: 1–27.
Greene, W. H. 1997. *Econometric Analysis,* 3d ed. Englewood Cliffs, NJ: Prentice Hall International.
Heywood, J. S., Hübler, O., and Jirjahn, U.. 1998. "Variable Payment Schemes and Industrial Relations: Evidence from Germany." *Kyklos* 51: 237–257.
Heywood, J. S., and Jirjahn, U. 2001. "Payment Schemes, Gender and Industrial Relations in Germany." *Industrial and Labor Relations Review,* forthcoming.
Heywood, J. S., Siebert, W. S., and Wei, X. 1997. "Payment by Results Systems: British Evidence." *British Journal of Industrial Relations* 35: 1–22.
Heywood, J. S., and Wei, X. 1997. "Piece-Rate Payment Schemes and the Employment of Women: The Case of Hong Kong." *Journal of Comparative Economics* 25: 237–255.
Holmström, B., and Milgrom, P. 1991. "Multitask Principal-Agent Analyses, Incentive Contracts, Asset Ownership, and Job Design." *Journal of Law, Economics, and Organization* 7: 24–52.
Hübler, O., and Jirjahn, U. 2000. "Works Councils and Collective Bargaining in Germany: The Impact on Productivity and Wages," Working Paper, University of Hannover, Germany.
———. 1998. *Zeit-, Leistungs-und Gruppenentlohnung—Empirische Untersuchungen mit Betriebsdaten zur Entlohnungsart* (Payment schemes—empirical analysis with established data) In *Ökonomische Analysen betrieblicher Strukturen und Entwicklungen: Das Hannoveraner Firmenpanel* (Economic analysis of establishments: The Hannover Firm panel), ed. K. Gerlach, O. Hübler, and W. Meyer. Frankfurt am Main: Campus, 148–172.

Hübler, O., and Klodt, T. 1995. *Anreize für Arbeitnehmer—Ein betrieblicher Erfolgsfaktor?* (Incentive pay for workers: Does it increase firm performance?) In *Erfolgreich Produzieren in Niedersachsen* (Successful production in Lower Saxony), ed. U. Schasse and J. Wagner. Hannover: Niedersaechsisches Institut fuer Wirtschaftforschung (NIW), 95–123.

Ichniowski, C., and Shaw, K. 1995. "Old Dogs and New Tricks: Determinants of the Adoption of Productivity-Enhancing Work Practices." In *Brookings Papers on Economic Activity*, ed. M. Baily, P. Reiss, and C. Winston, 1–65. Washington, D.C.: Brookings Institution.

Itoh, H. 1992. "Cooperation in Hierarchical Organizations: An Incentive Perspective." *Journal of Law, Economics, and Organization* 8: 321–345.

Jirjahn, U. 2000. "Incentives for Multitasking: Fixed Wages or Profit Sharing?" *Economic Analysis* 3: 137–148.

———. 1998. *Effizienzwirkungen von Erfolgsbeteiligung und Partizipation: Eine mikroökonomische Analyse*, (The efficincy of profit sharing and participation: A microeconomic analysis) Frankfurt am Main: Campus.

Jirjahn, U., and Klodt, T. 1999. *Lohnhöhe, industrielle Beziehungen und Produktmärkte* (Wages, industrial relations and product markets). In *Zur Entwicklung von Lohn und Beschäftigung auf der Basis von Betriebs-und Unternehmensdaten* (Analysis of wages and employment with establishment data), ed. L. Bellmann, S. Kohaut, and M. Lahner. Nürnberg: BeitrAB, 27–54.

Jirjahn, U., and Stephan, G. 2000. "Gender and Pay for Performance: The Impact of Tenure, Flexibility and Discrimination." Working paper, University of Hannover, Germany.

Kandel, E., and Lazear, E. P. 1992. "Peer Pressure and Partnerships." *Journal of Political Economy* 100: 801–817.

Kelly, M. R. 1996. "Participative Bureaucracy and Productivity in the Machined Products Sector." *Industrial Relations* 35: 374–399.

Kraft, K. 1991. "The Incentive Effects of Dismissals, Efficiency Wages, Piece-Rates and Profit-Sharing." *Review of Economics and Statistics* 73: 451–459.

Kreps, D. M. 1990. "Corporate Culture and Economic Theory." In *Perspectives on Positive Political Economy*, eds. J. E. Alt and K. A. Shepsle. Cambridge: Cambridge University Press, 90–143.

Kruse, D. L. 1996. "Why Do Firms Adopt Profit-Sharing and Employee Ownership Plans." *British Journal of Industrial Relations* 34: 515–538.

Lazear, E. P. 2000. "Performance Pay and Productivity." *American Economic Review* 90: 1346–1361.

———. 1989. "Pay Equality and Industrial Politics." *Journal of Political Economy* 97: 561–80.

———. 1981. "Agency, Earnings Profiles, Productivity, and Hours Restrictions." *American Economic Review* 71: 606–621.

Lindbeck, A., and Snower, D. J. 1997: "Centralized Bargaining, Multitasking and Work Incentives." Discussion Paper No. 1563. London, UK: Centre for Economic Policy Research.

Lindop, E. 1989. "The Turbulent Birth of British Profit Sharing." *Personnel Management* 21: 44–47.

MacDuffie, J. P. 1995. "Human Resource Bundles and Manufacturing Performance: Organizational Logic and Flexible Production." *Industrial and Labor Relations Review* 48: 197–221.

MacLeod, W. B. 1988. "Equity, Efficiency, and Incentives in Cooperative Teams." In

Advances in the Economic Analysis of Participatory and Labor-Managed Firms, vol. 3, eds. C. Jones and J. Svejnar. Greenwich, CT: JAI Press, 5–23.

Milgrom, P., and Roberts, J. 1995. "Continuous Adjustment and Fundamental Change in Business Strategy and Organization." In *Trends in Business Organization: Do Participation and Cooperation Increase Competitiveness?* ed. H. Siebert. Tübingen: JC. B. Mohr, 231–264.

———. 1992. *Economics, Organization and Management.* Englewood Cliffs, NJ: Prentice-Hall International.

Milkovich, G. T, and Newman, J. M. 1996. *Compensation,* 5th ed. Chicago: Irwin.

Müller-Jentsch, W. 1995. "Germany: From Collective Voice to Co-Management." In *Works Councils—Consultation, Representation and Cooperation in Industrial Relations,* eds. J. Rogers and W. Streeck. Chicago: University of Chicago Press, 53–78.

Nickell, S. 1999. "Product Markets and Labour Markets." *Labour Economics* 6: 1–20.

Osterman, P. 1994. "How Common Is Workplace Transformation and Who Adopts It?" *Industrial and Labor Relations Review* 47: 173–188.

Petersen, T. 1992. "Individual, Collective, and Systems Rationality in Work Groups: Dilemmas and Market-Type Solutions." *American Journal of Sociology* 98: 469–510.

Prendergast, C. 1999. "The Provision of Incentives in Firms." *Journal of Economic Literature* 37: 7–63.

Smith, S. C. 1991. "On the Economic Rationale for Codetermination Law." *Journal of Economic Behavior and Organization* 12: 261–281.

Statistisches Bundesamt (German statistical office). *Löhne und Gehälter: Arbeiterverdienste nach Wirtschaftszweigen und ausgewählten Merkmalen 1995,* Fachserie 16, Heft 2 (Wages and salaries, series16, no.2).

———. 1990. *Löhne und Gehälter: Arbeiterverdienste nach Wirtschaftszweigen und ausgewählten Merkmalen 1990,* Fachserie 16, Heft 2 (Wages and salaries, series 16, no.2).

———. 1978. *Löhne und Gehälter: Arbeiter-und Angestelltenverdienste im Produzierende Gewerbe, im Groß-und Einzelhandel, be Kreditinstituten und im Versicherungsgewerbe 1978,* Fachserie 16 (Wages and salaries, series 16, no.2).

———. 1972. *Preise, Löhne, Wirtschaftsrechnungen: Gehalts-und Lohnstrukturerhebungen– Arbeiterverdienste 1972,* Fachserie M, Reihe 17 (Prices and wages: Salary and wage structure, series M).

———. 1966. *Preise, Löhne, Wirtschaftsrechnungen: Gehalts-und Lohnstrukturerhebungen—Arbeiterverdienste 1966,* Fachserie M, Reihe 17 (Prices and wages: Salary and wage strucure, series M).

Svejnar, J. 1982. "On the Theory of a Participatory Firm." *Journal of Economic Theory* 27: 313–333.

Chapter 7
Performance Related Pay in Australia

John Shields

Introduction

While performance related pay in Australia may have lacked the prominence and notoriety attained in other Anglophone countries, its use is as old as European settlement itself. Since the first cargo of convicts arrived from Britain in 1788, Australian workers have labored under payment systems in which rewards have been linked directly to individual or work group performance. For most of the twentieth century, the Australian industrial landscape was dominated by systems of compulsory state arbitration and centralized award making. By according primacy to time-based occupational and national living, basic, or minimum wages, centralized arbitral regulation influenced the manner in which wage incentives, bonuses, and other forms of performance related pay were applied in Australian workplaces. Yet, as Wright (1991, 1994) has demonstrated, even during the heyday of arbitration in the mid-twentieth century, Australian employers engaged in significant experimentation with performance pay of various types. In this sense, recent interest in and experimentation with performance pay in Australian public and private sector workplaces has historical precedent. Equally, the available evidence indicates that the past decade has witnessed a significant resurgence in performance related pay usage; a resurgence primarily associated with a shift from "centralized" award making and collective bargaining to "decentralized" modes of bargaining and pay determination.

This chapter seeks both to assess these recent developments and to locate them in a historical context by exploring elements of continuity and discontinuity in Australian pay practice. The chapter is divided into three main sections and draws on data from a variety of sources. The first section overviews the historical development of performance pay in Australia until the mid-1980s. The second section examines the resurgence of performance pay in the context of an increasingly decentralized system of bargaining. The third section details recent developments in performance pay practices in both private and public sectors. A conclusion summarizes the main contours of temporal and spatial variation and considers the implications for the future of performance pay in twenty-first-century Australia.

Historical Background

This section examines secular changes in the type and incidence of performance pay in Australia since the beginning of permanent European settlement in 1788. Particular attention is paid to the impact of six key variables: (1) long-term structural change in the Australian economy, (2) short-term economic cycles, (3) trade union presence, (4) the role of the regulatory state, (5) changes in organizational structure, (6) and developments in management ideas and strategy. With these variables in mind, three main historical phases are identified: (1) the colonial or "pre-arbitral" era (1788–1900); (2) the early-twentieth-century or "early-arbitral" era (1900–1940); (3) the period of the long boom (1940–1980), which might also be characterized as the "high-arbitral" era. Each of these periods corresponds to major shifts in one or more of the key variables identified above, and in the political economy of Australian capitalism. It is also instructive to note that each of these periods was associated with a particular nomenclature and set of performance pay practices: "task" and "piece" work in the nineteenth century; "payment by results" in the early twentieth century; "wage incentives" in the mid-twentieth century; "financial participation" in the 1970s; "performance related pay" in the 1980s and 1990s; and, most recently, "contribution-based pay."

Working by "Task" and "Piece" (1788–1901)

Throughout the nineteenth century, as the economy shifted first from convictism to primary production and extraction (whaling, wool, gold-mining, coal mining, wheat and beef production) and then, starting in the 1860s, to nascent urban manufacturing, two specific types of payment by results, namely task work and straight piece work, vied with time rates. With labor in chronically short supply for most of the period up to 1840, British colonial administrators and managers soon came to appreciate both the limited currency of physical coercion in a land of permanent exile and the difficulties of extracting work effort from convict labor. With supervisory skills also in short supply, the first thirty years of European settlement witnessed a struggle between male convict workers and their keepers over effort levels. Along the way, male convicts became the focus of quite elaborate systems of performance and reward management. One of the first and most significant of these strategies was task work, which was employed widely in the "government" sector from 1793 onward. This involved using prototypical methods of work study to determine a minimum acceptable quantity of work for specific jobs. Task work applied both to work carried out individually and to work undertaken by teams. Those to whom the system was more readily applied were those whose work could most easily be quantified—sawyers, grass cutters, stonecutters, stone masons, brick makers, bricklayers, shell gatherers, carters, and the like (Robbins 1999). Yet, as Robbins explains, the practice amounted to "a crude motivational device": the more quickly the convicts completed their daily or weekly tasks, the more "free" time they could devote to working for wages in the emergent "private" sector. Other short-term incentives applied to convict workers included extra rations and day passes, while the main long-term incentive was the prized ticket of leave. In this sense, task work allowed reward for greater personal effort (Robbins 1999; Patmore 1991). The task work system retained its importance until the mid-1820s, when convict labor was redirected to the private sector by means of assignment and forced labor itself began to yield place to free wage labor (Robbins 1999).

By the 1830s, straight piece work established a strong presence in the private sector. In the towns, preindustrial work practices, including customary payment by the piece for trade journeymen, were common in craft workshops, with the first trade unions seeking to establish standard piece rates. Piece rates were common in tailoring, boot making and shoemaking, printing, and cabinetmaking. These schemes were perceived as unfair and arbitrary, with the result that these occupations were to be among the first to unionize (Thomas [1919] 1962; Patmore 1991). In the primary sector (agriculture and mining), payment by results was applied to a range of occupations, including whalers, shearers, reapers, threshers, and fencers (Sullivan 1985; Merritt 1986).

During the round of urban industrialization which followed the gold rushes of the 1850s, piece rates became even more common. In the burgeoning urban clothing and footwear industries of the 1870s and 1880s, piece rates were dominant for both factory-based employees and outwork-ers. Piece work was common in other urban mass-production, including brick making, tin smithing, furniture making, and coopering. (Markey 1988). Piece rates were also widely used in the urban building trades, particularly in subcontracting (Coolican 1988) and were common in maritime and road transport, especially among waterside workers and road carters. In the primary sector, piece rates emerged as the dominant mode of remuneration for sheep shearing and coal mining, and were virtually universal among seasonal rural workers, including sheep shearers, wool pressers, wool scourers, wool classers, carriers, ploughmen, harvesters, threshers, and fruit pickers (Lee and Fahey 1986; Merritt 1986).

Workers and their unions responded to piece rates in disparate ways. For coal miners and shearers, piece rates were an accepted fact of working life. On the New South Wales coalfields, beginning in the 1850s, miners organized to regulate rather than resist piece rates (Hagan and Fisher 1973). The advent of unionism among the itinerant sheep shearers in the 1880s also stemmed largely from the desire to achieve and uphold uniform rates per hundred sheep (Hearn and Knowles 1996; Merritt 1986). Similarly, newspaper hand compositors, who were among the most highly paid of all Australian workers, had a strong preference for piece rates, a preference undiminished by the introduction of mechanized typesetting in the mid-1890s. The nature of their skills and the level of workplace control they exercised through their unions allowed them to regulate both effort levels and piece rates (Hagan and Fisher 1973; Frances 1993).

Conversely, unionized tradesmen in the emergent engineering industry—fitters and turners, molders, blacksmiths, and boilermakers—consistently resisted the introduction of piece rates. That they were able to do this was due partly to their organizational resilience and partly to the fact that the staple activity of the late colonial engineering industry was jobbing and repair work rather than standardized mass production. (Shields 1997). In 1892, underground miners in the remote silver-lead-zinc mining locality of Broken Hill failed in an attempt to prevent the displacement of time rates by team-based contracting and payment by results (Kennedy 1978).

Between the two extremes of acceptance and resistance was the growing number of male urban industrial workers, such as boot makers and tailors, who found themselves caught between their attachment to customary piece-rate practices and factory employers' growing attraction to outwork. Initially, these workers strove to uphold customary piece rate standards while at the same time opposing cut-rate outwork. However, success in limiting outwork came at a cost, with employers in both industries intensifying task subdivision, mechanization, and work force feminization. During the depression of the 1890s, in those sections of factory production where productive reorganization had been most pronounced, piece work itself began to give way to time rates and task work.

Awarding Payment by Results (1901–1940)

The advent of an Australian nation state in 1901 and of compulsory industrial arbitration and award making, during the ensuing decade ushered in an era of systematic state involvement in the determination of both pay levels and methods (Deery, Plowman, and Walsh 1997; Patmore 1991). The most obvious and significant consequences of award making was the introduction of legally enforceable minimum time rates (base rates plus margins for skill) and a standard forty-eight-hour week across a wide spectrum of occupations and industries (Dabscheck and Niland 1981). In some industries, the application of time wages and standard hours clearly reduced the attractions to employers of straight piece work. For instance, in feminized sections of the footwear and clothing industries, where outwork and factory piece work were already giving way to time-based task work, the imposition of minimum award wages accelerated preexisting trends (Frances 1993). Yet, in these and other industries, enforcing minimum award standards proved highly problematic. In the clothing industry in particular, outwork remained a major presence and the enforcement of minimum standards posed constant challenges (Ellem 1989).

In recent years there has been a view that arbitration and national minimum wage setting were antithetical to flexible pay practices (Blandy and Niland 1986; Plowman 1992; Buchanan and Callus 1993). Yet, performance related pay not only survived under arbitration but, at times, actually flourished *beside* and *above* it. In the early decades of award making, piece rates were incorporated directly into a great many awards and consent agreements. In industries, occupations and tasks where use of simple piece rates was a long-established custom, early awards made by state wages boards and arbitration courts, and those made subsequently by the Commonwealth Court of Conciliation and Arbitration, served to confirm, codify, and regulate preexisting practice. This was the case, for example, in shearing, coal mining, and printing, and in certain sections of the footwear and clothing industries dominated by "skilled" male workers, most notably "making" and "pressing" (Hagan and Fisher 1973; Merritt 1986; Frances 1993). In many other occupations, where piece rates were used, the tendency was for piece rates to be incorporated into awards as a conditional alternative to minimum time rates. In fixing piece rates, tribunals generally incorporated controls to protect the workers affected and, in many cases, awards provided for union or worker participation in the setting of rates.

Typical piece-rate clauses stipulated that rates should be set such that an average worker could earn at least 10 percent above otherwise equal minimum award time rates (Cockfield 1993; Anderson 1929).

The Commonwealth Court of Conciliation and Arbitration demonstrated a preparedness to extend the scope of performance pay, union opposition notwithstanding. This was particularly the case in new tariff-protected manufacturing industries where mass production methods and repetitive work made piece rates appear feasible (Cockfield 1993; Anderson 1929). Piece rates were progressively incorporated in awards covering stove making, agricultural implement making, sheet-metal working, machine molding, metal manufacturing, and other mass production industries (Wright 1994). At the federal level a new generation of arbitration judges embraced a progressive campaign to alter remuneration methods, labor costs, and productivity levels in the interest of greater "national efficiency" and as a counter to union claims for a forty-four hour week (Blackburn 1996). Tribunals showed a willingness to sanction a range of new individual incentives and "scientific management" practices. During World War I, private and public sector employers alike experimented with systematic work measurement, and with forms of "scientific" payment by results.

One of the most controversial forms of performance pay was the premium bonus. Under premium bonus plans of the type advocated by F. A. Halsey, an engineer who developed the premium bonus as an alternative to scientific work management, workers who beat a task standard received a bonus based on the time saved and calculated according to time rates (Patmore 1998, Patmore 1994). Between 1915 and 1920, premium bonus schemes were introduced at the newly opened Broken Hill Proprietary Company Steelworks at Newcastle, at the state-owned Lithgow Small Arms Factory, and in the main metropolitan workshops operated by the government-owned New South Wales Railways. Each of these initiatives encountered direct but unsuccessful union resistance, particularly to the use of time study and job card techniques used to set "scientific" task standards.

In the manufacturing sector generally, Taylorist time-study methods were used extensively to reset task standards for new incentive schemes. Two of the first Australian firms to make use of time study methods were a Melbourne agricultural implement firm, the Sunshine Harvester Works, and a shirt manufacturer, Pelaco. In both cases, the adoption of scientific management techniques dates from 1911. In that year, following a major dispute, management at the Sunshine plant refused to recognize the union, introduced semiautomatic machine tools, piece rates, and American management methods. These initiatives were subsequently endorsed by State

Wages Boards and by the Commonwealth Arbitration Court (Cockfield 1998; Fahey and Lack 2000). At Pelaco, time study methods were used in conjunction with both task work and piece rates for female machinists (Frances 1993). Approval of these practices by state and federal tribunals encouraged their spread to other large clothing factories (Ellem 1989).

During the interwar years, subsidiaries and affiliates of U.S. manufacturing firms, including General Motors, Standard Telephone and Cable, Ducon, and Goodyear, made extensive use of time study techniques and "efficiency experts" in designing performance pay (Wright 1995). In the 1930s, consultants installed Bedaux time management and incentive systems at BHP's Newcastle steelworks and in a number of leading firms in retailing, clothing manufacture, and metal manufacturing (Wright 1995).

While individual incentives were certainly the primary focus, there was also cautious experimentation with collective incentives, most notably profit sharing. At this juncture, advocacy of profit sharing was closely associated with the tenets of "industrial welfare" and industry "copartnership." The reality, however, fell well short of the prescriptive rhetoric. A 1931 study found that, of seventy-six firms with organized "industrial welfare" plans, only six operated profit sharing schemes (Mauldon 1931). The one industry in which profit sharing was well established by this time was metal mining. Here, employers sought to establish a buffer against both arbitrated wage increases and increasingly wide fluctuations in international metal prices by introducing a price-linked "bonus" component to miners' wages.

In sum, the early decades of arbitration witnessed a significant widening of the scope of performance related pay, particularly individual output–based incentives. However, the extent of change is easily overstated. Notwithstanding the advocacy of "scientific" incentive plans by management journals, consultants, governments, and arbitration tribunals, there remained significant institutional and ideological limits to its adoption. For example, in general engineering, union and workforce resistance dramatically circumscribed the adoption of incentive plans. Union opposition thwarted plans for the introduction of piece rates in state shipbuilding after World War I (Anderson 1929). In the 1920s, resistance by the metal trades unions effectively limited its application to low-skilled repetition work (Cockfield 1993). The peak union body, the Australian Council of Trade Unions, also expressed strong opposition to all forms of payment by results, although this sometimes sat uncomfortably with the support for piece rates of some large unions, including those representing the powerful sheep shearers and coal miners (Anderson 1929; Hearn and Knowles 1996).

The Rise and Decline of Over-Award Incentives (1940–1980)

The changes wrought by World War II swept away many of the structural and technical barriers to the greater use of incentives. The war induced a rapid development of Australia's heavy and light manufacturing sectors, and the postwar years witnessed a surge in domestic demand for capital and consumer goods, and for residential housing. With massive public infrastructure projects absorbing much of the first wave of post-war immigration, and restive trade unions renewing their stalled wartime campaign for a forty-hour week and increased award margins for skill (Sheridan 1989), private sector employers turned increasingly to performance pay as a means of attracting and retaining labor and raising productivity and output.

By the late 1940s, "a wage incentives fad was sweeping through Australian industry" (Wright 1991). Chambers of Manufactures, other peak employer organizations, a new generation of management consultants, and emerging professional bodies, such as the Institute of Industrial Management, all took a hand in advocating performance pay. Interest was further intensified by a flood of direct investment in Australian manufacturing by U.S. and British multinational firms. The state promoted performance pay even more proactively than it had after the previous war. Both Labor and non-Labor governments openly supported a wider use of incentives, as did key sections of the Commonwealth bureaucracy, particularly the Department of Labour and National Service. The Commonwealth Court of Conciliation and Arbitration also continued its strong advocacy. In the Standard Hours Case in 1947, the court highlighted the broader use of performance pay as a means of offsetting a reduction in working hours (Wright 1991).

Much of this postwar advocacy focused on a wider range of incentives, including task-and-bonus plans and standard hour plans, progressive and regressive piece rate plans, and "merit pay" schemes based on supervisory performance ratings. While employers still showed considerable interest in straight piece work, and in simple incentives like attendance and seniority bonuses, the available survey evidence points to a significant increase in the use of more sophisticated schemes in the 1940s and 1950s. These newer schemes tended not to be incorporated directly in awards and were treated by tribunals as "over-award" payments falling within the province of management prerogative (Wright 1991).

The first detailed study of incentive use in Australian industry, conducted by the Commonwealth Statistician in 1949 (Commonwealth Bureau of Census and Statistics 1949), indicates that by this time Australian per-

Table 7.1

Manual Workers Receiving Incentive Payments, by Industry, 1949

Industry	Percentage receiving output bonuses (piece rates, commissions, or task bonuses)	Percentage receiving nonoutput bonuses	Percentage receiving incentive payments of any type*
Engineering and Vehicles	17.0	18.9	35.4
Textiles	39.9	23.4	54.6
Clothing	25.2	11.9	35.0
Food, drink, and tobacco	8.0	11.9	19.7
Wood, furniture, etc.	10.6	11.0	21.6
Paper and printing	9.5	20.8	29.2
Other manufacturing	15.4	18.5	31.3
All manufacturing	17.0	16.3	31.8
Mining	29.0	17.6	43.3
Building	4.9	2.8	7.7
Transport	2.7	8.4	10.0
Wholesale and retail trade	7.4	23.7	29.7
Other nonmanufacturing	3.1	4.3	7.4
All industries	13.8	15.0	27.5

Source: D. Anon, 1950, 17.
* Includes some employees receiving both output and nonoutput bonuses.

formance pay practice was comparable to that in larger industrialized countries. A summary of the results are presented in Table 7.1. The survey, which covered 25 percent of manual employees in nonrural private sector firms, revealed that 27.5 percent of all employees and 31.8 percent of employees in manufacturing received performance pay. These aggregate figures were very similar to prevailing usage in both Britain (26 percent) and the United States (30 percent) (Anon 1950, 16; Wright 1994, 14). Industry categories where incentives were widely applied included textiles, mining, engineering and vehicle building, and clothing; conversely, incentive use was much lower among firms in building, transport and "other" nonmanufacturing industries. Whereas overall usage was evenly divided "output-based" incentives (piece rates, commissions, and task bonuses) and non–"output-based" incentives (merit pay, attendance bonuses, profit-sharing), output-based incentives were favored far more heavily in textiles, clothing, and mining, while the converse applied in firms in paper and printing and the wholesale and retail trade. The 1949 data also reveal that female workers across all industries were more likely than males to receive performance pay (37 percent as against 25 percent) and were much more likely than males to receive output-based pay (26 percent compared to 10 percent) (Anon 1950; Commonwealth Bureau of Census and Statistics 1949).

Throughout the immediate postwar years the Australian Council of Trade Unions (ACTU) and key metal trades unions opposed all forms of performance pay. However, many individual unions were far less hostile, particularly those controlled by right-wing officials and those representing semiskilled factory workers for whom such schemes delivered earnings well above award rates. In 1953, members of the right-dominated Federated Ironworkers Association employed at one large Sydney foundry reportedly received performance earnings 30–100 percent in excess of award rates. At the same time, members of the Textile Workers' Union were receiving performance earnings averaging 25 percent-33 percent above award time rates (Evans 1959, 41, 46). Many unions continued to engage such pay practices directly by seeking to increase their control over rate setting by controlling work pace. As a consequence, the postwar years witnessed disputes over rate setting. Other unions, such as the Sheet Metal Workers, adopted a wholly pragmatic approach, opposing incentives in principle but seeking to influence them wherever members chose to accept them. (Wright 1991; Evans 1959). Either way, by the early 1950s, the ACTU's position had become untenable, and, in 1953, the ACTU Congress abandoned the policy of blanket opposition, despite continued resistance by the main metal trades unions (Wright 1991; Evans 1959).

A second major survey of incentive practice was undertaken in 1969 by the Commonwealth Department of Labour and National Service and the results are reported in Table 7.2. The survey covered over 1,300 firms with nonmanagerial employment equivalent to 21 percent of total private sector work force. It revealed that 41 percent of firms had at least one performance pay plan in place. Most firms (69 percent) had only one scheme in operation, while 23 percent had two schemes and only 7 percent operated three or four schemes (Gunzburg 1969, 279). The overall proportion of employees receiving performance pay was relatively unchanged over the previous two decades, with 26 percent of all employees covered. Manufacturing remained the main focus, with 47 percent of firms and 31 percent of employees receiving performance pay. The comparable figures for nonmanufacturing were 31 percent and 18 percent respectively. The industries with the highest proportion of employees covered by one or more incentive plans remained largely as before: textiles, clothing and footwear, engineering and metalworking, retail trade, and vehicles and ships. Taking all industries into account, employees of "average performance" received performance earnings averaging 22 percent of the award base—payments that

Table 7.2

Wage Incentive Payments in Australian Firms, by Industry Group and Gender, 1969*

Industry	Percentage of firms with incentive schemes of any type	Percentage of employees receiving incentive payments of any type		
		All employees	Males	Females
Engineering and metalworking	43	36	37	29
Vehicles and ships	42	29	30	22
Textiles, clothing, and footwear	70	56	47	61
Food, drink, and tobacco	44	13	9	23
Other manufacturing	45	23	23	24
All manufacturing	47	31	30	36
Building and construction	18	7	7	4
Finance and property	36	23	27	17
Retail trade	52	33	30	34
Other nonmanufacturing	17	4	4	4
All nonmanufacturing	31	18	15	23
All industries	41	26	25	29

Source: D. Gunzburg. 1969. "Wage Incentives in Australia 1—Extent." *Personnel Practice Bulletin* 25(4): 276–278. Reprinted with permission.
* Survey excluded executive, managerial and professional staff, as well as firms in forestry, fishing, mining, amusement, hotels, cafes, and personal service.

on average added 7.5 percent to firms' total payroll costs (Gunzburg 1969, 18–19).

Output-based schemes still predominated but the data on plan type also indicates an undercurrent of change, as can be seen in Table 7.3. Of those firms making any use of plans, 74 percent used either output bonuses, standard time plans or sales commissions, while merit pay, profit sharing and other plans remained much less common. Output bonuses and standard time plans were targeted mainly at direct production employees. Merit pay was used by 11 percent of incentive-using firms (chiefly in finance and property) and was most common among maintenance workers, supervisors, technicians, and clerical workers. While output bonuses remained the most widely used plan type overall, in engineering, in metal manufacturing, and in textiles, clothing, and footwear, standard hours plans were now the most commonly used type. Commission payments were also now widely applied, being applied by 24 percent of incentive-using firms (Gunzburg 1969, 1970).

While individual incentives remained to the fore, the postwar years saw a heightened use of group-based pay. Of all plans in operation, 30 percent

Table 7.3

Types of Wage Incentive Systems in Australian Firms, by Industry, 1969*

Industry	Output bonus %	Standard time %	Commission %	Merit rating %	Profit sharing %	Other %
Engineering and metalworking	26	33	12	11	4	14
Vehicles and ships	13	23	39	17	4	4
Textiles, clothing, and footwear	41	40	5	5	0	9
Food, drink, and tobacco	35	16	37	7	0	5
Other manufacturing	39	20	16	13	2	10
Building and construction	31	17	9	17	4	22
Finance and property	11	0	35	36	9	9
Retail trade	4	0	67	0	9	20
Other nonmanufacturing	31	0	38	15	6	10
All industries	28	22	24	11	3	12

Source: D. Gunzberg. 1969. "Wage Incentives in Australia—Extent." *Personnel Practice Bulletin* 25(4): 280–281. Reprinted with permission.
* Data relate to 763 systems in operation in 541 firms. Data exclude executive, managerial, and professional staff, as well as firms in forestry, fishing, mining, amusement, hotels, cafes, and personal service.

were based on group performance, 61 percent on individual performance, and 9 percent on a combination of the two (Gunzburg 1969, 17). Most collective schemes implemented during the 1950s and 1960s took the form of bonuses and commissions based on a single volume-based measure of group output. Moreover, profit sharing attracted little interest, being used by just 3 percent of firms and having its highest incidence in the finance and property and retailing industries and among supervisors and technicians.

The 1969 data also indicate a leveling of the gender imbalance. In both 1949 and 1969 the proportion of male workers covered by performance plans remained at 25 percent. By contrast, the proportion of female employees covered by performance plans fell from 37 percent to 29 percent. This probably reflects a refocusing of female employment from manufacturing to office work during the 1960s; that is from a sector of high output-based incentive use to a sector of relatively low use.

During the 1970s, the available qualitative evidence indicates a major decline in management and employee enthusiasm for output-based incentives. Many of the schemes implemented during the previous two decades proved increasingly difficult and costly to administer. In the face of accelerating technological change, output-based schemes required ongoing maintenance to ensure that rates became neither too "tight" nor too "loose"

(Wright 1991, 1994). Management's long-held proclivity for "rate-cutting" further eroded employee trust in surviving schemes, particularly those based on group output (Carey 1995). At the time of the 1969 survey, 13 percent of firms indicated that they had discontinued at least one scheme, with 29 percent of these indicating that they had discontinued a scheme because it was "generally ineffective" (Gunzburg 1969, 282, 284). Existing schemes became a major source of worker dissatisfaction and disputation in the latter half of the 1960s, with performance earnings being regarded increasingly as an entitlement rather than a reward. Twenty-eight percent of firms using incentives were experiencing labor relations problems by 1969 (Wright 1991).

In the period 1968–1974, strike activity and working days lost reached unprecedented heights, as unions pushed for wage increases outside arbitration in the face of gathering price inflation. The consequence was a "wages explosion" that saw the Commonwealth Commission temporarily lose control over "total wage" outcomes, with workers in many industries winning substantial increases in over-award payments through a combination of pattern bargaining and direct workplace action (Dabscheck and Niland 1981; Dabscheck 1994; Wright 1995). In manufacturing, unions successfully pressured employers to replace output-based bonuses with flat over-award allowances such as attendance bonuses (Wright 1991).

Amid the industrial turmoil and economic uncertainty of the early to mid-1970s, some employers turned to more consultative techniques, such as employee participation and industrial democracy, and to motivational methods associated with the Human Relations and Socio-Technical Systems models of labor management (Wright 1995). As a consequence, the tenets of time study, extrinsic motivation, and individual reward gave way to those of job enrichment, quality circles, joint consultation, and collective reward.

The Reemergence of Performance Related Pay

The economic recession of 1981–1982 presaged a series of changes that eventually had a dramatic impact on Australian remuneration practice. The ascendancy of neoliberalism across the political and policymaking spectrum saw the deregulation of financial markets, the floating of the dollar, and the dismantling of tariff protection for manufacturing. Now, more then ever before, Australian employers and employees alike felt the full force of global competition. In the private sector, a major round of industry restructuring was accompanied by mergers and acquisitions; the relocation offshore of many manufacturing operations, the contracting out of noncore activities; large-scale job reductions; and a resort to casual, contract, and agency labor (Australian Centre for Industrial Relations Research and Training 1999b). In the public sector, downsizing, delayering, and outsourcing brought a massive shrinkage in permanent full-time positions, while many key government enterprises and utilities (water, electricity, telecommunications, banks, and airlines) were either made public corporations or fully privatized. The result was a sustained decline in union membership density. In 1980, half of all Australian employees were union members; by 1995, union density had fallen to one-third (Deery, Plowman, and Walsh 1997). After the mid-1980s, a rising current account deficit, falling global commodity prices and weak performance in manufactured exports prompted policy initiatives aimed at enhancing national productivity and the "freeing up" of labor markets.

Beginning in 1987, centralized award regulation gave way to progressively more decentralized modes of pay determination at the federal level. First, the commision sponsored "managed decentralism" of award restructuring and industrywide "productivity bargaining" (1987–1991); then there was union-only "enterprise bargaining" (from 1991 on); and next there was nonunion enterprise bargaining (from 1993 on) (Deery, Plowman, and Walsh 1997; Wright 1995). Then, in late 1996, the passage of the Workplace Relations Act opened the way for the application of individual employment contacts (Australian Workplace Agreements) to workers hitherto covered by federal awards. The turn to industry bargaining, then enterprise bargaining, and finally to individual bargaining progressively widened the scope for the adoption of a new generation of "flexible" pay practices.

These institutional developments were accompanied by a widespread managerial embrace of human resource management (HRM), with its normative emphasis on the strategic necessity for increased labor "flexibility"—greater flexibility functionally, numerically, temporally, and financially (Wright 1995). The objective of financial flexibility became equated with the abandonment of "traditional" pay practices in favor of new practices referred to as "strategic pay," "contingent pay," the "new pay," "pay for the person," or "pay for performance" (Lawler 1990; Schuster and Zingheim 1992). In essence, these all required abandoning fixed, job-based pay in favor of "variable cash remuneration plans" and a "total" approach to reward management tailored to each organization's strategic objectives (Wright 1995; Jankelson 1990). Job-based pay structures were to make way for base pay configured according to personal skills, "high performance competencies," and "career broad bands." "Traditional" incentives, such as appraisal-based "merit" increments to base pay were to be succeeded by conditional merit bonuses, recognition awards, team incentives, business unit goal sharing, and employee share plans.

In the private sector, these ideas were diffused by the local advocates (e.g., Jankelson 1990; O'Neill 1995a, 1995b, 1995c) and by the rapidly growing management consulting industry. In the public sector, neoliberal politicians and policy advisors performed a similar function, launching a series of initiatives to transform traditional seniority-based public sector remuneration structures. Performance pay was first introduced for senior executive officers of the Australian Public Service in late 1992 as part of the Australian Public Service Workplace Bargaining Agreement (O'Donnell 1998). Similar schemes were also introduced for executives and senior managers in the state public services (Marshall 1998).

Evidence from the Australian Workplace Industrial Relations Surveys (AWIRS) of 1990 and 1995 (Callus et al. 1991; Morehead et al. 1997) indicates that the use of these "new pay" methods was neither wholesale nor uniform. In 1995, among workplaces with twenty or more employees, 33 percent had some form of performance pay for at least some nonmanagerial employees, as shown in Table 7.4. This compares with a usage rate of 34 percent in 1990. The AWIRS95 data reveal that performance pay was more common in workplaces with 200 or more employees than in smaller workplaces. Performance pay was most prevalent in finance, insurance, and wholesale trade. It was used in around half of all workplaces in mining, retailing, and property and business services; in just under 40 percent of workplaces in manufacturing and cultural and recreational services, and in 20–30 percent of workplaces in construction, utilities, transport and communications. By contrast, just 8 percent of education workplaces and 7 percent of health and community services workplaces had such schemes. Notwithstanding the introduction of performance payments for public sector senior managers, performance pay remained far more prevalent in private sector workplaces. In short, performance pay retained its greatest appeal to large firms in highly competitive environments and with a preference for competitive strategies based on cost minimization. Indeed, Drago and Heywood (1995) used multivariate techniques in 1990 to find that performance pay use correlated strongly with workforce size, management hierarchy, and exposure to high product market competition.

In the majority of workplaces using performance pay, coverage was limited to less than 25 percent of the workforce, and only 16 percent gave such payments to all their employees (Morehead et al. 1997). The AWIRS95 data suggests that overall coverage in 1995 may still have been lower than during the postwar boom. In 1995 among nonmanagerial employees, 20 percent had received a performance related payment during the previous twelve months. This compares with a coverage rate of 26 percent in firms participating in the 1949 and 1969 surveys.

Table 7.4

Workplaces Using Performance Related Pay and Employees Receiving Performance Payments, by Workplace Category, 1995 (percentages)

	Workplaces using performance payments for nonmanagerial employees	Employees receiving performance payments
All workplaces with 20+ employees	33	20
Workplaces with:		
20–49 employees	32	21
50–99 employees	31	20
100–199 employees	33	18
200–499 employees	41	24
500+ employees	41	19
Sector		
Private	41	26
Public	12	11
Industry		
Finance and insurance	77	49
Wholesale trade	70	45
Mining	52	40
Retail trade	50	35
Property and business services	48	31
Manufacturing	39	29
Cultural and recreational services	38	25
Construction	30	23
Electricity, gas, and water	28	20
Transport and storage	24	19
Communication services	22	17
Personal and other services	18	18
Accommodation, cafes, and restaurants	17	10
Government administration	16	8
Education	8	6
Health and community services	7	4
Union presence		
No union	51	36
Union, no delegate	31	20
Union and delegate	24	16

Source: A. Morehead et al., 1997, 220, 530, 557.

Table 7.5 shows that 26 percent of all workplaces used schemes based on "individual performance," 10 percent used "work group performance," 5 percent used "workplace performance," and 8 percent used "organizationwide performance" criteria of some sort, while only 5 percent used "profit sharing." Clearly, schemes emphasizing individual performance

Table 7.5

Workplaces Using Specific Types of Performance Related Pay, 1995 (percentages)

	Individual performance	Work group performance	Workplace performance	Profit sharing	Organization-wide performance	Employee share ownership*
All workplaces	26	10	5	5	8	22
Workplaces with:						
20–49 employees	26	9	4	5	6	16
50–99 employees	23	12	5	5	8	20
100–199 employees	27	9	6	7	9	37
200–499 employees	29	10	8	5	15	43
500+ employees	27	14	7	2	16	26
Workplaces in:						
The private sector	32	13	7	7	10	22
The public Sector	10	3	1	1	2	—
Workplaces with:						
No union	43	14	7	11	12	14
Union, no delegate	27	11	3	3	7	16
Union and delegate	16	8	4	3	5	32

Source: Morehead. et al., 1997, 531–532.
* Nonmanagerial and Managerial employees in private sector workplaces.

(merit pay, piece rates, commissions) remained predominant. Of those workplaces making performance payments of any type for nonmanagerial employees in 1995, 79 percent used individual performance criteria. However, the AWIRS95 data also indicate a solid use of work group incentives, with 32 percent of workplaces using performance payments basing those payments at least in part on work group performance (Morehead et al. 1997). Team commissions remained popular, but by the mid-1990s newer forms of group-based pay plans were establishing a presence, particularly team and business unit incentives based on performance indicators, gain sharing, and goal sharing (Leihy 1998).

One striking development of the early to mid-1990s was a growth in employee share ownership plans. In 1990 share ownership plans were present in just 16 percent of private sector workplaces with twenty or more employees; by 1995 this figure had risen to 22 percent. In 1995 share plans were present in 40 percent of workplaces in finance and insurance and in just under 40 percent of workplaces in mining and retailing (Morehead et al. 1997, 532–533). AWIRS data indicates that over half of the workplaces that had share plans in 1995 introduced them after 1990 (Department of Employment, Workplace Relations and Small Business 1999, 11–12). Such plans appealed not only as a way (quite literally) of achieving long-term employee "buy-in" to organizational change but also as a means for existing companies to forestall or offset increases in employee base pay. Despite the rise in the proportion of workplaces using share plans, the proportion of nonmanagerial employees participating in such plans remained small. In 1990, the proportion of nonmanagerial employees in private sector workplaces participating in share plans was just 2 percent; in 1995 the figure was still only 3 percent (Morehead et al. 1997, 532–533).

Although the proportion of workplaces using profit sharing had experienced a modest revival in the late 1980s (Jankelson 1990, 32), between 1990 and 1995, it fell from 8 percent to 5 percent (Callus et al. 1991, 244; Morehead et al. 1997, 531). The boom and bust of 1988–91—in theory the very circumstances for which such plans were best suited—caused many firms to abandon such plans in favor of more long-term means of fostering employee commitment. The move away from profit sharing may have been furthered by the requirement to engage in productivity bargaining under the "structural efficiency" principle set down by the Australian Industrial Relations Commission in 1988 (Deery, Plowman, and Walsh 1997, 9.6–9.7). By itself, organizationwide profit sharing was considered too blunt and too remote an instrument to enhance productivity. In the banking and financial services industry, for instance, the late 1980s witnessed the substitution of a range of newer group and individual plans for preexisting cash profit sharing schemes.

In sum, the initial move toward decentralized pay determination did not increase the formal provision of "flexible" remuneration practices in industrial agreements. A sample survey of 833 enterprise agreements certified federally between 1989 and 1995 indicates that only 5.1 percent made any provision for performance pay. Significantly, in the few agreements incorporating performance pay, provision was divided relatively evenly between individual and collective schemes (Brown 1997). Thus the main effect of enterprise bargaining may well have been to underwrite the importance of group schemes.

Performance Related Pay: Here to Stay?

In contrast to the modest changes of the early 1990s, the available evidence indicates a dramatic resurgence in the use of performance related pay since the mid-1990s. One significant influence in this regard has been the federal Workplace Relations Act of 1996. This legislation has a threefold intent: first, to marginalize even further the centralized arbitration system, with its emphasis on industrywide awards and union collective agreements; secondly, to uncouple enterprise bargaining from industry-wide "pattern bargaining"; and, third, and most important, to institute individual bargaining and individual contracts of employment. Among other things, the Workplace Relations Act provides for the introduction of statutory bipartite agreements between employers and individual employees. Known as Australian Workplace Agreements (AWAs), these are nonunion in nature and are intended to supercede both awards and collective agreements. The act also requires that the contents of each such agreement remain entirely confidential (MacDermott 1997; Deery et al. 2001).

Although AWAs still cover only a small fraction of the work force, their use as a vehicle for greater labor flexibility is increasing rapidly. The span of ordinary working hours is being increased, shift times are being extended, base pay is being annualized, penalty rates for overtime and weekend work are being stripped away, sick leave and annual leave entitlements are being cashed out, and time-off-in-lieu arrangements are being applied to further increase the flexibility of working hours. (Australian Centre for Industrial Relations Research and Training 1999; Department of Employment, Workplace Relations and Small Business 2000). In some sectors, pay is also being linked increasingly to individual performance. As of March 2000, there were approximately 100,000 approved AWAs in place, with the number growing by 5,000 per month. Many of these are located in specific industries: transport, manufacturing, government administration, and health and community services. The last two are primarily areas of public sector employment, where a concerted push has been made to use the public sector as a pacesetter for replacement of collective agreements with individual AWAs.

It is necessary to make several qualifications to these generalizations. First, the federal system presents human resource managers with a legal maze and many seem to prefer the administrative convenience of collective agreements. Second, individual AWAs are often simply replicated across the relevant workforce rather than being tailored to individual employees. Third, it is still possible for unions for negotiate collective agreements ("certified agreements") on behalf of their members—and many still seek to do just this. The 1996 act also makes provision for collective agreements of a nonunion nature (Deery et al. 2001).

Performance Related Pay in Collective and Individual Agreements

While the confidentiality provision precludes any comprehensive consideration of the contents of AWAs, it is possible to develop an approximate profile of performance pay provisions in such agreements. Using the Agreement Database and Monitor (ADAM) maintained by the Australian Centre for Industrial Relations Research and Training (ACIRRT) at the University of Sydney, ADAM provides detailed cross-sectional and comparative information on current pay practice under both collective and individual agreements. As of March 2000, the database contained encoded information on a total of 2,100 certified union and nonunion collective agreements and some 350 AWAs. While the latter represents only a tiny fraction of existing AWAs, analysis of their performance pay provisions highlights a number of major points of contrast to collective agreements.

The ADAM data reveals that AWAs are far less likely to provide for a pay increase than are either union or nonunion certified agreements: 21 percent as against 71 percent and 53 percent, respectively (ACIRRT 1999a, 8). However, as can be seen in Table 7.6, in those agreements that do provide for a pay increase, the pay increase is far more likely to be performance linked in AWAs (25.9 percent of current AWAs) than in either union or nonunion agreements (17.3 percent and 8.4 percent respectively). AWAs are also far more likely to utilize *individual* performance criteria for pay increases—including individual performance appraisal and piece rates—than are either type of collective agreement. Whereas 21.6 percent

Table 7.6

Performance Related Pay Provisions in Industrial Agreements, by Agreement Type, 2000

Provision	Percentage of union-certified agreements (n = 1610)	Percentage of nonunion certified agreements (n = 501)	Percentage of Australian workplace agreements (n = 347)
Part or all of pay increase performance linked in Agreements of this type for:			
All industries	17.3	8.4	25.9
Agriculture	28.6	7.1	16.7
Mining/construction	10.5	14.6	20.6
Food/beverage manufacturing	12.1	4.5	6.3
Metal manufacturing	15.3	16.2	32.1
Other manufacturing	19.5	2.7	20.6
Electricity, gas, and water	29.4	25.0	55.6
Wholesale/retail	8.1	6.0	5.4
Transport/storage	16.3	8.8	4.5
Communications	20.0	0	0
Property and financial services	15.6	7.3	29.6
Public administration	36.5	29.4	75.8
Community services	12.1	7.1	26.8
Recreational services	9.5	3.6	26.8
Increase linked to productivity improvements	10.0	3.4	4.0
Increase linked to KPI targets	9.6	4.4	7.2
Increase linked to individual performance appraisal	2.0	2.0	21.6
Individual performance payments	3.9	5.4	9.8
Piecework payments	1.3	3.2	3.5
Bonus payments	9.8	9.2	6.6
Gain sharing	4.2	2.2	1.7
Profit sharing	1.5	1.0	1.7
Employee share scheme	0.9	0.4	0.9

Source: J. Shields, 2001, 4.

of AWAs provide for pay increases linked to individual performance appraisal, this applies in only 2 percent of collective agreements.

In the industries of electricity, gas and water, and public administration, agreements of all types have a high incidence of performance-linked pay increases. Moreover, in agriculture, food and beverage manufacturing, wholesale and retail, transport and storage, and communications, union agreements make significantly greater provision for performance-linked

Table 7.7

Proportion of Performance Pay Increase in Industrial Agreements, by Agreement Type and Sector, 2000

	Quartile distribution of agreements of this type, according to the proportion of pay increase specified in agreement, which is performance linked			
	Less than 25% of specified increase is performance linked	25–50% of specified increase is performance linked	50–75% of specified increase is performance linked	75–100% of specified increase is performance linked
Certified agreements, all ($n = 309$)	16.8%	37.5%	24.6%	21.0%
Certified agreements, union ($n = 276$)	17.8	36.6	24.6	21.0
Certified agreements, nonunion ($n = 33$)	9.1	45.5	24.2	21.1
Certified agreements, public sector ($n = 134$)	4.5	41.8	32.1	21.6
Certified agreements, private sector ($n = 175$)	26.3	34.3	18.9	20.6
AWAs, all ($n = 35$)	8.6	25.7	34.3	31.4
AWAs, public sector ($n = 21$)	4.8	19.0	52.4	23.8
AWAs, private sector ($n = 14$)	14.3	35.7	7.1	42.9

Source: ADAM Database, Australian Centre for Industrial Relations Research and Training, University of Sydney.

pay increases than does either form of nonunion agreement. Union collective agreements are more likely have pay increases based on collective and transparent performance measures such as improvements in site productivity. For instance, Table 7.6 shows that gain sharing is provided for in 4.2 percent of union-certified agreements, but only 1.7 percent of AWAs.

A further point of contrast between AWAs and collective agreements is the proportion of any specified pay increase that is performance based. Looking at those agreements that do provide for a quantifiable performance-linked pay increase (Table 7.7), in AWAs over half of specified pay increases are performance based, whereas in certified agreements the figure is between 25 percent and 50 percent.

Information released by the federal Department of Employment, Workplace Relations and Small Business shows that of those employers entering into AWAs approved in 1998–1999, 30 percent offered performance pay to their employees, while approximately 45 percent of employees covered by these agreements were eligible to receive such payments. Young employees covered by AWAs had a significantly higher incidence of performance pay provisions (53 percent), whereas the incidence among females and part-time employees was lower (at 39 percent and 43 percent, respectively). The higher exposure of young workers possibly reflects the type of industries in which they tend to be most heavily concentrated, namely retail, accommodations, cafes, and restaurants (Department of Employment, Workplace Relations and Small Business 2000).

By far the most striking point of contrast revealed by the ADAM data is that between public and private sector agreements, irrespective of agreement type. Public sector agreements are far more likely to incorporate performance pay than those for private sector employees, as seen in Table 7.8. Public sector certified agreements are twice as likely to provide for a performance-linked pay rise as are their private sector counterparts (26 percent as opposed to 11.9 percent), while public sector AWAs are almost four times as likely to do so than those for private sector employees (67.3 percent as against 17.5 percent). Moreover, public sector AWAs are far more likely to provide for individual performance payments and for increases linked to individual performance appraisal. Similarly, compared to private sector certified agreements, those in the public sector are far more likely to provide for pay increases linked to productivity improvements, key performance indicators, individual performance appraisal, and gain sharing. Equally, in those collective agreements that quantify the performance-linked component of any pay increase, the proportion of the pay increase that is linked to performance tends to be substantially higher in public sector agreements.

These differences may reflect a concerted push by the architects of the Workplace Relations Act to create a "performance culture" in the Australian Public Service. New "policy parameters" set down by the Howard government in 1997 require federal public sector agencies to fund agreement provisions from within their budget appropriations and to introduce new staff classification structures coupled with performance related salary progression. These parameters apply to both certified agreements and AWAs (O'Donnell and O'Brien 2000).

Table 7.8

Incidence of Performance Related Pay Provisions in Industrial Agreements, by Sector and Agreement Type, 2000

	Public Sector		Private Sector	
	Certified agreements (n = 493)	Australian workplace agreements (n = 52)	Certified agreements (n = 1,618)	Australian workplace agreements (n = 274)
	Percentage of these agreements providing for:			
Part or all of pay increase performance linked	26.0	67.3	11.9	17.5
Increase linked to productivity improvements	15.6	3.8	6.3	4.4
Increase linked to key performance targets	15.2	23.1	6.2	4.4
Increase linked to individual performance appraisal	3.2	63.5	1.6	13.1
Individual performance payments	5.5	30.8	4.0	6.6
Piecework payments	0.6	0	2.1	4.4
Bonus payments	9.3	17.3	9.8	5.1
Gainsharing	6.5	0	2.8	2.2
Profit sharing	2.0	0	1.2	2.2
Employee share scheme	0	0	1.0	1.1

Source: J. Shields, 2001, 7.

Current Public and Private Sector Practice

Prior to 1996, public sector performance pay initiatives were confined largely to executive level officers. However, a recent official audit of performance management initiatives in forty-one agency agreements found that all agencies now link performance to pay in some way. The most widely used method was performance-linked pay progression, but agencies also used cash bonuses to reward high-performing groups and individuals (Australian National Audit Office 2000). The study reported that that in some large agencies, such as the Australian Taxation Office and Centrelink, considerable progress has been made toward implementing transparent and valid schemes for measuring and rewarding gains in unit productivity (Australian National Audit Office 2000). Yet, in most of the Australian Public Service the implementation of performance pay has not been systematic or cost effective. Many agencies have reportedly failed to establish proper systems for monitoring whether productivity gains occur or to implement appropriate procedures for full public disclosure of performance payments made. Moreover, most schemes fail to differentiate adequately between "effective" and "superior" job performance, with most agencies falling back on automatic annual "merit" increments to base pay for all employees achieving an "effective" performance rating. Even in "better practice" agencies "the wage increases staff were eligible to receive through performance-linked remuneration were significant, sometimes greater than the wage increases included in the certified agreement." Overall, the National Audit Office found little concrete evidence that performance payments had improved agency performance (Australian National Audit Office 2000, 13, 18–20, 24–25, 129–135).

A recent inquiry by the opposition-dominated Finance and Public Administration Committee of the Australian Senate has faulted the absence of transparency in the determination of performance payments for senior executives covered by AWAs. While the average proportion of performance payments to total remuneration for public sector executives remains low by private sector standards—ranging from 4.8 percent to 6 percent—such payments have reportedly been as high as 38 percent of base salary. The use of executive incentives has also been associated with increases in the upper limit of executive base salary bands and a consequent widening of base salary differences between executive and nonexecutive employees (Senate Finance and Public Administration References Committee 2000). The Senate Finance Committee also noted that in some agencies performance pay for nonexecutive employees had been "abandoned on the grounds that there was no evidence that it motivated people to work harder or better. On the contrary, there was evidence that it had tainted the performance management process." The departmental heads of several agencies, including the Department of Defense, have refused to use performance pay in their organizations (Senate Finance and Public Administration References Committee 2000, 51, 56, 59).

Research by O'Donnell and O'Brien points to widespread dissatisfaction among federal public sector employees with individual performance pay. In particular, there is resentment at the perceived violation of basic procedural justice, including supervisors' failure to provide regular feedback and the "moderation" of appraisal scores for purely budgetary or political reasons. In some agencies, employees have responded by taking the initiative away from supervisors 'to ensure that performance criteria and indi-

Table 7.9

Firms Using Specific Types of Performance Related Pay for Managerial and Nonmanagerial Employees, 1999 (percentages)

	Firms using method	
	For managerial employees	For nonmanagerial employees
Firms using at least one type of PRP for at least some employees	97.3	86.3
Individual performance pay	97.3	78.0
Piece rates	0.0	5.5
Sales commissions	24.7	26.0
Merit pay raises to base pay	89.0	63.0
Merit pay bonuses	64.4	30.1
Special purpose cash incentives	13.7	27.4
(broadbanding)	(46.6)	(45.2)
(Individual noncash recognition awards)	(36.6)	(41.1)
Group performance pay	34.2	35.6
Gain sharing plans	15.1	16.4
Goal sharing plans	20.5	17.8
Other group or team bonuses	8.2	13.7
(Group/team non-cash recognition awards)	(27.4)	(32.9)
Organization performance pay	47.9	39.7
Profit sharing	15.1	9.6
Share bonus plans	15.1	6.8
Share purchase plans	21.0	20.5
Share options	19.2	2.7
Other organizational performance plans	11.0	4.1

Source: J. Shields, 2001, 10.

cators were specific and job-related' and to insist on proper performance documentation and the provision of regular feedback during the appraisal cycle (O'Donnell and O'Brien 2000, 20).

The following observations on private sector pay follow from data generated by a 1999 survey of remuneration practices in Australian private sector firms conducted by Shields and Long (1999). The data set is based on responses from seventy-five medium-to large-scale enterprises with an average work force size of just over 2,000 employees and a combined work force equal to 2.3 percent of the total private sector work force.

As demonstrated in Table 7.9, the 1999 data imply a far higher overall incidence of performance related pay practices than that indicated by AWIRS95: 86.3 percent of firms participating in the 1999 survey made some use of performance related payments for some of their nonmanagerial employees. In 1995, by comparison 41 percent of the AWIRS workplaces with 200 or more employees made such payments. The 1999 respondents made greater use of all categories of performance pay: 78.0 percent used individual performance pay; 35.6 percent used systems geared to the business unit, work group, or team performance, and 39.7 percent used systems geared to performance of the organization. The most widely used individual methods were appraisal-based merit increments to base pay (63.0 percent of firms) and merit bonuses (30.1 percent). Goal sharing was the most commonly applied group-based method (17.8 percent), followed closely by gain sharing (16.4 percent) and team bonuses (13.7 percent). Of those methods linked to the performance of the organization, share purchase plans were by far the most prevalent (20.5 percent), with profit sharing used by only 9.6 percent of firms. One striking finding from the survey is the popularity of noncash recognition awards. Considerable use was also made of broad banding, another pivotal "new pay" technique, with 45.2 percent of respondent firms indicating that broad-banded pay structures were applied to at least some nonmanagerial employees.

The proportion of nonmanagerial employees covered by these reward practices in firms that use them was typically well over 50 percent, with the only exception being piece rates (41.8 percent of employees) and sales commissions (12.4 percent), as can be seen in Table 7.10. The 1999 survey data therefore suggest that firms are both making use of a wider range of payment methods and extending their use to a majority of employees. Even though most types of performance pay are still applied more widely among managers than among nonmanagers, the 1999 data indicate a significant (if belated and selective) turn away from older, output-based incentives and toward "new pay" methods for nonmanagerial employees.

Available proprietary remuneration survey data support the conclusion of a substantial growth in the incidence of particular performance pay methods among nonmanagerial employees in private firms. A 1997 survey of remuneration methods used in 260 Australian organizations by consulting firm Mercer Cullen Egan Dell pointed to a rapid growth in organizational usage of team incentives—from 6 percent in 1995–1996 to 11 percent in 1996–1997. In organizations that had self-directed work teams in place, 50 percent of these teams at "award staff" level were covered by team incentives, as were 75 percent of teams at "exempt staff" level. In 1999 the same consultants reported that over the preceding year the proportion of surveyed organizations providing performance-variable rewards to award staff increased by 10 percentage points, to 58 percent. For exempt staff the corresponding proportion was 72 percent. The same source also reported a shift away from cash profit sharing toward share bonus plans

Table 7.10

Employees Covered by Specific Types of Performance Related Pay in Firms Using Each Type, 1999

	Mean percentage of employees covered	
	Managerial	Nonmanagerial
Individual performance pay		
Piece rates	0.0	41.8
Sales commissions	9.6	12.4
Merit pay raises to base pay	89.6	80.5
Merit pay bonuses	56.0	69.3
Special purpose cash incentives	80.7	68.6
(Individual noncash recognition awards)	(69.4)	(82.3)
Group performance pay		
Gain sharing plans	55.6	63.8
Goal sharing plans	54.5	76.3
Other group or team bonuses	26.0	50.5
(Group/team noncash recognition awards)	(69.3)	(78.1)
Organization performance pay		
Profit sharing	67.2	79.3
Share bonus plans	54.8	100.0
Share purchase plans	86.3	94.0
Share options	27.1	100.0
Other organizational performance plans	42.3	100.0

Source: J. Shields, 2001, 10.

and a growing preference for such plans linked to individual performance (Mercer Cullen Egan Dell 1999).

When the continued growth in employee share purchase plans is compared with the ADAM data, an interesting conundrum appears. Even though fewer than 1 percent of certified and individual agreements make provision for employee share ownership, the practice continues to expand, albeit incrementally. Its extension has been underwritten by further rounds of privatization, particularly the sale of the Commonwealth Bank of Australia, Qantas, and the Telstra, and by the demutualization of major insurers like MMI General Insurance Limited (now Allianz Australia Limited); Australian Mutual Provident Society (AMP), and most recently the National Roads and Motorists Association (NRMA). Of the firms participating in the 1999 survey, over one-fifth operated share purchase plans for some non-managerial employees, 6.8 percent operated share bonus plans, and 2.7 percent operated share option plans. Discounted share purchase plans are the preferred mode of providing employees with access to equity in organizations undergoing privatization and demutulization. Official data indicate that 6 percent of all employees were participants in such schemes in 1999. (House of Representatives Standing Committee 2000).

The extension of share plans is partly attributable to a more supportive public policy. Prior to the mid-1990s such schemes attracted no significant taxation concessions, due in large part to resistance from the Australian Taxation Office. This contrasts starkly with the generous concessions available to employers and/or employees in the United States, Britain, and France but is similar to the stance in Japan. This began to change in 1995 when the federal labor government introduced modest tax concessions to corporations and individuals for participating in such plans (House of Representatives Standing Committee 2000). More recently, effective campaigning by support groups such as the Australian Employee Ownership Association (established in 1986) has elevated political and public awareness of such schemes. Ministers in the current federal government have demonstrated a strong philosophical commitment to employee ownership and the principle of "people's capitalism." In 2000 the government-dominated Commonwealth Parliamentary Standing Committee on Employment, Education and Workplace Relations released a majority report recommending further legislative encouragement and regulation (House of Representatives Standing Committee 2000).

In stark contrast to the moves in executive remuneration toward share option plans and other long-term incentives (O'Neill 1999), the spread of performance related pay practices to the nonmanagerial work force has not been accompanied by any significant deepening of the contribution. The 1999 survey data reported in Table 7.11 reveal that in the private sector the overall contribution of performance payments to nonmanagerial employees' total remuneration remains relatively low. Performance payments of all types typically made up just 5.9 percent of total nonmanagerial pay, mostly in the form of payments based on individual performance. This proportion is low both in comparison with that for managerial employees (11.5 percent) and by historical standards. As we have seen, during the postwar boom it was common for performance pay earnings to exceed 30 percent of award base pay.

In sum, performance pay has certainly been diffused more widely across the nonmanagerial workforce since the mid-1990s and does indeed seem to be here to stay. Yet, its adoption has been wide rather then deep and base pay remains the center piece of nonmanagerial pay.

Table 7.11

Performance Related Pay as a Proportion of Total Remuneration, 1999

	"Typical" managerial/ supervisory employee	"Typical" nonmanagerial employee
Nominal base pay plus loadings	72.6%	82.1%
Individual performance pay	8.0	3.7
Group performance pay	1.4	1.2
Organizational performance pay	2.1	1.0
Superannuation and other financial benefits	15.9	12.0
Total pretax remuneration	100.0	100.0
Total performance-linked remuneration	11.5	5.9

Source: J. Shields, 2001, 11.

Conclusion

The available evidence on performance pay type, incidence, and earnings impact suggests a pattern of development which is complex, diverse, and far from unilinear. The history of performance pay in Australia is one of both continuity and change. In one sense, experimentation with performance pay has now come full circle. As we have seen, among the earliest initiatives was the application of task work to Australia's first public sector workers—the convicts. Two centuries later, performance plans are once again being applied systematically to public sector workers.

The most significant changes have been in plan type and mix. During the nineteenth century, task work spread from the nascent public sector to private sector workplaces, where it vied with piece rates as the dominant form of individual payment by results. In the early twentieth century, employers experimented with premium bonus plans and time-study methods. Profit sharing also made its debut at this time. By the late 1960s, firms in the services sector were also applying appraisal-based merit pay to supervisory, clerical, and technical-professional employees. The economic and industrial turmoil of the 1970s saw some firms turn to pay plans of a collective and participative nature, particularly gain sharing, profit sharing, and employee share plans. While individual incentives remained the dominant mode of performance pay, the structural and organizational changes of the 1990s brought a resurgence in employee share plans. Recent years have also seen considerable experimentation in both public sector and private sector organizations with "new pay" techniques ranging from goal sharing and team incentives to broad banding and individual merit bonuses.

Any suggestion of a uniform secular trend toward performance pay and away from time pay is doubly misplaced. It is misplaced, first, because pay for performance has always been a feature of working life in Australia. Even during the heyday of centralized wage regulation in the mid-twentieth century, individual and group-based incentive plans had a substantial presence across a wide range of industries. Second, any suggestion of a decisive trend toward performance pay is misplaced. While "new pay" methods—from individual merit bonuses to team incentives—have certainly become far more widely diffused throughout the nonmanagerial work force since the mid-1990s, these practices have not displaced time pay as the principal determinant of nonmanagerial earnings. Indeed, the contribution of performance payments to the earnings of a nonmanagerial employee is significantly lower today than it was half a century ago. Moreover, for nonmanagerial women workers, the incidence of performance payments appears to have declined during the second half of the twentieth century.

Equally, it is important to resist the temptation to draw equivalence between arbitration and time rates, on the one hand, and between "decentralized bargaining" and performance pay, on the other. Performance pay practices not only survived under arbitral centralism but, at times, actually flourished. During the cyclical booms of the 1920s, 1950s, and 1960s, arbitration tribunals assumed a proactive role in promoting "payment-by-results" and "incentive" plans. The main effects of arbitral regulation in its initial period of existence were to codify existing pay practices and generally to support experimentation by large industrial employers with scientific management techniques. During the economically buoyant decades of the mid-twentieth century, employers resorted en masse to incentive payments in the hope of deriving some benefit from a labor market necessity to pay overaward wages. Moreover, while the move toward decentralized pay determination since the late 1980s has widened the scope of performance pay practices, it cannot be said to have precipitated a decisive shift away from time-based modes of payment.

The central argument of this chapter has been that the past and present contours of Australian remuneration practice must be understood in multicausal rather than monocausal terms. In particular, while developments in remuneration practice undoubtedly owe something to shifts in management fads and fashions, the role of other more material factors must be recognized. Of these, the most decisive have been long-term structural change in the Australian economy, short-term economic cycles, the trade union presence, the nature of the regulatory and "deregulatory" state, and changes in organizational structure. The historical record indicates that both institutional and market factors have contributed materially to the shaping of Australian remuneration practice. Like market forces, regulatory environments can, and often do, change in unpredictable ways. We have argued that the Workplace Relations Act of 1996 has provided major encouragement to the spread of individual performance pay plans.

References

Anderson, G. 1929. *Fixation of Wages in Australia.* Melbourne: Macmillan.

Anon, D. 1950. "Incentive Payments in Australian Industry." *Bulletin of Industrial Psychology and Personnel Practice* 6: 13–17.

Australian Centre for Industrial Relations Research and Training. 1999a. *Agreements Database and Monitor Report,* no. 22, September. Sydney: Commercial Clearing House (CCH).

———. 1999b. *Australia At Work.* Sydney: Prentice Hall.

Australian Chamber of Commerce and Industry. 1997. "Performance Related Pay in Enterprise Agreements." "Best Practice" Information Paper No. 1.

Australian National Audit Office. 2000. *Certified Agreements in the Australian Public Service,* The Auditor-General Audit Report No.13 2000–2001. Canberra, Commonwealth of Australia.

Blackburn, K. 1996. "Preaching 'The Gospel of Efficiency': The Promotion of Ideas About Profit-Sharing and Payment by Results in Australia, 1915–29." *Australian Historical Studies* 107: 257–280.

Blandy, R., and Niland, J. R., eds. 1986. *Alternatives to Arbitration.* Sydney: Allen and Unwin.

Brown, M. 1997. "Performance Pay Choices: Evidence from Certified Agreements." *Journal of Industrial Relations* 39: 349–368.

Buchanan, J., and Callus, R. 1993. "Efficiency and Equity at Work: The Need for Labour Market Regulation in Australia." *Journal of Industrial Relations* 35: 515–537.

Callus, R., Morehead, A., Cully, M., and Buchanan, J. 1991. *Industrial Relations at Work: The Australian Workplace Industrial Relations Survey.* Canberra, Australian Government Publishing Service.

Carey, P. 1995. "Gain Sharing: A Metal Industry Case Study." In *Australian Human Resource Management,* eds. G. O'Neill and R. Kramar. Melbourne: Pitman, 179–190.

Cockfield, A. 1998. "McKay's Harvester Works and the Continuation of Managerial Control." *Journal of Industrial Relations* 40: 383–400.

Cockfield, S. 1993. "Arbitration, Mass Production and Workplace Relations: Metal Industry Developments in the 1920s." *Journal of Industrial Relations* 35: 19–38.

Coolican, A. 1988. "Solidarity and Sectionalism in the Sydney Building Trades: The Role of the Building Trades Council, 1886–1895." *Labour History* 54: 16–29.

Commonwealth Bureau of Census and Statistics. 1949. *Quarterly Business Survey No. 10. Preliminary Results.* Canberra, Commonwealth Bureau of Census and Statistics.

Dabscheck, B. 1994. "The Arbitration System Since 1967." In *State, Economy and Public Policy in Australia,* eds. S. Bell and B. Head. Melbourne: Oxford University Press, 142–168.

Dabscheck, B., and Niland, J. 1981. *Industrial Relations in Australia.* Sydney: George Allen and Unwin.
Deery, S., Plowman, D., and Walsh, J. 1997. *Industrial Relations: A Contemporary Analysis.* Sydney: McGraw-Hill.
Deery, S., Plowman, D., Walsh, J., and Brown, M. 2001. *Industrial Relations: A Contemporary Analysis,* 2d ed. Sydney: McGraw-Hill.
Department of Employment, Workplace Relations and Small Business, and Office of the Employment Advocate. 2000. *Agreement Making in Australia Under the Workplace Relations Act 1998 and 1999.* Canberra: Department of Employment, Workplace Relations and Small Business.
Department of Employment, Workplace Relations and Small Business. 1999. " 'Submission to House of Representatives Standing Committee on Employment, Education and Workplace Relations Inquiry into Employee Share Ownership in Australian Enterprises." http://www.aph.gov.au/house/committee/eewr/ESO/.
Drago, R., and Heywood, J. S. 1995. "The Choice of Payment Schemes: Australian Establishment Data." *Industrial Relations* 34: 507–531.
Ellem, B. 1989. *In Women's Hands? A History of Clothing Trades Unionism in Australia.* Sydney: University of New South Wales Press.
Evans, W. P. 1959. "Union Attitude and Policy." In *Payment by Results,* ed. D. Oxnam. Nedlands: University of Western Australia Press, 28–54.
Fahey, C., and Lack, J. 2000. "We Have to Train Men from Labourers: The Agricultural Implement Trade 1918–1945." *Journal of Industrial Relations* 42: 551–572.
Frances, R. 1993. *The Politics of Work: Gender and Labour in Victoria, 1880–1939.* Melbourne: Cambridge University Press.
Gunzburg, D. 1969. "Wage Incentives in Australia 1—Extent." *Personnel Practice Bulletin* 25: 278–287.
———. 1970. "Wage Incentives in Australia 2—Operation." *Personnel Practice Bulletin* 26: 10–24.
Hagan, J., and Fisher, C. 1973. "Piece-Work and Some of its Consequences in the Printing and Coal Mining Industries in Australia, 1850–1930." *Labour History* 25: 19–39.
Hearn, M., and Knowles, H. 1996 *One Big Union: A History of the Australian Workers Union 1886–1994.* Melbourne: Cambridge University Press.
House of Representatives Standing Committee on Employment, Education and Workplace Relations, Parliament of the Commonwealth of Australia. 2000. *Shared Endeavours. Inquiry into Employee Share Ownership in Australian Enterprises,* September, Canberra, http://www.aph.gov.au/house/committee/eewr/ESO/.
Jankelson, M. B. 1990. "Remuneration Trends and Issues: Looking Forward, Looking Back." *Asia Pacific Human Resource Management* (May): 27–43.
Kennedy, B. 1978. *Silver, Sin and Sixpenny Ale.* Carlton: Melbourne University Press.
Lawler, E. E. 1990. *Strategic Pay: Aligning Organizational Strategies and Pay Systems.* San Francisco: Jossey-Bass.
Lee, J., and Fahey, J. 1986. "A Boom for Whom? Some Developments in the Australian Labour Markey, 1870–1891," *Labour History* 50: 1–27.
Leihy, D. 1998. "Variable Reward and Share Plans in the 90s—Results of a Recent Survey." *Australian Company Secretary,* May, 160–164.
MacDermott, T. 1997. "Industrial Legislation in 1996: The Reform Agenda." *Journal of Industrial Relations* 39: 52–76.
Markey, R. 1988. *The Making of the Labor Party in New South Wales 1880–1900.* Sydney: University of New South Wales Press.

Marshall, N. 1998. "Pay for Performance Systems: Experiences in Australia." *Public Productivity and Management Review* 21: 403–418.

Mauldon, F. R. E. 1931. "Cooperation and Welfare in Industry." In *An Economic Survey of Australia,* ed. D. Copeland, published in *Annals of the American Academy of Political and Social Science,* November, 183–192.

Mercer Cullen Egan Dell. 1999. *1999/2000 Australian Benefits Review.* Sydney: Mercer Cullen Egan Dell.

———. 2000. *Executive Incentive Plans 2000.* Sydney: Mercer Cullen Egan Dell.

Merritt, J. 1986. *The Making of the AWU.* Melbourne: Oxford University Press.

Morehead, A., Steele, M., Alexander, M., Stephen, K., and Duffin, L. 1997. *Changes at Work: The 1995 Australian Workplace Industrial Relations Survey.* Melbourne: Longman.

O'Donnell, M. 1998. "Creating a Performance Culture? Performance-Based Pay in the Australian Public Service." *Australian Journal of Public Administration* 57: 28–40.

O'Donnell, M., and O'Brien, J. 2000. "Performance-Based Pay in the Australian Public Service: Employee Perspectives." *Review of Public Personnel Administration* 20: 20–34.

O'Neill, G. 1995a. "Linking Pay to Performance: Conflicting Views and Conflicting Evidence." *Asia Pacific Journal of Human Resource Management* 33: 20–35.

———. 1995b. "Framework for Developing a Total Reward Strategy." *Asia Pacific Journal of Human Resources* 33: 103–117.

———. 1995c. "Trends and Issues in Pay Design and Management." In *Australian Human Resource Management,* eds. G. O'Neill and R. Kramar. Melbourne: Pitman, 155–178.

———. 1999. *Executive Remuneration in Australia: An Overview of Trends and Issues.* Melbourne: Australian Human Resource Institute.

Patmore, G. 1988. "Systematic Management and Bureaucracy: The NSW Railways Prior to 1932."*Labour and Industry* 1:306–321.

———. 1991. *Australian Labour History.* Cheshire: Longman, 1991.

———. 1994. "American Hustling Methods: The Lithgow Small Arms Factory 1912–1922." *Labour History* 67: 42–56.

Plowman, D. H. 1992. "Industrial Relations and the Legacy of the New Protection." *Journal of Industrial Relations* 34: 48–64.

Robbins, W. M. 1999. "Contested Terrain: The Convict Task Work System, 1788–1830." In Hood, R., and Markey, R., eds. *Labour and Community. Proceedings of the Sixth National Conference of the Australian Society for the Study of Labour History,* Australian Society for the Study of Labour History. Wollongong: Illawarra Branch, 256–260.

Schuster, J. R., and Zingheim, P. K. 1992. *The New Pay: Linking Employee and Organizational Performance.* San Francisco: Jossey-Bass.

Senate Finance and Public Administration References Committee. 2000. *Australian Public Service Employment Matters. First Report: Australian Workplace Agreements.* Canberra: Parliament of the Commonwealth of Australia.

Sheridan, T. 1989. *Division of Labour: Industrial Relations in the Chifley Years, 1945–1949.* Melbourne: Oxford University Press.

Shields, J. 1997. " 'Lead Bonus Happy: Profit-sharing, Productivity and Industrial Relations in the Broken Hill Mining Industry, 1925–83." *Australian Economic History Review* 37: 222–255.

———. 2001. "Pay-for-Performance: What's Really Happening." *Human Resource Management Bulletin* 16.

Shields, J., and Long, R. 1999. "A Survey of Remuneration Practices in Australian Firms." Unpublished database.

Sullivan, M. 1985. *Men and Women of Port Phillip.* Sydney: Hale and Iremonger.
Thomas, L. [1919] 1962. *The Development of the Labour Movement in the Sydney District of New South Wales.* Canberra, Australian Society for the Study of Labour History.
Wright, C. 1991. "The Development of Incentive Payment Systems in Australian Manufacturing Industry, 1945–1970." *Labour and Industry* 4: 95–118.
———. 1994. "A History of Incentive Payment Systems in Australia." In *Incentive Payment Systems in Australia,* ed. C. Wright. Industrial Relations Research Series, No. 9, Department of Industrial Relations, 3–24.
———. 1995. *The Management of Labour: A History of Australian Employers.* Melbourne: Oxford University Press.

Chapter 8
Financial Participation and Pay for Performance in Japan

Takao Kato

Introduction

In many countries around the world, pay systems are rapidly changing away from a contractual fixed wage (Ben-Ner and Jones 1995) to reflect a greater emphasis on performance. Prominent among these changes is the explosion in the use of financial participation, such as employee stock ownership plans (ESOPs) and profit sharing plans (PSPs). This paper considers the postwar Japanese experience with financial participation and pay for performance.

After reviewing the scope and nature of ESOPs and PSPs in Japan, which represent nearly all financial participation schemes used by Japanese firms (gain sharing is rare), we examine the pay system that evolved during Japan's economic slowdown of the 1990s. In particular, we document the response of Japanese employee stock ownership plans to the burst of the previously booming economy and the subsequent financial trouble. We also present new evidence on the use of performance pay in Japanese pay systems.[1] The paper's key findings include: (1) as a result of favorable environments in the postwar Japanese economy, financial participation schemes

---

I am grateful to Motohiro Morishima, Takamasa Nakashima, and Rengo-Soken for facilitating the data collection. I benefited greatly from comments made by the editors, Michelle Brown and John Heywood.

spread widely and are firmly established; (2) such schemes have positive effects on company performance in the long run; (3) there exists synergy between financial participation schemes; (4) financial participation appears to be surviving intact during the economic slowdown in the 1990s; and (5) the "seniority wage" of the Japanese pay system is giving ground to increasing use of pay for performance during recent years.

A closer look at the postwar Japanese experience with financial participation is of particular interest. As Levine and Tyson (1990) suggest, the relative job security (often ensured by transfers within the firm and to related firms) and the strong group cohesiveness (supported by compression of wage and status differentials) of Japanese workers in large manufacturing firms results in an industrial relations system favorable to successful financial participation. Moreover, rapid and stable growth in the postwar period, low unemployment, and stable financial corporate groupings (banks and institutional shareholders as stable, long-term suppliers of capital) point to an external environment favorable to successful financial participation.

Probably as a result of these favorable environments, in particular in manufacturing, financial participation spread widely and is firmly established as documented below. Indeed financial participation schemes have become an important ingredient of "Japanese management." Many corporations around the world have adopted (sometimes by necessity) elements of this management style, including financial participation (see, for instance, Levine 1995, 5). In short, the postwar Japanese economy (especially in manufacturing) clearly represents one of the most important examples of experimentation with financial participation.

The economic slowdown in the 1990s and a rapidly aging work force have allegedly eroded the aforementioned participation-friendly environments. Have financial participation schemes successful in the 1960s, 1970s, and 1980s survived in Japan in the 1990s? If so, how have they been evolving? Are there differences between sectors in the survival of such schemes? A closer look at the recent Japanese experience with financial participation will help answer two key questions regarding participation: (1) What are the conditions under which financial participation schemes are best introduced and best sustained? (2) How do financial participation schemes evolve when external environments change?

Even as financial participation grew after World War II, Japanese employers always felt a need to introduce flexible employment practices. Indeed, they attempted to weaken traditional employment practices, such as "lifetime employment" (an implicit long-term employment contract for the regular work force) and the seniority-based pay system, as early as the late 1960s. Until recently, however, employers' attempts to weaken these traditional employment practices have not produced any major changes.[2] Therefore, it is of great interest whether or not Japan's economic slowdown in the 1990s has put pressure on these traditional employment practices. While the rhetoric of "the replacement of traditional seniority-based pay with pay for performance" is currently rampant, concrete data on changes in traditional employment practices remain scarce. This paper presents the first main findings from analysis of data collected on the evolving pay system during Japan's economic slowdown in the 1990s.

The paper is organized as follows. The next section discusses the scope and nature of financial participation in postwar Japan and its diffusion over time. The following section summarizes theoretical arguments on the effects of financial participation on company performance, in particular on labor productivity, and reviews the evidence on such effects. This is followed by evidence on the evolving pay system in the 1990s. The final section makes some concluding observations.

The Scope, Nature, and Diffusion of Financial Participation in Japan

Employee Stock Ownership Plans

Japanese ESOPs are perhaps best understood by contrasting their key characteristics with the better-known U.S. ESOPs.[3] Unlike U.S. ESOPs, Japanese firms establishing a *mochikabukai* (ESOP) do not receive any tax incentive to do so. To induce individual workers to participate in the ESOP, firms offer subsidies (usually the firm matches each worker's contribution by paying 5 to 10 percent of the contribution as well as bearing administrative costs). Whereas ESOPs elsewhere are frequently structured in order to promote participation by top executives, in Japan executives (as well as part-time and temporary employees) are typically ineligible for membership. As is the norm elsewhere, individual participants' shares (and dividends) in the ESOP are held in trust. Unusually, however, each participant has a right to withdraw his or her shares, and share withdrawals are privately owned. Withdrawals are permitted only in round lots of 1,000 shares. While members may freely exit completely from the ESOP, reentry is restricted. Exiting employees will receive their shares in 1,000 shares (again, round lots) and must sell the remaining shares to the trust at the prevailing market price. Upon retirement, model rules adopted by most ESOPs require retiring workers to exit completely from the ESOP. Finally, the *rijicho* (general director) represents stockholders in the ESOP. The general director is chosen by the participants, on a one-participant, one-vote basis. At the general meeting of shareholders, the general director votes the stock held by the plan, deciding independently, rather than by tabulating votes of employee participants. The general director must be a participant in the ESOP and thus is not an executive (Jones and Kato 1995).

ESOPs have existed in Japan at least since 1919, with the introduction of a plan in the Kanematsu Gosho (a major general trading company). For the next two decades employee ownership was steadily diffused. By the end of World War II, however, these original plans had vanished. A second phase began when, as part of the Occupation reforms, almost one-third of the shares of certain designated companies were purchased by employees. In this process, ESOP trusts were formed for employee holdings. These trusts faced serious financial problems, however, and eventually all disappeared. The current form of employee ownership began in the 1960s. In 1967, a special government committee on foreign capital advocated employee ownership as a way to help prevent takeovers of domestic firms by foreign capital. The government, using informal channels, encouraged firms to set up new ESOP trusts to accommodate employee investments in their stock. While the fear of foreign takeovers diminished in the 1970s, the idea of employee ownership took root (Jones and Kato 1993).

In the 1970s and 1980s, the incidence of ESOPs grew remarkably in Japan. Table 8.1 and Figure 8.1, using different measures of ESOPs, demonstrate this growth. The data were taken from the *Kabushiki Bunpu Jyokyo Chosa* (survey of stock distribution), conducted annually since 1973 by the *Zenkoku Shoken Torihikijyo Kyogikai* (National Association of Stock Exchanges). All firms listed on Japan's eight stock exchange markets respond to the survey every year. Thus, the survey provides the most accurate picture of the diffusion of ESOPs among Japanese firms listed on the stock markets.

In terms of the incidence of ESOPs, the proportion of firms listed on the Japanese stock markets that have ESOPs grew steadily from 60.51 percent in 1973 to 91 percent in 1988. In terms of participation rates, the proportion of the labor force in publicly traded firms with ESOPs who participate in ESOPs also grew steadily from 30 percent in 1973 to almost 50 percent in 1988.

The employee stake, shown in Figure 8.1, has also been rising. The share prices of most large corporations in Japan have risen steadily, and so it is not surprising that steady growth of corporate profitability caused ESOPs to gain increasing popularity in Japan. The real market value of outstanding shares owned by ESOPs more than quadrupled, and the real market value of outstanding shares owned by ESOPs per participant (the real value of the average stake) more than doubled in the 1980s. The Na-

Table 8.1

Diffusion of ESOPs in All Firms Listed on the Japanese Stock Markets, 1973–1998

Year	Number of firms	Number of firms with ESOPs	Proportion of firms with ESOPs (in percents)[a]	Number of employees in firms with ESOPs (in thousands)	Number of employees participating in ESOPs (in thousands)	ESOP Participation rate (in percents)[b]
1973	1,684	1,019	60.51	3,333	991	29.73
1974	1,706	1,105	64.77	3,582	1,157	32.30
1975	1,710	1,174	68.65	3,820	1,280	33.51
1976	1,719	1,225	71.26	3,851	1,350	35.06
1977	1,723	1,274	73.94	3,860	1,438	37.25
1978	1,707	1,304	76.39	3,875	1,482	38.25
1979	1,723	1,345	78.06	3,928	1,548	39.41
1980	1,734	1,387	79.99	4,004	1,622	40.51
1981	1,749	1,439	82.28	4,128	1,713	41.50
1982	1,771	1,505	84.98	4,275	1,783	41.71
1983	1,790	1,556	86.93	4,330	1,826	42.17
1984	1,806	1,588	87.93	4,404	1,847	41.94
1985	1,834	1,630	88.88	4,418	1,895	42.89
1986	1,881	1,686	89.63	4,721	2,212	46.85
1987	1,924	1,738	90.33	4,760	2,272	47.73
1988	1,975	1,797	90.99	4,816	2,370	49.21
1989	2,030	1,877	92.46	5,031	2,477	49.23
1990	2,078	1,942	93.46	5,253	2,575	49.02
1991	2,106	1,980	94.02	5,360	2,603	48.56
1992	2,120	2,008	94.72	5,536	2,671	48.25
1993	2,160	2,058	95.28	5,641	2,713	48.09
1994	2,211	2,109	95.39	5,608	2,710	48.32
1995	2,277	2,174	95.48	5,534	2,682	48.46
1996	2,339	2,238	95.68	5,452	2,705	49.61
1997	2,387	2,290	95.94	5,396	2,682	49.70
1998	2,426	2,337	96.33	5,313	2,628	49.46

Year	Number of outstanding shares owned by firms with ESOPs (in millions)	Number of outstanding shares owned by ESOPs (in millions)	Proportion of shares owned by ESOPs (in percents)[c]	Market value of outstanding shares owned by ESOPs (in 1995 billions of yen)	Share price in 1995 yen	Market value of outstanding shares owned by ESOPs per participant (in 1995 thousands of yen)
1973	102,701	672.94	0.66			
1974	115,603	938.46	0.81			
1975	133,688	1,266.65	0.95			
1976	146,264	1,633.61	1.12			
1977	159,052	2,000.00	1.26			
1978	168,369	2,169.00	1.29			

(continued)

Table 8.1 *(continued)*

Year	Number of outstanding shares owned by firms with ESOPs (in millions)	Number of outstanding shares owned by ESOPs (in millions)	Proportion of shares owned by ESOPs (in percents)[c]	Market value of outstanding shares owned by ESOPs (in 1995 billions of yen)	Share price in 1995 yen	Market value of outstanding shares owned by ESOPs per participant (in 1995 thousands of yen)
1979	177,960	2,412.00	1.36	1,062.56	440.53	686.41
1980	187,819	2,616.00	1.39	1,224.39	468.04	754.86
1981	203,277	2,792.00	1.37	1,232.96	441.60	719.77
1982	216,105	3,074.00	1.42	1,446.87	470.68	811.48
1983	226,542	3,194.00	1.41	1,965.82	615.47	1,076.57
1984	236,433	3,229.00	1.37	2,183.88	676.33	1,182.39
1985	246,981	3,148.00	1.27	2,712.71	861.73	1,431.51
1986	298,334	3,345.00	1.12	3,471.70	1,037.88	1,569.49
1987	315,478	3,181.00	1.01	4,067.73	1,278.76	1,790.37
1988	335,254	3,127.00	0.93	4,675.73	1,495.28	1,972.88
1989	363,335	3,185.00	0.88	4,526.68	1,421.25	1,827.49
1990	375,109	3,374.00	0.90	4,049.73	1,200.28	1,572.71
1991	385,304	3,703.00	0.96	3,038.76	820.62	1,167.41
1992	406,478	4,228.00	1.04	3,277.47	775.18	1,227.06
1993	419,238	4,525.00	1.08	3,713.18	820.59	1,368.66
1994	438,608	4,897.00	1.12	3,224.88	658.54	1,189.99
1995	450,711	5,298.00	1.18	4,153.50	783.98	1,548.66
1996	470,601	5,696.00	1.21	3,604.80	632.86	1,332.64
1997	487,819	6,269.00	1.29	3,259.37	519.92	1,215.28
1998	508,543	6,900.00	1.36	3,524.88	510.83	1,341.28

Source: Kabushiki Bunpu Jyokyo Chosa (Survey of stock distribution).
[a] The proportion of firms with ESOPs in percent was calculated by dividing the third column by the second column.
[b] The ESOP participation rate was calculated by dividing the fifth column by the fourth column. The number of employees participating in ESOPs includes a small number of employees in subsidiaries.
[c] The proportion of shares owned by ESOPs was calculated by dividing the seventh column by the sixth column.

tional Conference Board also published the average price of shares owned by ESOPs (the market value of outstanding shares owned by ESOPs divided by the total number of shares owned by ESOPs). The real value of this average price tripled in the 1980s. In 1988 (the peak of Japan's bubble economy), ESOPs owned stock worth 4.1 trillion yen in nominal value (about US$32 billion); this amounts to 1.7 million yen in nominal value (about US$14,000) per participant.

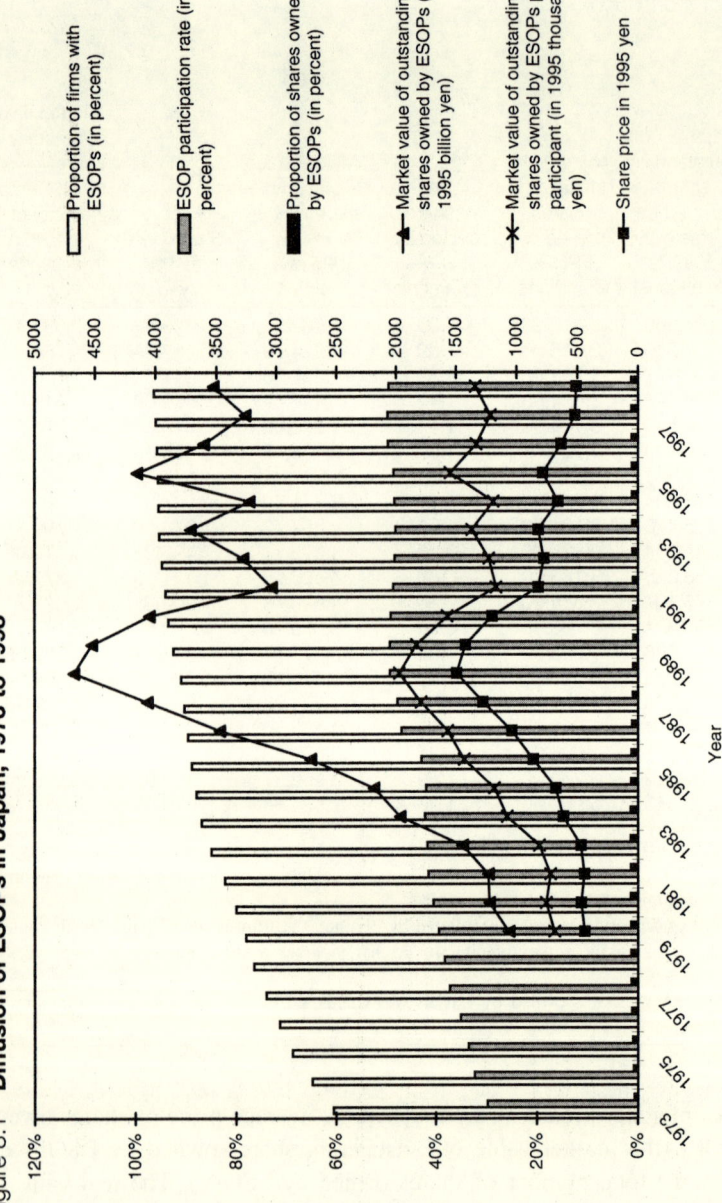

Figure 8.1 **Diffusion of ESOPs in Japan, 1973 to 1998**

These plans, however, do not own large percentages of company stock. As shown in Table 8.1, the proportion of stock owned by ESOPs for listed companies has been between 0.66 percent and 1.42 percent. In 1988 the average is lower than 1 percent and holdings over 5 percent are rare. However, while the total percentage of equity owned by plans is small, according to Nomura Securities (1990), in 21 percent of all listed Japanese firms, the ESOP is one of the ten largest shareholders. We will discuss the effects of an economic downturn on the use of ESOPs in the 1990s in a subsequent section.

Profit Sharing Plans

A profit sharing plan (PSP) is a pay system in which the total amount of bonuses is linked to a measure of firm performance, such as profit.[4] The Japanese bonus payment system has attracted considerable attention and controversy (e.g., Freeman and Weitzman 1987; Nakamura and Nakamura 1989; Hashimoto 1990; Hart and Kawasaki 1995). In light of the ongoing debate between those who stress the profit sharing aspect of the Japanese bonus system (e.g., Freeman and Weitzman 1987) and those who downplay it (e.g., Ohashi 1989; Brunello 1991), we consider only the least controversial (with respect to the profit-sharing aspect of the bonus payment system) type of the bonus payment system, that is, the bonus payment system containing an explicit profit sharing plan.

Japanese PSPs were adopted in the hope of making employees more conscious of the firm's sales and production targets, and of motivating them to work harder to accomplish these goals. According to Kato and Morishima (1999), one in four publicly traded firms had a PSP in 1993 (with no appreciable difference between manufacturing and nonmanufacturing firms). Figure 8.2 shows the diffusion of PSPs over time among these firms. The proportion of firms with PSPs was a little over 5 percent in the 1960s and then grew steadily to 14 percent by 1980. A significant diffusion occurred during the 1980s, however, with the proportion of firms with PSPs growing to over 20 percent by 1990.

PSPs are more popular among firms without unions than among firms with unions. Specifically, over 40 percent of firms without unions use a PSP, whereas only 23 percent of firms with unions use a PSP.[5]

PSPs are more prevalent among firms with employee participation at the grass roots, such as Shop-Floor Committees (SFCs), in which supervisors and employees on shop floor discuss issues such as shop-floor operation and shop-floor environments; Small Group Activities (SGAs), or

Figure 8.2 **Proportion of Firms with PSPs, 1965 to 1992**

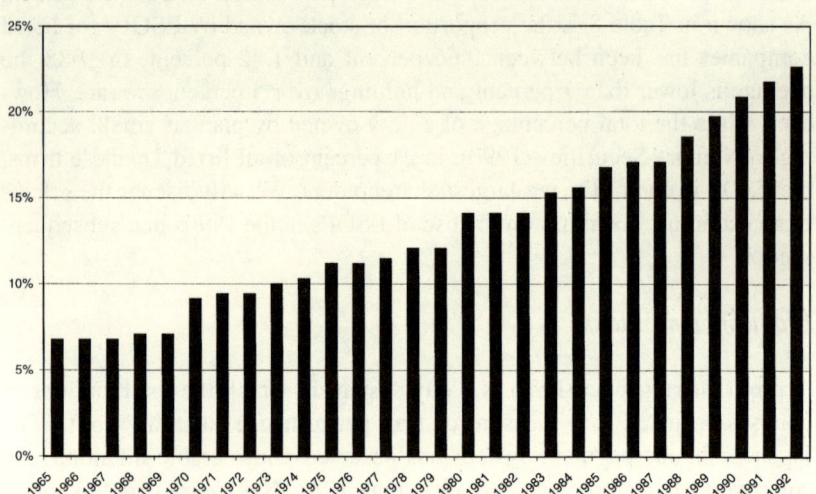

activities such as quality control (QC) circles; and Zero Defects, in which small groups at the workplace level voluntarily set plans and goals concerning operations and work together toward accomplishing these plans and goals.

In comparison with non-PSP firms, PSP firms have smaller labor forces, less value added, and higher ROA. Over 70 percent of firms with PSPs reported separate plans for executives and nonexecutives. However, Japanese PSPs do not normally distinguish between union and nonunion members (only one-third of firms with PSPs reported separate PSPs for union and nonunion members). PSPs are mostly companywide, with only 12 percent of firms with PSPs reporting separate plans for different divisions and occupations. Moreover, nearly all Japanese PSPs are cash plans (98 percent), which is in sharp contrast to the United States, where deferred plans are more popular (see Kruse 1993, 16–17). Being almost always cash plans, Japanese PSPs have no tax advantage. A little over 50 percent of Japanese PSPs do not have set formulas for how contributions are tied to profit, which also contrasts with PSPs in the United States, where only 22 percent are fully discretionary (Kruse 1993, 75). The most popular formula used by Japanese PSPs sets a specific percentage of profit in excess of predetermined target profit (26 percent of all profit sharing firms with explicit formula use this formula). A specific percentage of profit with no reference to any targets is used by 24 percent of all profit sharing firms with explicit formula. A little over 10 percent of profit sharing firms with explicit formula use a specific percentage of profit in excess of an amount reserved for dividends. Other formulas involve alternative firm performance measures such as sales and value added. The average age of Japanese PSPs is a little over eighteen years.

Effects of Financial Participation

In general, formal economic theory is ambiguous as to the expected effect of financial participation on productivity and firm performance. (For reviews, see the essays in Blinder 1990.) Focusing on individual motivation and performance, however, several hypotheses predict positive effects, of which the following are the most important.

PSPs help align the interest of the firm with the interest of its employees by linking pay for employees to firm performance, as measured by profitability. Likewise, the most direct positive effects of ESOPs result from enterprise success being reflected in a higher price of its equity, and thus in higher wealth for employees who own stock in the ESOP. Again, the interest of the firm is more aligned with the interest of its employees.

These interest alignment effects of financial participation can be expected to be more significant in Japan than in the United States. First, Japanese firms receive no tax incentive to establish financial participation with either PSPs or ESOPs. In this sense, the intent of Japanese firms to introduce financial participation can be interpreted by their employees as more "genuinely participatory" than in the United States or Britain. Second, executives are normally ineligible for membership in Japanese ESOPs, whereas ESOPs in the U.S. are often structured to encourage strong participation by top management (Jones and Kato 1995). Indeed, U.S. ESOPs are frequently designed to prevent participation by groups of nonexecutive employees, especially union members (Blasi 1988). In Japan all full-time nonexecutive employees are typically eligible for membership, and, based on our interviews with managers of several Japanese manufacturing corporations, it appears that blue-collar workers actively participate in ESOPs. Third, Kruse (1993) shows that cash PSPs tend to have a greater productivity effect than deferred plans. As discussed, almost all Japanese PSPs are cash plans. Finally, the average Japanese ESOP participant owns a substantial amount of stock, worth US$14,000 on average.

Another critical element of Japanese ESOPs is the vesting feature. In order to own shares privately, the average employee participant must stay with the firm for a substantial number of years (over twenty years, according to Jones and Kato 1995). This vesting feature can be expected to discourage employee turnover and promote the formation of more firm-specific human capital. As such, Japanese ESOPs may lead to higher labor productivity.

In spite of the importance of the postwar Japanese experience with financial participation, there exists little systematic investigation of the economic effects of financial participation in Japan. The Japanese bonus payment system has attracted considerable attention and controversy, in particular the claim that it represents a form of a PSP. Earlier studies focused on the effects on employment of the Japanese bonus payment system. Freeman and Weitzman (1987) use industry-level aggregate data to show a statistically significant positive correlation between bonuses and employment levels. However, Brunello (1991) uses firm-level micro data, and finds *no* statistically significant positive correlations between bonuses and employment levels for the electric machinery, car, and steel industries.[6] Recent studies have turned to the issue of the productivity effects of the Japanese bonus payment system. Jones and Kato (1995) use firm-level panel data to find that there is a modest productivity gain from the bonus system. Ohkusa and Ohtake (1997) find that firms with a statistically significant positive correlation between their wages and per capita profit are 9 percent more productive than firms without such a correlation. Jones and Kato (1995) again use firm-level panel data to find that the introduction of an ESOP leads to a 4–5 percent increase in productivity but that this productivity payoff does not appear immediately. Jones and Kato (1995) also provide evidence of the complementarity between ESOPs and bonuses in Japan. That is, the productivity effect of bonuses is enhanced by the existence of ESOPs, suggesting that ESOPs may create a climate conducive to bonuses by enhancing long-term commitment and peer monitoring. Most recently, Kato and Morishima (2000) use firm-level micro data from nearly 100 Japanese firms with PSPs. Their data contains detailed information on attributes of the PSPs, and they estimate the effects on enterprise performance of these varying attributes of Japanese PSPs. They find a statistically significant gain in firm performance from using an explicit formula in PSPs as opposed to not using an explicit formula. In addition, they show that including certain targets in the formula appears to further improve firm performance.

PAY FOR PERFORMANCE IN JAPAN   225

The Evolving Pay System in the 1990s[7]

ESOPs in the 1990s

As shown in Figure 8.1, the steady growth of share prices ended rather abruptly at the end of the 1980s. For instance, the average firm listed in the Tokyo Stock Exchange lost more than half its value in the early 1990s (Kang and Stulz 1998). Reflecting this rapid asset price deflation in the early 1990s, the real market value of outstanding shares owned by ESOPs, the real value of the average stake, and the real value of the average price of shares owned by ESOPs fell sharply in the early 1990s. As shown in Figure 8.1, recovery from this sharp drop has been anemic.

The substantial drop in the value of ESOPs does not appear to have discouraged employees from participating in ESOPs. As shown in Figure 8.1, the ESOP participation rate has not fallen in any significant way in the 1990s, although its steady increase during the 1980s did stop in the 1990s: The ESOP participation rate rose in the 1980s by 9 percentage points from 40 to 49 percent and has remained at the 49 percent level in the 1990s. It is, however, unclear whether the stagnation of the participation rate in the 1990s is caused by the adverse financial shocks.[8] At any rate, there has not been any sign of a frenzied exit of participants from ESOPs in response to the adverse financial shock in the 1990s.

Consistent with this relatively calm response of employees, very few employers have terminated their ESOPs in response to the adverse financial shock. Thus, as shown in Figure 8.1, the proportion of firms with ESOPs has not fallen in the 1990s and ESOPs have continued to be a near-universal phenomenon among publicly traded firms in Japan (95 percent of all publicly traded firms currently have ESOPs).

Overall, it appears that neither employees nor employers have panicked in the face of the adverse financial shock in the 1990s. In addition to the summary table for all publicly traded firms, the National Conference Board publishes the summary table for two-digit industries. Conceivably the adverse shock might have been hitting certain industries particularly hard and for those hard-hit industries, many ESOPs might have been terminated and the ESOP participation rate might have fallen significantly. As shown in Figures 8.3 and 8.4, there are no dramatic examples of such industries, although, as shown in Figure 8.4, the ESOP participation rate has fallen to some extent from 1988 to 1997 for mining, textiles, steel, primary metals, transportation equipment, wholesale and retail trade, finance and insurance, real estate, and service. Somewhat surprisingly, however, the ESOP partic-

Figure 8.3 **Changes in Proportion of Firms with ESOPs, 1988–97 by Industry**

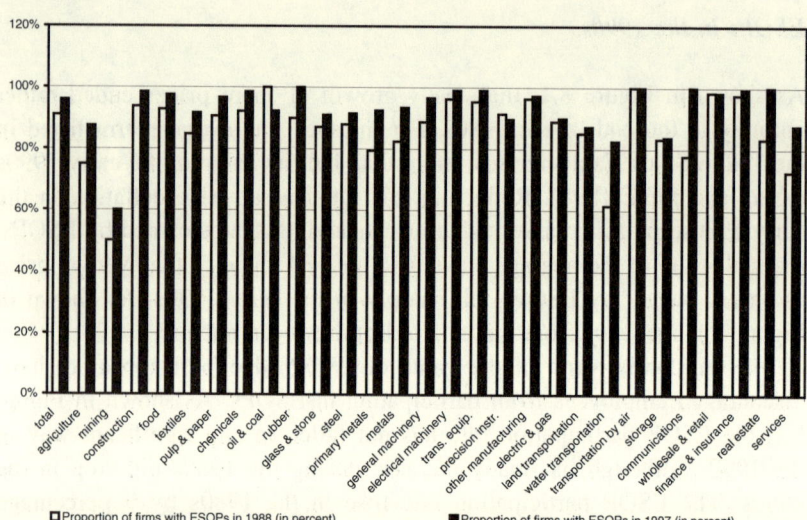

□ Proportion of firms with ESOPs in 1988 (in percent)   ■ Proportion of firms with ESOPs in 1997 (in percent)

ipation rate has risen substantially over the same time period for oil and coal, land transportation, water transportation, and transportation by air.

Shifts Towards Pay for Performance in the 1990s

Chingin Rodojikan Seido to Sogo Chosa (The general survey of wages and hours worked system), conducted in 1999 by the Ministry of Labor, provides the most recent aggregate data on other important changes in the pay systems of Japanese firms. The same survey was also conducted in 1996 by the Ministry.[9] Using various cross-tabulations published from the 1999 survey as well as those from the 1996 survey, tables 8.2–8.4 have been generated.

With Japan's rapidly aging labor force, Japanese firms have been finding their seniority-based wages increasingly costly and have been shifting their pay systems away from seniority-based wages and toward performance-based wages during the late 1990s. In addition, such a shift has often been proposed by employers as a necessary response to the allegedly dwindling productivity of white-collar workers.[10]

As shown in Table 8.2, about half of all firms changed their pay systems in late 1990s. Specifically, in 1999, about 30 percent of firms decreased their automatic pay raises (pre-determined pay raises that employees re-

Figure 8.4 **Changes in ESOP Participation Rate, 1988–1997 by Industry**

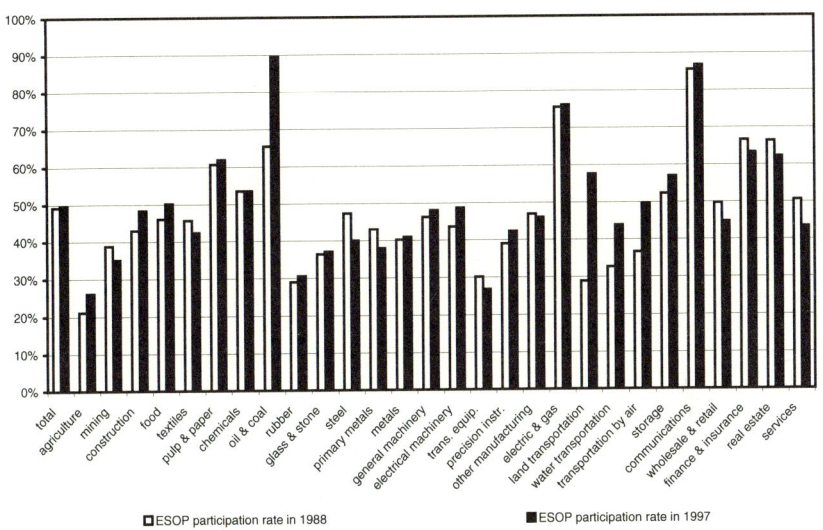

ceive as they spend an additional year with the firm) during the previous three years and over 10 percent abolished their automatic pay raises altogether. In other words, about 40 percent of firms decreased the importance of seniority-based pay during the previous three years. The corresponding figure for 1996 was 30 percent. Thus, the tendency away from seniority-based pay appears to be accelerating in late 1990s.

On the other hand, 15 percent of firms expanded the portion of their pay determined by outcome and performance in late 1990s. As shown in Table 8.3, over 20 percent of firms plan to expand the portion of their pay determined by outcome and performance in the next three years.

Table 8.4 shows the prevalence of individual incentive pay and gain sharing. As shown, over 15 percent of firms used individual incentive pay in the late 1990s. Individual incentive pay was particularly popular among firms in transportation and communication (over 40 percent of such firms used individual incentive pay). Firms in finance and insurance increased the use of individual incentive pay substantially in the late 1990s.

Gain sharing is less prevalent among Japanese firms. As shown in Table 8.4, fewer than 4 percent of Japanese firms use gain sharing. Gain sharing is most widely used among firms in mining. There is also no evidence for an increase in the incidence of gain sharing.

Table 8.2

Proportion of Firms That Changed Their Pay Systems in the Previous Three Years, as of 1996 and 1999

	1996	1999
Percentage of firms that changed their pay systems in the last three years	49.7	53.0
Increased automatic pay raise	11.9	10.5
Decreased automatic pay raise	23.3	30.1
Abolished automatic pay raise	3.8	10.5
Expanded the part of pay determined by the content of tasks and jobs	12.1	11.3
Expanded the part of pay determined by ability to carry out jobs	15.7	15.8
Expanded the part of pay determined by outcome and performance	15.0	15.5
Reduced benefits and integrated them into base pay	4.9	6.4
Introduced wage tables	6.8	5.2
Introduced and revised job grade systems	7.8	8.7
Introduced and revised multitrack pay systems	1.3	1.9
Introduced and revised annual salary systems	3.0	5.4
Limited base wage and increased weights for bonuses	3.5	2.7

Source: Chingin Rodojikan Seido to Sogo Chosa (General survey of wages and hours worked system), 1999, 1996.

Table 8.3

Proportion of Firms That Planned to Change Their Pay Systems in the Next Three Years, as of 1996 and 1999

	1996	1999
Percentage of firms that plan to change their pay systems in the next three years as follows:	49.4	39.7
Increase automatic pay raise	12.2	6.8
Decrease automatic pay raise	6.3	15.1
Abolish automatic pay raise	5.3	7.0
Expand the part of pay determined by the content of tasks and jobs	19.8	13.5
Expand the part of pay determined by ability to carry out jobs	27.2	20.8
Expand the part of pay determined by outcome and performance	27.2	22.3
Reduce benefits and integrate them into base pay	5.3	5.2
Introduce wage tables	12.6	7.1
Introduce and revise job grade systems	16.1	12.5
Introduce and revise multitrack pay systems	5.7	5.0
Introduce and revise annual salary systems	8.8	8.4
Limit base wage and increase weights for bonuses	8.3	6

Source: Chingin Rodojikan Seido to Sogo Chosa (General survey of wages and hours worked system), 1999, 1996.

Table 8.4

Proportion of Firms with Individual Incentive Pay and Gain Sharing, 1996 and 1999

	Percentage of Firms with individual incentive pay		Percentage of firms with gain sharing	
	1996	1999	1996	1999
All	15.6	16.4	3.6	3.0
1,000+	12.9	12.9	4.2	3.5
100–999	14.6	17.1	3.5	4.9
300–999	18.0	13.7	5.2	4.8
100–299	13.5	18.1	3.0	5.0
30–99	16.2	16.3	3.6	2.3
Mining	3.2	4.8	9.1	
Construction	15.1	12.8	1.6	0.4
Manufacturing	6.9	8.5	2.2	2.1
Electric, gas, heat and water	5.1	5.4	1.7	
Transportation and communication	40.3	41.1	4.9	4.1
Wholesale and retail trade	20.3	19.2	6.0	5.7
Finance and insurance	19.4	30.5	2.8	3.2
Real estate	13.7	17.8	2.0	2.3
Services	16.0	16.3	5.1	3.0

Source: Chingin Rodojikan Seido to Sogo Chosa (General survey of wages and hours worked system), 1999, 1996.

Recent Attitudes of Employees Toward Pay for Performance

In May 1998, the *Rengo Sogo Seikatsu Kaihatsu Kenkyu Jo* (Rengo Research Institute of General Life Development) mailed a questionnaire to 33,400 union members, asking them about their attitudes toward their pay systems and other employment policies. This resulted in 20,761 usable responses (a response rate of 62.2 percent). Of these, 44 percent of respondents worked in manufacturing firms, 39 percent in nonmanufacturing firms, and 17 percent in governments and other public service agencies.[11]

As shown in Table 8.5, the majority of employees felt that their pay system had changed to reflect more individual performance and merit. Such changes were felt most widely among workers in finance, insurance and real estate, and wholesale and retail trade, whereas they were felt least widely among workers in governments and other public service agencies.

Table 8.6 shows employee attitudes toward such changes in the pay

Table 8.5

Perceptions of Changes in the Pay System Toward Pay for Individual Performance and Merit, 1998

	Total	Manufacturing	Wholesale and retail trade	Finance, insurance, and real estate	Governments and other public service agencies
Proportion of employees who felt such changes strongly	16.10%	18.80%	22.90%	31.60%	4.50%
Proportion of employees who felt such changes somewhat	35.00	38.20	42.70	42.20	21.10
Proportion of employees who did not feel such changes a lot	17.40	17.20	11.80	8.80	20.60
Proportion of employees who did not feel such changes at all	7.60	5.50	4.00	2.20	16.10

Source: Wage and Personnel Policy Supplement to *Rengo Seikatsu Jittai* survey, 1998.

Table 8.6

Attitudes on Changing the Pay System Toward Pay for Individual Performance and Merit, 1998

	Total	Four-Year college degrees or postgraduate degrees	Two-year college degrees or other post-secondary degrees	High school diplomas	Junior high school diplomas
Proportion of employees who agreed strongly	10.70%	6.00%	9.50%	8.10%	6.90%
Proportions of employees who agreed somewhat	37.00	43.90	35.60	34.10	27.70
Proportion of employees who disagreed somewhat	11.40	8.50	10.20	12.90	15.60
Proportion of employees who disagreed strongly	4.40	3.50	3.30	5.10	4.90

Source: Wage and Personnel Policy Supplement to *Rengo Seikatsu Jittai* survey, 1998.

system. Overall, nearly half of employees agreed with such changes; and more educated workers are more receptive to such changes.

Finally, Table 8.7 presents the proportion of employees who agree that a larger component of their pay should reflect individual performance and merit, and the portion who agree that a larger component should reflect firm performance. Overall, employees are most receptive to changes in their bonus system to reflect pay for individual performance and merit (54.5 percent) and are next most receptive to changes in their bonus system to reflect firm performance (49.8 percent). They are least receptive to changes in their base wages to reflect firm performance (27.7 percent).

The rest of the table shows the figures disaggregated by educational attainment, age, tenure, and occupations. First, more educated workers are more receptive to changes that reflect individual performance and merit, and that reflect firm performance. In particular, over 70 percent of workers with at least four-year college degrees agreed that their bonus systems should be changed to reflect more individual performance and merit. Over 65 percent of such workers agreed that their bonuses should be more linked to firm performance. Second, workers in their late twenties and thirties were most open to changes in their pay system designed to reflect individual performance and merit, and to reflect firm performance. In general, workers tended to be less receptive to such changes as they aged. Third, a similar pattern was found for tenure; that is, in general more senior workers were less receptive to such changes than junior workers. Fourth, production workers were the least receptive to such changes while professional/technical and sales/marketing/service workers were most receptive.

Concluding Observations

This chapter has examined important aspects of the postwar Japanese experience with financial participation and with pay for performance. First we reviewed the scope and nature of financial participation schemes in Japan and their diffusion among Japanese firms over time. We then turned to the evidence on the effects of such schemes on company performance. Third we provided findings from our most recent research on the pay system evolving during Japan's economic slowdown in the 1990s. In particular, we documented the response of Japanese employee stock ownership plans to the burst of the bubble economy and subsequent financial trouble of the Japanese economy in the 1990s. Finally, we presented new evidence on the recent shift of the Japanese pay system toward pay for performance.

The paper's key findings include that as a result of favorable environments in the postwar Japanese economy, financial participation schemes

Table 8.7

Proportion of Employees Who Agreed on Pay System Changes, 1998

	Changing monthly base wage, based on Firm performance	Changing bonus, based on firm performance	Changing monthly base wage, based on individual performance	Changing bonus, based on individual performance
Total	27.70%	49.80%	44.40%	54.50%
Highest educational attainment:				
Four-year college degrees or post-graduate degrees	36.70	66.30	57.00	71.50
Two-year college degrees or other post-secondary degrees	26.80	46.60	43.60	52.70
High school diplomas	23.50	42.20	38.90	46.90
Junior high school diplomas	16.50	32.00	25.00	31.70
Age:				
Under 24	26.60	35.60	42.00	45.30
25–29	35.30	52.40	52.00	59.70
30–34	33.70	60.80	54.80	67.20
35–39	26.40	53.00	46.40	59.00
40–44	24.10	48.50	39.70	51.40
45–49	20.80	43.90	35.00	44.10
50–54	20.20	39.90	30.60	39.70
55+	18.00	33.30	25.60	33.20
Tenure:				
Less than 3 years	33.80	46.20	47.70	54.10
3–4 years	32.90	48.10	50.90	57.80
5–9 years	34.60	55.00	52.60	61.90
10–14 years	29.70	56.20	50.80	62.20
15–19 years	25.50	49.00	44.30	55.10
20–24 years	23.50	46.00	36.90	47.40
25–29 years	20.80	44.70	35.50	46.60
30 + years	19.20	40.80	29.00	39.50
Production	22.20	41.20	37.30	44.60
Professional/technical	31.50	58.40	52.10	65.20
Clerical	29.30	50.60	45.20	55.50
Sales/marketing/service	38.80	59.50	51.90	64.40

Source: Wage and Personnel Policy Supplement to *Rengo Seikatsu Jittai* survey, 1998.

spread widely and were firmly established. The balance of the evidence suggests that such schemes have positive effects on company performance in the long run. Moreover, evidence was found for synergy between financial participation schemes. Somewhat surprisingly, financial participation appears to be surviving intact during the economic slowdown in the 1990s. While it is impossible to say what would have happened had the economy remained robust, it is clear that financial participation remains a critical part of the pay system. Largely unrecognized, Japanese pay systems have been shifting in recent years away from seniority-based pay and toward performance pay.

Notes

1. For a growing literature on the burst of the booming economy and subsequent transformation of the Japanese financial system, see, for example, Hoshi and Kashyap, 1999 and Patrick (1998).
2. See, for instance, Morishima (1992).
3. See, for example, Jones and Kato (1993, 1995) for Japanese ESOPs.
4. For instance, Jones, Kato, and Pliskin (1997) provide a recent review of the literature on profit sharing in general.
5. See Kato and Morishima (2000) for various attributes of Japanese PSPs.
6. Brunello (1991) does find, however, the statistically significant positive correlation between bonuses and employment level for the textiles industry.
7. We focus on ESOPs and recent shifts from seniority-based wage toward pay for individual performance. Unfortunately, since our survey of 1993, no systematic data have been collected on PSPs. Based on my recent interviews with HR managers at a number of Japanese firms in the summer of 1999, Japanese employers' interest in PSPs appears to have diminished somewhat in recent years, giving way to surging interest in pay for individual performance.
8. The ESOP participation rate has seemingly reached a plateau in the 1990s, perhaps in part due to the rising availability of mutual funds. When ESOPs were initially introduced, they were the only means for the average worker in Japan, in particular the average production worker in Japan to own any stock.
9. The sample universe of the survey is all firms in Japan that employ thirty or more employees. The response rates were 92.9 percent and 95.2 percent for 1996 and 1999, respectively.
10. Nearly all HR managers whom we interviewed in the summer of 1999 mentioned thse two reasons (aging labor force and dwindling productivity growth of white-collar workers) for the shift toward performance-based wages.
11. Cross-tabulations of the survey results are available in Rengo Research Institute of General Life Development (1999).

References

Ben-Ner, Avner, and Jones, Derek C. 1995. "Employee Participation, Ownership, and Productivity: A Theoretical Framework." *Industrial Relations* 34: 532–554.

Blasi, Joseph R. 1988. *Employee Ownership: Revolution or Ripoff?* Cambridge: Balinger.

Blinder, Alan S., ed. 1990. *Paying for Productivity.* Washington, DC: Brookings Institution.

Brunello, Giorgio. 1991. "Bonuses, Wages and Performances in Japan: Evidence from Micro Data." *Ricerche Economiche* 45: 377–396.

Freeman, Richard B., and Weitzman, Martin L. 1987. "Bonuses and Employment in Japan." *Journal of the Japanese and International Economies* 1: 168–194.

Hart, Robert A., and Kawasaki, Seiichi. 1995. "The Japanese Bonus System and Human Capital." *Journal of the Japanese and International Economies* 9: 225–44.

Hashimoto, Masanori. 1990. *The Japanese Labor Market in a Comparative Perspective with the United States.* Kalamazoo, MI: Upjohn Institute for Employment Research.

Hoshi, Takeo, and Kashyap, Anil. 1999. "The Japanese Banking Crisis: Where Did it Come from and Where did it End." National Bureau of Economic Research, Working Paper No. 7250. Boston, MA.

Jones, Derek C., and Kato, Takao. 1993. "On the Scope, Nature and Effects of Employee Stock Ownership Plans in Japan." *Industrial and Labor Relations Review* 46: 352–367.

———. 1995. "The Productivity Effects of Employee Stock Ownership Plans and Bonuses: Evidence from Japanese Panel Data." *American Economic Review* 85: 391–414.

Jones, Derek, Kato, Takao, and Pliskin, Jeffrey. 1997. "Profit Sharing and Gain Sharing: A Review of Theory, Incidence, and Effects." In *The Human Resource Management Handbook,* Part 1, ed. David Lewin, Daniel J. B. Mitchell, and Mahmood A. Zaidi. Greenwich, CT: JAI Press, 153–174.

Kang, Jun-Koo, and Stulz, Rene M. 1998. "Is Bank-Centered Corporate Governance Worth It? A Cross-Sectional Analysis of the Performance of Japanese Firms During the Asset Price Deflation." Paper presented at the NBER Japan Project Meeting, Cambridge, MA, April 18.

Kato, Takao. 2000. "The End of 'Lifetime Employment' In Japan? Evidence from National Surveys and Field Research." Paper presented at the joint NBER–CEPR–TCER Conference on Unemployment, Tokyo, December 15.

Kato, Takao, and Morishima, Motohiro. 1999. "The Productivity Effects of Participatory Employment Practices: Evidence from New Japanese Panel Data." Mimeograph, Department of Economics, Colgate University, Hamilton, NY, May.

———. 2000. "The Nature, Scope and Effects of Profit Sharing in Japan: Evidence from New Survey Data." Mimeograph, Department of Economics, Colgate University, Hamilton, NY, November.

Kruse, Douglas L. 1993. *Profit Sharing: Does It Make a Difference?* Kalamazoo, MI: W. E. Upjohn Institute for Employment Research.

Levine, David I. 1995. *Reinventing the Workplace.* Washington, DC: Brookings Institution.

Levine, David I., and Tyson, Laura D'Andrea. 1990. "Participation, Productivity and the Firm's Environment." In *Paying for Productivity,* ed. Alan S. Blinder. Washington, DC: Brookings Institution, 183–236.

Morishima, Motohiro. 1992. "Use of Joint Consultation Committees by Large Japanese Firms." *British Journal of Industrial Relations* 30: 405–423.

Nakamura, Masao, and Nakamura, Alice. 1989. "Risk Behavior and the Determinants of Bonus versus Regular Pay in Japan." *Journal of the Japanese and International Economies* 3: 270–291.

Nomura Securities. 1990. *Mochikabu Seido no Unci Jitsumu* (Handbook of ESOPS). Tokyo: Shoki Homu Kenktu Kai.
Ohashi, Isao. 1989. "On the Determinants of Bonuses and Basic Wages in Large Japanese Firms." *Journal of the Japanese and International Economies* 3: 451–479.
Ohkusa, Yasushi, and Ohtake, Fumio. 1997. "The Productivity Effects of Information Sharing, Profit-Sharing and ESOPs." *Journal of the Japanese and International Economies* 11: 385–402.
Patrick, Hugh. 1998. "The Causes of Japan's Financial Crisis." Working Paper No. 146, Center on Japanese Economics and Business. Columbia University. New York, NY.
Rengo Research Institute of General Life Development. 1999. *"Koyo To Jinjishogu No Shorai Tenbo Ni Kansuru Chosa Kenkyu Houkokusho"* (Research report on the future of employment and personnel policies.) (In Japanese.) May.

Chapter 9

The Brazilian Case
Performance Pay as Workers' Right

Hélio Zylberstajn

Introduction

Performance pay in Brazil is quite a peculiar case study. For decades, the law prevented Brazilian firms from adopting flexible compensation policies. In recent years, however, the legal restraints have been replaced by a combination of economic incentives and new restrictions. As a result, performance pay can now lower the total cost of compensation and, for reasons explained in the text, has become a mandatory bargaining issue. This chapter describes and explores the extent to which Brazilian firms use performance pay to reduce compensation cost and the extent to which it is used to enhance labor productivity. The chapter also addresses the connection between performance pay and Brazilian unions.

The author expresses his appreciation to Antonio Tiago Loureiro Junior, Beraca Chen, Cristiane Gerosa Kisil, Daniel Augusto Motta, Ignez Miranda Tristão, Letícia Mina Hara, Marina Bitelman, and Yeung Luk Tai. As graduate students at the Department of Economics of the University of São Paulo, they helped collect and classify collective agreements from 1995 to the present. The author also thanks Anderson Stancioli for his important assistance with the econometric treatment of the data. Finally, the author thanks the editors of this volume for important comments on an earlier version of the chapter. Mistakes and omissions remain the responsibility of the author.

Legal and Institutional Background

In 1946, after fifteen years of dictator Getulio Vargas, democracy was restored, Brazilians elected a new president and Congress and passed a new Constitution. The new Constitution gave Brazilian workers the explicit right to share their employers' profits. Congress saw profit sharing as a means to promote social equity and correct income inequality. While subsequent constitutional reforms in 1967 and 1988 kept this right, it was not actually implemented until 1994. To understand this fifty-one-year wait, it is necessary to describe three features of Brazilian industrial relations: (1) unions and collective bargaining, (2) labor costs, and (3) the doctrine of acquired rights.

Unions and Collective Bargaining

Brazil is one of the few countries not to have signed Convention 87 of the International Labor Organization (ILO). The Convention, regarded as important by ILO, establishes the "freedom to organize." Under the Convention, workers are entitled to decide on the matters of union organization and structure without interference. In particular, workers decide whether the union structure should be unified, with a single union, or organized, with more than one union. In Brazil, the structure of representation is a matter of law and constitution, and workers do not have the freedom to organize unions of their own.

Until 1988, the Labor Code was very restrictive about union organization, and unions were subject to interference and even intervention by the government. The law restricted the size of union boards of directors to twenty-five members. To exist, the union needed a formal authorization from the labor secretary, known as the *Carta Sindicale* (Union Letter). Unions could organize only workers belonging to "categories" that were narrowly defined in the law. If a category was not listed in the Labor Code, there could not be a union for these workers. The law never recognized the right to organize or to represent workers at the plant level. The smallest representative and bargaining unit was at the level of the city.

Together with restrictions on union activities, the law provided rights to the unions, including the monopoly of representation. Once recognized by the government, the union becomes the single representative of the workers. In addition, the law created the "union tax," a compulsory fee taken from all workers belonging to the category. The union tax is equal in value to earnings from one day of work. The revenue is distributed in the following proportions: 60 percent to the local (city) union, 15 percent to the state federation, 5 percent to the national confederation, and 20 percent to the Labor Department.

Brazilian labor law created within the Labor Department many tripartite structures, with some positions reserved for labor union officers. The Labor Court system was also a tripartite structure, with hundreds of positions to be filled. The appointment decisions were highly political, and were used by governments to coopt labor leaders. Through this system, the government was able to control the labor movement, and the industrialization of the country proceeded with minimal industrial conflict.

The 1988 Constitution changed old provisions and created an ambiguous situation. On the one hand, the new Constitution eliminated all forms of government interference and intervention in union affairs. On the other hand, it kept the monopoly of representation and the union tax, and it created a second compulsory contribution, the size of which was to be decided by the union-organized "workers assembly." Thus, unions achieved more freedom without assuming the risks and responsibilities that typically come with freedom. As a result, Brazilian unions today retain the guarantee of monopolistic representation and the right to collect compulsory fees from all workers; they were made free to define their own categories of workers, and yet they still do not represent workers at the plant level.

The maintenance of both the union tax and the union monopoly has provided incentives to create new unions even as union officers remain relatively insulated from rank-and-file pressures to represent workers interests. Figures from the Brazilian Labor Department show there are now about 18,000 unions. There is, however, an important part of the Brazilian labor movement, within Central Única dos Trabalhadores (CUT [Unique center of workers]—the largest peak organization), which advocates the signing of Convention 87. Some Brazilian unions give back to the workers they represent the fees collected by the government, and some unions fight to establish formal representation at the plant level through Works Councils, and to establish direct negotiations with management. However, the majority of Brazilian unions are probably more concerned with collecting compulsory fees; they prefer to keep their monopoly representation and to engage in local industry-wide bargaining.

In sum, Brazilian workers in an organized firm are represented by a single union. The union engages in collective bargaining at least once a year. Bargaining outcomes are automatically extended to all workers in the industry, regardless of membership status. The bargaining unit is the industry, typically at the municipal level. A local (city) union bargains with either a local or a state employers' association over the wage rate and over

Table 9.1

Union Density in Brazil, 1979–1999
(union members as a percentage of the labor force)

Year	Union density
1979	22.5
1988	24.0
1990	22.6
1995	14.1
1996	15.7
1997	15.3
1998	15.1
1999	15.0

Source: PNAD-IBGE (National Household Sample Survey, Brazilian Institute of Geography and Statistics).

other issues. Bargaining outcomes then apply to the entire industry at the city level. The law provides workers with a long list of individual rights.[1] Unions exist regardless of workers' will. Workers are always represented and there is always only one labor organization occupying the space, but workers do not have a union representing their interests at the plant level.

Union membership in Brazil has declined. In 1999, union members make up about 15 percent of the Brazilian labor force, down from 22.5 percent in 1979 (Table 9.1). These figures reflect three limitations: first, the institutional restrictions already described; second, a more open and competitive market structure in Brazil; and third, the existence of a large informal sector, where organizing workers is a very difficult job for unions.

Individual and collective industrial disputes can be taken to the Labor Courts. Individual grievances, however, are rarely raised during the employment relationship, as workers wait until the termination of their employment to raise a grievance with the Labor Courts. Unions have a very secondary role in solving individual disputes, while lawyers and judges play a major role. Thus, a government-sponsored system of conflict resolution, a generous Labor Code, and industrywide bargaining at the local level have each accommodated union leaders and moved most union activity away from the plant. As will become apparent, the structure and operation of unions play an important role in the evolution of profit and gain sharing programs in Brazil.

Labor Costs

Brazil's comprehensive and generous labor rights were gradually created during the period of Getulio Vargas (1930–1945) and consolidated in the Labor Code in 1943. After Getulio Vargas, the country experienced several political regimes with democratic periods followed by authoritarian periods, but the Labor Code and the paternalistic approach to labor market regulation remains largely unchanged. The rights provided by the code include: (1) a weekly break pay (pay for the seventh day); (2) a Christmas bonus equivalent to a month of regular pay; (3) thirty days of annual vacation, plus a cash vacation bonus equivalent to one-third of a month's regular pay; (4) thirty days of severance pay for dismissal with no cause; (5) overtime pay; (6) an 8 percent pay complement, deposited every month into a government-managed fund, intended as a Length-of-Service Security Fund (the fund may be cashed in after dismissal); (7) compensation for dismissal with no cause, (40 percent of the accumulated deposits in the Length-of-Service Security Fund); (8) complementary pay to compensate for risky working conditions and/or risky environment; (9) daily working time limited to eight hours; and (10) weekly working time limited to forty-four hours.

In 1988, the Constitution was again reformed, and workers' rights were enlarged. In all, thirty-four labor rights were specified. Among the new rights are unemployment insurance and complementary pay for uninterrupted shift work. The labor rights specified in the Constitution are complemented by those in the Labor Code and in several other pieces of legislation.

In addition to labor rights, there are many payroll taxes and obligations, created to fund both public policy (such as Social Security) and private activities (such as training programs provided by employers' associations). Payroll taxes and legally provided pay complements increase the base wage by 88 percent (Table 9.2, row 15), and the ratio of total labor cost to worker net immediate pay is 1.79 (Table 9.2, row 20). This means that when a Brazilian firm hires a worker for a base wage of $100, the final cost is actually $188. If other taxes and legally provided complements were included, the difference between the cost and the net pay would be even larger.

Together, payroll taxes and legally provided pay complements are important disincentives. The combination of a large labor supply, payroll taxes, legal obligations, and legally provided pay complements make it not surprising that Brazilian wages are among the lowest in the world (Amadeo

Table 9.2

Impact of Legally Provided Pay Complements and Payroll Taxes on Base Wage in Brazil, 2000

Components of labor bosts	Cost
Direct pay	
1. Base wage	100.0
2. Weekly break	16.7
3. Total weekly pay	116.7
4. Christmas bonus (1/12 of weekly pay)	9.7
5. Thirty-day vacation plus cash vacation bonus	12.1
6. Total direct pay	**138.5**
Taxes and obligations collected by the government (% on total direct pay)	
7. Length-of-Service Guarantee Fund (8%)	11.1
8. Employer contribution to Social Security (20%)	27.7
9. Working Place Risks Insurance (2%, average)	2.8
10. Employers' Associations Training and Social Programs (2.5%)	3.5
11. Education tax (2.5%)	3.5
12. Land Reform Program Tax (0.2%)	0.3
13. Small Business Promotion Program (0.6%)	0.8
14. Total payroll taxes and obligations	**49.7**
15. Total labor cost (6 + 14)	**188.2**
16. Worker contribution to Social Security (10%, average)	13.9
17. Worker net pay (90% of 6)	124.6
18. Worker net deferred pay (90% of 4 + 5)	19.6
19. Worker net immediate pay (90% of 3)	105.0
20. Ratio: Total labor cost/Worker net immediate pay (15/19)	**1.79**

Notes: First, there are other legally provided pay complements, not linked to the payroll, which are not included in the table. One example would be the transportation bonus. Second, for most of the Brazilian workers, net pay is lowered by the income tax.
Source: Author's computation, based on provisions of the Brazilian constitution and Brazilian labor laws.

1994; DIEESE 1993) or that the informal sector composes about 65 percent of the labor market (Table 9.3).

The high costs associated with the labor rights set out in the Constitution and the Labor Code have promoted interest in the use of profit and gain sharing programs, as will be demonstrated shortly.

Doctrine of Acquired Rights

The Labor Courts have adopted the doctrine of acquired rights. The doctrine applies whenever the firm "customarily" pays some amount to any

Table 9.3

Structure of the Brazilian Labor Market, 1999

	Number (millions)	Percentage
Formal wage or salary earners	26.1	35
Informal wage earners	12.7	17
Self-employed	17.3	23
Not-paid employees	6.1	9
Domestic employees	6.0	8
Employers	3.0	4
Self-consumption	3.8	5
Total labor force	**75**	**100**

Source: PNAD-IBGE (National Household Sample Survey, Brazilian Institute of Geography and Statistics, 1999).

worker. In such a situation, the "customary" pay becomes an explicit part of the total wage. As soon as this happens, all legally provided pay complements and payroll must be based on the new higher total wage. The doctrine of acquired rights has prevented Brazilian firms from engaging in performance pay policies. Performance pay may be considered as "customary" pay and the firm would have to pay for performance even when workers do not perform. In fact, until 1995, Enunciation 251 of the Supreme Labour Court considered "customary" profit sharing as having "the nature of wages, for all legal effects."[2] Even though Brazilian workers had the right to share profits, the acquired rights doctrine as applied to "customary" pay prevented Brazilian firms from engaging in any kind of performance pay, until 1995.

Major Change: The 1988 Constitution

The 1988 Constitution, which enlarged workers' rights, kept the right to share profits, but promoted two important changes. First, Brazilian workers were given the right to share either "profits" or "outcomes." As the right applies either to profit sharing or to gain sharing, workers and firms may choose the kind of incentive they prefer. Second, the Constitution explicitly declares that such sharing "is not linked to compensation." This qualification had two important consequences. First, it eliminated the restriction imposed by the doctrine of acquired rights. In fact, in April 1994, almost six years after the constitutional reform, the Supreme Labor Court canceled Enunciation 251, and opened up the way to large-scale adoption of performance pay policies in Brazil. Second, if profit sharing and gain sharing are not considered part of compensation, they do not contribute to the basis for payroll taxes and legally provided pay complements. Thus, the 1988 Constitution transformed profit sharing and gain sharing into pay that was "taxfree" pay (except for income tax), and "complements free." Profit and gain sharing became cheap forms of compensation.

One would expect performance pay to have spread rapidly following the 1988 Constitution. However, before the constitutional provision could be implemented, a series of regulations had to be passed. In December 1994, two days before leaving his job, President Itamar Franco signed those regulations as Provisional Measure 794.[3]

Some Features of Profit and Gain Sharing Regulation

Provisional Measure 794 introduced worker participation at the plant level. Profit and gain sharing programs cannot be unilaterally implemented by a firm and must be negotiated with representatives of the employees. This provision was innovative, because the Labor Code and bargaining were limited to pay issues and because Brazilian management was not used to dealing directly with employees' representatives at the plant level.

The first provisional measures had used the expression "negotiation" and mentioned that employees should choose representatives to negotiate with the firm. With this wording, it was inevitable that the issue of union participation would emerge. When the Constitution deals with collective rights, it establishes that only the union has the right to represent workers in collective as well in individual issues "of interest in the (occupational) category." Since performance pay must be negotiated at the plant level, this would be a collective negotiation. Thus, unions have the right to assist employees' representatives and to participate in the negotiations. In June 1997, the government changed the provisional measure to integrate a union representative into the council of employee representatives.

The regulation of performance pay has brought a major change in labor relations and has posed Brazilian management a double challenge. First, management has to accept that employees can choose their representatives to bargain over a topic that is usually considered a management prerogative. Second, the union, which was traditionally excluded from plant-level issues, is now, in part, a partner in the negotiation. Old-fashioned labor organizations were challenged too, since they were not used to bargaining directly with firms and preferred the industrywide bargain structure. As a result of pressures from both management and old union leadership, the provisional measure was again changed to allow for three kinds of bargaining structures over performance pay: (1) direct negotiation involving the firm and employees representatives with the participation of a union representative, (2) direct negotiation involving the firm and the union, (3) industrywide bargaining involving the employers association and the labor union.

The old-fashioned model of workers' representation and bargaining structure was preserved. However, an important opening was created, since those firms unwilling to accept performance pay rules negotiated at the industry level may engage in direct negotiations with their union or with their employees representatives. In December 2000, the provisional measure became law, keeping these three models of bargaining structures.[4]

Brazilian firms have a strong financial incentive to adopt performance pay, but in order to take advantage of the incentive, they must bargain directly with labor unions. At the same time, labor unions have the opportunity to establish themselves at the firm level, through the bargaining of profit and gain sharing programs. Management lobbied the executive branch to eliminate the unions from the negotiation over performance pay. Management's aim was to establish direct bargaining with employees, without the participation of unions. Some labor organizations have fought to keep the bargaining right. Such disagreement may undermine the prospects of successful gain sharing and profit sharing because it generates hostility and lack of trust about the concept of performance pay. As will be seen in a subsequent section of this chapter, many authors consider trust a necessary condition for performance pay to work as an incentive device.

Further Features of Regulation

Costs of payroll taxes and legal pay complements create a strong incentive for firms and workers to disguise earnings as profit and gain sharing. To prevent firms and workers from substituting profit and gain sharing payments for regular monthly wages, the provisional measure established that any profit or gain sharing payments should be made at least six months apart. Thus, payments made monthly, bimonthly, and quarterly would not be considered performance pay, and would not be exempted from payroll taxes and legal complements. Few workers would agree to have large parts of their monthly paychecks postponed for six or more months.

The transformation of profit and gain sharing into a constitutional labor right is just one more manifestation of Brazilian populism. Performance pay choices are typically made according to the objectives of an organization, its history, and its environment. Performance pay may work in some circumstances but fail in others. This is ignored when the Constitution mandates that all workers are entitled to share either profits or gains. As a consequence, this requirement was subsequently amended by regulations establishing performance pay as a mandatory subject of bargaining. Thus, profit-and gain sharing are no longer absolute rights, but negotiable issues.

What if bargaining reaches an impasse? The Provisional Measure established that, if parties cannot agree on the program of profit or gain sharing, they "may use either mediation or final offer arbitration." This was another departure in Brazilian labor law with its historical and cultural dependence upon the Labor Court to solve labor conflicts. While the Constitution guarantees the right to take grievances and impasses to the Labor Court, for the first time, the law acknowledged that parties could use private, alternative mechanisms for conflict resolution.

Brazilian labor law has traditionally focused on outcomes rather than processes, but there are no details on the formula to be used nor on the minimum value to be paid to workers under a profit or gain sharing plan. The Constitution and the provisional measure establish only a framework for bargaining about performance pay, providing unions and management the opportunity to design and implement performance pay schemes that reflect their particular circumstances.

Summary of the Legal and Institutional Background

Table 9.4 presents a summary of the changes in the provisions of who are the partners in the negotiation of conditional pay bargaining. It summaries changes in Provisional Measure 794 from December 1994, when the first version of the regulation was adopted, until it became a law in December 2000.

The actual extent of performance pay in Brazil is unclear. Surveys conducted by consulting firms and released to the media indicate high proportions of firms adopting performance pay. However, samples in such surveys are likely biased, as firms adopting performance pay program are more likely to participate in such surveys. Yet, given the economic incentives, one would expect that performance pay is spreading. In the survey conducted by the author, and examined in a subsequent section, bonuses paid to workers were, on average, equivalent to one and a half times the monthly wage. At this level, performance pay would constitute about 10 percent of total annual compensation.

The economic incentives and the legal restrictions raise at least two questions. First, are profit and gain sharing programs being used to improve labor productivity and worker satisfaction? Or are they simply being

Table 9.4

Changes in Bargaining Structure Under Provisional Measure 794, 1994–2000

Month and year	Negotiation partners
December, 1994	Collective bargaining with the labor union.
January, 1995	"To convention" with representatives, elected by the employees. Text of the agreement is to be sent to the labor union.
June, 1997	Negotiation with representatives, elected by the employees. One more member, indicated by the union, integrates the group of employees' representatives.
June, 1998	Negotiation with representatives, elected by the employees. One more member, indicated by the union, integrates the group of employee's representatives.
	Two other structures are acknowledged and permitted: (1) direct firm-union negotiations, without elected employee representatives, and (2) industrywide negotiations, between the union and the industry employers' association.
December, 2000	The provisional measure is approved by the Congress and transformed into law, keeping the June 1998 content.

adopted to reduce labor costs because they are exempt from payroll tax and legal compliments? Second, since performance pay cannot be unilaterally implemented by firms, what are the implications of union involvement for profit and gain sharing programs? Those two questions are addressed in the next sections. A theoretical evaluation of both issues is followed by an examination of empirical evidence.

Performance Pay as an Incentive

According to the New Institutional Economics (NIE), employment contracts are incomplete and transaction costs are associated with information asymmetries (Dow 1997). Similar to other incomplete contracts, labor contracts demand governance structures to be implemented. Governance structures are necessary to solve problems arising from either adverse selection at the time contracts are negotiated, or moral hazard that emerges after that, or asset specificity that both firms and workers build when their relationship is lengthy enough to allow investments to be made on it by both sides. Incentive mechanisms, such as efficiency wages and tournaments, are often seen as a way to reduce these problems.

Profit and gain sharing are alternative mechanisms designed to have workers increase their effort—and, thus, their productivity. These incentives help to overcome the asymmetry of information a firm faces, since the true productivity of workers is difficult to assess, and, even if it is known, it is costly to monitor. One way to do it is to offer rewards tied to individual performance, whenever individual productivity is often easy to monitor. When individual productivity is not easy to monitor, bonuses are offered to the team of workers, in exchange for increased group productivity (or profitability).

Group incentives must be designed carefully to combine workers' risk aversion with the firm's neutrality regarding risk. Profit- and gain-sharing programs solve this problem with a combination of fixed pay (base wage) and conditional pay (gain or profit sharing bonuses). Yet, gain or profit indicators must also be carefully chosen to prevent paying workers for performance not conducive to economic gains.

Dow (1977) summarizes four important conclusions for the success of incentive policies: First, the program should provide incentives for both firms and workers. Second, cooperation between workers and firms (leading to efficient levels of effort) is sustainable, even if there is a predictable terminal date for the employment relationship. Third, incentives are only feasible when surplus can be generated for at least one of the parties. Fourth, ongoing management is required because inefficient combinations may emerge and remain permanent. In sum, although NIE literature is optimistic about incentives, gain and profit sharing policies must be carefully designed and implemented since success is not guaranteed.

Since profit and gain sharing may overcome some of the imperfections of labor contracts, many suggest creating tax incentives for firms adopting such policies. Yet, a tax incentive may be given to firms which would adopt a profit or a gain sharing program anyway. Moreover, the tax incentives may help firms fuel other unrelated inefficient activities.

Whether aided by tax policy or not, performance pay usage has increased worldwide following the transformation of labor markets and the global economy. According to Elvira (1997), the weakening of unions, foreign competition, and automation are forcing firms to modify their traditional employment structures. Performance pay and incentives are replacing old compensation policies of secure pay rules and predictable job ladders. Firms need to adjust their pay policies to less predictable environments, and to prefer more flexible policies, such as performance pay.

Agency theory predicts that since agents are risk averse, they (the workers) prefer fixed salaries. Thus, an inverse relationship exists between the base salary and the value of the bonus. The higher the base salary, the lower the bonus. On the other hand, power (sociological) theories predict that powerful workers would get both—higher base pay as well as higher bonuses. Elvira (1997) tests both hypotheses and concludes that there is a quadratic relationship between the two pay components. When salaries are low (less powerful workers), the risk hypothesis holds. In this case, the higher the wage, the lower the bonus. Yet, when salaries are high (more powerful workers), the opposite holds. In this case, the higher the salary, the higher the bonus.

Poole and Glenville (1998) argue that linking reward to performance depends on structural features of the firm and action (strategic) choices of management, and this dependence may explain the distance observed between discourse (laudatory of performance related pay) and actual practice (traditional pay) in compensation policies. The author's argument reinforces the idea, very present in NIE, that a firm's history and culture influences its present institutions. In other words, even if a more efficient arrangement is available, partners may take a long time before implementing it.

Drago and Heywood (1995) present evidence that pay policies depend on a wide variety of firm-level variables. Hypotheses suggested by the new economics of personnel were confirmed. Thus, profit sharing is more likely to be used in less conflictive environments, as well as in firms with higher monitoring costs. Kruse (1996), using U.S. panel data, finds evidence that profit sharing is chosen as an incentive and to deal with organizational instability. Specifically, the adoption of profit sharing by firms is more likely when research and development expenditures are large, involvement and motivation are promoted, profits are unstable, and monitoring costs are high.

As this very brief review shows, the literature on performance pay acknowledges both its potential as an incentive device and the difficulties firms may face in implementing such compensation policies. Risk-averse workers may feel uncomfortable with performance pay and may resist its implementation, and performance pay can be a conflictual issue in labor relations.

Despite these potential problems, performance pay is emerging in Latin America. Garza (1997) identifies a move towards the "flexibilization" of labor rules in Latin America and identifies "productivity agreements" as part of this move. In the case of Brazil, "productivity agreements" are the outcome of profit and gain sharing negotiations, and have all been group oriented. Unions in Brazil have opposed the adoption of individual criteria in performance pay. Moreover, there remains risk that individual performance pay may be considered an "acquired right" by the Labor Courts. In the following sections, an assessment is made of such group performance pay programs. Two questions are addressed: Is performance pay working as incentive? What is the role of labor unions in the adoption of performance pay?

The Effectiveness of Performance Pay as an Incentive

In this section, we examine data collected by an Internet questionnaire for human resource managers from April to July 2000 and in April, 2001.[5] A total of 121 firms answered the questionnaire (50 in 2000 and 71 in 2001). Of the 121 firms, only 26 reported that they did not have profit or gain sharing programs (10 in 2000 and 16 in 2001). Thus, the frequency of performance pay is very high (79 percent, corresponding to 95 firms), which is consistent with the findings of other surveys.[6] Table 9.5 depicts some characteristics of the firms in the sample.

The survey data are used to evaluate if profit and gain sharing had any impact on labor productivity, on workers' commitment, and on the relationship between workers and supervisors. The actual estimations used had the following specification:

$$\text{Dependent variable} = \text{Intercept} + \alpha \text{ Coverage} + \qquad (9.1)$$
$$\chi \text{ Coverage Type} + \delta \text{ Usefulness} +$$
$$\varepsilon \text{ Payroll} +$$
$$\phi \text{ Wage ratio} + \upsilon \text{ Year} +$$
$$\text{Random error term}$$

Four **dependent variables** are identified. The first isolates the labor productivity (**Imp_Prod**) and is the perceived percentage change in productivity. The HR manager was asked to state the increase in labor productivity attributable to the performance pay program, since the program was implemented (with intervals of 10 percentage points from zero to 100 percent). Two other dependent variables are the impact on workers' commitment (**Imp_Com**), and on their relationships with the supervisor (**Imp_Rel**), both measured with the perceived percentage change indicated by HR managers in the questionnaire (with intervals of 10 percentage points from zero to 100 percent). The fourth dependent variable is **Impact,** an arithmetic average of the three previous variables.

Coverage is a dummy variable, with 0 indicating that the performance pay program covers the entire industry and 1 indicating that the program was created for a single firm. Firm-specific programs are more likely to be designed in accordance with firm needs, while industrywide programs should have a smaller effect as incentive mechanism.

Table 9.5

Distribution of Firms Answering the Author's Questionnaire, 2000 and 2001 (N = 95)

Characteristics	2000		2001		Total	
	Number	Percent	Number	Percent	Number	Percent
Sectoral Distribution						
Commerce and services	4	10	10	18	14	15
Manufacturing	32	80	42	76	74	78
Others	4	10	3	5	7	7
Total	**40**	**100**	**55**	**100**	**95**	**100**
Total number of employees	70,521		109,461		179,982	
Average number of employees	1,763		1,990		1,895	

Type is a series of two dummy variables with three combinations of values. The reference value (0, 0) indicates that the program does not offer performance pay. In this case, the firm simply pays an unconditional biannual bonus. The bonus is not conditioned to any previously adjusted goal. This would be a disguised performance pay program, in which part of the base pay is simply paid on a biannual basis, and the firm saves the expenditures with all legally imposed additional costs to base pay. The value (1, 0) of the dummy variable indicates that the firm has a profit sharing plan, and the value (0, 1) indicates that there is a gain sharing program. Some firms use both profit and gain criteria to determine performance pay. These firms were included in the gain sharing type. For the later two values, the hypothesis is a positive impact, indicating that, keeping all other variables unchanged, whenever the firm evolves from a non-conditional program to a performance pay program, workers would respond with increased productivity, higher identification with firm goals, and improved relationship with supervisors.

Coverage_Type is an interaction of the two previous variables.

Usefulness represents the opinion of the manager about the usefulness of profit and gain sharing as a management tool. The hypothesis is a positive impact, reflecting that the more management perceives performance pay as a tool, the larger management effort and involvement with the program, and the larger the effect of the program on the three impact variables.

Payroll represents the monthly compensation expenditures, in millions of Reais *(R$)*, the Brazilian currency. It reflects both the size of the firm and the level of the wages and/or salaries. Given the minimum pay frequency of six months, performance pay is more likely to work as an incentive in large firms where wages or salaries are higher. Better paid workers are more likely to accept and to be motivated by biannual bonuses. Their higher pay means that they can afford to wait six months for the next bonus. In economic terms, we could say that large payroll expenditures correspond to smaller workers' discount rates. Thus, the hypothesis is a positive impact.

Wage ratio is the size of the average performance payment as a proportion of the average wage or salary. When the bonus is larger, the influence on effort is expected to be larger.

Year is a dummy variable to designate the two periods in which the questionnaire was answered.

Results of the estimation, depicted in Table 9.6, indicate that performance pay does have a positive overall impact on perceived productivity. At any level of coverage (the firms without programs are excluded), productivity is positively and significantly impacted by either a profit or a gain sharing program when compared to plans that disguise earnings. Productivity increases significantly with the perceived usefulness of performance pay and with the wage ratio. Coverage of a disguised program (when the two type variables are zero) does not affect the impact on perceived productivity. When industrywide programs are compared to firm-specific programs, the impact on productivity is the same. However, when industrywide programs are compared to firm-specific profit sharing and gain sharing programs, significant impacts are estimated. This is again shown by the significant coefficients on the interactions. This may indicate that firm-specific programs more closely link bonuses to collective performance.

Even though the models have similar capacities to explain variation, as represented by their respective R-squareds, performance pay seems to have more modest impacts on perceived workers commitment and on perceived worker-supervisor relationship, as shown by models 2 and 3, respectively. In both models, the only significant coefficient is that for the gain sharing interaction. The fourth model captures the combined effect of performance pay on the three dimensions. In this model, three variables have positive, significant coefficients: gain sharing type, usefulness, and wage ratio.

Results of the estimated models indicate that, in the sample of ninety-five firms that reported having programs, performance pay is perceived to be working as an economic incentive by positively affecting labor productivity. Brazilian HR managers may not be exploring performance pay as a

Table 9.6

Impact of Performance Pay on Productivity, Commitment, and Relations

Variable	Model 1 Imp_prod	Model 2 Imp_com	Model 3 Imp_rel	Model 4 Impact
Coverage	−0.52	−0.41	−0.08	−0.34
	(0.54)	(0.66)	(0.93)	(0.68)
Coverage: Profit sharing	2.63	1.86	1.44	1.97
	(0.02)	(0.12)	(0.26)	(0.06)
Coverage: Gain sharing	2.48	3.04	2.51	2.68
	(0.00)	(0.00)	(0.01)	(0.00)
Usefulness	0.48	0.44	0.39	0.44
	(0.00)	(0.00)	(0.00)	(0.00)
Payroll	0.02	0.02	0.00	−0.28
	(0.48)	(0.62)	(0.92)	(0.64)
Wage ratio	1.04	0.90	0.49	0.81
	(0.00)	(0.00)	(0.13)	(0.00)
Year	−0.11	−0.08	0.12	−0.02
	(0.76)	(0.85)	(0.79)	(0.95)
Constant	−0.35	−0.27	−0.21	−0.28
	(0.55)	(0.68)	(0.76)	(0.63)
R^2	64.7	60.9	49.5	63.9
F-Test	22.82	19.34	12.18	21.99
	(0.00)	(0.00)	(0.00)	(0.00)

Note: Values in parenthesis are *p*-numbers, and they represent the probability of the estimated coefficient's being different from zero.

device to improve other aspects labor relations, such as improvement on workers' commitment or on worker-supervisor relationships. The disguised biannual bonus shows that no programs seem to have similar effects. When performance pay is linked to profits or to gains, significant differences between the two kinds of negotiation structures do emerge. Impacts seem to be significantly greater in firm-specific programs.

Unions and Performance Pay Bargaining

To examine the outcomes of performance pay bargaining, a sample of 1,201 agreements negotiated since 1995 has been collected. The description of the sample is presented in Table 9.7 and shows two trends: First, performance pay negotiations were initially limited almost entirely to the metallurgical sector of the economy, and second, they were conducted almost entirely in São Paulo, the most developed state of the Brazilian federation. After five years, performance pay has devolved to all sectors of

Table 9.7

Distribution of the Sample of 1,201 Performance Pay Agreements According to Industry and Region, 1995–1999

Industry and Region	1995		1996		1997		1998		1999		Total	
	N	%	N	%	N	%	N	%	N	%	N	%
Industry												
Metalurgical industries	129	53.1	152	53.1	140	44.4	142	47.5	19	27.5	582	48.4
Other manufacturing industries	85	37.1	106	37.1	139	44.2	118	39.5	32	46.3	481	40.0
Commerce/services	13	8.6	25	8.6	30	9.6	33	11.1	13	18.8	114	9.5
Agriculture and mining	5	1.0	3	1.0	6	1.9	6	2.0	5	7.2	25	2.1
Total	**232**	**100.0**	**286**	**100.0**	**315**	**100.0**	**299**	**100.0**	**69**	**100.0**	**1201**	**100.0**
Region												
São Paulo	190	84.3	241	84.3	230	73.0	225	75.3	42	60.9	928	77.3
South East except São Paulo	20	3.8	11	3.8	38	12.1	27	9.0	14	20.3	110	9.1
Remaining regions	21	10.8	31	10.8	46	14.6	47	15.7	12	17.4	157	13.0
Nacional agreements	1	1.0	3	1.0	1	0.3	0		1	1.4	6	0.5
Total	**232**	**100.0**	**286**	**100.0**	**315**	**100.0**	**299**	**100.0**	**69**	**100.0**	**1201**	**100.0**

the economy, and to all regions. This evolution indicates that performance pay was initially established in the sector and state where unions are most active and powerful, suggesting that unions have played a key role in the growing use of performance pay.

Data on performance pay bargaining outcomes are used as a dependent variable to estimate three models: a multinomial logit model, an ordered logit model, and an OLS model. Specifications of the three models are described below.

For the dependent variable, five bargaining structures are defined: (1) industrywide (in which an employers' associations negotiates with a labor union; (2) firm-union; (3) firm–employee representatives, with the participation of the union; (4) firm–employee representatives, without the participation of the union; and (5) firm decision, in which there is no bargaining and performance pay is created as a result of the firm's discretion and decision. The five bargaining structures may be regarded as a succession of situations, with increasing firm autonomy. In the first structure, the firm has no autonomy in defining the program of performance pay since it is determined at the industry level by the employers' association and the labor union. In this case, firm influence may exist only if the firm participates in the planning and preparation of the bargaining. In the second situation, in which the firm bargains with the labor union, the firm may exert much more influence on the program. The third situation is similar, but the firm may have even more influence since the employees are part of the bargaining, together with the union representative. In the fourth situation, the influence of the firm may be larger, because the union is not part of the bargaining. Finally, the last situation would be the one with the largest firm influence because the firm itself makes the decision.

The independent variables are built up from clauses of the collective agreements. These were classified into twenty-six categories, of which nine are used in this model. For more detail on this classification see Zylberstajn (1998). The nine kinds of clauses are transformed into nineteen dummy variables, as described in Table 9.8. For each of these variables, a coefficient was estimated in the three models. The interpretation of the coefficients is offered in the next paragraphs.

OLS Model

If the probabilities associated with the set of bargaining structures could be regarded as a continuum varying linearly with the dependent variables, then ordinary least squares (OLS) would be appropriate. In this case, the coefficients would simply indicate the estimated impact of the change in

Table 9.8

Transformation of Nine Qualitative Variables into Nineteen Dummy Variables

Variables	Reference level (0)	Other levels
1. Sector of activity	Other sector	1. Manufacturing (MNF)
2. Region	São Paulo	2. Southeast (RSE)
		3. South (RSO)
		4. Other regions (ROT)
3. Duration of agreement	Less than 1 year	5. 1 year (DU1)
		6. 2+ years (DU2)
4. Advance pay	No	7. Yes (ADV)
5. Period of pay	Semester	8. Year (PDY)
		9. Less than semester (PDL)
		10. Other period (PDO)
6. Period of measurement	Month	11. Not specified (MNS)
		12. No measurement (MNE)
7. Employees' council	No	13. Yes (EEC)
8. Number of criteria	None	14. 1–2 (C1_2)
		15. 3–4 (C3_4)
		16. 5+ (C5+)
9. Type of program	Not conditioned	17. Profit sharing (SHP)
		18. Gain sharing (SHG)
		19. Profit and gain sharing (SPG)

one qualitative variable on the scale of probabilities associated to the set of bargaining structure. A positive coefficient would indicate, for instance, that the change in the variable from its reference level to the value associated with the coefficient would increase the probability that the firm would move from a less autonomous toward a more autonomous kind of bargaining structure. Unfortunately, this kind of association between our variables may not be plausible. Nonetheless, the OLS model was estimated, as shown in the first column of Table 9.9 and may be considered as a reference.

Ordered Logit Model

In this model, the estimation procedure computes a weighted scale of probabilities associated with each of the bargaining structures. Coefficients may be interpreted similarly to the OLS case. This model is more acceptable, because, contrary to the OLS model, the scale of probabilities does not behave linearly. Results of the estimation, which are depicted in the second column of Table 9.9 are very similar to the OLS case. Not only are the

Table 9.9

Estimation of the Probabilities of Bargaining Structures

Variable	OLS	ODL	1-2	2-3	3-4	4-5
MNF (manufacturing)	0.19 (0.000)	1.21 (0.000)	7.43 (0.000)	1.63 (0.699)	0.28 (0.347)	0.38 (0.907)
RSE (Southeast)	−0.05 (0.404)	−0.14 (0.500)	−0.71 (0.004)	0.59 (0.871)	0.27 (0.391)	−0.83 (0.582)
RSO (South)	0.09 (0.099)	0.29 (0.228)	−0.59 (0.120)	0.31 (0.921)	0.40 (0.170)	20.53 (0.251)
ROT (other regions)	−0.14 (0.144)	−0.32 (0.282)	−0.55 (0.271)	−0.95 (0.609)	1.01 (0.136)	−1.00 (1.000)
DU1 (duration 1 year)	0.04 (0.361)	0.25 (0.129)	−0.24 (0.416)	0.27 (0.927)	0.66 (0.005)	−0.96 (0.297)
DU2 (duration 2 + years)	−0.05 (0.487)	−0.13 (0.582)	−0.64 (0.191)	0.45 (0.912)	−0.03 (0.910)	−0.92 (0.496)
ADV (advance pay)	0.02 (0.645)	0.07 (0.664)	2.95 (0.014)	−0.96 (0.192)	−0.09 (0.614)	−0.51 (0.792)
PDY (period of pay, 1 year)	0.07 (0.106)	0.28 (0.110)	3.36 (0.001)	5.77 (0.303)	0.12 (0.547)	−0.78 (0.419)
PDL (period of pay, less 1 semester)	−0.07 (0.177)	−0.19 (0.297)	1.74 (0.020)	3.90 (0.574)	−0.28 (0.201)	−0.90 (0.454)
PDO (period of pay, other)	−0.15 (0.003)	−0.36 (0.028)	1.61 (0.040)	0.56 (0.840)	−0.52 (0.010)	−1.00 (1.000)
MNS (nonspecified measurement)	0.03 (0.433)	0.20 (0.266)	−0.38 (0.661)	−1.00 (0.975)	0.29 (0.159)	1.04E+24 (0.998)
MNE (no measurement)	0.15 (0.005)	0.62 (0.016)	−0.71 (0.291)	−1.00 (0.987)	0.64 (0.026)	3.19E+15 (0.000)
EEC (employees' council)	1.40 (0.000)	1179.09 (0.000)	206388.0 (0.993)	4.50E+21 (0.968)	6.70E+06 —	−1.00 (0.000)

C1_2 (1–2 criteria)	−0.27	−0.70	−0.66	−1.00	−0.75	5.55E+07
	(0.004)	(0.001)	(0.326)	(0.995)	(0.001)	(0.999)
C3_4 (3–4 criteria)	−0.25	−0.62	3.33	−1.00	−0.75	−1.00
	(0.005)	(0.006)	(0.311)	(0.995)	(0.001)	(1.000)
C5+ (5+ criteria)	−0.24	−0.62	18.63	−1.00	−0.77	2.59E+07
	(0.006)	(0.005)	(0.027)	(0.995)	(0.000)	(0.999)
SHP (profit sharing)	0.77	13.06	1.21	1.40E+09	12.78	−1.00
	(0.000)	(0.000)	(0.593)	(0.998)	(0.000)	(0.000)
SHG (gain sharing)	0.52	5.25	−0.20	23213.50	4.63	−1.00
	(0.000)	(0.000)	(0.849)	(0.999)	(0.000)	(1.000)
SPG (profit and gain sharing)	0.77	12.43	1.73E+09	6249.86	9.67	−0.98
	(0.000)	(0.000)	(0.998)	(0.999)	(0.000)	(1.000)
R^2	64.18	41.05	54.13	54.13	54.13	54.13
***F* test**	110.40					
Likelihood ratio		1267.01	1670.82	1670.82	1670.82	1670.82
***P* value**	0,000	0,000	0,000	0,000	0,000	0,000

Note: Values in parenthesis are *p* values which represent the probability of the estimated coefficient's being different from zero.

variables with significant coefficients approximately the same, but the directions of the relative magnitudes also coincide. In short, in both models the role of manufacturing (a proxy for strong unions), period of pay and the sharing plans emerges. These are further detailed below.

Multinomial Logit Model

Results are depicted in columns 3, 4, 5, and 6 of Table 9.9. Each column represents the transition from a bargaining structure with less firm autonomy to a bargaining structure with more firm autonomy. Estimated coefficients in column 3, for instance, indicate the impact of a change in the qualitative variables from its reference level on the probability of the firm changing from industrywide bargaining to firm-union bargaining. Similarly, estimated coefficients in column 4 indicate the impact of a change in the qualitative variables from its reference level on the probability of the firm's changing from firm-union bargaining to firm–employee representatives bargaining, with the participation of a union representative. In the last column of Table 9.9, coefficients represent the impact on the probabilities of the firm's changing from firm–employee representatives bargaining to the situation in which the firm unilaterally decides about performance pay.

Transition from industrywide bargaining to firm-union bargaining is more likely to occur in "Manufacturing," with "Advance pay" (in essence, a signing bonus), with pay being made in other than a biannual basis, and with five or more criteria to link performance to pay. There seems to be no significant differences in the transition from firm-union bargaining to firm–employee representatives bargaining, with the participation of a union representative. Transition from this structure to the next (firm–employee representatives bargaining) is negatively associated with the number of criteria (from one to five or more). At the same time, however, it is strongly and positively associated with performance pay (gain sharing, profit sharing, or both). Finally, there seems to be little impact on the dependent variables of the last transition, to the most autonomous status of the firm.

In sum, results indicate two main impacts. First, the transition from industrywide to firm-specific bargaining with the involvement of a labor union is strongly associated with the manufacturing sector. Not surprisingly, this is the sector with the most powerful unions. This transition is negatively associated with advance pay and with other than biannual frequency of pay. The second important transition is from firm-specific bargaining with participation of a union to firm specific programs, without the participation of a union (3–4). This transition is associated with annual duration of the programs (as opposed to duration of less than one year). It is also associated with reduced number of criteria, and strongly associated with profit sharing and associated to a smaller extent with gain sharing. These last coefficients indicate that preference for profit sharing is more characteristic of autonomous decision making. When a union is present, preferences tend to favor gain sharing and a large number of criteria.

Conclusions

This chapter has described the institutional and legal background under which performance pay has emerged in Brazil. Legal restraints and economic incentives have driven Brazilian firms and workers to choose collective criteria to link pay to performance. Brazilian firms must negotiate with representatives of the workers over the design of the program. Firms not willing to engage in direct bargaining may transfer this task to the employer association, which negotiates an industrywide program. Many labor unions prefer to deal once a year with one employers' association rather than with all firms in the industry. Many Brazilian workers are paid performance pay. Industrywide programs appear to be less likely to work as incentive, because they are not designed to attend the needs of specific firms. Firms with their own performance pay programs have engaged in direct bargaining to create them. Results presented in this chapter indicate that HR managers perceive performance pay as a mechanism that increases productivity. Labor unions in manufacturing contribute to the spread of performance pay, enlarge the number of criteria to link pay to performance, and prefer gain sharing to profit sharing.

Notes

1. For the union, it may be somewhat irrelevant to try to organize workers, since the union is provided with guaranteed revenue.
2. Federal Labor Court "enunciations" are rulings that should apply to similar cases, and are issued to standardize State Labor Court rulings.
3. Brazilian presidents may issue a provisional measure, which is valid for thirty days, and the Congress is supposed to examine the measure within this period. If the Congress does not examine the provisional measure, the president may issue a new one, valid for another thirty days. The provisional measure that regulates profit and gain sharing was renewed every month between December 1994 and December 2000, when the Congress transformed it into law.
4. Law No. 10,101 was passed on December 19, 2000.
5. The questionnaire is part of a permanent research project conducted by the author, at the Foundation Institute of Economic Research (FIPE), a research body linked to the Department of Economics of the University of São Paulo. The project (named MEDIAR; on-line at http://www.fipe.com/mediar) releases monthly questionnaires, to col-

lect information from firms and unions on labor relations issues. The objective of the project is to promote strategic mediation of labor and capital.

6. In a 1997 survey conducted by the author, with 566 participating firms, the frequency of performance pay was 48 percent. In a survey conducted in 1996, by the Brazilian branch of the consulting firm Arthur Andersen, with 127 large firms, the reported frequency was 71 percent.

References

Amadeo, E. 1994. *Análise Comparativa da Indústria Manufatureira Brasileira (com ênfase nos determinantes do custo do trabalho)* (Comparative analysis of Brazilian manufacturing industries [with emphasis on determinants of labor cost]). Mimeograph, BNDES.
Departamento Intersindical de Estatísticas e Estudos Socio Econômicos (DIEESE). 1993. *Os encargos trabalhistas no Brasil* (Payroll costs in Brazil). Mimeograph.
Dow, G. K. 1997. "The New Institutional Economics and Employment Regulation." In *Government Regulation of the Employment Relationship*, ed. B. E. Kaufman, pp. 57–90, Industrial Relations Research Association Series.
Drago, R., and Heywood, J. S. 1995. "The Choice of Payment Schemes: Australian Establishment Data." *Industrial Relations* 34: 507–531.
Elvira, Marta M. 1997. "When Is a Bonus a Bonus? Incentive Pay, Risk Sharing, and Wage Levels."; *In Proceedings of the Forty-Ninth Annual Meeting*, ed. P. B. Voos. Industrial Relations Research Association Series.
Garza, Enrique de la. 1997. "*La flexibilidad del trabajo en América latina*" (Labor Felxibility in Latin America). *Revista Latino-americana de Estudos do Trabalho No. 3*: 133–157.
Kruse, D. L. 1996. "Why Do Firms Adopt Profit Sharing and Employment Ownership Programs?" *British Journal of Industrial Relations* 34: 515–538.
Poole, M., and Glenville J., 1998: "Human Resource Management and the Theory of the Rewards: Evidence from a National Survey" *British Journal of Industrial Relations* 36: 227–247.
Zylberstajn, H. 1998. *Participação nos Lucros ou Resultados: Balanço de Três Anos de Regulamentação* (Profit- or gain-sharing: An evaluation after three years of regulation). Mimeograph, FIPE/MTb.

Chapter 10
Paying for Performance
What Has Been Learned?

Michelle Brown and John S. Heywood

The Form and Incidence of Performance Pay

This project began with the expectation that we would find secular increases in the use of performance pay that, albeit different in form and extent by country, would be qualitatively similar. Clearly, that expectation has not been realized. The initial combinations of performance pay methods differ by country, and the recent emphasis and growth among those methods is far from uniform. Nonetheless, this has clearly been a period of great experimentation with performance pay across countries. The initial patterns of both performance pay use and those experiments deserve summary.

Among the countries studied, Japan, France, and Brazil made the greatest use of performance pay based on the organization. In Japan, employee stock ownership plans (ESOPs) and profit sharing are tools, among others, building worker commitment to the long-run success of firms. The Japanese government provides no tax breaks or subsidies to explicitly encourage such financial performance. Nonetheless, over 90 percent of listed firms provide ESOPs and more than half of all workers participate. The French government provides generous tax benefits to both firms and workers as part of a largely mandated plan of profit sharing. The plan originated not as a way to create performance incentives or build commitment but as a way to encourage savings. Nonetheless, as Fakhfakh and Pérotin show in chapter 4, the result has been that those firms with profit sharing have greater productivity.

Profit and gain sharing plans in Brazil had a particularly long genesis. While profit sharing was first provided for in the 1946 Constitution, it was not until the mid-1990s that facilitating provisions established legal standing to profit and gain sharing plans. The Brazilian provisions are intended to promote social equity and reduce income inequality and now exist in a majority of organizations. Moreover, as was found in France, organizations with profit and gain sharing plans are associated with improvements in worker productivity.

Australia provides a historical contrast with France, having little profit sharing, no preferred tax treatment until very recently, and even some history of an institutional bias against profit sharing. In chapter 7 Shields describes how government-sponsored productivity bargaining sought to link earnings with increased productivity but ruled out profit sharing as such a mechanism because it was "too blunt" an instrument to influence productivity. Thus, the Australians ruled out profit sharing because it could not influence productivity, and the French increased productivity without meaning to do so.

Despite substantial financial participation in France, profit sharing has not been integrated with worker participation in decision making. Next door, Germany has substantial legislated decision-making participation, but unions and workers remain skeptical of profit sharing. In Brazil, profit and gain sharing plans were made mandatory subjects of bargaining, effectively requiring employee representatives and/or union involvement in scheme design and operation. In Japan the combination of financial and decision-making participation remains the domain of firms and company unions, largely without governmental intervention.

The most prevalent form of performance pay in the United States, Australia, Canada, and the United Kingdom was that based on the individual. Parent reports that nearly half of all American workers claim to be paid some type of individual merit pay or profit sharing. There are a number of features of American society that may make performance pay more palatable. First, the influence of "American exceptionalism" (Voss 1993; Kaufman 1993) with its emphasis on the individual. The establishment of a "classless society" via the right to vote, own property, and have access to education meant that individuals were to succeed without recourse to collective organization and action. This history is seen to have resulted in weak and politically conservative labor unions. Second, Guest (1990) argues that this emphasis on the individual provided a context highly amendable to the tools and techniques of human resource management (HRM), including performance pay. Individuals through hard work and education would be recognized and rewarded for their efforts. This is reflected in the common U.S. notion that workers are "in business for themselves." Third, relatively high mobility between jobs, low termination costs, and flexible labor markets may imply that reputation effects emerge which actually act to enforce nonunion performance pay arrangements (Bull 1987). Thus, workers allocate *themsleves* jobs based, in part, on the variety of payment methods; they anticipate that employers will roughly keep the terms constant, and they threaten, credibly, to change jobs if firms renege. While overly stylized, this suggests that a highly competitive labor market with more nearly full information for all parties could generate "implicit contracts" which allows workers and firms to agree to and enforce the terms of performance pay schemes.

The emphasis on individual performance pay in the United States has also been linked to the economic performance of the country over the last decade. The deregulated nature of American labor markets has facilitated a climate in which real wage increases have been low, even in the face of relatively high levels of labor demand and aggregate growth.[1] As Shields demonstrates, Australia moved to deregulate its labor markets along the lines of the American model, with a view to capturing some of the presumed economic benefits of this approach. Part of the move to a more deregulated labor market has involved the greater use of individual performance pay.

Long, in his study of Canadian private sector organizations (chapter 3), demonstrates the popularity of individual forms of performance pay, particularly merit raises. Almost three-quarters of the firms in his sample operated a system of merit raises. He also finds that there has been a dramatic increase in the use of organization-level schemes in the last quarter of the twentieth century, a finding attributed to a belief in the perceived benefits of these schemes. The study of performance pay in the United Kingdom by Marsden and French (chapter 5) provides an interesting contrast. Successive UK governments have moved away from a seniority-based pay system to one based on supervisory assessments of individual performance. The magnitude of the change is such that public sector organizations are now as likely to use performance pay for their managers as are private sector organizations.

The third major variety of performance pay schemes uses the group as the unit of performance assessment. Long shows that Canada has seen growth in group-based schemes and that such schemes are used in conjunction with individual and organization-level schemes. The success of the Japanese economy in the 1980s and the early 1990s has been linked to its greater use of a performance pay system that encouraged workers to cooperate, which subsequently generated benefits for the whole organization. Kato, however, demonstrates in chapter 8 that Japanese firms are beginning to shift the balance toward more individualized performance pay.

Japanese interest in individual forms of performance pay has been partly driven by organizational concerns about the costs and inflexibilities associated with seniority-based wages in the context of an aging work force. It has also been driven by the aspirations of Japanese workers. More than half of all workers support the move toward pay for individual performance either "somewhat" or "strongly." Further, Kato has shown that workers with higher levels of education and young Japanese workers are particularly interested in being paid on the basis of individual performance. This "age effect" has also been identified in studies in the United Kingdom (Torrington 1993) and in Australia (Brown 2001). The challenge for Japanese organizations is to translate this in-principle support for performance pay into productive outcomes. As Marsden and French demonstrate in chapter 5, there was a high level of in-principle support for performance pay, though many employees subsequently reported concerns with many operational aspects of the scheme.

The Milkovich and Widgor (1992) matrix of performance pay provided in chapter 1 implies that organizations are limited to using just one scheme. Long identifies this implication as the "substitution argument." According to this argument, using two or more types of performance pay represents duplication. The alternative view argues that performance pay schemes can be complementary. Using several types of performance pay can result in a pay system that provides the advantages of each and minimizes the deficiencies. Long argues that the high level of use of individual performance pay and the growth in the use of group and organizational level schemes in Canada provides evidence in support of the complementary argument. In France and Japan, the authors demonstrate the complementarity of schemes utilizing the same unit of performance measurement. Thus, ESOPs and profit sharing are shown to work in harmony.

The second element of the Milkovich and Widgor (1992) matrix is the relationship of performance payments to base pay. These payments can accumulate in base pay or have to be reearned each evaluation cycle. The predominance of individual merit pay plans in the United Kingdom, Canada, and Australia suggests that accumulating schemes are the more popular. In the United States, there have been moves toward nonaccumulating schemes, though LeBlanc and Mulvey demonstrate a wide discrepancy in the preferred approaches to pay by American employers and their employees. "[W]orkers prefer permanent base increases based on merit, while management is fonder of one-time variable pay systems, since these systems cost less and are more short-term focused" (LeBlanc and Mulvey 1998, 25). In Brazil, the legal framework attempts to ensure that profit sharing and gain sharing payments do not substitute for base pay by specifying the intervals at which payments can be made in order to be eligible for favorable tax treatment.

The Nature of Change

Perhaps the most remarkable finding to emerge from the studies in this volume is the accelerating nature of experimentation and change in payment methods. These patterns are, again, far from uniform. Australia experienced an explosion in ESOPs involving large shares of workers but not large shares of compensation. At the same time, changes in the institutions of industrial relations resulted in decentralized pay setting in the hope of fostering more performance pay. The prevailing view is that increasingly nonunion employment relations will result in more individual performance pay, although the evidence from the individual level contracts remains scarce. The future would seem to hold both more organization-level performance pay and more individual-level performance pay.

Japan's continued expansion of organization-level performance pay came to a halt in the 1990s. While not reversing, performance pay innovations came in other forms. More than a quarter of all firms in 1996 had either eliminated or reduced automatic pay raises in the preceding three years. In the years between 1996 and 1999, such raises were either eliminated or reduced by 40 percent of firms. Conversely, in 1996 more than 15 percent of firms increased the portion of pay determined by ability to carry out jobs and another 15 percent increased the portion of pay determined by outcome or performance. This trend accelerated between 1996 and 1999. Thus, as the Australians are having their first widespread experience with organization-level incentives, the Japanese have shifted to a greater reliance on individual-level incentives.

The Canadian study provides evidence of an association between growth in the use of group and organizational level schemes such as gain sharing, profit sharing, and stock option plans and high-commitment management. This evidence sheds light on the debate about the appropriateness of performance pay in high-commitment organization. Huselid and Becker (1996) view performance pay as a significant component of high-commitment management as it provides a means of directly affecting the goals of workers and rewarding their achievement. S. Wood (1999), on the other hand, views performance pay as inconsistent with high-commitment management. He identifies the level of management control associated with individual forms of performance pay as a feature more typically associated with Taylorism. Long reports that high-commitment firms use a greater number of group- and organization-level performance pay plans, which he views as consistent with promoting employee commitment to, and identification with, with overall goals of the organization.

The country with the most dramatic change in the incidence of performance pay was Brazil. Until 1995 the law and its interpretation by the Labor Courts effectively prevented the use of performance pay. Zylberstajn demonstrates in chapter 9 that, by 2001, just over three-quarters of firms use profit and/or gain sharing plans. He attributes the predominance of collective performance pay plans to union preferences. This union preference effect is evidenced by the spread of collective performance pay from the highly unionized sectors to the less well unionized sectors of the Brazilian economy.

German manufacturing presents a more stable picture. The share of blue-collar workers receiving piece rates or premium pay either regularly or occasionally has changed little if at all over the period 1966–1995 despite enormous changes in technology. Yet, the picture behind this stability is a much more complex pattern. In chapter 6, Jirjahn demonstrates enormous churning in performance pay plans among manufacturing firms even over just a few years. As an illustration, 8.9 percent of firms had profit sharing in 1994 only, 6.7 percent had it in 1996 only, and 8.1 percent of firms had it in both years. Put differently, the share of firms that dropped old plans or started new ones is 14.8 percent, while the share that kept existing plans is 8.1 percent. Across five of the six types of performance pay examined, the share of firms having the scheme in either 1994 or 1996 exceeds the share having it both 1994 and in 1996. This striking degree of instability runs counter to the notion that payment systems reflect a long-term strategy designed to optimize worker effort and achieve enterprise goals. At a minimum, the process of establishing pay structures in Germany seems one of trial and error.

This view behind the scenes is replicated in Australia. Panel data from the Australian Workplace Industrial Relations Survey (Morehead et al. 1997) shows that 35.6 percent of commercial establishments report using individual-level performance pay in 1990 and 31.4 percent report such use in 1995. Yet, this modest decline hides substantial variation, as the establishments that dropped such pay between 1990 and 1995, combined with the firms that newly adopted such pay between 1990 and 1995, represent fully a quarter of all establishments in the panel (Brown and Heywood 2001).

Another major change involves which groups newly face performance pay. Both the United Kingdom and Australia have experienced substantial deregulation in employment relations, and the government has led by example, by implementing performance pay schemes for its own employees. The central governments make increasing use of performance pay usually in the form of merit rewards. As R. Wood (1995, 81) notes, performance pay is a "highly contentious component in the public sector reform programs of many Organization for Economic Cooperation and Development (OECD) countries." On the one hand, performance pay is a response to pressures to create and run more cost-effective and responsive public sector departments and agencies. However, the use of performance pay in the public sector rests on the assumption that this system of pay will promote marketlike efficiencies and improve effectiveness (Perry 1996). In other words, the public sector work force is largely similar to the private sector work force.[2] Marsden and French suggest that experience with merit pay in the Inland Revenue Service in the United Kingdom should allow managers to refine its workings and employees to become accustomed to new rules and incentives. Yet, to the contrary, their evidence indicates that five years of experience with merit pay has served only to increase and solidify the resentment of employees.

This evidence may reflect the finding that public sector workers attach greater importance to the intrinsic value of their work. Public sector pay researchers (Perry 1996) have found that public employees have more interest in altruistic or ideological goals, such as helping others or doing something worthwhile for society, and less interest in monetary rewards than do their private sector counterparts. Crewson (1997) found that public employees rate extrinsic rewards lower in importance than do employees from the private sector. In turn, intrinsic rewards are more important to public employees than to those employed in the private sector.[3]

Another group of employees now facing performance pay is nonmanagerial employees. Performance pay has typically been a feature of managerial employment in many of the countries included in this volume. Managers' comparatively high incomes allow them to weather performance-related pay fluctuations, and their jobs provide enough discretion to permit meaningful distinctions in performance assessments. In four of the countries studied, the United Kingdom, the United States, Canada, and Australia, the authors provide evidence of the spread of performance pay to groups of nonmanagerial employees. This may represent the extension of the early findings of Dyer et al. (1976), who reported that managers who work under a performance pay system feel it would also be appropriate for the employees they managed. In other words, as performance pay has become an entrenched feature of managerial employment, managers have encouraged its spread to their subordinates. Interestingly,

Kato provides the exception to this finding, noting that Japanese executives are not eligible to be members of an ESOP.

In many of the countries studied, the impetus for change derived from cost and competitive pressures on the organization. Organizations sought to find more efficient ways to operate and saw performance pay as a useful option. The introduction of performance pay in the context of cost consciousness does raise issues about the implications for employees. As Marsden and French point out, in the United Kingdom performance pay had the effect of putting pressure on workers, rather than providing an incentive. This has the effect of reducing levels of organizational commitment. Marsden and French also raise questions about the sustainability of the productivity increases achieved under a system that forces workers to work harder. Financial pressures in Japan have had quite different consequences. The collapse in the value of ESOPs in Japan appears to have had only a negligible effect. Kato reports that the number of ESOPs and the participation rate in ESOPs has not changed significantly in recent years.

In Brazil, the government attempted to eliminate the use of performance pay as a cost-cutting device. Each firm had a substantial economic incentive to shift a greater proportion of its compensation to a performance pay system to avoid taxes. Legal provisions limiting the intervals of payments were designed to reduce such shifting, and the evidence suggests that managers largely view performance pay as a method to increase productivity rather than simply to cut costs.

Participation and the Use of Performance Pay

German employment relations provide dual representation, and the works councils have been given statutory participation rights regarding the creation of certain types of performance pay. The evidence presented by Jirjahn indicates that such participation increases the likelihood of using performance pay. Indeed, German manufacturing has a very high incidence of piece rates and premium pay, with a quarter of blue-collar women and a third of blue-collar men receiving them. Moreover, the presence of works councils increases the probability of using such schemes. Interestingly, works councils also increase the likelihood of adopting the HRM strategy of lean production.

The German experience may well be part of a broader pattern in which the adoption of performance pay depends on the ability of workers and firms to agree upon and mutually "enforce" specific provisions. Thus, German legislation on works councils ensures that workers will be represented in the creation of performance pay and in enforcement of its provisions. In a related way, the award system in Australia codified performance pay plans often requiring worker participation as a condition of the reward. French profit sharing flourishes, in part, due to a formulaic approach in which the government sets many of the terms for such schemes, thereby providing certainty and continuity. Performance pay in Japan lacks a governmental overlay but may, nonetheless, fall into the pattern. Mechanisms both formal and cultural bind workers and firms together, generating long-term relationships and fostering performance pay arrangements perceived as fair.

The more flexible labor markets of the United States and the United Kingdom may point out the consequences of a general inability to mutually agree upon and enforce the provisions of performance pay. Thus, employee dissatisfaction with the merit pay scheme in the Inland Revenue may flow from its unilateral imposition and the absence of bipartite review. Indeed, labor unions in both countries generally oppose performance pay (Heywood, et al. 1997), a far cry from the German works councils, which seem to facilitate it (Heywood, Huebler, and Jirjahn 1998). While some of this opposition simply reflects the desire to create solidarity wages (Balkin 1989), it also reflects the view that the individualization of earnings can create unfair treatment that is either not detected or not remedied. Nonetheless, as Parent highlights, collective bargaining in the United States has the potential to be a mechanism that fosters mutually agreed upon and enforced performance pay schemes. The resulting contract binds the parties to specific provisions that cannot be unilaterally changed by the firm (Lazear 1986). Without these binding provisions, fear of unilateral changes can result in counterproductive effort reduction.

Yet, both the United States and the United Kingdom have large nonunionized sectors where the opposition of organized labor should not matter and in which collective bargaining cannot act as an enforcement mechanism. Thus, there appear fewer options for mutually agreed upon and enforceable performance standards suggesting that performance pay should be the province of senior management or imposed on only the lowest paid who have little bargaining power. Certainly, case studies of nonunion call centers in both the United States and the United Kingdom present bleak pictures of low-wage, high-stress jobs made worse by computerized monitoring and piece rates (Fernie and Metcalf 1999; Drago 1996). More generally, Heywood and Wei (2001) find that U.S. workers paid piece rates report less job satisfaction that those not paid piece rates, even controlling for earnings, benefits, and working conditions.

A participative approach has also been associated with productivity increases. Ohkusa and Ohtake (1997) report a 9 percent gain in productivity due to profit sharing in Japan. This is almost identical to the productivity increase identified in France by Fakhfakh and Pérotin under profit sharing. Further, both the Japanese and the French studies show that the productivity increase is dependent on good information sharing.

The country chapters also provide insights into the process of changing pay systems. In the United Kingdom, the shift to a system of individual performance pay took place over a five-year period and involved substantial changes both to the structure of management and in decision-making systems. Marsden and French, however, find that the extended time frame and the revisions undertaken throughout the change process did not produce a system which had employee support.

Zylberstajn demonstrates that in Brazil change required the involvement of employees and/or their union representatives in the negotiation of profit and gain sharing plans. In that country the difficulties encountered appear to have stemmed from the absence of experience of union and management officials in local-level bargaining. The combination of highly prescriptive labor laws and centralized bargaining limited the opportunities for union and management officials to develop the skills necessary to negotiate firm-specific collective performance pay schemes.

Lawler (1990) has recommended a participative approach to change. His reasoning is that participation provides better information for design decisions and builds commitment and acceptance. Yet, this approach is not always effective in practice. Heneman and Young (1991, 44) found in a U.S. longitudinal study that school administrators (who were involved in the design and implementation of a performance pay scheme) did not support its use prior to its introduction and that subsequent experience did nothing to alter their skepticism. In fact it "may have heightened negative reactions to the program" (Heneman and Young 1991, 44). Yet, the German experience seems to fit Lawler's prescription and suggests that participation can be highly effective. Thus, comparative researchers point to a difference between the United States and Germany in the use of participation as a management tool (Weaver 1995). In the United States participation is used to achieve employee commitment to a change, but in Germany there exists a societal commitment to meaningful participation in a broad range of organizational decisions as a method to make change more successful.

Organizational Characteristics and the Use of Performance Pay

In chapter 1, we noted that the choice of pay system can be made on the basis of a "best practice" or "strategic fit" approach. The emphasis in many of the country chapters was on investigating the role of organizational characteristics as predictors of the use of performance pay, an approach consistent with the notion of "strategic fit."

The country studies provide evidence of the importance of organizational characteristics in understanding pay system choices. Long reports that, in Canada, the competitive strategy, ownership, geographical dispersion, the proportion full time, the proportion with degrees, and the proportion of the work force unionized predict the use of merit raises. In Australia, Shields records that the individual performance pay is associated with work force size, management hierarchy, and exposure to high product market competition.

What the country chapters also demonstrate is the role played by institutions and laws in the choice, and incidence, of performance pay schemes. In Brazil the absence of facilitating measures and interlocking legal interpretations virtually eliminated performance pay despite the 1946 Constitution, which identified such pay as a right. New provisions in the mid-1990s resulted in rapid and widespread adoption of profit and gain sharing plans. In Japan, ESOPs were initially part of a government initiative to block foreign ownership, and profit sharing originated from a desire to make employees conscious of the firms' sales and production targets. In France, profit sharing was a government initiative largely designed to promote national savings. Ironically, in both Japan and France, organizations experienced productivity gains that might well be described as unintended. In Australia, the centralized system of awards did not preclude performance pay, but neither was it encouraged. The move to a decentralized approach shifted responsibility for the development and implementation of employment conditions to the workplace, providing scope for a greater variety of pay practices. The recent growth of such practices in Australia, together with the Canadian and U.S. experiences, appear to highlight the role of deregulated labor regulation in facilitating the use of performance pay systems.

Future Directions and Conclusions

The country chapters provide evidence of broad interest in performance pay around the globe, particularly over the last ten to fifteen years. This interest comes at a time of increasing income inequality for many of the countries studied. In the United States (Freeman and Katz 1994) and Australia (Borland 1999) there has been a growth in the number of high- and low-income workers and a collapse in the number of middle-income earners. Further, in Australia there is evidence (ACTU 1999) of growth in the gap between the earnings of men and women. It is important to investigate the role of performance pay in these two income trends.

The Human Rights and Equal Opportunity Commission in Australia (1998) is actively discouraging the use of performance pay out of concern about the scope it provides for the use of subjective (and potentially discriminatory) criteria in pay decision making. This would seem to be especially true of merit pay schemes in which supervisors' judgments play such a critical role. On the other hand, piece rates and related payment schemes may be less subjective, as they present a clear formulaic approach which may be more difficult to manipulate (Belman and Heywood 1992). The evidence on this point is mixed and varies by country. Parent (1999) shows that the earnings increase associated with piece rates is smaller for women than for men in the United States, but Jirjahn and Stephan (2000) show that the earnings increases associated with piece rates and premium pay are larger for women than for men. The latter finding generates a smaller gender gap among those paid performance pay and is interpreted as being consistent with the limited range for discrimination within such "objective" pay schemes.

The growth in the use of performance pay demonstrated by this volume has been accompanied by increased research attention. While the United States has the longest record of research on performance pay, academics and practitioners in many other countries are now actively studying performance pay processes and outcomes. Their approach, however, is often country specific. This volume extends our understanding of performance pay by comparing and contrasting the rationale for, and the operation of, performance pay schemes across countries. The preceding chapters demonstrate that a form of performance pay that is widely used in one country is an anathema in another. The country studies demonstrate the importance of specific historical, cultural, and institutional factors in understanding the form and incidence of performance pay schemes across countries. These factors, in turn, set limits on the transferability of performance pay practices across international boundaries.

Pay is a powerful tool in the employment relationship. This volume demonstrates the variety of ways in which organizations in eight countries have sought to use this tool, how employees and unions have responded, and how governments have sought to influence performance pay choices. Too often, researchers limit their enquires to the effectiveness of a particular performance pay scheme, an inquiry plagued by measurement issues and generating findings often specific to a time and place. A comparative approach to performance pay represents an alternative methodology. We encourage others to investigate a broad range of performance pay issues, using the full range of methodologies typical of the various disciplines that study pay systems.

Notes

1. The U.S. pattern of wages over the last two decades has largely been one of relatively small growth hiding two offsetting patterns. The wages of the less skilled have declined in real terms, while the wages of the more skilled have increased substantially (Freeman and Katz 1994).

2. Belman and Heywood (2001) show that one-third of the U.S. federal government is composed of occupations that are completely absent from the private sector, leaving open the question of whether or not performance pay can easily be adapted for these workers.

3. Heywood, Siebert, and Wei (2001) demonstrate that government workers report greater job satisfaction, given the same earnings and fringe benefits, than do private sector workers.

References

Australian Council of Trade Unions (ACTU). 1999. *Equal Pay: A Union Priority.* Melbourne: ACTU.
Balkin, D. B. 1989. "Union Influences on Pay Policy: A Survey." *Journal of Labor Research* 10: 299–307.
Bartol, K. M., and Locke, E. A. 2000. "Incentives and Motivation." In *Compensation in Organisations,* eds. S. L. Rynes and B. Gerhart. San Francisco: Jossey-Bass.
Belman, D., and Heywood, J. 2001. "The Role of Unique Occupations in the Public Sector Wage Differential." Working paper, Department of Economics, University of Wisconsin–Milwaukee.
———. 1992. "Wages, Incentive Schemes and the Role of Gender." *Review of Social Economy* 50: 141–158.
Borland, J. 1999. "Earnings Inequality in Australia: Changes, Causes and Consequences." *Economic Record* 75: 177–202.
Brown, M. 2001. "An Analysis of Employee Merit Pay Preferences: Evidence from the Public Sector." *Human Resource Management Journal* 11, no. 4: 38–54.
Brown, M., and Heywood, J. 2001. "The Determinants of Incentive Schemes: Australian Panel Data." Working paper, Department of Economics, University of Wisconsin–Milwaukee.
Bull, C. 1987. "The Existence of Self-Enforcing Implicit Contracts." *Quarterly Journal of Economics* 52: 147–159.
Crewson, P. E. 1997. "Public-Service Motivation: Building Empirical Evidence of Incidence and Effect." *Journal of Public Administration Research and Theory* 7(4): 499–518.
Drago, Robert. 1996. "Workplace Transformation and the Disposable Workplace: Employee Involvement in Australia." *Industrial Relations* 35: 526–544.
Dyer, L., Schwab, D. P., and Theriault, R. D. 1976. "Managerial Perceptions Regarding Salary Increase Data." *Personnel Psychology* 29: 233–242.
Fernie, S., and Metcalf, D. 1999. "(Not) Hanging on the Telephone: Payment Systems in the New Sweatshop." In *Advances in Industrial and Labor Relations,* vol. 9, 23–68, eds. D. Lewin and B. Kaufman. Stamford, CT: JAI Press.

Freeman, R., and Katz, L. 1994. "Rising Wage Inequality: The United States vs. Other Advanced Countries." In *Working Under Different Rules,* ed. R. Freeman. New York: Russell Sage Foundation.

Guest, D. 1990. "Human Resource Management and the American Dream." *Journal of Management Studies* 27: 377–397.

Heneman, H., and Young, P. I. 1991. "Assessment of a Merit Pay Program for School District Administrators." *Public Personnel Management* 20: 35–48.

Heywood, J., Huebler, O., and Jirjahn, J. 1998. "Variable Payment Schemes and Industrial Relations: Evidence from Germany." *KYKLOS* 51: 237–257.

Heywood, J., Siebert, W. S., and Wei, X. 1997. "Payment by Results Systems: British Evidence." *British Journal of Industrial Relations* 35: 1–22.

———. 2001. "Worker Sorting and Job Satisfaction: The Case of Union and Government Jobs." *Industrial and Labor Relations Review,* forthcoming.

Heywood, J., and Wei, X. 2001. "Performance Pay and Job Satisfaction." Working paper, Department of Economics, University of Wisconsin–Milwaukee.

Human Rights and Equal Opportunity Commission. 1998. *The Equal Pay Handbook.* Commonwealth of Australia: Sydney.

Huselid, M. A., and Becker, B. E. 1996. "Methodological Issues in Cross Sectional and Panel Estimates of the Human Resource-Firm Performance Link." *Industrial Relations* 35: 400–422.

Jirjahn, U., and Stephan, G. 2000. "Gender and Pay for Performance: The Impact of Tenure, Flexibility and Discrimination." Working paper, Institute for Quantitative Economics, University of Hannover, Germany.

Kaufman, B. E. 1993. *The Origins and Evolution of the Field of Industrial Relations in the United States.* Ithaca, NY: Industrial and Labor Relations (ILR) Press.

Lawler, E. E. 1990. *Strategic Pay.* San Francisco: Jossey-Bass.

Lazear, E. P. 1995. *Personnel Economics.* Cambridge, MA: Massachusetts Institute of Technology Press.

Lazear, E. 1986. "Salaries and Piece Rates." *Journal of Business* 59: 405–432.

LeBlanc, P., and Mulvey, P. 1998. "How American Workers See the Rewards of Work." *Compensation and Benefits Review* 30: 24–31.

Milkovich, G. T. and Widgor, A. K. 1992. *Pay for Performance: Appraisal and Merit Pay.* Washington, DC: National Academy Press.

Morehead, A., Steele, M., Alexander, M., Stephen, K., and Duffin, L. 1997. *Changes at Work: The 1995 Australian Workplace Industrial Relations Survey.* Melbourne: Longman.

Parent, D. 1999. "Methods of Pay and Earnings: A Longitudinal Analysis." *Industrial and Labor Relations Review* 53: 71–86.

Perry, J. 1996. "Measuring Public Service Motivation: An Assessment of Construct Reliability and Validity." *Journal of Public Administration Research and Theory* 6: 5–22.

Ohkusa, Y., and Ohtake, F. 1997. "The Productivity Effects of Information Sharing, Profit-Sharing and ESOPs." *Journal of the Japanese and International Economies* 11: 385–402.

Torrington, D. 1993. "Sweets to the Sweet: Performance Related Pay in Britain." *International Journal of Employment Studies* 1: 149–164.

Voss, K. 1993. *The Making of American Exceptionalism.* Ithaca, NY: Cornell University Press.

Weaver, K. 1995. *Negotiating Competitiveness: Employment Relations and Organiza-*

tion Innovation in Germany and the United Sates. Cambridge, MA: Harvard University Press.

Wood, R. 1995. "Performance Pay as a Coordinating Mechanism in the Australian Public Service." *Australian Journal of Public Administration* 54: 81–96.

Wood, S. 1999. "Getting the Measure of the Transformed High Performance Organization." *British Journal of Industrial Relations* 37(3): 391–417.

About the Editors and Contributors

Michelle Brown is a lecturer in human resource management in the Department of Management at the University of Melbourne, Australia. Prior to this appointment, she served as assistant director of the Masters in Industrial and Labor Relations Program at the University of Wisconsin–Milwaukee (now the Masters in Human Resources and Labor Relations Program). She has published in Australia and overseas on a range of topics, including pay systems, the labor market effects of layoffs, employee participation, and the industrial relations system of the Australian state of Victoria. Her current interests include the pay referents of workers and their consequences for pay-level satisfaction, the relationship between performance pay and the quality of jobs, and the pay adjustment preferences of workers.

Fathi Fakhfakh is a *Maître de Conférences* teaching economics at the University of Paris–II and a research fellow of Equipe de Recherche sur les Marchés, l'Emploi et la Simulation (ERMES) (Centre National de la Recherche Scientifique). He received his Ph.D. in economics from the University of Paris–II and his masters in economic analysis and policy from Ecole des Hautes Etudes en Sciences Sociales (EHESS) and Ecole Nationale de la Statistique et de l'Administration Economique (ENSAE). Prior to joining Paris–II, he held research positions at the Centre d'Etude des Revenus et des Coûts and Centre d'Etudes de l'Emploi (Paris). His research focuses on the effects of employee involvement and human resource management on firm performance, and has appeared in *Industrial and Labor Relations Review, Labour Economics, Travail et Emploi,* and other periodicals.

Stephen French is a lecturer in industrial relations at Keele University in Staffordshire, U.K. Prior to undertaking his doctoral studies at the Institute for German Studies at the University of Birmingham, he worked for the

Inland Revenue Service. During that time he was an active lay representative in the Inland Revenue Staff Federation (IRSF) union now the Public and Commercial Services Union (PCS). A specialist in comparative industrial relations, he is currently working, with colleagues from the University of Göttingen, on a project financed by the Anglo-German Foundation, examining racial discrimination in the workplace.

John S. Heywood is a professor of economics and director of the graduate program in human resources and labor relations at the University of Wisconsin–Milwaukee, and also senior research fellow in the Department of Commerce at the University of Birmingham, U.K. His research interests include the economics of trade unions, public sector labor markets, the economics of job satisfaction, and the economics of personnel. He has done comparative research on performance pay in the United States, the United Kingdom, Germany, Australia, and Hong Kong. This and related research has been published in the *Journal of Political Economy,* the *Review of Economics and Statistics,* and the *Industrial and Labor Relations Review.*

Uwe Jirjahn earned his Ph.D. in economics from the University of Hannover in Germany, with a thesis focusing on the efficiency of profit sharing and worker participation in firm decision making. He works as a research economist with the Institute for Quantitative Economic Research at the University of Hannover, studying markets and incentives within firms. He also teaches labor economics at the same university. He has published research on performance pay and human resources management systems, industrial relations, employer-provided training, and labor demand.

Takao Kato is a professor of economics at Colgate University, Hamilton, New York and research associate with the Center on Japanese Economy and Business at Columbia University, New York and research associate with the Tokyo Center for Economic Research. An expert in participatory work practices, incentives within careers, and executive compensation, he has published his research results in the *American Economic Review, Industrial and Labor Relations Review, Economic Inquiry,* and the *Journal of the Japanese and International Economies,* among other leading journals. As a research associate of the Tokyo Center for Economic Research, he has been a visiting scholar at several Japanese universities. He has strong interests in cross-country comparisons and has attracted research grants from sources such as the Social Science Research Council, the Russell Sage Foundation, and the Rockefeller Foundation.

Richard J. Long is a professor of industrial relations and organizational behavior at the University of Saskatchewan, Canada. Since he received his

Ph.D. from Cornell University, Ithaca, New York, in 1977, his main research focus has been performance pay systems, including employee stock ownership and profit sharing plans. He also has an interest in the impact of information technology on organizations and the way they are managed, as represented by his 1987 book *The New Office Information Technology: Human and Managerial Implications*. His work has appeared in the *Academy of Management Journal, Industrial and Labor Relations Review, Industrial Relations,* and *Human Relations,* among other journals. He is also the author of *Compensation in Canada: Strategy, Practice and Issues* (2002, 2d ed.).

David Marsden is a professor of industrial relations at the London School of Economics and Political Science. Member of the Centre for Economic Performance, he is currently engaged on research on performance pay for teachers in the UK; on whether a "procedural justice" role for unions can replace the "common rule"; and on a study of the effects of pay inequalities on economic performance in the European Union, the United States, and Japan. Recently he published *A Theory of Employment Systems: Micro-Foundations of Societal Diversity*.

Daniel Parent earned his Ph.D. in economics from the University of Montreal and is currently an assistant professor in the Department of Economics at McGill University, Montreal. His past positions include assistant professor at the University of Sherbrooke, Québec, and visiting fellow at Princeton University, Princeton, New Jersey. His research expertise lies in wage determination and dynamics, the impact of private sector training, the school-to-work transition, methods of pay, and the effects of performance pay. He has published in the *Journal of Labor Economics, Industrial and Labor Relations Review,* and *Research in Labor Economics,* among other leading journals.

Virginie Pérotin is a professor of economics at the Leeds University Business School, U.K. She received her Ph.D. and M.A. from Cornell University, Ithaca, New York, and a degree in management from Ecole Supérieure de Commerce de Paris. Her previous positions include senior research economist at the International Labor Office in Geneva and research positions at the London School of Economics (UK) and the Centre d'Etude des Revenus et des Coûts (Paris). Her research examines the effects of governance, employee involvement, and human rights at work on firm efficiency as well as on the creation and survival of labor-managed firms. Her work has been published in various journals, including the *British Journal of Industrial Relations,* the *European Economic Review,* and the *International Journal of Industrial Organization*.

John Shields is a senior lecturer in work and organizational studies in the School of Business at the University of Sydney, Australia, where he teaches human resource management. His research includes examination of performance and reward management practices in Australian and international organizations, and he is writing a book on these subjects. Together with Richard Long, he is researching comparative remuneration practice and management strategy in Australian and Canadian firms. Shields has a long-standing interest in labor history, and, with his colleague Bradon Ellem, he is working on a history of social relations in the Australian metal mining region of Broken Hill. He is coeditor of the *Biographical Register of the Australian Labour Movement, 1788–1975*.

Hélio Zylberstajn is a professor of economics at the University of São Paulo, Brazil, and is a staff researcher at the Foundation Institute of Economic Research (FIER), which is linked to the University. Since earning his Ph.D. at the University of Wisconsin–Madison, he has been conducting research in the area of unions and collective bargaining. This work has involved evaluating the training programs of the Metalworkers Union in São Paulo and examining concession bargaining and labor market adjustment in Brazil. At FIER he has been conducting an ongoing research project to collect data from firms and unions on labor relations issues, including the use of performance pay.

Index

Australia
  bonuses
    development (1940–1980), 187, 189, 190, 191
    directions, 205–6
    premium bonus, 184
  commission
    development (1940–1980), 187, 189, 190
    development (1980–1995), 194, 196
  employee share ownership plans (ESOPs)
    development (1980–1995), 196
    directions, 206–7
  gain sharing
    development (1980–1995), 196
    directions, 201
  gender impact
    system development (1788–1901), 182
    system development (1901–1940), 183, 185
    system development (1940–1980), 187–88, 190
    system directions, 201
  goal sharing, 196
  group schemes
    development (1940–1980), 189–90
    development (1980–1995), 194, 196–97
    directions, 10, 198–202
  human resource management (HRM)
    development (1940–1980), 191
    development (1980–1995), 192–93
  individual schemes
    development (1980–1995), 194, 196–97
    directions, 198–202

Australia *(continued)*
  international contrast
    change impetus/response, 265, 266–67
    employee participation, 269
    form/incidence, 262, 264
    legislation impact, 271
    organizational characteristics, 271
  legislation impact, 192, 197, 198, 201, 271
  merit pay
    development (1940–1980), 186, 187, 189
    development (1980–1995), 194, 196
    directions, 5, 205
  overview, 13, 179–80
  piece rate
    development (1788–1901), 180–83
    development (1901–1940), 183–85
    development (1940–1980), 186, 187
    development (1980–1995), 194, 196
    directions, 198
  premium bonus, 184
  profit sharing
    development (1901–1940), 183–85
    development (1940–1980), 187, 189, 190
    development (1980–1995), 194, 196–97
  standard pay
    development (1901–1940), 183–84
    development (1940–1980), 186, 189
    directions, 197, 203
  stock bonuses, 206–7
  stock options, 206–7
  stock purchases, 206–7
  summary, 208–10

Australia *(continued)*
  system development (1788–1901)
    economic impact, 180–82
    gender impact, 182
    managerial strategy, 181
    organizational structure, 181–83
    piece rate, 180–83
    task work, 180–83
    union impact, 181, 182
  system development (1901–1940)
    gender impact, 183, 185
    managerial strategy, 184–85
    organizational structure, 183–85
    payment-by-results, 183–85
    piece rate, 183–85
    premium bonus, 184
    profit sharing, 183–85
    scientific management, 184, 185
    standard pay, 183–84
    state regulation, 183–85
    union impact, 183–85
  system development (1940–1980)
    bonuses, 187, 189, 190, 191
    commission, 187, 189, 190
    economic impact, 186, 190–91
    gender impact, 187–88, 190
    group schemes, 189–90
    human resource management (HRM), 191
    incentives, 186–91
    managerial strategy, 186, 189–91
    merit pay, 186, 187, 189
    organizational structure, 186–90
    piece rate, 186, 187
    profit sharing, 187, 189, 190
    standard pay, 186, 189
    state regulation, 186, 188, 191
    union impact, 186, 188, 191
  system development (1980–1995)
    commission, 194, 196
    economic impact, 191–92, 193, 196–97
    employee share ownership plans (ESOPs), 196
    gain sharing, 196
    goal sharing, 196
    group schemes, 194, 196–97
    human resource management (HRM), 192–93
    individual schemes, 194, 196–97
    managerial strategy, 192–97

Australia
  system development (1980–1995) *(continued)*
    merit pay, 194, 196
    organizational structure, 191–93, 196–97
    piece rate, 194, 196
    profit sharing, 194, 196–97
    state regulation, 192, 196–97
    system reemergence, 191–97
    union impact, 192, 193
  system directions, 271–72
    Australian Workplace Agreements (AWAs), 197–202
    bonuses, 205–6
    broad banding, 205
    economic impact, 203
    employee share ownership plans (ESOPs), 206–7
    gain sharing, 201
    gender impact, 201
    group schemes, 10, 198–202
    individual schemes, 198–202
    managerial/nonmanagerial contrast, 203–8
    merit pay, 5, 205
    nested schemes, 11
    organizational structure, 197–201
    pay progression, 201
    piece rate, 198
    profit sharing, 205–6
    public/private sector, 201–8
    standard pay, 197, 203
    state regulation, 197, 198, 201, 203, 206, 207
    stock bonuses, 206–7
    stock options, 206–7
    stock purchases, 206–7
    union impact, 197, 198–200
    Workplace Relations Act (1996), 192, 197, 198, 201
  union impact
    system development (1788–1901), 181, 182
    system development (1901–1940), 183–85
    system development (1940–1980), 186, 188, 191
    system development (1980–1995), 192, 193
    system directions, 197, 198–200

Best-practice approach
 defined, 7
 organizational contrast, 270–71
 United Kingdom, 131
Bonuses
 Australia
  development (1940–1980), 187, 189, 190, 191
  directions, 205–6
 Canada
  determinants, 79–80t, 81
  employee monitoring, 59
  high-involvement management, 54
  incidence, 64, 66–67
 France, 92, 93, 94, 95
 Japan, 224
 United States
  evidence summary, 35–38
  group schemes, 36
  human resource management (HRM), 39
  incidence, 19, 20t, 21t, 35–36, 47n.3
  individual schemes, 35–39
  National Longitudinal Survey of Youth (NLSY), 36
  Panel Study of Income Dynamics (PSID), 36, 37f, 38
  theoretical perspective, 35–38
  union impact, 37f, 38
Brazil
 Constitution (1988)
  gain sharing, 242–43, 244–45
  Labor Code, 240, 241
  labor cost impact, 240, 241
  Labor Court, 242–43
  legislation impact, 238, 240, 241, 242–43, 244–45
  profit sharing, 242–43, 244–45
  union impact, 238, 243, 245
 gain sharing
  Constitution (1988), 242–43, 244–45
  determinants, 246–49
  effects, 249–52
  Provisional Measure 794, 243–46, 259n.3
  union impact, 239, 252–59
 international contrast
  change impetus/response, 266, 268
  employee participation, 270
  form/incidence, 261, 262, 265

Brazil
 international contrast *(continued)*
  legislation impact, 271
 Labor Code
  Constitution (1988), 240, 241
  labor cost impact, 240, 241
  legislation impact, 237–38, 239, 240, 241, 243
  Provisional Measure 794, 243
  union impact, 237–38, 239
 Labor Court
  Constitution (1988), 242–43
  doctrine of acquired rights, 241–43, 248
  Enunciation 251, 242–43, 259n.2
  legislation impact, 238, 239, 241–43, 248
  profit sharing, 242, 259n.2
  union impact, 238, 239, 245, 248
 legislation impact
  Constitution (1988), 238, 240, 241, 242–43, 244–45
  doctrine of acquired rights, 241–43, 248
  Enunciation 251, 242–43, 259n.2
  international contrast, 271
  Labor Code, 237–38, 239, 240, 241, 243
  labor costs, 240–41
  Labor Court, 238, 239, 241–43, 248
  Provisional Measure 794, 243–46, 259n.3
  unions, 237–39, 243–44, 245, 248
 overview, 13–14, 236
 profit sharing, 6
  Constitution (1988), 242–43, 244–45
  determinants, 246–49
  effects, 249–52
  Labor Court, 242, 259n.2
  Provisional Measure 794, 243–46, 259n.3
  union impact, 239, 252–59
 Provisional Measure 794
  features, 243–46
  gain sharing, 243–46, 259n.3
  Labor Code, 243
  legislation impact, 243–46, 259n.3
  profit sharing, 243–46, 259n.3
  union impact, 243–44, 245, 259n.4
 summary, 259

Brazil *(continued)*
system determinants
gain sharing, 246–49
policy success, 247
principal-agent model, 247–48
profit sharing, 246–49
union impact, 252–59
system effects
gain sharing, 249–52
profit sharing, 249–52
union impact
bargaining process, 238–39, 259n.1
Constitution (1988), 238, 243, 245
Convention 87, 237, 238
gain sharing, 239, 252–59
Labor Code, 237–38, 239
Labor Court, 238, 239, 245, 248
Labor Department, 237–38
legislation, 237–39, 243–44, 245, 248
membership, 239
profit sharing, 239, 252–59
Provisional Measure 794, 243–44, 245, 259n.4
system determinants, 252–59
union monopoly, 238
union tax, 237–38
works councils, 238

Canada
bonuses
determinants, 79–80t, 81
employee monitoring, 59
high-involvement management, 54
incidence, 64, 66–67
commission
determinants, 79–80t, 81
education impact, 59
employee monitoring, 59
incidence, 64, 65–67
retail industry, 60
employee share ownership plans (ESOPs)
incidence, 66t, 69, 70–71
organizational growth, 60
organizational size, 58–59
public trade organizations, 60
union impact, 58–59
gain sharing
determinants, 79–80t, 81
employee monitoring, 60

Canada
gain sharing *(continued)*
high-involvement management, 55
incidence, 66t, 68–69
gender impact, 58
goal sharing
determinants, 79–80t, 81
incidence, 66t, 68, 69
group schemes
alternative plans, 53
complementary argument, 72–75
determinants, 79–80t, 81, 86n.1
gain sharing, 53
goal sharing, 53
high-involvement management, 54–55
incidence, 67–69
independent benefits argument, 72–75
organizational characteristics, 60
organizational structure, 54–60
strategic-fit approach, 56–57
substitution argument, 72–75
union impact, 56–60
work force characteristics, 59–60
individual schemes
bonuses, 53
commission, 53
complementary argument, 72–75
determinants, 78–81, 86n.1
employee monitoring, 55–56, 59
high-involvement management, 54
incidence, 64–67
independent benefits argument, 72–75
merit pay, 53
organizational characteristics, 60
organizational structure, 54, 55–60
piece rate, 53
special incentives, 53
strategic-fit approach, 56–57
substitution argument, 72–75
union impact, 56–60
work force characteristics, 59–60
international contrast
change impetus/response, 265–66, 267
form/incidence, 262, 263, 264
legislation impact, 271
organizational characteristics, 271

Canada *(continued)*
merit pay
  determinants, 78–81
  education impact, 59
  employee monitoring, 55–56, 59
  incidence, 64, 65–67
  union impact, 56, 78, 81
nested schemes, 11
organizational characteristics
  determinants, 76–78, 82–83
  group schemes, 60
  individual schemes, 60
  organizational schemes, 60
  study measurement, 63
organizational schemes
  alternative plans, 53
  complementary argument, 72–75
  determinants, 79–80t, 81–82, 86n.1
  free-rider problem, 57
  high-involvement management, 54–55
  incidence, 69–72
  independent benefits argument, 72–75
  organizational characteristics, 60
  organizational structure, 54–60
  profit sharing, 53
  stock bonuses, 53
  stock options, 53
  stock purchase, 53
  strategic-fit approach, 56–57
  substitution argument, 72–75
  union impact, 56–60
  work force characteristics, 59–60
organizational structure
  determinants, 76–78, 82
  employee monitoring, 55–56, 59, 60
  group schemes, 54–60
  high-involvement management, 52–53, 54–55
  individual schemes, 54, 55–60
  organizational schemes, 54–60
  size, 56–60
  study measurement, 63
  union impact, 56–60
overview, 12–13, 52–53
piece rate
  determinants, 79–80t, 81
  education impact, 59
  employee monitoring, 55–56, 59
  gender impact, 58

Canada
piece rate *(continued)*
  high-involvement management, 54
  incidence, 64–67
  manufacturing industry, 60
  organizational size, 57–58
  union impact, 56–58, 65
profit sharing
  casual employees, 60
  determinants, 79–80t, 82
  employee monitoring, 60
  employee participation, 55
  high-involvement management, 54–55
  incidence, 69–70
  organizational size, 58
  union impact, 58
research study
  data collection, 61
  sample, 61
  variable measurement, 61–64, 84–86
special incentives, 64, 67
standard pay
  employee monitoring, 55–56
  union impact, 56, 60
stock bonuses
  determinants, 79–80t, 82
  incidence, 66t, 69, 70–71
stock options
  determinants, 79–80t, 81–82
  incidence, 66t, 69, 70–71
stock purchases
  determinants, 79–80t, 81
  incidence, 66t, 69, 70–71
summary, 83–84
union impact
  determinants, 76–83
  employee share ownership plans (ESOPs), 58–59
  group schemes, 56–60
  individual schemes, 56–60
  merit pay, 56, 78, 81
  organizational schemes, 56–60
  organizational structure, 56–60
  piece rate, 56–58, 65
  profit sharing, 58
  standard pay, 56, 60
  work force characteristics, 59–60
work force characteristics
  determinants, 76–78, 83
  group schemes, 59–60

Canada
  work force characteristics *(continued)*
    individual schemes, 59–60
    organizational schemes, 59–60
    study measurement, 63–64
    union impact, 59–60
Commission
  Australia
    development (1940–1980), 187, 189, 190
    development (1980–1995), 194, 196
  Canada
    determinants, 79–80t, 81
    education impact, 59
    employee monitoring, 59
    incidence, 64, 65–67
    retail industry, 60
  France, 92
  United States
    determinants, 20, 22–30, 31t
    effects, 30, 32–35
    gender impact, 26–27, 30
    human resource management (HRM), 35
    incidence, 18–20, 21t
    union impact, 26, 27
Complementary argument
  Canada, 72–75
  Germany, 169
  nested schemes, 264

Employee share ownership plans (ESOPs), 10–11
  Australia
    development (1980–1995), 196
    directions, 206–7
  Canada
    incidence, 66t, 69, 70–71
    organizational growth, 60
    organizational size, 58–59
    public trade organizations, 60
    union impact, 58–59
  France, 90–91
  international contrast
    change impetus/response, 265, 267–68
    form/incidence, 261–62
    legislation impact, 271
  Japan, 214
    alignment effects, 223–24
    characteristics, 216–17

Employee share ownership plans (ESOPs)
  Japan *(continued)*
    diffusion of, 217–21
    effects, 223–24
    employee reactions, 229–31, 232t, 233n.11
    incidence, 217–21, 225–27, 233n.8
    1990s, 225–27, 233n.10
    United States contrast, 216–17, 223
    vesting feature, 224

France
  bonuses, 92, 93, 94, 95
  commission, 92
  employee share ownership plans (ESOPs), 90–91
  gender impact, 93–95
  group schemes, 92–96, 97t
  individual schemes, 92–96, 97t
  legislation impact
    compulsory participation plan, 96–97, 99–100
    profit sharing, 90, 91, 95–100, 112n.5
    voluntary subsidized plan, 95–99
  merit pay, 92, 93
  organizational schemes, 92–96, 97t
  piece rate, 92, 93
  profit sharing
    characteristics, 96–100
    compulsory participation plan, 96–97, 99–100, 112n.12
    employee participation objective, 90–91
    employment effects, 100–101, 103–5
    incidence, 90, 92, 93, 95–96
    legislation impact, 90, 91, 95–100, 112n.5
    overview, 4, 6, 11, 13, 90–92
    payment exemptions, 97, 98, 112n.4
    productivity effects, 100–103, 105–8, 112n.15
    savings objective, 91, 98, 112n.9
    substitution argument, 95–96
    summary, 108–9
    voluntary subsidized plan, 95–99, 112n.5
  Weitzman model, 91
  substitution argument, 95–96

INDEX 287

France *(continued)*
  system incidence
    bonuses, 92, 93, 94, 95
    commission, 92
    data sources, 109–11
    gender impact, 93–95
    group schemes, 92–96, 97t
    individual schemes, 92–96, 97t
    merit pay, 92, 93
    organizational schemes, 92–96, 97t
    piece rate, 92, 93
    profit sharing, 90, 92, 93, 95–96
    skill level, 95, 96t
    standard pay, 95–96, 97t
Free-rider problem
  Canada, 57
  Germany, 154, 155, 172
  group schemes, 7, 9
  United States, 39–40

Gain sharing
  Australia
    development (1980–1995), 196
    directions, 201
  Brazil
    Constitution (1988), 242–43, 244–45
    determinants, 246–49
    effects, 249–52
    Provisional Measure 794, 243–46, 259n.3
    union impact, 239, 252–59
  Canada
    determinants, 79–80t, 81
    employee monitoring, 60
    high-involvement management, 55
    incidence, 66t, 68–69
    international contrast
      change impetus/response, 265, 266
      legislation impact, 271
  Japan, 214, 227, 229t
Gender impact
  Australia
    system development (1788–1901), 182
    system development (1901–1940), 183, 185
    system development (1940–1980), 187–88, 190
    system directions, 201
  Canada, 58

Gender impact *(continued)*
  commission, 26–27, 30
  France, 93–95
  Germany
    human resource management (HRM), 168, 170, 172
    piece rate, 150, 151t, 157, 174n.7
    premium pay, 150, 151t, 157
    profit sharing, 157–58
    system determinants, 157–58
    system incidence, 150, 151t
  piece rate
    Canada, 58
    Germany, 150, 151t, 157, 174n.7
    United States, 26–27, 30
  premium pay, 150, 151t, 157
  profit sharing
    Germany, 157–58
    United States, 40–41, 49n.30
  United States
    commission, 26–27, 30
    piece rate, 26–27, 30
    profit sharing, 40–41, 49n.30
Germany
  gender impact
    human resource management (HRM), 168, 170, 172
    piece rate, 150, 151t, 157, 174n.7
    premium pay, 150, 151t, 157
    profit sharing, 157–58
    system determinants, 157–58
    system incidence, 150, 151t
  human resource management (HRM)
    complementary argument, 169
    determinants, 168–72
    forms of, 165, 166–68
    gender impact, 168, 170, 172
    industrial relations, 168–69, 170
    managerial incentives, 168, 169, 170
    meetings, 166–68
    production technology, 168, 169, 172
    product markets, 168, 169, 170, 172
    tenure, 168, 169–70, 172
    training, 165, 166–68
    union impact, 168–69, 170
    works councils, 168–69, 170
    work teams, 165, 166–68
  international contrast
    change impetus/response, 266
    employee participation, 268–69, 270
    form/incidence, 262

Germany *(continued)*
  overview, 13, 148–49
  piece rate
    characteristics, 149–52
    gender impact, 150, 151*t*, 157, 174*n*.7
    group schemes, 150, 152–54, 155, 157, 160, 161, 164–68
    human resource management (HRM), 166–68
    incidence, 150–54
    individual schemes, 150, 152–58, 160–63, 164–68
    job security impact, 156–57
    product market impact, 164–65
    racial impact, 158
    skill level impact, 154–55, 174*n*.3
    tenure impact, 156–58
    union impact, 160–63
    work organization impact, 154–55
    works councils impact, 160, 162–63
  premium pay
    characteristics, 149–52
    gender impact, 150, 151*t*, 157
    group schemes, 150, 152–54, 155, 157, 160, 161, 166–68
    human resource management (HRM), 166–68
    incidence, 150–54
    individual schemes, 150, 152–54, 155, 157, 160, 161, 163, 166–68
    job security impact, 156
    product market impact, 164
    union impact, 160–63
    work organization impact, 155
    works councils impact, 160, 162–63
  profit sharing
    characteristics, 4, 6, 150
    free-rider problem, 154, 155, 172
    gender impact, 157–58
    human resource management (HRM), 166–68, 169, 170, 172
    incidence, 152–54
    job security impact, 156
    product market impact, 164–65
    skill level impact, 154–55, 174*n*.4
    union impact, 160–63
    work organization impact, 154–55, 173*n*.2
    works councils impact, 160, 162–63

Germany *(continued)*
  promotions, 156, 174*n*.5
  study methodology, 149–50, 152, 167–68
  summary, 172–73
  system determinants
    empirical studies, 148–49, 154–65
    gender impact, 157–58
    importance of, 148–49
    industrial relations, 158–64
    job security, 156–57
    legislation impact, 159
    managerial incentives, 164–65
    production technology, 154–55
    product markets, 164–65
    tenure, 156–57
    theoretical perspective, 148–49, 154–65
    union impact, 159, 160–64, 175*n*.9
    work organization, 154–55
    works councils, 159–60, 162–63
  system forms
    group schemes, 150, 152–54
    individual schemes, 150, 152–54
    piece rate, 8, 149–52
    premium pay, 149–52
    profit sharing, 4, 6, 150
    standard pay, 150
  system incidence
    gender impact, 150, 151*t*
    piece rate, 150–54
    premium pay, 150–54
    profit sharing, 152–54
  union impact
    human resource management (HRM), 168–69, 170
    piece rate, 160–63
    premium pay, 160–63
    profit sharing, 160–63
    system determinants, 159, 160–64, 175*n*.9
  works councils
    codetermination, 159–60, 162–63
    human resource management (HRM), 168–69, 170
    organizational schemes, 159–60, 162–63
    piece rate, 160, 162–63
    premium pay, 160, 162–63
    system determinants, 159–60, 162–63
    Works Constitution Act (1952), 159

Goal sharing
  Australia, 196
  Canada
    determinants, 79–80*t*, 81
    incidence, 66*t*, 68, 69

Human resource management (HRM)
  Australia
    system development (1940–1980), 191
    system development (1980–1995), 192–93
  Canada, 52–53, 54–55
  Germany
    complementary argument, 169
    determinants, 168–72
    forms of, 165, 166–68
    gender impact, 168, 170, 172
    industrial relations, 168–69, 170
    meetings, 166–68
    production technology, 168, 169, 172
    product markets, 168, 169, 170, 172
    training, 165, 166–68
    union impact, 168–69, 170
    works councils, 168–69, 170
    work teams, 165, 166–68
  high-commitment management
    Canada, 52–53, 54–55
    change impetus/response contrast, 265–66
  United States, 35, 39

Independent benefits argument, 72–75

Japan
  bonuses, 224
  economic impact, 214–16, 224, 225–26
  employee share ownership plans (ESOPs), 214
    alignment effects, 223–24
    characteristics, 216–17
    diffusion of, 217–21
    effects, 223–24
    employee reactions, 229–31, 232*t*, 233*n*.11
    incidence, 217–21, 225–27, 233*n*.8
    1990s, 225–27, 233*n*.10
    United States contrast, 216–17, 223
    vesting feature, 224
  gain sharing, 214, 227, 229*t*

Japan *(continued)*
  international contrast
    change impetus/response, 265, 267–68
    employee participation, 269–70
    form/incidence, 216–17, 223, 261, 262, 263–64
    legislation impact, 271
  lifetime employment, 215–16
  overview, 13, 214–16
  profit sharing, 4, 6, 214
    alignment effects, 223–24
    characteristics, 221
    diffusion of, 221, 222*f*
    effects, 223–24
    employee reactions, 229–31, 232*t*, 233*n*.11
    incidence, 221–23
    1990s, 225, 233*n*.7
    United States contrast, 223
  seniority-based pay system, 215–16, 226–27
  summary, 231, 233

Legislation impact
  Australia, 192, 197, 198, 201, 271
  Brazil
    Constitution (1988), 238, 240, 241, 242–43, 244–45
    doctrine of acquired rights, 241–43, 248
    Enunciation 251, 242–43, 259*n*.2
    international contrast, 271
    Labor Code, 237–38, 239, 240, 241, 243
    labor costs, 240–41
    Labor Court, 238, 239, 241–43, 248
    Provisional Measure 794, 243–46, 259*n*.3
    unions, 237–39, 243–44, 245, 248
  France
    compulsory participation plan, 96–97, 99–100
    profit sharing, 90, 91, 95–100, 112*n*.5
    voluntary subsidized plan, 95–99
  Germany, 159
  international contrast, 271
  United Kingdom
    Civil Service Act (1992), 120
    Education Reform Act (1988), 121

290 INDEX

Merit pay
  advantages, 9
  Australia
    development (1940–1980), 186, 187, 189
    development (1980–1995), 194, 196
    directions, 5, 205
  Canada
    determinants, 78–81
    education impact, 59
    employee monitoring, 55–56, 59
    incidence, 64, 65–67
    union impact, 56, 78, 81
  defined, 9
  disadvantages, 9–10
  France, 92, 93
  group schemes, 9–10
  individual schemes, 9–10
  international contrast
    change impetus/response, 267
    employee participation, 269
    form/incidence, 262, 263
    organizational characteristics, 271
  management assessment, 9–10

Nested schemes
  advantages, 11
  Australia, 11
  Canada, 11
  complementary argument, 264
  defined, 11
  disadvantages, 11
  form/incidence contrast, 264
  substitution argument, 264

Performance pay schemes
  accumulating payment schemes
    advantages, 7
    defined, 7
    form/incidence contrast, 264–65
  award system
    employee participation contrast, 269
    legislation impact, 271
  best-practice approach
    defined, 7
    organizational contrast, 270–71
  change impetus/response contrast
    Australia, 265, 266–67
    Brazil, 266, 268
    Canada, 265–66, 267

Performance pay schemes
  change impetus/response contrast *(continued)*
    employee share ownership plans (ESOPs), 265, 267–68
    gain sharing, 265, 266
    Germany, 266
    group schemes, 265–68
    high-commitment management, 265–66
    individual schemes, 265, 266
    Japan, 265, 267–68
    merit pay, 267
    nonmanagerial employees, 267–68
    organizational schemes, 265–68
    overview, 14
    piece rate, 266
    premium pay, 266
    profit sharing, 265, 266
    public/private sector, 266–67, 273$n.3$
    stock options, 265
    union impact, 266
    United Kingdom, 266–67, 268
    United States, 267, 273$n.2$
  comparative research, 4, 11–14, 272–73
  employee participation contrast
    Australia, 269
    award system, 269
    Brazil, 270
    France, 269, 270
    Germany, 268–69, 270
    individual schemes, 270
    Japan, 269–70
    merit pay, 269
    overview, 14
    piece rate, 268, 269
    premium pay, 268
    profit sharing, 269–70
    union impact, 269, 270
    United Kingdom, 269, 270
    United States, 269, 270
    works councils, 268–69
  employee share ownership plans (ESOPs), 10–11
    change impetus/response contrast, 265, 267–68
    form/incidence contrast, 261–62
    legislation impact, 271

Performance pay schemes *(continued)*
form/incidence contrast
accumulating payment schemes, 264–65
Australia, 262, 264
Brazil, 261, 262, 265
Canada, 262, 263, 264
employee share ownership plans (ESOPs), 261–62
France, 261–62
gain sharing, 262, 265
Germany, 262
group schemes, 263–64
individual schemes, 262–63, 264
Japan, 216–17, 223, 261, 262, 263–64
management assessment, 263
merit pay, 262, 263
nested schemes, 264
nonaccumulating payment schemes, 264–65
organizational schemes, 261–62, 264
overview, 14
profit sharing, 261–62, 265
seniority-based system, 263, 264
union impact, 262, 263
United Kingdom, 262, 263, 264
United States, 262–63, 264–65, 273*n*.1
future directions
Australia, 271–72
comparative research, 272–73
income trends, 271–72
United States, 271, 272
gain sharing
change impetus/response contrast, 265, 266
legislation impact, 271
group schemes
Australia, 10
change impetus/response contrast, 265–68
disadvantages, 7, 8–9
form/incidence contrast, 263–64
free-rider problem, 7, 9
merit pay, 9–10
piece rate, 8–9
individual schemes
advantages, 7, 9
change impetus/response contrast, 265, 266

Performance pay schemes
individual schemes *(continued)*
disadvantages, 7, 9–10
dysfunctional individualism, 7, 10, 14*n*.4
employee participation contrast, 270
form/incidence contrast, 262–63, 264
merit pay, 9–10
organizational characteristics contrast, 271
piece rate, 8–9
legislation impact
Australia, 271
award system, 271
Brazil, 271
Canada, 271
employee share ownership plans (ESOPs), 271
France, 271
gain sharing, 271
Japan, 271
policy importance, 6, 14*n*.1
profit sharing, 271
United States, 271
merit pay
advantages, 9
Australia, 5
change impetus/response contrast, 267
defined, 9
disadvantages, 9–10
employee participation contrast, 269
form/incidence contrast, 262, 263
group schemes, 9–10
individual schemes, 9–10
management assessment, 9–10
organizational characteristics contrast, 271
United Kingdom, 5
United States, 5–6, 10
nested schemes
advantages, 11
Australia, 11
Canada, 11
complementary argument, 264
defined, 11
disadvantages, 11
form/incidence contrast, 264
substitution argument, 264

Performance pay schemes *(continued)*
  nonaccumulating payment schemes
    advantages, 7
    defined, 7
    disadvantages, 7
    form/incidence contrast, 264–65
  objectives, 8–11
  organizational characteristics contrast
    Australia, 271
    best-practice approach, 270–71
    Canada, 271
    individual schemes, 271
    merit pay, 271
    overview, 14
    strategic-fit approach, 270–71
    union impact, 271
  organizational schemes
    advantages, 10–11
    change impetus/response contrast, 265–68
    employee share ownership plans (ESOPs), 10–11
    form/incidence contrast, 261–62, 264
    profit sharing, 10–11
  piece rate
    advantages, 8, 14*n*.2
    change impetus/response contrast, 266
    disadvantages, 8–9
    employee participation contrast, 268, 269
    equipment maintenance impact, 8
    Germany, 8
    group schemes, 8–9
    individual schemes, 8–9
    production gains, 8
    quality reduction, 8
    scrap rate increase, 8
    strategic fit approach, 8
  policy importance
    comparative research, 4, 11–14
    to employee, 4
    international interest, 4–6
    international variation, 4, 5–6, 11–14
    legislation impact, 6, 14*n*.1
    to organization, 3–4
    personnel economics, 3
    scientific management, 4–5
    terminology variation, 11–12

Performance pay schemes *(continued)*
  premium pay, 8
    change impetus/response contrast, 266
    employee participation contrast, 268
  profit sharing
    Brazil, 6
    change impetus/response contrast, 265, 266
    employee participation contrast, 269–70
    form/incidence contrast, 261–62, 265
    France, 4, 6, 11
    Germany, 4, 6
    Japan, 4, 6
    legislation impact, 271
    organizational schemes, 10–11
    United States, 4, 6, 14*n*.1
  strategic-fit approach
    defined, 8
    organizational contrast, 270–71
    piece rate, 8
  taxonomies, 6–8
  time/production schemes, 6–7
    employee retention, 9, 14*n*.3
  union impact
    change impetus/response contrast, 266
    employee participation contrast, 269, 270
    form/incidence contrast, 262, 263
    organizational characteristics contrast, 271
  works councils, 268–69
Piece rate
  advantages, 8, 14*n*.2
  Australia
    development (1788–1901), 180–83
    development (1901–1940), 183–85
    development (1940–1980), 186, 187
    development (1980–1995), 194, 196
    directions, 198
  Canada
    determinants, 79–80*t*, 81
    education impact, 59
    employee monitoring, 55–56, 59
    gender impact, 58
    high-involvement management, 54
    incidence, 64–67
    manufacturing industry, 60

INDEX   293

Piece rate
Canada *(continued)*
  organizational size, 57–58
  union impact, 56–58, 65
disadvantages, 8–9
equipment maintenance impact, 8
France, 92, 93
Germany
  characteristics, 149–52
  gender impact, 150, 151*t*, 157, 174*n*.7
  group schemes, 150, 152–54, 155, 157, 160, 161, 164–68
  human resource management (HRM), 166–68
  incidence, 150–54
  individual schemes, 150, 152–58, 160–63, 164–68
  job security impact, 156–57
  product market impact, 164–65
  racial impact, 158
  skill level impact, 154–55, 174*n*.3
  tenure impact, 156–58
  union impact, 160–63
  work organization impact, 154–55
  works councils impact, 160, 162–63
group schemes, 8–9
individual schemes, 8–9
international contrast
  change impetus/response, 266
  employee participation, 268, 269
production gains, 8
quality reduction, 8
scrap rate increase, 8
strategic fit approach, 8
United States
  determinants, 20, 22–30, 31*t*, 47*n*.4
  effects, 30, 32–35
  gender impact, 26–27, 30
  human resource management (HRM), 35
  incidence, 18–20, 21*t*
  union impact, 26, 27
Premium pay, 8
Germany
  characteristics, 149–52
  gender impact, 150, 151*t*, 157
  group schemes, 150, 152–54, 155, 157, 160, 161, 166–68
  human resource management (HRM), 166–68

Premium pay, 8
Germany *(continued)*
  incidence, 150–54
  individual schemes, 150, 152–54, 155, 157, 160, 161, 163, 166–68
  job security impact, 156
  product market impact, 164
  union impact, 160–63
  work organization impact, 155
  works councils impact, 160, 162–63
international contrast
  change impetus/response, 266
  employee participation, 268
Principal-agent model
Brazil, 247–48
United Kingdom, 116–17, 131
United States, 23–26
Profit sharing
Australia
  development (1901–1940), 183–85
  development (1940–1980), 187, 189, 190
  development (1980–1995), 194, 196–97
Brazil, 6
  Constitution (1988), 242–43, 244–45
  determinants, 246–49
  effects, 249–52
  Labor Court, 242, 259*n*.2
  Provisional Measure 794, 243–46, 259*n*.3
  union impact, 239, 252–59
Canada
  casual employees, 60
  determinants, 79–80*t*, 82
  employee monitoring, 60
  employee participation, 55
  high-involvement management, 54–55
  incidence, 69–70
  organizational size, 58
  union impact, 58
France
  characteristics, 96–100
  compulsory participation plan, 96–97, 99–100, 112*n*.12
  employee participation objective, 90–91

Profit sharing
  France *(continued)*
    employment effects, 100–101, 103–5
    legislation impact, 90, 91, 95–100, 112n.5
    overview, 4, 6, 11, 13, 90–92
    payment exemptions, 97, 98, 112n.4
    productivity effects, 100–103, 105–8, 112n.15
    savings objective, 91, 98, 112n.9
    substitution argument, 95–96
    summary, 108–9
    voluntary subsidized plan, 95–99, 112n.5
    Weitzman model, 91
  free-rider problem
    Canada, 57
    Germany, 154, 155, 172
    group schemes, 7, 9
    United States, 39–40
  Germany
    characteristics, 4, 6, 150
    free-rider problem, 154, 155, 172
    gender impact, 157–58
    human resource management (HRM), 166–68, 169, 170, 172
    incidence, 152–54
    job security impact, 156
    product market impact, 164–65
    skill level impact, 154–55, 174n.4
    union impact, 160–63
    work organization impact, 154–55, 173n.2
  international contrast
    change impetus/response, 265, 266
    employee participation, 269–70
    form/incidence, 261–62, 265
    legislation impact, 271
  Japan, 4, 6, 214
    alignment effects, 223–24
    characteristics, 221
    diffusion of, 221, 222f
    effects, 223–24
    employee reactions, 229–31, 232t, 233n.11
    incidence, 221–23
    1990s, 225, 233n.7
    United States contrast, 223
  organizational schemes, 10–11

Profit sharing *(continued)*
  United States, 4, 6, 14n.1
    effects, 40–41
    free-rider problem, 39–40
    gender impact, 40–41, 49n.30
    group schemes, 39–41
    incidence, 18, 19, 21t, 40, 47n.2
    individual schemes, 39–40
    National Longitudinal Survey of Youth (NLSY), 40–41
    Quality of Employment Survey (QES), 40
Promotions
  Germany, 156, 174n.5
  United States
    evidence summary, 35–38
    human resource management (HRM), 39
    incidence, 19, 20t, 21t, 35–36, 47n.3
    individual schemes, 35–39
    Panel Study of Income Dynamics (PSID), 36, 37f
    theoretical perspective, 35–38

Scientific management
  Australia, 184, 185
  policy importance, 4–5
Standard pay
  Australia
    system development (1901–1940), 183–84
    system development (1940–1980), 186, 189
    system directions, 197, 203
  Canada
    employee monitoring, 55–56
    union impact, 56, 60
  France, 95–96, 97t
  Germany, 150
Stock bonuses
  Australia, 206–7
  Canada
    determinants, 79–80t, 82
    incidence, 66t, 69, 70–71
Stock options
  Australia, 206–7
  Canada
    determinants, 79–80t, 81–82
    incidence, 66t, 69, 70–71
Stock purchases
  Australia, 206–7

Stock purchases *(continued)*
  Canada
    determinants, 79–80*t*, 81
    incidence, 66*t*, 69, 70–71
Strategic-fit approach
  Canada, 56–57
  defined, 8
  organizational contrast, 270–71
  piece rate, 8
Substitution argument
  Canada, 72–75
  France, 95–96
  nested schemes, 264

Union impact
  Australia
    system development (1788–1901), 181, 182
    system development (1901–1940), 183–85
    system development (1940–1980), 186, 188, 191
    system development (1980–1995), 192, 193
    system directions, 197, 198–200
  Brazil
    bargaining process, 238–39, 259*n*.1
    Constitution (1988), 238, 243, 245
    Convention 87, 237, 238
    gain sharing, 239, 252–59
    Labor Code, 237–38, 239
    Labor Court, 238, 239, 245, 248
    Labor Department, 237–38
    legislation, 237–39, 243–44, 245, 248
    membership, 239
    profit sharing, 239, 252–59
    Provisional Measure 794, 243–44, 245, 259*n*.4
    system determinants, 252–59
    union monopoly, 238
    union tax, 237–38
    works councils, 238
  Canada
    determinants, 76–83
    employee share ownership plans (ESOPs), 58–59
    group schemes, 56–60
    individual schemes, 56–60
    merit pay, 56, 78, 81
    organizational schemes, 56–60

Union impact
  Canada *(continued)*
    organizational structure, 56–60
    piece rate, 56–58, 65
    profit sharing, 58
    standard pay, 56, 60
    work force characteristics, 59–60
  Germany
    human resource management (HRM), 168–69, 170
    piece rate, 160–63
    premium pay, 160–63
    profit sharing, 160–63
    system determinants, 159, 160–64, 175*n*.9
  international contrast
    change impetus/response, 266
    employee participation, 269, 270
    form/incidence, 262, 263
    organizational characteristics, 271
  United Kingdom, 126–28
  United States
    bonuses, 37*f*, 38
    commission, 26, 27
    piece rate, 26, 27
United Kingdom
  best-practice approach, 131
  education system
    Education Reform Act (1988), 121
    employee reaction, 126
    Local Management of Schools, 121, 122
    Office for Standards in Education, 122–23
    public sector reform history, 118, 119, 121, 122–23, 124, 125
  Employment Service scheme
    employee reaction, 126
    performance indicators, 121–22
  Inland Revenue scheme (1988), 126
  Inland Revenue scheme (1991)
    best-practice approach, 131
    commitment factor, 140–42, 143–44, 145*n*.6
    deterioration causation, 131–42, 145*n*.3
    employee reaction, 117–18, 125–26, 128–30, 137–42
    line management reaction, 136–37
    performance indicators, 121–22
    performance targets, 123

United Kingdom
  Inland Revenue scheme (1991)
      (continued)
    stress factor, 137–42, 145n.6
    study methodology, 127–28
    summary, 142–43
    union impact, 127–28
  Inland Revenue scheme (1993),
      126–27
  Inland Revenue scheme (1996)
    best-practice approach, 131
    commitment factor, 140–42, 143–44,
        145n.6
    deterioration causation, 131–42,
        145n.3
    employee reaction, 117–18, 125–26,
        129t, 130–31, 137–42
    line management reaction, 136–37
    performance indicators, 121–22
    performance targets, 123
    stress factor, 137–42, 145n.6
    study methodology, 127–28
    summary, 142–43
    union impact, 127–28
  Inland Revenue Staff Association
      (IRSF), 126–27
  international contrast
    change impetus/response, 266–67,
        268
    employee participation, 269, 270
    form/incidence, 262, 263, 264
  legislation impact
    Civil Service Act (1992), 120
    Education Reform Act (1988), 121
  merit pay, 5
  National Health Service (NHS)
    employee reaction, 126
    public sector reform history, 118,
        120–21, 124–25, 145n.1
  overview, 13, 115–18
  public sector performance pay
    appropriateness debate, 116–18
    managerial incidence, 115–16
    nonmanagerial incidence, 116
    principal-agent model, 116–17, 131
  public sector reform history
    appraisal-based pay, 117, 126,
        135–37
    Civil Service Act (1992), 120
    contract system, 126–27
    cost control, 124–25

United Kingdom
  public sector reform history *(continued)*
    Department of Health and Social
        Security (DHSS), 121
    Department of the Environment, 121
    Education Reform Act (1988), 121
    education system, 118, 119, 121,
        122–23, 124, 125
    Inland Revenue, 121–22, 123,
        126–27
    legislation impact, 120, 121
    Local Management of Schools, 121,
        122
    managerial responsibility, 119–20
    managerial structures, 120–21
    National Audit Office (NAO),
        121–22
    National Health Service (NHS), 118,
        120–21, 124–25, 145n.1
    Office for Standards in Education,
        122–23
    pay structures, 120–21
    performance indicators, 121–25
    performance targets, 121–25
    quotas, 127
    union impact, 126–27
  union impact
    Inland Revenue scheme (1988), 126
    Inland Revenue scheme (1991),
        127–28
    Inland Revenue scheme (1993),
        126–27
    Inland Revenue scheme (1996),
        127–28
United States
  bonuses
    evidence summary, 35–38
    group schemes, 36
    human resource management
        (HRM), 39
    incidence, 19, 20t, 21t, 35–36, 47n.3
    individual schemes, 35–39
    National Longitudinal Survey of
        Youth (NLSY), 36
    Panel Study of Income Dynamics
        (PSID), 36, 37f, 38
    theoretical perspective, 35–38
    union impact, 37f, 38
  commission
    determinants, 20, 22–30, 31t
    effects, 30, 32–35

United States
commission *(continued)*
  gender impact, 26–27, 30
  human resource management
    (HRM), 35
  incidence, 18–20, 21*t*
  union impact, 26, 27
education system, 5–6
future directions, 271, 272
gender impact
  commission, 26–27, 30
  piece rate, 26–27, 30
  profit sharing, 40–41, 49*n*.30
human resource management (HRM)
  bonuses, 39
  commission, 35
  piece rate, 35
  promotions, 39
international contrast
  change impetus/response, 267,
    273*n*.2
  employee participation, 269, 270
  form/incidence, 262–63, 264–65,
    273*n*.1
  legislation impact, 271
merit pay, 5–6, 10
overview, 12, 17–18
piece rate
  determinants, 20, 22–30, 31*t*, 47*n*.4
  effects, 30, 32–35
  gender impact, 26–27, 30
  human resource management
    (HRM), 35
  incidence, 18–20, 21*t*
  union impact, 26, 27
profit sharing, 4, 6, 14*n*.1
  effects, 40–41
  free-rider problem, 39–40
  gender impact, 40–41, 49*n*.30
  group schemes, 39–41
  incidence, 18, 19, 21*t*, 40, 47*n*.2
  individual schemes, 39–40
  National Longitudinal Survey of
    Youth (NLSY), 40–41
  Quality of Employment Survey
    (QES), 40
promotions
  evidence summary, 35–38
  human resource management
    (HRM), 39
  incidence, 19, 20*t*, 21*t*, 35–36, 47*n*.3

United States
promotions *(continued)*
  individual schemes, 35–39
  Panel Study of Income Dynamics
    (PSID), 36, 37*f*
  theoretical perspective, 35–38
summary, 41–42
system determinants
  commission, 20, 22–30, 31*t*
  evidence summary, 27–30, 31*t*
  gender impact, 26–27, 30
  group schemes, 25–26, 27, 30
  individual schemes, 20, 22–30, 31*t*
  Informativeness Principle, 25–26
  institutional impact, 26–27
  Lazear model, 22–23
  measurement error, 27, 29, 45–47
  National Longitudinal Survey of
    Youth (NLSY), 27, 29*t*
  occupation breakdown, 27–30
  piece rate, 20, 22–30, 31*t*, 47*n*.4
  principal-agent model, 23–26
  Quality of Employment Survey
    (QES), 27, 28*t*, 30*f*
  theoretical perspective, 22–26
  union impact, 26, 27
system effects
  Bureau of Labor Statistics (BLS), 32
  commission, 30, 32–35
  cross-sectional evidence, 32–33, 34,
    47*n*.14
  human resource management
    (HRM), 35
  individual schemes, 30, 32–35
  Industry Wage Surveys, 32
  longitudinal evidence, 33–35,
    47*n*.16
  National Longitudinal Survey of
    Youth (NLSY), 32, 34
  piece rate, 30, 32–35
  profit sharing, 40–41
system incidence
  bonuses, 19, 20*t*, 21*t*, 35–36, 47*n*.3
  commission, 18–20, 21*t*
  Current Population Survey (CPS),
    18–19, 45
  individual schemes, 18–20, 21*t*
  National Longitudinal Survey of
    Youth (NLSY), 18–19, 21*t*,
    43–44
  occupation breakdown, 19, 20*t*, 21*t*

United States
  system incidence *(continued)*
    Panel Study of Income Dynamics
      (PSID), 18–19, 44–45
    piece rate, 18–20, 21*t*
    profit sharing, 18, 19, 21*t*, 40, 47*n*.2
    promotions, 19, 20*t*, 21*t*, 35–36,
      47*n*.3
    Quality of Employment Survey
      (QES), 18–20, 42–43
  union impact
    bonuses, 37*f*, 38
    commission, 26, 27
    piece rate, 26, 27

Works councils
  Brazil, 238
  employee participation contrast, 268–69
  Germany
    codetermination, 159–60, 162–63
    human resource management
      (HRM), 168–69, 170
    organizational schemes, 159–60,
      162–63
    piece rate, 160, 162–63
    premium pay, 160, 162–63
    system determinants, 159–60,
      162–63
  Works Constitution Act (1952), 159